London

The Tower of London

Copyright 1999 by The Palancar Company Limited
All rights reserved
Printed by EBS, Verona, Italy

Publishers Cataloguing in Publication
Lown, Patricia Twohill
All London : the source guide / by Patricia
Twohill Lown and David Amory Lown ; illustrated
by Megan Green.— 1st ed.
p. cm.
Includes index.
ISBN: 0-9643256-4-0

1. Decorative arts—England—London—
Directories. 2. Artisans—England—London—
Directories. 3. Interior decoration—England—
London—Directories. I. Lown, David. II.
Title

NK931.L6L68 1999   745'.025'421
QBI99-212

Library of Congress Catalog Card Number 99 - 702 90
CIP

The Palancar Company Limited,
111 East 80th Street, New York, NY 10021
E-mail: twolowns@aol.com
The Palancar Company Limited,
The Courtyard, 12 Hill Street, St. Helier, Jersey JE2 4UB

ALL LONDON

The Source Guide

by

Patricia Twohill Lown

and

David Amory Lown

Illustrated by Megan Green

The Palancar Company Limited
New York • Paris • United Kingdom

The Editors have selected artisans, dealers and suppliers who are considered the best in their fields. Amongst all these, however, are a select few who are outstanding.

The reader will find these indicated by a Crown.

TELEPHONE CALLERS PLEASE TAKE NOTE: When calling London and the Counties from abroad, you will need to dial the country code (44) and eliminate the zero (0) which precedes all the telephone numbers. When in England you dial the zero and the rest of the number.

The endpapers represent a survey of London, by Stowe, published by Act of Parliament in 1754. Courtesy of The Trowbridge Gallery, London.

INTRODUCTION

When you read these lines, you are on the threshold of one of life's great experiences: London. London is a wonderland of all those beautiful things created by the minds and hands of humankind since the beginning of history. Here, in this astonishing city, surprises await around every corner.

London is the home of many of the greatest fine art and antique dealers in the world. Most of them are clustered in certain neighbourhoods making it convenient for the browser and buyer to develop, through comparisons, his "eye", as well as his or her individual taste. There are also the Markets where one can find authentic antiques and exciting collectibles in amazing profusion at very low, as well as very high, prices.

London is also home to many of the great Guilds representing some of the finest craftsmen in the world.

Wherever you go in London, you will have a strong feeling of living history. This sense of the "past" will be fortified when you walk along the streets of this amazing city or into the Antique Shops or the Art Galleries and begin to realize the tremendous legacy our ancestors have left us.

Regardless of where we come from, the culture we were born into or the language we speak, there is always a sense of homecoming when we arrive in England. And here in London, we experience the unique humour and English courtesy which make our search for beauty more delightful.

The authors have had a marvellous time researching and preparing this book. There are literally thousands of people to thank for their friendly cooperation. Our special thanks to Joan Mullen, our Assistant, to Serena Torrey, Interior Decorator Grant White, Joan Penn and George Hayim. We hope the reader will have as much fun as we have had.

CATEGORY INDEX

ANTIQUE DEALERS

For the antique lover, whether dealer, collector, curator or casual browser, London is one of the world's greatest treasure troves. History and the mementos of the past help us to focus on who and what we are in the great scheme of life. A piece of antique furniture, beautifully designed and lovingly wrought by a skillful craftsman, can humble all who look upon it or touch it.

London is rich in history and equally rich in antiques and works of art. England's role as a world empire and a great trading nation have brought to its shores the wonders of man's creativity. You will find in London the products of this genius from the four corners of the earth.

This guide was conceived to help the designer, the dealer, the collector and all who love the treasure hunt, to navigate this great city and make the search a trifle easier.

There are three organizations you should be aware of: BADA (The British Antique Dealers Association), LAPADA (The Association of Art and Antique Dealers) and ADA (The Antiquities Dealers Association). Some dealers belong to all three organizations, but, when you see the symbol of one of these organizations on the façade of a dealer's shop, or in his promotional material, you can be quite sure that he is honest, reputable and the objects he offers for sale are genuine, are accurately presented, have not been stolen and any restoration or alteration from the original is properly done.

ABERDEEN HOUSE ANTIQUES
75 St. Mary's Road, London W5 5RH ■ Tel: (0181) 567-5194 ■ Fax: (0181) 840-2362 ■ Mon-Sat 10:00-5:00 ■ French and Portuguese spoken ■ Prices medium to high ■ Trade discount ■ Major credit cards ■ LAPADA

18th and 19th century furniture, mirrors, lighting, decorative objects and some porcelain.

ALAN ADRIAN
66-67 South Audley Street, London W1Y 5FE ■ Tel: (0171) 495-2324 ■ Fax: (0171) 495-0204 ■ Mon-Fri 10:00-6:00 ■ BADA

18th and 19th century Continental furniture, Georgian furniture, clocks and barometers; European ceramics, decorations. Architectural and garden ornaments, decorative objects, country and pine furniture, sculpture and bronzes.

ALAN ADRIAN
219 Kensington Church Street, London W8 7LX ■ Tel: (0171) 727-4783 ■ Fax: (0171) 727-7353 ■ Mon-Fri 10:00-6:00, Sat 11:00-4:00 ■ BADA

18th and 19th century Continental furniture, clocks and barometers.

♕ MARIA ANDIPA & SON ICON GALLERY
162 Walton Street, Knightsbridge, London SW3 2JL ■ Tel: (0171) 589-2371 ■ Fax: (0171) 225-0305 ■ E-mail: art@andipa.com ■ Tue-Sat 11:00-6:00 ■ Maria and Acoris Andipa ■ Greek, French and Arabic spoken ■ Prices low to very high ■ Major credit cards ■ Trade discount ■ LAPADA

Icons, 18th and 19th century furniture, glass, jewellery and works of art. Restoration, research and valuations.

ARENSKI FINE ART LTD
185 Westbourne Grove, London W11 2SB ■ Tel: (0171) 727-8599/(0171) 727-7584 ■ Mon-Sat 10:00-5:30 ■ BADA, LAPADA

19thcentury bronzes, furniture, glass, objets d'art. Gothic Revival.

ARTEMIS DECORATIVE ARTS LTD.
36 Kensington Church Street, London W8 4DB ■ Tel: (0171) 376-0377 ■ Mon-Fri 10:00-6:00, Sat by appointment ■ French spoken ■ Prices medium to high ■ Professional discount ■ Major credit cards ■ LAPADA

19th and 20th century clocks, glass, bronzes and sculpture.

♛ ASPREY

165-169 New Bond Street, London W1Y 0AR ■ Tel: (0171) 493-6767 ■ Fax: (0171) 491-0384 ■ Telex: 25110 ASPREY G ■ Mon-Fri 9:00-5:30, Sat 9:00-1:00 ■ BADA

An excellent collection of fine 18th and 19th century furniture, silver and old Sheffield plate; clocks and barometers; glass; Russian works of art.

B & T ANTIQUES

79-81 Ledbury Road, London W11 2AG ■ Tel: (0171) 229-7001 ■ Fax: (0171) 229-2033 ■ Mon-Sat 10:00-6:00 ■ Mrs. Bernadette Lewis ■ French spoken ■ Prices medium to high ■ Visa, MC, Switch ■ Trade discount

Eclectic collection of French and English furniture from the 18th century to 1940. Restoration. New showroom by appointment only.

H. BALDWIN & SONS LTD

11 Adelphi Terrace, London WC2N 6BJ ■ Tel: (0171) 930-6870 (coins)/(0171) 839-1310 (medals) ■ Fax: (0171) 930-9450 ■ Mon-Fri 9:00-5:00 ■ BADA

Coins, medals, decorations, tokens, numismatic books. Valuations.

EDDY BARDAWIL ANTIQUES

106 Kensington Church Street, London W8 4BH ■ Tel: (0171) 221-3967 ■ Fax: (0171) 221-5124 ■ Mon-Fri 10:00-1:00, 2:00-5:30, Sat 10:00-1:00 ■ BADA

18th and early 19th century English furniture, glass, metalwork, paintings, drawings and prints.

J & A BEARE LTD

7 Broadwick Street, London W1V 1FJ ■ Tel: (0171) 437-1449 ■ Fax: (0171) 439-4520 ■ Mon-Fri 9:00-12:15, 1:30-5:00, appointment advisable ■ BADA

Musical instruments of the violin family. Valuations.

H. BLAIRMAN & SONS LTD

119 Mount Street, London W1Y 5HB ■ Tel: (0171) 493-0444 ■ Fax: (0171) 495-0766 ■ Mon-Fri 9:00-5:30, Sat by appointment ■ Martin Levy ■ French spoken ■ BADA

Furniture. Later 19th and early 20th century Western applied arts.

CLAUDE BORNOFF

20 Chepstow Corner, Pembridge Villas, London W2 4XE ■ Tel: (0171) 229-8947 ■ Mon-Fri 9:30-5:30, other times by appointment ■ BADA

Furniture, porcelain and pottery. Valuations.

BUTCHOFF ANTIQUES

220 and 229 Westbourne Grove, London W11 2SE ■ Tel: (0171) 221-8174 ■ Fax: (0171) 792-8923 ■ Mon-Sat 9:30-6:00 ■ Ian Butchoff ■ Italian spoken ■ Prices medium to high ■ Amex, Visa, Diners ■ Professional discount ■ LAPADA

English and Continental 18th and 19th century furniture. Restoration.

BARNET CATTANACH ANTIQUES

79 Kensington Church Street, London W8 4BG ■ Telfax: (0171) 396-2817 ■ Restoration Studio: Tel: (0181) 207-6792 ■ Tue-Sat 10:00-5:30 ■ R.J. Gerry and A.M Cattanach ■ French spoken ■ Prices medium to high ■ Trade discount ■ Major credit cards ■ BADA, LAPADA

18th century and early 19th century English and Continental furniture. Restoration workshop.

ANTOINE CHENEVIERE FINE ARTS LTD

27 Bruton Street, London W1X 7DP ■ Tel: (0171) 491-1007 ■ Fax: (0171) 495-6173 ■ Mon-Fri 9:30-6:00 ■ BADA

18th and 19th century Russian, Austrian, German, and Italian furniture and objets d'art.

THE COACH HOUSE

189 Westbourne Grove, London W11 2SB ■ Tel: (0171) 229-8311 ■ Fax: (0171) 229-4297 ■ Mon-Sat 9:00-5:30 ■ Arenski, Peter Farlow, Peter Petrov ■ Prices medium to high ■ Professional discount ■ Major credit cards ■ BADA, LAPADA

Wide range of antique furniture, paintings and objects d'art.

DYALA SALAM ANTIQUES

174A Kensington Church Street, London W8 4DP ■ Tel: (0171) 229-4045 ■ (0171) 229-2433 ■ Mon-Sat 11:00-5:30 ■ Dyala Salam ■ French and Arabic spoken ■ Prices low to very high ■ Amex accepted ■ Trade discount

Antiques from the Ottoman Empire. 18th and 19th century furniture, textiles, glass, porcelain and cushions.

EMANOUEL CORPORATION (UK) LTD

64 South Audley Street, London W1Y 5FA ■ Tel: (0171) 493-4350 ■ Fax: (0171) 629-3125 ■ French and Arabic spoken ■ Professional discount ■ Major credit cards ■ LAPADA

Antiquities, clocks, 19th century furniture, glass, Oriental items, porcelain and pottery, paintings, sculpture, bronzes and Islamic objects.

END OF THE WORLD ANTIQUES

490A King's Road, London SW10 ■ Tel: (0171) 823-3394 ■ Mon-Sun 10:00-7:00 ■ Gervase Thorp ■ French and Spanish spoken ■ Prices low to medium ■ Trade discount

Victorian and Georgian furniture.

FLUSS AND CHARLESWORTH LIMITED

1 Lauderdale Road, London W91LT ■ Telfax: (0171) 286-8339 ■ By appointment only ■ John Charlesworth, Mrs. Elfrieda Fluss ■ German spoken ■ LAPADA

18th and early 19th century fine furniture and decorative works of art. Fine reproduction of special commissions. Interior decoration.

JUDY FOX ANTIQUES

81 Portobello Road, London W11 2QB ■ Tel: (0171) 229-8130 ■ Fax: (0171) 229-6998 ■ Saturdays ■ French and Italian spoken ■ Prices medium to high ■ Professional discount ■ MC and Visa ■ LAPADA

19th century furniture, porcelain and objects.

UN FRANCAIS A LONDRES

202 Ebury Street, London SW1W 8UN ■ Tel: (0171) 730-1771 ■ Fax: (0171) 730-1661 ■ Mon-Fri 10:00-6:00, Sat 10:00-4:00 ■ Paul Sumner ■ French spoken ■ Prices medium to high ■ Major credit cards ■ Trade discount

French 18th and 19th century antique furniture, lighting, sculpture and paintings.

GAVINA EWART

Bond Street Galleries, 2nd floor, 111-112 New Bond Street, London W1Y 9AB ■ Tel: (0171) 491-7266/(01242) 254940 ■ Fax: (0171) 491-7211/(01242) 526994 ■ Mon-Fri 9:30-1:00/2:00-5:30 ■ BADA

Table silver and cutlery, Old Sheffield plate, glass, maps, prints, porcelain, pottery and enamels.

GROVE ANTIQUES
220 Westbourne Grove, London W11 2RH ■ Telfax: (0171) 792-8028
■ Mon-Sat 10:00-6:00 ■ Paul Crann ■ Prices medium to very high ■
Amex accepted ■ Trade discount

18th and 19th century French clocks, English and French long case clocks, ormolu with Sèvres panels. Some French furniture, credenzas.

HALYCON DAYS LTD.
14 Brook Street, London W1Y 1AA ■ Tel: (0171) 629-8811 ■ Fax:
(0171) 409-0280 ■ Internet http://www.halcyon.days.co.uk ■ Mon-Fri
9:15-5:30 ■ BADA

Enamels, snuff boxes, objets de vertu, tôle peinte, papier maché, porcelain and pottery.

HANCOCKS & CO. (JEWELLERS) LTD
52-53 Burlington Arcade, London W1X 2HP ■ Tel: (0171) 493-8904 ■
Fax: (0171) 493-8905 ■ Mon-Fri 9:30-5:00, Sat 10:00-4:00 ■ BADA

Antique jewellery, antique silver, art objects.

ROBERT HARMAN ANTIQUES
140-142 Kensington Church Street, London W8 4BN ■ Tel: (0171)
221-6790 ■ Mobile: (0860) 549797 ■ Mon-Fri 10:00-6:00, Sat 10:00-
4:00 ■ BADA

Furniture and works of art.

♛**JONATHAN HARRIS**
9 Lower Addison Gardens, London W14 8BG ■ Tel: (0171) 602-6255
■ Fax: (0171) 602-0488 ■ Mon-Fri 9:30-6:00 ■ Jonathan Harris and
Bruce Lindsay ■ French spoken ■ Prices high ■ BADA

European and Oriental furniture and works of art.

♛**BRIAN HAUGHTON ANTIQUES**
3B Burlington Gardens, Old Bond Street, London W1X 1LE ■
Tel: (0171) 734-5491 ■ Fax: (0171) 494-4604 ■ E-mail:
info@haughton.com ■ Brian Haughton ■ Mon-Fri 10:00-5:00 ■ Prices
high to very high ■ Professional discount ■ Visa

Fine ceramics and works of art of the 18th and 19th century.

JEANETTE HAYHURST FINE GLASS
32A Kensington Church Street, London W8 4HA ■ Tel: (0171) 938-
1539 ■ Mon-Fri 10:00-5:00, Sat 12:00-5:00 ■ BADA

British glass from the 17th to the 20th century.

JONATHAN HORNE (ANTIQUES) LTD

66B and 66C Kensington Church Street, London W8 4BY ■ Tel: (0171) 221-5658 ■ Fax: (0171) 792-3090 ■ Mon-Fri 9:30-5:30 or by appointment ■ BADA

Early English pottery and works of art.

HOWARD-JONES SILVER SHOP

43 Kensington Church Street, London W8 4BA ■ Telfax: (0171) 937-4359 ■ Mon-Fri 10:00-5:00 and by appointment ■ LAPADA

Desk and writing accessories, porcelain, silver, sculpture and bronzes.

J & B ANTIQUES

Chelsea Galleries, 67 Portobello Road, London W11 2QB ■ Tel: (01295) 711689 ■ Tel 2: (0836) 684133 ■ Saturdays ■ LAPADA

Clocks, glass, jewellery, Oriental items, objects of art, silver, sculpture and bronze.

STEVE JOHNSON DECORATIVE ARTS

The Antique Centre, 58 Kensington Church Street, London W8 4DB ■ Tel: (0171) 937-8318 ■ Fax: (0171) 937-3400 ■ Mon-Sat 11:00-5:30 ■ French spoken ■ Prices low to high ■ Professional discount

19th and 20th century decorative arts: pewter, cameo glass, ceramics, sculpture, Art Nouveau, Art Deco and Secession.

KIKUCHI TRADING CO. LTD.

Grays Antiques Market, 58 Davies Street, London W1Y 2LP ■ Tel: (0171) 629 6808 ■ LAPADA

Antiquities, glass, jewellery and works of art.

KLEANTHOUS ANTIQUES

144 Portobello Road, London W11 2DZ ■ Tel: (0171) 727-3649 ■ Fax: (0171) 243-2488 ■ E-mail: antiques@kleanthous.com ■ Sat 8:00-4:00, other days by appointment ■ Chris and Costas Kleanthous ■ Greek spoken ■ Trade discount ■ Major credit cards ■ LAPADA

British 18th to 20th century silver, porcelain, furniture, clocks and objets de vertu. Vintage watches by the big names and Georgian, Victorian, Art Nouveau and Art Deco Jewellery.

KOOPMAN RARE ART

London Silver Vaults, Chancery House, Vaults 13-15, 53-64 Chancery Lane, London WC2A 1QX ■ Tel: (0171) 242-7624/(0171) 405-9968 ■ Fax: (0171) 831-0221 ■ Mon-Fri 9:00-5:30, Sat 9:00-1:00 ■ BADA

Beautiful English and Continental antique silver.

D. S. LAVENDER ANTIQUES LTD

26 Conduit Street, London W1R 9TA ■ Tel: (0171) 629-1782 ■ Fax: (0171) 629-3106 ■ E-mail: dslavender@clara.uk• Mon-Fri 9:30-5:30 ■ David Lavender ■ French and German spoken ■ Major credit cards ■ Professional discount ■ BADA

16th to early 19th century portrait miniatures, snuff boxes, fine jewels, objets d'art. Repair.

LEWIS & LLOYD

65 Kensington Church Street, London W8 4BA ■ Tel: (0171) 938-3323 ■ Fax: (0171) 361-0086 ■ Mon-Fri 10:15-5:30 ■ BADA

18th and 19th century English furniture.

J. LIPITCH LTD

177 Westbourne Grove, London W11 2SB ■ Tel: (0171) 229-0783 ■ Mon-Fri 10:00-5:30, Sat 10:00-1:30 ■ Prices medium to high ■ Major credit cards ■ BADA

English and Continental furniture, porcelain and pottery. Valuations.

CLIVE LOVELESS

54 St. Quintin Avenue, London W10 6PA ■ Tel: (0181) 969-5831 ■ Fax: (0181) 969-5292 ■ By appointment ■ BADA

18th and 19th century Oriental tribal rugs. 17th to 19th century Ottoman, Central Asian, African and Pre-Colombian textiles.

MALLETT & SON (ANTIQUES) LTD

141 New Bond Street, London W1Y 0BS ■ Tel: (0171) 499-7411 ■ Fax: (0171) 495-3179 ■ Mon-Fri 9:00-6:00, Sat: 11:00-4:00 ■ CEO: Lanto M. Synge ■ French and Spanish spoken ■ Prices high ■ Amex and Visa ■ Trade discount ■ BADA

Finest English antique furniture, paintings, watercolours, objets d'art, antique glass. Range of catalogues and publications. Restoration.

E & H MANNERS

66a Kensington Church Street, London W8 4BY ■ Telfax: (0171) 229-5516 ■ Mon-Fri 10:00-5:30 appointment advised ■ Errol Manners ■ Prices high ■ BADA

18th century European ceramics.

MARK GALLERY

9 Porchester Place, Marble Arch, London W2 2BS ■ Tel: (0171) 262-4906 ■ Fax: (0171) 224-9416 ■ Mon-Fri 10:00-1:00/2:00-6:00, Sat 11:00-1:00 and by appointment ■ Helen Mark ■ French, German and Italian spoken ■ Prices low to very high ■ Visa, Amex ■ BADA

16th to 19th century Russian icons and modern and contemporary French lithographs and etchings. Valuation, verification and framing.

MORELLE DAVIDSON LTD.

45-46 New Bond Street, London W1Y 9HB ■ Tel: (0171) 408-0066 ■ Fax: (0171) 495-8885 ■ Mon-Fri 9:30-5:30 ■ LAPADA

Jewellery, silver and Russian works of art.

NAMARA FINE ART

25 Shepherd Market, London W1Y 7HR ■ Tel: (0171) 499-2901 ■ Fax: (0171) 499-2914 ■ Mon-Fri 9:30-5:30 ■ French spoken ■ Trade discount ■ Major credit cards ■ BADA

18th and 19th century European antiques and works of art including silver, glass, ceramics, furniture and sculpture.

THE OLD CINEMA

160 Chiswick High Road, London W4 1PR ■ Tel: (0181) 995-4166 ■ Fax: (0181) 995-4167 ■ E-mail: theoldcinema@antiques-uk.co.uk ■ Mon-Sat 9:30-6:00, Sun 12:00-5:00 ■ Martin Hanness ■ Prices medium to high ■ Professional discount ■ Visa, MC ■ LAPADA

Antique furniture, silver, ceramics. Restoration and upholstery.

OLIVER-SUTTON ANTIQUES

34c Kensington Church Street, London W8 4HA ■ Tel: (0171) 937-0633 ■ Mon-Fri 10:00-5:00, closed August ■ BADA

Fine collection of Staffordshire pottery figures. He has written several books on his subject.

PELHAM GALLERIES LTD
24 & 25 Mount Street, London W1Y 5RB ■ Tel: (0171) 629-0905 ■ Fax: (0171) 495-4511 ■ Mon-Fri 9:00-5:30, Sat by appointment ■ BADA

18th century and Regency English and Continental furniture and works of art. Clocks and barometers, musical instruments, tapestries, needlework and fabrics. Oriental works of art.

👑 RONALD PHILLIPS LTD
26 Bruton Street, London W1X 8LH ■ Tel: (0171) 493-2341 ■ Fax: (0171) 495-0843 ■ Mon-Sat 9:00-5:30 ■ Prices high to very high ■ BADA

Fine 18th century English furniture, mirrors and decorative objects.

PORTOBELLO FINE ART LTD.
286 Westbourne Grove, London W11 ■ Tel: (0171) 284-3030 ■ Fax: (0171) 636-3878 ■ Mobile: 0958 437043 ■ Saturdays ■ LAPADA

Decorative objects, prints and maps, furniture of the 18th, 19th and early 20th century, paintings, sculpture and bronzes. Restoration.

JONATHAN POTTER LTD
125 New Bond Street, First floor, London W1Y 9AF ■ Tel: (0171) 491-3520 ■ Fax: (0171) 491-9754 ■ E-mail: jpmaps@ibm.net ■ Mon-Fri 10:00-6:00, Sat by appointment ■ BADA, LAPADA

Maps and atlases, books and manuscripts. Valuations.

👑 REINDEER ANTIQUES LTD
81 Kensington Church Street, London W8 4BG ■ Telfax: (0171) 937-3754 ■ Fax: (0171) 937-7199 Mon-Sat 9:00-6:00, other times by appointment ■ Adrian Butterworth, Viviana Hieber ■ French, Italian and German spoken ■ Prices medium to high ■ Major credit cards ■ Trade discount ■ BADA, LAPADA

Fine 17th to 19th century English furniture, paintings, clocks and barometers, silver, ceramics and porcelain. Restoration.

JOAN ROGER (ANTIQUES) LTD
London W14 0RRn Tel: (0171) 381-2884 or Tel: (0171) 381-2884 or (0171) 603-7627 or (0171) 603-7627 ■ By appointment only ■ BADA

18th and early 19th century furniture, especially small elegant pieces; prints; porcelain; decorative items.

BRIAN ROLLESTON (ANTIQUES) LTD
104A Kensington Church Street, London W8 4BU ■ Telfax: (0171) 229-5892 ■ Mon-Fri 10:00-1:00, 2:30-5:30 ■ BADA

Fine 18th century English furniture.

⚱ALISTAIR SAMPSON ANTIQUES
120 Mount Street, London W1Y 5HB ■ Tel: (0171) 409-1799 ■ Fax: (0171) 409-7717 ■ Mon-Fri 9:30-5:30, Sat by appointment ■ Alistair Sampson, Christopher Banks ■ Prices medium ■ Amex and Visa accepted ■ Trade discount ■ BADA

English 18th century furniture, treen, brass, pottery, needlework.

PATRICK SANDBERG ANTIQUES
140-142 and 150-152 Kensington Church Street, London W8 4BN ■ Tel: (0171) 229-0373 ■ Fax: (0171) 792-3467 ■ Mon-Fri 10:00-6:00, Sat 10:00-4:00 ■ BADA

18th and early 19th century English furniture.

SCHREDDS OF PORTOBELLO
107 Portobello Road, London W11 2QB ■ Tel: (0181) 348 3314 ■ Website: www.schredds.com ■ Sat 7:30-2:00 ■ LAPADA

18th and 19th century European silver. Some porcelain.

M & D SELIGMANN
37 Kensington Church Street, London W8 4LL ■ Tel: (0171) 937-0400 ■ Fax: (0171) 722-4315 ■ Mon-Fri 10:30-5:30, Sat 11:00-4:00, other times by appointment ■ BADA

English country furniture, works of art and unusual items; early English pottery.

JEAN SEWELL (ANTIQUES) LTD
3 & 4 Campden Street, London W8 7EP ■ Tel: (0171) 727-3122 ■ Fax: (0171) 229-1053 ■ Mon-Fri 10:00-5:30, Sat 10:00-2:00 ■ BADA

English, Continental and Oriental porcelain, pottery and enamels.

⚱STAIR & COMPANY LTD
14 Mount Street, London W1Y 5RA ■ Tel: (0171) 499-1784 ■ Fax: (0171) 629-1050 ■ Website: www.artnet.comstair&company.htm1 ■ Mon-Fri 9:30-5:30 or by appointment ■ Robert Luck, Michael Pick ■ French and German spoken ■ Prices medium to very high ■ Amex accepted ■ Professional discount ■ BADA

Since 1911 the finest English antique furniture and works of art. Design and decoration. Restorations. They also help form collections and bid at auction. You might also try their STAWAX furniture wax for your precious furniture.

LOUIS STANTON

299-301 Westbourne Grove, London W11 2QA ■ Tel: (0171) 727-9336 ■ Fax: (0171) 727-5424 ■ Mon-Fri 9:30-5:30 and by appointment ■ BADA

16th to 19th century furniture, specializing in early oak, medieval sculpture and works of art, curiosities and unusual items; metalwork and pewter.

JACOB STODEL

116A Kensington Church Street, London W8 4BH ■ Tel: (0171) 221-2652 ■ Fax: (0171) 229-1293 ■ By appointment ■ BADA

18th century English and Continental furniture. Oriental and European ceramics and works of art.

♛ JUNE & TONY STONE FINE ANTIQUE BOXES

75 Portobello Road, London W11 2QB ■ Tel: (01273) 500212 ■ Tel 2: (0468) 382424 ■ Fax: (01273) 500024 ■ E-mail: jts@boxes.co.uk ■ Tue-Fri 10:30-4:30, Sat 7:00-5:00 ■ Prices high ■ Major credit cards ■ Trade discount ■ LAPADA

An astonishing collection of boxes, caskets, humidors, portable writing desks, tea caddies, dressing cases, knife boxes, sewing boxes. Some of the items are in tortoise shell and shagreen. Seeing this collection is believing.

TURPIN

27 Bruton Street, London W1X 7DB ■ Tel: (0171) 493-3275 ■ Fax: (0171) 408-1869 ■ Mon-Fri 10:00-6:00 or by appointment ■ M. Turpin and J. Mann ■ Prices high to very high ■ Trade discount ■ LAPADA

A large stock of fine English furniture and mirrors of the 17th, 18th and early 19th century. Some Continental antiques and art objects.

GRAHAM WALPOLE ANTIQUES

187 Westbourne Grove, London W11 2RS ■ Tel: (0171) 229-0267 ■ Mon-Sat 10:00-5:30 ■ Prices medium to high ■ Trade discount ■ Visa, Amex ■ LAPADA

19th century furniture, fireplaces, decorative items, lighting, mirrors, metalwork, needlework, paintings, watercolours and drawings, works of art, sculpture, bronzes and brass.

TRUDE WEAVER (ANTIQUES)

71 Portobello Road, London W11 2QB ■ Tel: (0171) 229-8738 ■ Wed-Fri 10:00-5:00, Sat 8:00-5:00 and by appointment ■ LAPADA

18th and 19th century furniture, fireplaces, Oriental textiles, treen, and works of art.

MARY WISE AND GROSVENOR ANTIQUES

27 Holland Street, London W8 4NA ■ Tel: (0171) 937-8649 ■ Fax: (0171) 937-7179 ■ Mon-Fri 9:30-5:30 or by appointment ■ Mary Wise ■ French spoken ■ Prices medium to high ■ Major credit cards ■ Trade discount ■ BADA

English porcelain, 18th and 19th century bronzes, Chinese watercolours on pith paper and works of art.

SOUTH LONDON

DIDIER AARON (LONDON) LTD

21 Ryder Street, London SW1Y 6PX Tel: (0171) 839-4716 ■ Fax: (0171) 930- 6699 ■ Open Mon-Fri by appointment only ■ BADA

18thcentury furniture, Old Master drawings and paintings.

ACANTHUS ART LTD

PO Box 211, London SW11 4BS ■ Tel: (0171) 622-0734 ■ By appointment only

Ceramics, French textiles and antiques.

NORMAN ADAMS LTD

8-10 Hans Road, Knightsbridge, London SW3 1RX ■ Tel: (0171) 589-5266 ■ Fax: (0171) 589-1968 ■ Mon-Fri 9:00-5:30, Sat & Sun by appointment ■ BADA

Exceptional 18th and 19th century furniture. European ceramics, decorations.

ADAMS ROOM ANTIQUES

20 The Ridgway, London SW19 4LN ■ Tel: (0181) 946-7047 ■ Fax: (0181) 946-7476 ■ Mon-Sat 10:00-5:00 ■ Grace Seymour-Cole ■ Prices medium to high ■ Trade discount ■ Major credit cards ■ LAPADA

18th and 19th century French and English furniture, lighting, paintings and mirrors.

DAVID ALEXANDER ANTIQUES

102 Waterford Road, London SW6 2HA ■ Tel: (0171) 731-4644 ■ Fax: (0171) 731-1622 ■ Tue-Fri 10:00-6:00 ■ BADA

16th to 18th century English and Continental Furniture.

PETER ALLEN ANTIQUES LTD.

17-17A Nunhead Green, Peckham SE15 3QQ ■ Tel: (0171) 732-1968 ■ Mon-Fri 8:00-4:00 ■ 111 Portobello Road, W11 ■ Tel: (0171) 727-3397 ■ Sat 9:00-4:00 ■ LAPADA

Continental furniture, clocks, porcelain and pottery, Oriental items, silver.

ANNO DOMINI ANTIQUES

66 Pimlico Road, London SW1W 8LS ■ Tel: (0171) 730-5496/(0171) 352-3084 when closed ■ Mon-Sat 10:00-1:00, 2:15-5:30 and by appointment ■ Frederick Bartman and David Cohen ■ German spoken ■ Prices medium ■ Trade discount ■ BADA

English furniture of the 18th and early 19th century, mirrors, glass and decorative objects.

APTER FREDERICKS LTD

265-267 Fulham Road, London SW3 6HY ■ Tel: (0171) 352-2188 ■ Fax: (0171) 376-5619 ■ Mon-Fri 9:30-5:30, other times by appointment ■ BADA

Beautiful 18th and early 19th century English furniture, specializing in dining room furniture and bookcases.

CHRISTOPHER BANGS

PO Box 6077, London SW6 7XS ■ Tel: (0171) 381-3532 ■ Fax: (0171) 381-2192 ■ Mon-Thu 10:00-4:00 by appointment ■ LAPADA

Early metalware, metalwork and works of art, together with early lighting, candelabra and candlesticks. Consultancy and research.

ROBERT BARLEY ANTIQUES

48 Fulham High Street, London SW6 3LQ ■ Telfax: (0171) 736-4429 ■ Mon-Fri 9:30-5:30 ■ Robert Barley and Chris Loesch ■ Prices low to very high ■ Major credit cards ■ Trade discount

Highly unusual furniture, pictures, sculpture and objects from 500BC to 1950.

JOANNA BARNES FINE ARTS

14 Mason's Yard, Duke Street, London SW1Y 6BU ■ Tel: (0171) 930-4215 ■ Mon-Fri 10:00-5:30 ■ BADA

European sculpture.

NIGEL BARTLETT

67 St. Thomas Street, London SE1 3QX ■ Tel: (0171) 378-7895 ■ Fax: (0171) 378-0388 ■ Mon-Fri 9:30-5:30 ■ BADA

Architectural antiques, mainly English chimney pieces.

HILARY BATSTONE DECORATIVE ANTIQUES

8 Holbein Place, London SW1W 8NL ■ Tel: (0171) 730-5335 ■ Mon-Fri 10:30-5:30, Sat 10:30-3:30 ■ Prices medium to high ■ Professional discount ■ Major credit cards ■ LAPADA

European 18th, 19th and early 20th century decorative antiques and textiles. Decorative objects, painted furniture and lighting.

H. C. BAXTER & SONS

40 Drewstead Road, London SW16 1AB ■ Tel: (0181) 769-5869/5969 ■ Fax: (0181) 769-0998 ■ Mon-Fri 8:30-4:00 by appointment ■ Prices medium ■ Trade discount ■ BADA, LAPADA

Fine 18th century English furniture.

JOHN BLY

27 Bury Street, St. James's, London SW1Y 6AL ■ Tel: (0171) 930-1292 ■ Fax: (0171) 839-4775 ■ Mon-Fri 9:00-5:30, Sat 10:30-2:00, other times by appointment ■ John Bly and James Bly ■ French, Italian and Portuguese spoken ■ Prices medium to very high ■ Trade discount ■ BADA, LAPADA

17th, 18th and 19th century furniture, antiquities, works of art, fine paintings and objets d'art.

JOANNA BOOTH

247 King's Road, Chelsea, London SW3 5EL ■ Tel: (0171) 352-8998 ■ Fax: (0171) 376-7350 ■ Mon-Sat 10:00-6:00, other times by appointment ■ Joanna Booth ■ French and Spanish spoken ■ Prices low to very high ■ Major credit cards ■ Trade discount ■ BADA

Sculptured wood carvings, tapestries, textiles, Old Master drawings.

ROBERT BOWMAN

PO Box 13393, London SW3 4RP ■ Tel: (0171) 730-8057 ■ Fax: (0171) 259-9195 ■ By appointment only ■ BADA

19th and early 20th century sculpture in bronze and marble.

HUMPHREY CARRASCO

43 Pimlico Road, London SW1W 8NE ■ Tel: (0171) 730-9911 ■ Fax: (0171) 730-9944 ■ Mon-Fri 10:00-6:00, Sat 10:00-5:00 ■ David Humphrey and Marylise Carrasco ■ French and Spanish spoken ■ Prices medium to very high ■ Trade discount

18th and 19th century English furniture and lighting. Furniture designed and reproduced to order.

RICHARD COURTNEY LTD

112-114 Fulham Road, South Kensington, London SW3 6HU ■ Tel: (0171) 370-4020 ■ Fax: (0171) 370-4020 ■ Mon-Fri 9:30-6:00, other times by appointment ■ BADA

18th century English furniture.

ZAL DAVAR ANTIQUES

273 Lillie Road, London SW6 7LL ■ Tel: (0171) 381-2500 ■ Fax: (0171) 381-8320 ■ Mon-Fri 9:30-5:30 ■ Prices medium to high ■ Trade discount ■ Major credit cards ■ LAPADA

Architectural and garden ornaments, 19th century furniture, mirrors, barometers and decorative items.

JESSE DAVIS ANTIQUES

Antiquarius Antiques Market, 131-141 King's Road, London SW3 4PW ■ Tel: (0171) 352 4314 ■ Mon-Sat 10:00-6:00 ■ Prices medium to high ■ Professional discount ■ Major credit cards ■ LAPADA

Ceramics: specialists in Staffordshire, majolica and decorative objects.

ROBERT DICKSON & LESLEY RENDALL ANTIQUES

263 Fulham Road, London SW3 6HY ■ Tel: (0171) 351-0330 ■ Fax: (0171) 352-0078 ■ Mon-Fri 9:30-5:30, Sat 10:30-1:00 and by appointment ■ BADA

Late 18th and early 19th century works of art.

CHARLES EDWARDS

582 King's Road, London SW6 2DY ■ Tel: (0171) 736-8490 ■ Fax: (0171) 371-5436 ■ Mon-Sat 9:30-6:00 ■ Prices medium to high ■ Professional discount ■ Major credit cards ■ BADA

Antique lighting, furniture, pictures, garden objects. Late 19th and early 20thcentury Western applied arts.

ERMITAGE LTD

23 Stanhope Gardens, London SW7 5QX ■ Telfax: (0171) 731-1810
■ By appointment only ■ BADA

Fabergé, Continental silver and Russian works of art.

EYRE & GREIG LTD

2 Rosenau Crescent, London SW11 4RZ ■ Tel: (0171) 738-0652 ■ Fax:
(0171) 738-0652 ■ Mobile: 0468 410764 ■ By appointment ■ BADA

18th century English furniture and paintings related to India.

NICOLE FABRE

592 King's Road, London SW6 2DX ■ Tel: (0171) 384-3112 ■ Fax
(0171) 610-6410 ■ Mon-Fri 9:00-6:00, Sat 10:00-5:00 ■ French spoken ■ Prices medium to high ■ Professional discount ■ Major credit
cards ■ LAPADA

**French 18th to mid 19th century provincial fruit wood furniture
and mirrors. French textiles, toiles de Jouy and linen of the 18th
to late 19th century.**

FERNANDES & MARCHE

23 Motcomb Street, Belgrave Square SW1X 8LB ■ Telfax: (0171)
235-6773 ■ Mon-Fri 10:00-5:30 ■ Prices high ■ Professional discount
■ Major credit cards ■ LAPADA

**18th century Georgian furniture, mirrors and decorative
objects.**

THE GENERAL TRADING COMPANY

144 Sloane Street, London SW1X 9BL ■ Tel: (0171) 730-0411 ■ Fax:
(0171) 823-4624 ■ Mon-Sat 9:30-6:00 ■ Michael MacRae ■ French and
German spoken ■ Trade discount ■ Major credit cards ■ LAPADA

**Large store with 19th century furniture, prints and maps. A won-
derful collection of porcelain and china from hand-painted
Herend to Raynaud and Wedgwood, Royal Worcester, Spode,
Emma Bridgewater, and Holdenby design earthenware. Crystal:
Waterford, Baccarat, Dartington and many others. Bridal registry.**

BIRDIE FORTESCUE ANTIQUES

London SW6 ■ Telfax: (0171) 371-8600 ■ By appointment only ■
LAPADA

18th and 19th century English furniture.

MICHAEL FOSTER

118 Fulham Road, London SW3 6HU ■ Tel: (0171) 373-3636 ■ Fax:
(0171) 373-4042 ■ Mon-Fri 9:30-6:00, Sat by appointment ■ BADA

18th and early 19th century furniture and works of art. Valuations.

♛ VICTOR FRANSES GALLERY

57 Jermyn Street, St. James's, London SW1Y 6LX ■ Tel: (0171) 493-6284/(0171) 629-1144 ■ Fax: (0171) 495-3668 ■ Mon-Fri 10:00-5:00, other times by appointment ■ Prices high to very high ■ Professional discount ■ Major credit cards ■ BADA

19th century animalier sculpture, rare carpets, tapestries and rugs. Valuations.

FREDERICKS & SON

92 Fulham Road, London SW3 6HR ■ Tel: (0171) 589-5847 ■ Fax: (0171) 589-7893 ■ Mon-Fri 9:00-5:30 and by appointment ■ BADA

18th century English furniture.

NICHOLAS GIFFORD-MEAD ANTIQUES

68 Pimlico Road, London SW1W 8LS ■ Tel: (0171) 730-6233 ■ Fax: (0171) 730-6239 ■ Mon-Fri 9:30-5:30, Sat 9:30-1:30 ■ Prices medium to high ■ Professional discount ■ Major credit cards ■ LAPADA

Splendid fireplaces and accessories. Some architectural and garden ornaments, furniture, metalwork, sculpture and bronzes.

A & F GORDON

C/O 20 Rutland Gate, London SW7 1BB ■ Tel: (0171) 935-5627 ■ By appointment only ■ BADA

18th and 19th century English and Continental furniture. 17th to 20th century paintings, decorative arts. Valuations.

ROSS HAMILTON LTD.

95 Pimlico Road, London SW1W 8HP ■ Telfax: (0171) 730-3015 ■ Mon-Fri 9:30-6:00, Sat 11:00-1:30 ■ Mark Boyce ■ Prices medium to high ■ Trade discount ■ LAPADA

English period furniture and unusual Continental furniture, objects, paintings, clocks, candelabra, lighting, sculpture and bronzes.

RONALD HARMAN ANTIQUES

533 King's Road, London SW10 OTZ ■ Tel: (0171) 352-3775 ■ Fax: (0171) 352-3759 ■ Mon-Sat 10:00-6:00, Sun 11:00-4:00 ■ Prices medium to high ■ Professional discount ■ Major credit cards ■ LAPADA

18th and 19th century furniture and some decorative objects. Some nice 1920s leather chairs.

KENNETH HARVEY ANTIQUES

Ground floor, Furniture Cave, 533 King's Road, London SW10 OTZ
■ Tel: (0171) 352-8645 ■ Fax: (0171) 352-3759 ■ Mon-Sat 10:00-6:00,
Sun 11:00-4:00 ■ Prices medium to high ■ Professional discount ■
Major credit cards ■ LAPADA

**Large display of 18th and 19th century Continental and English
furniture, lighting and decorative objects.**

BRIAN HAWKINS ANTIQUES

Bermondsey Antique Traders, 158 Bermondsey Street, London SE1
3TQ ■ Telfax: (0171) 378-1000 ■ Mon-Thu 9:30-5:00, Fri 7:00-5:00 ■
Brian Hawkins ■ Some French and Spanish ■ Prices medium ■ Trade
discount ■ Major credit cards ■ LAPADA

**Antique furniture from the 18th to the early 20th century.
Restorations.**

HEMPSON

C/O 20 Rutland Gate, London SW7 1BD ■ Tel: (0171) 584-8058 ■ By
appointment only ■ BADA

Continental furniture and works of art.

ROBERT E. HIRSCHHORN

London SE5 8JA ■ Tel: (0171) 703-7443 ■ Mobile: 0831 405937 ■ By
appointment only ■ Prices low to high ■ Professional discount ■ Visa
and MC accepted ■ BADA

Early oak and country furniture and objects.

CARLTON HOBBS LTD

46A Pimlico Road, London SW1W 8LP ■ Tel: (0171) 730-3640/3517
■ Fax: (0171) 730-6080 ■ Mon-Fri 9:00-6:00, Sat 10:00-5:00, other
times by appointment ■ BADA

**18th century and early 19th century English and Continental
furniture and works of art.**

JOHN HOBBS LTD

105-107A Pimlico Road, London SW1W 8PH ■ Tel: (0171) 730-8369
■ E-mail: hobbs.co.uk ■ Mon-Fri 9:30-6:00, Sat 11:00-4:00 ■ BADA

Furniture and works of art.

CHRISTOPHER HODSOLL LTD

89-91 Pimlico Road, London SW1W 8PH ■ Tel: (0171) 730-3370 ■ Fax: (0171) 730-1516 ■ Mon-Fri 9:30-6:00, Sat 10:00-5:00 ■ Christopher Hodsoll ■ French and German spoken ■ Prices high to very high ■ Amex accepted ■ Trade discount

Country house furniture on the grand scale. 18th and 19th century English and Continental furniture, carpets, lamps, paintings and decorative objects. Item search, interiors re-designed and furnished.

WILLIAM HOTOPF ANTIQUES

24 Pimlico Road, London SW1W 8LJ ■ Tel: (0171) 730-3971 ■ Fax: (0171) 730-8703 ■ Mon-Fri 10:00-6:00, Sat-Sun by appointment ■ Prices high ■ Professional discount ■ Major credit cards ■ LAPADA

19th century furniture and glass.

HOTSPUR LTD

14 Lowndes Street, London SW1X 9EX ■ Tel: (0171) 235-1918 ■ Fax: (0171) 235-4371 ■ E-mail: hotspurltd@msn.com. ■ Mon-Fri 9:00-6:00, Sat 9:00-1:00 ■ Mr. Robin Kern ■ French spoken ■ BADA

Fine 18th century English furniture, mirrors, chandeliers and works of art.

HRW ANTIQUES (LONDON) LTD.

26 Sullivan Road, London SW6 3DT ■ Tel: (0171) 371-7995 ■ Fax: (0171) 371-9522 ■ Mon-Fri 9:00-5:00 ■ Iain Henderson Russell ■ Spanish, Italian and French spoken ■ Prices medium to high ■ Trade discount ■ Major credit cards ■ LAPADA

18th and 19th century English and Continental furniture, porcelain and decorative objects.

ANTHONY JAMES & SON LTD

88 Fulham Road, London SW3 6HR ■ Tel: (0171) 584-1120 ■ Fax: (0171) 823-7618 ■ Mon-Fri 9:30-5:45, Sat by appointment ■ BADA

18th and 19th century English and Continental furniture and objects.

LUCY JOHNSON ANTIQUES

2 Chester Street, London SW1X 7BB ■ Tel: (0171) 235-2088 ■ Fax: (0171) 235-2098 ■ E-mail: lucy-johnson@lucy-johnson.com ■ By appointment ■ Professional discount ■ LAPADA

Fine English furniture, Delftware and period interiors from 1660 to 1714.

TOBIAS JELLINEK ANTIQUES

20 Park Road, East Twickenham, Middlesex TW1 2PX ■ Tel: (0181) 892-6892 ■ Fax: (0181) 744-9298 ■ E-mail: toby@jellinek.com ■ Website: www.jellinek.com/oak/ ■ By appointment only ■ BADA

Early English furniture, European ceramics, European sculpture and works of art; early metalworks, treen and bygones.

JEREMY LTD

29 Lowndes Street, London SW1X 9HX ■ Tel: (0171) 823-2923 ■ Fax: (0171) 245-6197 ■ Mon-Fri 8:30-6:00, Sat 9:00-5:00 ■ Prices high ■ Professional discount ■ Major credit cards ■ BADA

A good collection of English and Continental furniture, chandeliers, wall lights, glass pictures and works of art.

JOHN KEIL LTD

154 Brompton Road, London SW3 1HX ■ Tel: (0171) 589-6454 ■ Fax: (0171) 823-8235 ■ Mon-Fri 9:30-6:00 and by appointment ■ Prices medium to high ■ Professional discount ■ Major credit cards ■ BADA

17th, 18th and early 19th century English furniture and works of art.

KIRKWOOD

Suffolk Road, Barnes, London SW13 9PH ■ Tel: (0181) 748-7418 ■ By appointment only ■ BADA

Late 18th and early 19th century English furniture and decorative items.

LAMONT ANTIQUES LTD.

Tunnel Avenue Antique Warehouse, Tunnel Avenue Trading Estate, Greenwich SE10 OQH ■ Tel: (0181) 305-2230 ■ Mon-Fri 9:30-5:30 ■ Prices medium ■ Trade discount ■ Major credit cards ■ LAPADA

Architectural antiques, 18th, 19th and early 20th century furniture and glass.

LINDA SMITH ANTIQUES

London SE3 ■ Tel: (0181) 856-1668 ■ Mobile: 0374 952888 ■ By appointment only ■ LAPADA

Porcelain and glass, 19th century furniture and lighting.

MICHAEL LIPITCH LIMITED

98 Fulham Road, London SW3 6HS ■ Tel: (0171) 589-7327 ■ Fax: (0171) 823-9106 ■ Mon-Fri 9:00-6:00, Sat 10:00-5:00 ■ Prices high ■ Professional discount ■ Major credit cards ■ BADA

Excellent 18th and 19th century furniture and works of art from the Queen Anne to Regency periods.

J. LIPITCH LTD
177 Westbourne Grove, London W11 2SB ■ Tel: (0171) 229-0783
Mon-Fri 10:00-5:30, Sat 10:00-1:30 ■ Prices medium to high ■ Professional discount ■ Major credit cards ■ BADA

English and Continental furniture, porcelain and pottery.

PETER LIPITCH LTD
120 & 124 Fulham Road, London SW3 6HU ■ Tel: (0171) 373-3328 ■
Fax: (0171) 373-8888 ■ Mon-Fri 9:30-5:30, Sat by appointment ■
Melvyn Lipitch ■ Prices high to very high ■ Professional discount ■
Major credit cards ■ BADA

18th and 19th century English furniture and mirrors, objects, glass pictures.

MEGAN MATHERS ANTIQUES
571 King's Road, London SW6 2EB ■ Tel: (0171) 371-7837 ■ Fax: (0171) 371-7895 ■ Mon-Fri 9:30-5:30, Sat 10:30-5:00 ■ Prices medium to high ■ Professional discount ■ Major credit cards ■ LAPADA

Architecture and garden ornaments, 18th and 19th century Continental furniture, painted furniture and works of art.

ANTONIO MENDOZA - EUROPA HOUSE ANTIQUES
160 Tower Bridge Road, London SE13LS ■ Tel: (0171) 357-8951 ■
Mon-Sun 10:00-5:00 ■ French, Spanish, Italian and Portuguese spoken ■ Prices medium ■ Major credit cards ■ Trade discount

Some good quality 18th and 19th century furniture. All types. Some very good dining room tables.

OAKSTAR LTD.
London SW1 ■ Tel: (0171) 630-1822 ■ Fax: (0171) 630-8509 ■ By appointment only ■ LAPADA

18th and 19th century English and Continental furniture, carpets and rugs.

THE OLD CINEMA
157 Tower Bridge Road, Bermondsey SE1 3LW ■ Tel: (0171) 407-5371 ■ Fax: (0171) 403-0359 ■ E-mail: theoldcinema@antiques-uk.co.uk ■ Mon-Sat 9:30-5:30, Sun 12:00-5:00 ■ Martin Hanness ■ Prices medium ■ Trade discount ■ Visa, MC ■ LAPADA

Furniture, shop fittings, architectural antiques. Antiques and decorative furniture from 1850-1950.

JACQUELINE OOSTHUIZEN

23 Cale Street, London SW3 3QR ■ Tel: (0171) 352-6071 ■ Telfax: (0171) 376-3852 ■ Mon-Sat 10:00-5:00 ■ Dutch and German spoken Bourbon-Hanby Antiques Centre, 151 Sydney Street, London SW3 6NT ■ Tel: (0171) 460-8561 ■ Mon-Sun 10:00-5:00 ■ Prices medium to high ■ Professional discount ■ Major credit cards ■ LAPADA

Staffordshire figures 1760-1890: animals, cottages and Toby jugs. Estate jewellery.

PIETER OOSTHUIZEN

Bourbon-Hanby Antiques Centre, 151 Sydney Street, London SW3 6NT ■ Tel: (0171) 352-6071/460-3078 ■ Mon-Sun 10:00-5:00 ■ Dutch and German spoken ■ Prices medium to high ■ Trade discount ■ Major credit cards

Dutch Art Nouveau pottery and Boer War memorabilia.

♛ OSSOWSKI

83 Pimlico Road, London SW1W 8PH ■ Tel: (0171) 730-3256 ■ Fax: (0171) 823-4500 ■ Mon-Fri 10:00-6:00, Sat 10:00-1:00 ■ BADA

Fine gilded mirrors, consoles and woodcarvings.

ANTHONY OUTRED (ANTIQUES) LTD

533 King's Road, London SW10 0TZ ■ Tel: (0171) 352-8840 ■ Fax: (0171) 376-3627 ■ Mon-Sat 10:00-6:00, Sun 11:00-4:00 ■ Prices medium to high ■ Professional discount ■ Major credit cards ■ BADA

18th and 19th century English and Continental furniture.

LE PAVILLON DE SEVRES

9 Halkin Arcade, Morcomb Street, London SW1X 8JT ■ Tel: (0171) 603-5599 ■ Fax: (0171) 221-6378 ■ Mon-Fri 10:00-5:30 ■ French spoken ■ Prices medium to high ■ Major credit cards

Unusual collection of European ceramics and glass.

DAVID PETTIFER LTD

73 Glebe Place, London SW3 4JB ■ Telfax: (0171) 352-3088 ■ Telfax: (01572) 757572 ■ By appointment only ■ BADA

Furniture and works of art. Glass pictures and bygones.

MARIE RANSOM LTD

62 & 105 Pimlico Road, London SW1W 8LS ■ Tel: (0171) 259-0220 ■ Fax: (0171) 259-0323 ■ Mon-Sat 10:00-6:00 ■ Marie Ransom ■ French, Russian and Spanish spoken ■ Prices medium to very high ■ Major credit cards ■ Trade discount

French and Russian furniture from the early 19th century. Objects, paintings and some antiquarian books.

RICHARDSON & KAILAS

65 Rivermead Court, Ranelagh Gardens, London SW6 3RY ■ Tel: (0171) 371-0491 ■ By appointment only ■ BADA

15th and 19th century icons and frescoes.

ROGERS & CO

604 Fulham Road, London SW6 5RP ■ Tel: (0171) 731-8504 ■ Fax: (0171) 610-6040 ■ Mon-Fri 10:00-6:00, Sat 10:00-5:00 ■ Prices medium to high ■ Professional discount ■ Major credit cards ■ LAPADA

18th to early 20th century furniture and decorative objects. Large selection of fabrics, wallpapers and home furnishings. Will make curtains and blinds.

ROGERS DE RIN

76 Royal Hospital Road, Chelsea SW3 4HN ■ Tel: (0171) 352-9007 ■ Fax: (0171) 351-9407 ■ Mon-Fri 10:00-5:30, Sat 10:00-1:00 ■ Victoria de Rin ■ French spoken ■ Prices medium to high ■ Professional discount ■ Major credit cards ■ LAPADA

Specialists in Wemyss ware. Good collection of tea caddies, snuff boxes, 18th century enamels and Vienna bronzes.

ROGIER ANTIQUES

20A Pimlico Road, London SW1W 8LJ ■ Telfax: (0171) 823-4780 ■ Mon-Fri 0:00-6:00, Sat 11:00-4:00 ■ Lauriance Rogier ■ French and Italian spoken ■ Prices medium to high ■ Trade discount

French and Continental decorative antiques and reproductions. Lamps, sconces, lanterns, mirrors. Reproduction lighting. Restoration of painted and lacquered furniture and murals.

JANE SACCHI

Chelsea, London SW3 ■ Tel: (0171) 589-5643 ■ Fax: (0171) 581-3564 ■ By appointment only ■ LAPADA

Specialists in antique linen: 19th to early 20th century French linen sheets and bed linen. Upholstery and curtains in all qualities.

♔SEAGO

22 Pimlico Road, London SW1W 4LL ■ Tel: (0171) 730-7502 ■ Fax: (0171) 730-9179 ■ Mon-Fri 9:30-5:30 and by appointment ■ Trade discount ■ Major credit cards ■ BADA

Fabulous garden ornaments, sculpture and works of art of the 17th, 18th and 19th century.

GERALD SATTIN LTD
14 King Street, St. James's, London SW1Y 6QU ■ Tel: (0171) 493-6557 ■ Fax: (0171) 493-6557 ■ Mon-Fri 9:00-5:30, Sat 9:00-1:00 and by appointment ■ Prices high ■ Trade discount ■ Major credit cards ■ BADA

Excellent collection of glass, porcelain and silver.

DAVID MARTIN-TAYLOR ANTIQUES
558 King's Road, London SW6 2DZ ■ Tel: (0171) 731-4135 ■ Fax: (0171) 371-0029 ■ Mon-Fri 10:00-6:00 ■ French and Dutch spoken ■ Prices medium to high ■ Trade discount ■ Major credit cards ■ LAPADA

Boxes and caskets, Continental and painted furniture, candelabra and candlesticks, paintings, drawings and watercolours, singerie (also known as "monkey business"). Everything is from the 18th and 19th century.

WILLIAM TILLMAN LTD
30 St. James's Street, London SW1A 1HB ■ Tel: (0171) 839-2500 ■ Fax: (0171) 930-8106 ■ Mon-Fri 10:00-6:00, Sat by appointment ■ Prices high ■ Professional discount ■ Major credit cards ■ BADA

18th and early 19th century English furniture and works of art.

TWO ZERO C APPLIED ART
56 Abbey Business Centre, Ingate Place, off Queenstown Rd., Battersea, London SW8 3NS ■ Tel: (0171) 720-2021 ■ Mobile: 0370 520725 ■ Fax: (0171) 720-1015 ■ E-mail: appliedart@twozeroc.co.uk ■ Website: www.twozeroc.co.uk ■ By appointment ■ Michael Playford ■ French, Italian and Japanese spoken ■ Trade discount ■ LAPADA

All 20th century applied art including Wiener Werkstatte, Loetz glass, Art Deco and Modernist furniture, ceramics and glass.

ALEXANDER VON MOLTKE
46 Bourne Street, London SW1W 8JD ■ Tel: (0171) 730-9020 ■ Fax: (0171) 730-2945 ■ Mon-Fri 10:00-6:00, Sat 10:00-2:00 ■ Alexander Von Moltke ■ German and French spoken ■ Prices low to high ■ Major credit cards ■ Trade discount

Classically designed French furniture of the late 18th to the early 19th century. Mirrors, pictures, lamps and objects. Will source Continental and English furniture.

MARK J. WEST

Cobb Antiques Ltd, 39B High Street, Wimbledon Village, London SW19 5BY ■ Telfax: (0181) 946-2811 ■ Mon-Sat 10:00-5:30 ■ Prices medium to high ■ Trade discount ■ Major credit cards ■ BADA

18th and 19th century English and Continental glass.

♕ WESTENHOLZ ANTIQUES LTD

76-78 Pimlico Road, London SW1W 8PL ■ Tel: (0171) 824-8090 ■ Fax: (0171) 823-5913 ■ E-mail: shop@westenholzco.uk ■ Mon-Fri 9:00-6:00 ■ French and Spanish spoken ■ Prices high ■ Trade discount

Excellent collection of 19th century British decorative furniture and lighting.

ARNOLD WIGGINS & SONS LTD

4 Bury Street, St. James's, London SW1Y 6AB ■ Tel: (0171) 925-0195 ■ Fax: (0171) 839-6928 ■ Mon-Fri 9:00-5:30 ■ Prices high to very high ■ Professional discount ■ Major credit cards ■ BADA

16th to 19th century picture frames.

O.F. WILSON LTD.

3-6 Queens Elm Parade, Old Church Street, London SW3 6EJ ■ Tel: (0171) 352-9554 ■ Fax: (0171) 351-0765 ■ Mon-Fri 9:30-5:30, Sat 10:30-1:00 ■ E-mail: ofw@email.msn.com. ■ Peter Jackson, Grant White, Margo Briscoe Knight ■ Prices medium to very high ■ Trade discount ■ LAPADA

French and Continental and painted English 18th century furniture and chimney pieces. Mirrors and decorative objects.

CHRISTOPHER WOOD

20 Georgian House, 10 Bury Street, St. James's, London SW1Y 6AA ■ Tel: (0171) 839-3963 ■ Fax: (0171) 839-3963 ■ By appointment only ■ BADA

Victorian, Pre-Raphaelite and European 19th century paintings and drawings. Gothic furniture and Arts and Crafts movement.

CLIFFORD WRIGHT ANTIQUES LTD

104-106 Fulham Road, London SW3 6HS ■ Tel: (0171) 589-0986 ■ Fax: (0171) 589-3565 ■ Mon-Fri 10:00-6:00, Sat by appointment ■ Prices medium to high ■ Trade discount ■ BADA

18th and early 19th century English furniture and giltwood looking glasses. Glass pictures and prints.

YORK & WHITING

Furniture Cave, 533 King's Road, London SW10 OTZ ■ Tel: (0171) 376-8530 ■ Fax: (0171) 352-7994 ■ Mon-Sat 10:00-6:00, Sun 11:00-5:00 ■ German, French and Spanish spoken ■ Trade discount ■ Major credit cards ■ LAPADA

18th and 19th century furniture, paintings and carpets.

RAINER ZIETZ LTD

1A Prairie Street, London SW8 3PX ■ Tel: (0171) 498-2355 ■ Fax: (0171) 720-7745 ■ Mon-Fri 9:30-5:30 (appointment advisable) ■ Prices medium to high ■ Trade discount ■ Major credit cards ■ BADA

European works of art and sculpture.

EAST LONDON

HALCYON DAYS LTD

4 Royal Exchange, London EC3V 3LL ■ Tel: (0171) 626-1120 ■ Mon-Fri 10:00-5:30 ■ Prices medium to high ■ Trade discount ■ Major credit cards ■ BADA

Enamels, snuff boxes, objets de vertu, tôle, papier maché, porcelain and pottery.

♛ LONDON ARCHITECTURAL SALVAGE & SUPPLY CO.

St. Michael's Church, Mark Street, London EC2A 4ER ■ Tel: (0171) 739-0448 ■ Fax: (0171) 729-6853 ■ Prices medium to high ■ Trade discount ■ Major credit cards ■ LAPADA

Very large choice of architectural elements and garden ornaments, fireplaces, Art Deco and Art Nouveau, mirrors, metalwork, carpets and rugs, sculptures and bronzes. Everything that can be salvaged.

🏰 W. AGNEW & COMPANY LTD
58 Englefield Road, London N1 4HA ■ Tel: (0171) 254-7429 ■ Mobile: 0973 188272 ■ Fax: (0171) 254-7429 ■ By appointment only ■ Prices medium to high ■ Trade discount ■ BADA

Sculpture, works of art, Majolica and pottery.

B.C. METAL CRAFTS LTD.
London NW9 ■ Tel: (0181) 204-2446 ■ By appointment only ■ Prices medium to high ■ Professional discount ■ LAPADA

Clocks, glass, lighting, silver, sculpture, bronzes.

PATRICIA BECKMAN ANTIQUES
London NW3 ■ Tel: (0171) 435-5050 ■ By appointment only ■ Prices medium to high ■ Trade discount ■ LAPADA

18th and 19th century English and Continental furniture.

PETER CHAPMAN ANTIQUES
10 Theberton Street, London N1 OQX ■ Tel: (0171) 226-5565 ■ Fax: (0181) 348-4846 ■ Mon-Sat 9:30-6:00 ■ Trade discount ■ Major credit cards ■ LAPADA

Almost everything and anything: 18th and 19th century English and Continental furniture, architectural and garden ornaments, desk and writing accessories, decorative items, lighting, mirrors, paintings, watercolours, drawings.

DOME ANTIQUES
75 Upper Street, London N1 ONU ■ Tel: (0171) 226-7227 ■ Fax: (0171) 704-2950 ■ Mon-Fri 9:30-5:30 ■ Adam Woolfe ■ Prices medium to high ■ Trade discount ■ Major credit cards ■ LAPADA

19th century furniture in fine marquetry, bookcases, sets of chairs. Mainly English.

G. & F. GILLINGHAM LTD.
West Hampstead, London NW2 ■ Tel: (0171) 435-5644 ■ By appointment only ■ Prices medium ■ Trade discount

19th and early 20th century oak furniture.

THE GRAHAM GALLERY

104 Islington High Street, Camden Passage, Islington N1 8EG ■ Tel: (0171) 354- 2112 ■ Fax: (0171) 704-0728 ■ Wed, Sat 9:30-5:30 ■ Prices medium to high ■ Trade discount ■ Major credit cards ■ LAPADA

19th century furniture, candelabra, candlesticks, desk and writing accessories, mirrors, oil paintings and silver.

PATRICIA HARVEY ANTIQUES

42 Church Street, Marylebone NW8 8EP ■ Tel: (0171) 262-8989 ■ Fax: (0171) 625-8326 ■ Mon-Sat 10:00-5:30 ■ Prices medium to high ■ Trade discount ■ Major credit cards ■ LAPADA

Decorative antiques, porcelain, glass and oil paintings.

W. R. HARVEY & CO (ANTIQUES) LTD

70 Chalk Farm Road, London NW1 8AN ■ Tel: Witney: (01993) 706501 ■ Fax: (01993) 706601 ■ By appointment only ■ BADA

English furniture, clocks, barometers, mirrors and other works of art, 1650-1830.

HERITAGE ANTIQUES

PO Box 2974, Brighton BN1 3QG ■ Telfax: (01273) 326850 ■ Mobile: 0802 473422 ■ Trade discount ■ LAPADA

Specialist in antique domestic and decorative metalware.

HIGHGATE ANTIQUES

PO Box 10060, London N6 5JH ■ Tel: (0181) 340-9872/(0181) 348-3016 ■ Fax: (0181) 340-1621 ■ By appointment only ■ Prices medium to high ■ Trade discount ■ BADA, LAPADA

18th and early 19th century English and Welsh porcelain and glass.

ISLINGTON ANTIQUES

12-14 Essex Road, London N1 8LN ■ Telfax: (0171) 226-6867 ■ Mon-Sat 9:30-5:30 ■ R.A. Bent ■ French spoken ■ Prices low to high ■ Major credit cards ■ Trade discount

English and European pine and dark wood antique furniture. Restoration.

JONATHAN JAMES

52-53 Camden Passage, London N1 8AE ■ Tel: (0171) 704-8266 ■ Wed & Sat 9:30-5:30 ■ Prices medium to high ■ Trade discount ■ Major credit cards ■ LAPADA

Furniture from the 18th to the 20th century, plus country furniture and clocks.

JULIAN ANTIQUES

54 Duncan Street, Islington N1 8BL ■ Tel: (0171) 833-0835/(01273) 832145 ■ Wed, Sat 9:30-5:30 ■ Prices medium to high ■ Trade discount ■ Major credit cards ■ LAPADA

Antiquities, clocks, candelabra, candlesticks, Continental furniture, fireplaces, decorative objects, sculpture and bronzes.

♕ CAROL KETLEY ANTIQUES

PO Box 16199, London N1 7WD ■ Tel: (0171) 359-5529 ■ Mobile: 0831 827284 ■ Fax: (0171) 226-4589 ■ Showroom by appointment ■ Carol Ketley ■ French spoken ■ Prices medium ■ Professional discount ■ Major credit cards

Speciality: glassware. Large selection of Georgian decanters in stock. Good choice of early 19th century antiques, mainly mirrors and gilded furniture. Her daughter, Sophie, has a gilding restoration studio.

KLABER & KLABER

PO Box 9445, London NW8 1WD ■ Tel: (0171) 435-6537 ■ Fax: (0171) 435-9459 ■ By appointment ■ Prices medium to high ■ Trade discount ■ BADA

18th century English and Continental porcelain and enamels.

MICHAEL LEWIS ANTIQUES

16 Essex Road, London N1 8LM ■ Tel: (0171) 359-7733 ■ Fax: (0171) 354-3603 ■ By appointment ■ Prices medium to high ■ Trade discount ■ LAPADA

18th, 19th and early 20th century English and Continental furniture.

A.J. MANGION ANTIQUES

85 De Beauvoir Road, London N1 4EL ■ Telfax: (0171) 249-3745 ■ By appointment only ■ Prices medium to high ■ Trade discount ■ LAPADA

English and Continental furniture of the 18th, 19th and early 20th century.

D.M. & P. MANHEIM (PETER MANHEIM) LTD

PO Box 1259, London N6 4TR ■ Tel: (0181) 340-9211 ■ By appointment only ■ Prices medium to high ■ Professional discount

18th and early 19th century English porcelain, pottery and enamels.

DUNCAN R. MILLER FINE ARTS

17 Flask Walk, Hampstead, London NW3 1HJ ▪ Tel: (0171) 435-546 ▪ Fax: (0171) 431-5352 ▪ Mon-Sat 11:00-6:00, Sun 2:00-5:00 ▪ Prices medium to high ▪ Trade discount ▪ Major credit cards ▪ BADA

Paintings 1840-1950, including Scottish paintings and watercolours, carpets and rugs.

LAURENCE MITCHELL ANTIQUES

13 Camden Passage, London N1 8EA ▪ Tel: (0171) 359-7579 ▪ Wed, Sat 9:00-5:00 ▪ Prices medium to high ▪ Trade discount ▪ Major credit cards ▪ LAPADA

Glass and porcelain, Oriental items, sculpture and bronzes.

PORTOBELLO FINE ART LTD – YOUNG & SON

88 The Stables Market off Chalk Farm Road, London NW1 ▪ Tel: (0171) 284-3030 ▪ Mobile: 0958 437043 ▪ Fax: (0171) 636-3878 ▪ E-mail:Leon@dircon.co.uk ▪ Appointment suggested ▪ Prices medium to high ▪ Trade discount ▪ Major credit cards ▪ LAPADA

19th century furniture and country oak furniture. Lots of dining tables and chairs. Prints and maps.

KEITH SKEEL ANTIQUES

94 Islington High Street, London N1 8EG ▪ Tel: (0171) 359-9894 ▪ Fax: (0171) 700-6387 ▪ By appointment ▪ Prices medium to high ▪ Trade discount ▪ LAPADA

Continental furniture, fireplaces, sculpture, bronze and works of art.

MALCOLM D. STEVENS

9-10 Lower Mall, The Mall, 359 Upper Street, London N1 OPD ▪ Tel: (0171) 359-1020 ▪ Wed & Sat only ▪ Prices medium to high ▪ Trade discount ▪ LAPADA

18th, 19th and early 20th century furniture, desk and writing accessories.

28 ANTIQUES

28 Church Street, London NW8 8EP ▪ Tel: (0171) 724-4631 ▪ Mon-Sat 10:00-6:00 ▪ David Tulissio, Dominic de Beaumont, Alan Isenberg ▪ Italian spoken ▪ Prices medium to high ▪ Trade discount

Chandeliers, wall lights, lamps, decorative objects and furniture. All from the late 18th century to the mid-20th century. Mostly European.

LEASK WARD

64A South Hill Park, London NW3 ■ Telfax: (0171) 435-9781 ■ 7 days by appointment ■ Trade discount ■ LAPADA

European and Oriental antiques and paintings.

WELLINGTON GALLERY

1 St. John's Wood, High Street, London NW8 6AP ■ Tel: (0171) 586-2620 ■ Fax: (0171) 483-0716 ■ Mon-Sat 10:30-6:00 ■ Mrs. Maureen Barclay ■ Prices medium to high ■ Trade discount ■ LAPADA

Antiques and decorative objects, picture framing, restoration, upholstery.

Antique Clocks

ARCHAIC TEMPO

298 Westbourne Grove, London W11 (Nr. Portobello Road) ■ Telfax: (0171) 482-2442 ■ Sat only 8:30-4:00 ■ Anthony Wisdom ■ Spanish, Portuguese and some French spoken ■ Prices medium ■ Major credit cards ■ Trade discount

Late 19th and early 20th century clocks. Also repair and restoration.

BIG BEN CLOCKS

5 Broxholme House, New King's Road, London SW6 3HR ■ Tel: (0171) 731-0072 ■ Fax: (0171) 384-1957 ■ By appointment only ■ Roger Lascelles ■ French, German, Italian and Spanish spoken ■ Prices medium ■ Visa accepted ■ Trade discount

Antique clocks, especially English long-case clocks. 15 to 20 long-case clocks in stock. Some furniture as well.

BOBINET LTD

PO Box 2730, London NW8 9PL ■ Tel: (0171) 266-0783 ■ Fax: (0171) 289-5119 ■ By appointment only ■ BADA

Clocks and watches; scientific instruments.

♛ AUBREY BROCKLEHURST

124 Cromwell Road, South Kensington, London SW7 4ET ■ Tel: (0171) 373-0319 ■ Fax: (0171) 373-7612 ■ Mon-Fri 9:00-1:00, 2:00-5:30, Sat 10:00-1:00 ■ Aubrey Brocklehurst ■ French and some German spoken ■ Major credit cards ■ Professional discount ■ BADA

Antique clocks and barometers. Repairs of clocks and barometers. Furniture restoration.

PATRIC CAPON

350 Upper Street, Islington, London N1 0PD ■ Tel: (0171) 354-0487/(0181) 467-5722 anytime ■ Fax: (0181) 295-1475 ■ Wed 8:00-5:00, Sat 9:30-5:00, and by appointment ■ Patric Capon ■ French spoken ■ Prices low to very high ■ Trade discount ■ BADA

17th to 19th century clocks, marine chronometers, barometers. Specialist in fine carriage clocks. Restorations.

JOHN CARLTON-SMITH

17 Ryder Street, St James's, London SW1Y 6PY ■ Tel: (0171) 930-6622 ■ Fax: (0171) 930-9719 ■ Mon-Fri 9:30-5:30 ■ BADA

Antique clocks and barometers.

THE CLOCK CLINIC LTD.

85 Lower Richmond Road, Putney, London SW15 1EU ■ Tel: (0181) 788-1407 ■ Fax: (0181) 780-2838 ■ Tue-Fri 9:00-6:00, Sat 9:00-1:00 ■ Robert S. Pedler ■ Prices medium ■ Major credit cards ■ LAPADA

Antique barometers and clocks, Also repair and restoration.

GAVIN DOUGLAS

75 Portobello Road, London W11 2QB ■ Tel: (0171) 221-1121 ■ Fax: (01825) 724418 ■ Tue-Sat 10:30-4:30 ■ Gavin Douglas ■ Prices medium to high ■ Visa, Amex ■ Professional discount

French Empire clocks, fine 18th and 19th century ormolu, candelabra, vases. Clock cleaning and restoration.

GROVE ANTIQUES

220 Westbourne Grove, London W11 2RH ■ Telfax: (0171) 792-8028 ■ Mon-Sat 10:00-6:00 ■ Paul Crann ■ Prices medium to very high ■ Amex accepted ■ Trade discount

French clocks of the 18th and 19th century. Ormolu with Sèvres panels. French long-case clocks.

JILLINGS DISTINCTIVE ANTIQUE CLOCKS

17 Croft House, Church Street, Newent, Gloucestershire GL18 1YN ■ Tel: (01531) 822-100 ■ Fax: (01531) 822-666 ■ Mobile: 0973 830110 ■ By appointment only ■ John and Doro Jillings ■ Prices medium to high ■ Major credit cards ■ Trade discount ■ LAPADA

18th and 19th century English and Continental antique clocks and small scientific instruments. Free delivery and set-up throughout the UK. Shipping arranged.

WILLIAM MANSELL

24 Connaught Street, Marble Arch, London W2 2AF ■ Tel: (0171) 723-4154 ■ Fax: (0171) 724-2273 ■ Mon-Fri 9:00-6:00, Sat 10:30-12:00 ■ William Salisbury ■ Prices medium ■ Major credit cards

Clocks, watches and some silver.

NEWCOMBE & SON

89 Maple Road, London SE20 8UL ■ Telfax: (0171) 778-0816 ■ Mike Newcombe ■ Prices medium ■ Trade discount

Antique clocks and barometers. Repairs and restoration.

TERENCE PLANK

23 The Mall, 359 Upper Street, London N1 OPD ■ Tel: (0171) 226-2426 ■ Wed & Sat by appointment ■ LAPADA

Antique barometers and clocks.

♛RAFFETY

34 Kensington Church Street, London W8 4HA ■ Telfax: (0171) 938-1100 ■ Mon-Fri 10:00-5:30, Sat 10:00-2:00 ■ Howard Walwyn and Nigel Raffety ■ Spanish and French spoken ■ Major credit cards ■ Professional discount ■ BADA

English longcase and bracket clocks and barometers of the 17th to 19th century, scientific instruments and 19th century mechanical musical instruments. Some English antique furniture.

RAFFETY

39 Ledbury Road, London W11 2AA ■ Tel: (0171) 229-4947 ■ Mon-Fri 10:00-5:00, Sat 11:00-3:00, or by appointment ■ BADA, LAPADA

English longcase and bracket clocks, barometers, scientific instruments and 19th century mechanical musical instruments.

RODERICK ANTIQUES

23 Vicarage Gate (Junction with Kensington Church Street), London W8 4AA ■ Telfax: (0171) 937-8517 ■ Mon-Fri 10:00-5:30, Sat 10:00-3:30 ■ LAPADA

Clocks and barometers from 1700 to 1900.

SOMLO ANTIQUES

7 Piccadilly Arcade, London SW1Y 6NH ■ Tel: (0171) 499-6526 ■ Fax: (0171) 499-0603 ■ Mon-Fri 10:00-5:30 ■ Prices medium to high ■ Trade discount ■ Major credit cards ■ BADA

Antique watches.

STRIKE ONE (ISLINGTON) LTD
48A Highbury Hill, London N5 1AP ■ Tel: (0171) 354-2790 ■ Fax: (0171) 354-2790 ■ By appointment only ■ BADA

Clocks and barometers; music boxes.

W.F. TURK ANTIQUE CLOCKS
London SW19 ■ Telfax: (0181) 543-3231 ■ Mobile: 0385 583500 ■ By appointment only ■ LAPADA

Barometers and clocks.

Antique Country Furniture

CHALK FARM ANTIQUES
60 Chalk Farm Road, London NW1 8N ■ Telfax: (0171) 267-1612 ■ Mon-Sun 11:00-6:00 ■ Regina Barter ■ Prices medium ■ Major credit cards

Antique country furniture.

JOHN FELL CLARK
84 Ledbury Road, London W11 2AH ■ Tel: (0171) 229-0224 ■ By appointment ■ LAPADA

Country and pine furniture, mirrors, textiles and treen.

ROBERT E. HIRSCHHORN
London SE5 8JA ■ Tel: (0171) 703-7443 ■ Mobile: 0831 405937 ■ By appointment only ■ Prices low to high ■ Professional discount ■ Visa and MC accepted ■ BADA

Early oak and country furniture and objects.

P. & S. LEHMANN
18 Narrow Street, Limehouse, London E14 8DQ ■ Telfax: (0171) 790-9006 ■ Mobile: 0802 897224 ■ By appointment ■ Peter and Stephanie Lehmann ■ German spoken ■ Prices medium ■ Professional discount ■ Major credit cards

19th century French furniture and decorative items. French country furniture is their specialty. Assisted buying trips to France.

M. & D. SELIGMANN
37 Kensington Church Street, London W8 4LL ■ Tel: (0171) 937-0400 ■ Fax: (0171) 722-4315 ■ Mon-Fri 10:30-5:30 ■ Maja and David Seligmann ■ French spoken ■ Prices medium to high ■ Major credit cards ■ Trade discount

Country furniture of the 17th to early 19th century, especially English tables. Treen, objets d'art and some early English pottery.

ROBERT YOUNG ANTIQUES

68 Battersea Bridge Road, London SW11 3AG ■ Tel: (0171) 228-7847 ■ Fax: (0171) 585-0489 ■ Tue-Fri 10:00-6:00, Sat 10:00-5:00 ■ Robert and Josyane Young ■ French spoken ■ Prices medium to high ■ Major credit cards ■ Trade discount

Fine English and Northern European country furniture.

Antique Country House Furniture

♛ CHRISTOPHER HODSOLL LTD

89 Pimlico Road, London SW1W 8PH ■ Tel: (0171) 730-3370 ■ Fax: (0171) 730-1516 ■ Mon-Fri 9:30-6:00, Sat 10:00-5:00 ■ Christopher Hodsoll ■ French and German spoken ■ Prices high to very high ■ Amex accepted ■ Trade discount

Country house furniture on the grand scale. 18th and 19th century English and Continental furniture, carpets, lamps, paintings, mirrors, chandeliers and decorative objects. Item search, interiors re-designed and furnished.

♛ CHRISTOPHER HOWE

93 Pimlico Road, London SW1W 8PH ■ Tel: (0171) 730-7987 ■ Fax: (0171) 730-0157 ■ Mon-Fri 9:00-5:30, Sat 10:30-2:30 ■ Christopher Howe ■ French, Spanish and German spoken ■ Prices medium to high ■ Major credit cards ■ Professional discount

English country house furniture and lighting from the 17th to the 19th century and 20th century European furniture. Fine copies of classic furniture and lighting with the capability to cater for large projects and commercial contracts. A wide and interesting range of leather and suede.

♛ MCCLENAGHAN

69 Pimlico Road, London SW1W 8NE ■ Telfax: (0171) 730-4187 ■ Mon-Sat 10:00-6:00 ■ Bob Gilhooly and John McClenaghan ■ Prices medium to very high ■ Major credit cards ■ Trade and export discount

A large selection of 19th century English country house furniture, objects, mirrors and lighting. Console tables, William IV armchairs, lamps, an extensive range of hanging lanterns. Some Gothic Revival, Arts and Crafts and Aesthetic movement. Lamp conversions and restorations.

Antique Painted Furniture

👑 ODYSSEY FINE ARTS LTD.

24 Holbein Place, London SW1W 8NL ■ Tel: (0171) 730-9942 ■ Fax: (0171) 259-9941 ■ Mon-Fri 10:30-5:30, Sat 10:30-3:30 ■ Martin MacRodain ■ Major credit cards ■ LAPADA

Superb 18th and 19th century painted furniture, mainly Italian, decorative objects, textiles, framed watercolours and prints.

Antique Porcelain, Pottery and Ceramics

👑 ALEXANDRA ALFANDARY

9 The Mall, Camden Passage, 359 Upper Street, London N1 OPD ■ Tel: (0171) 354-9762 ■ Fax: (0171) 727-4352 ■ Wed & Saturday ■ Persian and French spoken ■ Prices medium to high ■ Trade discount ■ Major credit cards ■ Stand 16, Lipka's Arcade, Portobello Road, London W11 2DY ■ Mobile: 0956 993233 ■ Saturdays

Fine European ceramics: Meissen, Dresden, Sèvres, Vienna and objets d'art.

GARRY ATKINS

107 Kensington Church Street, London W8 7LN ■ Tel: (0171) 727-8737 ■ Fax: (0171) 792-9010 ■ E-mail: garryatkins@mcmail.com ■ Mon-Fri 10:00-5:30 ■ Garry Atkins ■ Prices low to high ■ MC and Visa accepted ■ Trade discount

Early English and Continental pottery from 1650 to 1850. Antique Delftware, Creamware, saltglazed stoneware.

JESSE DAVIS ANTIQUES

Antiquarius Antiques Market, 131-141 King's Road, London SW3 4PW ■ Tel: (0171) 352 4314 ■ Mon-Sat 10:00-6:00 ■ Prices medium to high ■ Professional discount ■ Major credit cards ■ LAPADA

Ceramics: specialists in Staffordshire, majolica and decorative objects.

A.J. GREENACRE LTD.

Wimbledon ■ Tel: (0181) 946-9413 ■ By appointment only ■ LAPADA

Porcelain and pottery.

BRIAN HAUGHTON ANTIQUES
3B Burlington Gardens, Old Bond Street, London W1X 1LE ■ Tel: (0171) 734-5491 ■ Fax: (0171) 494-4604 ■ E-mail: info@haughton.com ■ Brian Haughton ■ Mon-Fri 10:00-5:00 ■ Prices high to very high ■ Professional discount ■ Visa

Fine ceramics and works of art of the 18th and 19th century.

HIGHGATE ANTIQUES
PO Box 10060, London N6 5JH ■ Tel: (0181) 340-9872/Telfax: (0181) 348-3016 ■ Fax: (0181) 340-1621 ■ By appointment only ■ Jean Horsman and Enid Thomas ■ BADA, LAPADA

18th and early 19th century English and Welsh porcelain and glass.

JONATHAN HORNE (ANTIQUES) LTD
66B and 66C Kensington Church Street, London W8 4BY ■ Tel: (0171) 221-5658 ■ Fax: (0171) 792-3090 ■ Mon-Fri 9:30-5:30 or by appointment ■ BADA

Early English pottery and works of art.

VALERIE HOWARD
2 Campden Street, off Kensington Church Street, London W8 7EP ■ Tel: (0171) 792 9702 ■ Fax: (0171) 221-7008 ■ Mobile: 0976 204755 ■ Mon-Fri 10:00-5:30, Sat 10:00-4:30 ■ Valerie Howard ■ French spoken ■ Major credit cards ■ Professional discount ■ LAPADA

Masons and ironstone china. French pottery, especially Quimpers.

DIANA HUNTLEY
8 Camden Passage, London N1 3ED ■ Tel: (0171) 226-4605 ■ Wed, Sat by appointment ■ Prices medium to high ■ Trade discount ■ Major credit cards ■ LAPADA

Porcelain, glass and decorative objects.

RODERICK JELLICOE AT STOCKSPRING ANTIQUES
114 Kensington Church Street, London W8 4BH ■ Telfax: (0171) 727-7995 ■ E-mail: jellicoe@mcmail.com ■ Website: www.jellicoe.mcmail.com ■ Mon-Fri 10:00-5:30, Sat 10:00-1:00 ■ Prices high ■ Professional discount ■ Major credit cards

18th century English porcelain.

KLABER & KLABER
PO Box 9445, London NW3 1WD ■ Tel: (0171) 435-6537 ■ Fax: (0171) 435-9459 E-mail: info@klaber.com ■ Website: www.klaber.com ■ By appointment ■ BADA

18th century English and Continental porcelain and enamels.

ANDREW LINEHAM FINE GLASS

The Mall, Camden Passage, London N1 8ED ■ Tel: (0171) 704-0195/(01243) 576241 ■ Wed & Sat 10:00-3:00, and by appointment ■ BADA

Rare and unusual 19th and 20th century coloured glass and European porcelain.

MERCURY ANTIQUES

1 Ladbroke Road, London W11 3PA ■ Tel: (0171) 727-5106 ■ Fax: (0171) 229-3738 ■ Mon-Sat 10:00-5:30 ■ BADA

Good collection of 18th and early 19th century porcelain, pottery, Delft and glass.

♔ OLIVER-SUTTON ANTIQUES

34c Kensington Church Street, London W8 4HA ■ Tel: (0171) 937-0633 ■ Mon-Fri 10:00-5:00, closed August ■ BADA

Fine collection of Staffordshire pottery figures. He has written several books on his subject.

NADINE OKKER

5 The Mall Antiques Arcade, 359 Upper Street, London N1 OPD ■ Tel: (0171) 354-9496 ■ Wed, Sat by appointment ■ Prices medium to high ■ Trade discount ■ Major credit cards ■ LAPADA

Porcelain and glass.

JACQUELINE OOSTHUIZEN

23 Cale Street, London SW3 3QR ■ Tel: (0171) 352-6071 ■ Telfax: (0171) 376-3852 ■ Mon-Sat 10:00-5:00 ■ Dutch and German spoken Bourbon-Hanby Antiques Centre, 151 Sydney Street, London SW3 6NT ■ Tel: (0171) 460-8561 ■ Mon-Sun 10:00-5:00 ■ Prices medium to high ■ Professional discount ■ Major credit cards ■ LAPADA

Staffordshire figures1760-1890: animals, cottages and Toby jugs.

ROBYN ROBB

43 Napier Avenue, London SW6 3PS ■ Telfax: (071) 731-2878 ■ By appointment only ■ BADA

18th century English porcelain.

♔ STOCKSPRING ANTIQUES

114 Kensington Church Street, London W8 4BH ■ Telfax: (0171) 727-7995 ■ Website: www.antique-porcelain.co.uk ■ Mon-Fri 10:00-5:30, Sat 10:00-1:00 ■ Felicity Marno ■ Prices high ■ Professional discount ■ Major credit cards ■ BADA, LAPADA

18th and early 19th century English porcelain.

RAY WALKER ANTIQUES

Burton Arcade, 296 Westbourne Grove, London W11 2PS ■ Tel: (0171) 727-7920 or (0181) 464-7981 ■ Fax: (0181) 464-8065 ■ Sat 7:00-2:00 or by appointment ■ Ray Walker ■ French and German spoken ■ Prices medium ■ Major credit cards ■ Trade discount

Staffordshire figures and animals, Sunderland Lustre Pottery and reference books.

Antique Collectibles

ARMS, ARMOUR, MILITARIA

CHARLES DAGGETT GALLERY

153 Portobello Road, London W11 2DY ■ Tel: (0171) 229-2248 ■ Fax: (0171) 229-0193 ■ LAPADA

Militaria and paintings.

PETER DALE LTD.

11/12 Royal Opera Arcade, Pall Mall, London SW1Y 4UY ■ Tel: (0171) 930-3695 ■ LAPADA

Arms and armour and assorted militaria.

ELLIOTT AND SNOWDON LTD.

61A Ledbury Road, London W11 2AA ■ Tel: (0171) 229-6900 ■ LAPADA

Arms and armour, objects for decoration, icons, metalwork, sculpture and bronzes. Also Indian and Tibetan items.

♚ PETER FINER

Ilmington, Warwickshire ■ Tel: (01608) 682267 ■ Fax: (01608) 682575 ■ By appointment only

One of the world's best collections of antique arms and armour. He participates in the important international antique shows.

♚ MICHAEL C. GERMAN

38B Kensington Church Street, London W8 4BX ■ Tel: (0171) 937-2771 ■ Fax: (0171) 937-8566 ■ Mon-Fri 10:00-5:00, Sat 10:00-3:00 and by appointment ■ Michael German ■ French spoken ■ Major credit cards ■ Trade discount ■ BADA, LAPADA

Exceptional collection of antique European arms and armour.

PORTOBELLO ARMS & ARMOUR SHOPPE

Rear of 117 Portobello Road, London W11 2DZ ■ Tel: (01782) 394397 ■ Mobile: 0889 137308 ■ Sat 8:00-4:00 ■ John Burgess ■ Prices low to medium ■ Major credit cards

Wide range of armour and weapons. Approximately 100 swords always in stock.

ROBERT J. TREDWEN

Shop 3, Phelps Cottage, 357 Upper Street, Islington, London N1 ■ Tel: (0171) 359-2224 ■ Fax: (0181) 461-7027 ■ Tue-Sat 11:00-4:30 ■ Prices low to high ■ Major credit cards ■ Trade discount

Military antiques from all periods up to World War II specializing in fine British head-dress, edged weapons, uniforms.

AUTOGRAPHS

ALAN BRETT LTD

24 Cecil Court, London WC2N 4HE ■ Tel: (0171) 836-8222 ■ Fax: (0171) 497-0473

The largest collection of Vanity Fair prints in London. Antique maps and books, celebrity photos and autographs.

FRASERS AUTOGRAPHS

1st Floor, Stanley Gibbons, 399 Strand, London WC2R 0LX ■ Tel: (0171) 836-9325 ■ Fax: (0171) 836-7342 ■ Mon-Sat 9:00-5:30 ■ Major credit cards ■ Trade discount

Extensive collection of autographs and film and music-related memorabilia. Catalogue available.

MAGGS BROS LTD

50 Berkeley Square, London W1X 6EL ■ Tel: (0171) 493-7160 ■ Fax: (0171) 499-2007 ■ Mon-Fri 9:30-5:30 ■ BADA

Rare books, autographs, manuscripts and miniatures.

STAGE DOOR PRINTS

9 Cecil Court, St. Martins Lane, London WC2N 4EZ ■ Tel: (0171) 240-1083 ■ Fax: (0171) 379-5598 ■ Mon-Sat 11:00-6:00 ■ Al Reynold ■ Prices low to very high ■ Visa and MC ■ Trade discount

Autographs from the performing arts. Antique prints and film posters and memorabilia.

BRASS, COPPER AND PEWTER

JACK CASIMIR LTD
23 Pembridge Road, London W11 3HG ■ Telfax: (0171) 727-8643 ■
Mon-Sat 10:00-5:30 and by appointment ■ M. & R. Casimir ■ Major
credit cards ■ BADA, LAPADA

**Extensive and unusual collection of British and European 16th
through to 19th century brass, copper and pewter. Candelabra,
candlesticks and fireplaces.**

BUTTONS

THE BUTTON QUEEN
19 Marylebone Lane, London W1M 5FE ■ Telfax: (0171) 935-1505 ■
Mon-Tue-Wed 10:00-5:00, Thu-Fri 10:00-6:00, Sat 10:00-4:00 ■ Martyn
Frith ■ Prices low to very high ■ Major credit cards ■ Trade discount

**Antique and old buttons of every description, Art Deco, Art Nou-
veau, Victorian. Blazer and tailor buttons, fashion buttons, buttons in quantity and button covering services.**

CANES

♛ MICHAEL C. GERMAN
38B Kensington Church Street, London W8 4BX ■ Tel: (0171) 937-
2771 ■ Fax: (0171) 937-8566 ■ Mon-Fri 10:00-5:00, Sat 10:00-3:00
other times by appointment ■ Michael German ■ French spoken ■
Major credit cards ■ Trade discount ■ BADA, LAPADA

**Extraordinary collection of antique walking canes. Both deco-
rative and system canes. Cane stands. Books and videos on
canes.**

COINS AND MEDALS

A.H. BALDWIN & SONS LTD
11 Adelphi Terrace, London WC2N 6BJ ■ Tel: (0171) 930-6897 ■ Fax:
(0171) 930-9450 ■ Mon-Fri 9:00-5:00 ■ Timothy Millett ■ French and
German spoken ■ Prices low to very high ■ Major credit cards ■
Trade discount

Antique coins and medals. Numismatic books.

COINCRAFT

45 Great Russell Street, London WC1B 3LU ■ Tel: (0171) 636-1188 ■ Fax: (0171) 323-2860 ■ Barry Clayden

Greek, Roman, Egyptian antiquities and coins.

HESPERIDES LTD

4 Davies Mews, London W1Y 2LP ■ Telfax: (0171) 355-1565 ■ Mon-Fri 10:00-6:00 ■ Louis Thomas and D. Lauro ■ French, Italian, Spanish and German spoken ■ Prices low to high ■ Visa and MC accepted ■ Trade discount

All types of coins from ancient through modern. Foreign and U.S. paper money. Antiquities, Classical and Eastern.

See also: Ancient Art and Antiquities

DOLLS AND DOLLS HOUSES

THE DOLL CUPBOARD

The Admiral Vernon Market, 141-149 Portobello Road, London W11 2DY ■ Telfax: (0181) 559-8176 ■ Sat only 8:30-3:30 ■ Vivien Seip ■ Prices medium to high ■ Visa and MC

Antique dolls, furniture and related items. Some doll houses. Restoration and doll dressing.

GOODIES

11 East Street, Coggeshall, Essex CO6 1SH ■ Tel: (01376) 562885 ■ Fax: (01376) 563885 ■ Mon-Sat 9:30-5:30, Sun 11:30-5:30 ■ Belinda Opies ■ Prices low to very high ■ Major credit cards

Dolls houses, doll furniture, accessories. Many items exclusive to their shop. Telephone orders with credit cards.

LONDON DOLLS HOUSE COMPANY

29 Covent Garden Market, London WC2E 8RE ■ Tel: (0171) 240-8681 ■ Fax: (0171) 240-2288 ■ Mon-Sat 10:30-7:00, Sun 12:00-5:00 ■ Charlotte Brandelli ■ Prices low to very high ■ Major credit cards ■ Trade discount

Hand-made English miniatures for dolls houses from Tudor to contemporary. Furniture and some DIY items. Catalogue and mail-order available.

THE SINGING TREE
69 New King's Road, London SW6 4SQ ■ Tel: (0171) 736-4527 ■ Fax: (0171) 736-0336 ■ Mon-Sat 10:00-5:30 ■ Prices low to very high ■ Major credit cards ■ Trade discount

Remarkable replicas of period houses. Also doll house furniture, porcelain, glass, silver and garden statuary made exclusively for The Singing Tree by British craftsmen. Catalogue available.

YESTERDAY CHILD
Angel Arcade, 118 Islington High Street, London N1 8EG ■ Telfax: (01908) 583403 ■ Wed & Sat 9:00-3:30 ■ David & Gisela Barington ■ German and French spoken ■ Trade discount

Antique dolls. Also a dolls hospital for surgery and intensive care.

GLASS

♔ CHRISTINE BRIDGE ANTIQUES
78 Castelnau, Barnes, London SW13 9EX ■ Telfax: (0181) 741-5501 ■ Mobile: 0831 126668 ■ By appointment ■ Christine Bridge and Darryl Bowles ■ Prices medium to high ■ Major credit cards ■ Trade discount ■ LAPADA

18th century collectors' glass, 19th century coloured glass samplers, needlework and small antiques. Glass restoration service and glass de-clouding, chips reduced, enamels repaired and silver re-plating.

W.G.T. BURNE (ANTIQUE GLASS) LTD
PO Box 9465, London SW20 9ZD ■ Mobile: (0374) 725834 ■ Telfax: (0181) 543-6319 ■ By appointment only ■ BADA

English and Irish glass. Chandeliers.

JEANETTE HAYHURST FINE GLASS
32A Kensington Church Street, London W8 4HA ■ Tel: (0171) 938-1539 ■ Mon-Fri 10:00-5:00, Sat 12:00-5:00 ■ BADA

British glass from the 17th to the 20th century.

ANDREW LINEHAM FINE GLASS
The Mall, Camden Passage, London N1 8ED ■ Tel: (0171) 704-0195/(01243) 576241 ■ Wed & Sat 10:00-3:00, other times by appointment ■ BADA

Rare and unusual 19th and 20th century coloured glass and European porcelain.

MARK J. WEST

Cobb Antiques Ltd, 39B High Street, Wimbledon Village, London SW19 5BY ■ Telfax: (0181) 946-2811 ■ Mon-Sat 10:00-5:30 ■ Prices medium to high ■ Trade discount ■ Major credit cards ■ BADA

18th and 19th century English and Continental glass.

GOLF MEMORABILIA

GOLFIANA

Grays South, Davies Mews, off Davies Street, London W1 ■ Tel: (0171) 408-1239 ■ Fax: (0171) 493-9344 ■ Mon-Fri 10:30-5:30 ■ Sarah Fabien Baddiel ■ Prices medium ■ Visa accepted ■ Trade discount

Tin toys, diecast toys, golf art, golf books and paper.

ICONS

♟ MARIA ANDIPA & SON ICON GALLERY

162 Walton Street, Knightsbridge, London SW3 2JL ■ Tel: (0171) 589 2371 ■ Fax: (0171) 225-0305 ■ E-mail: art@andipa.com ■ Tue-Sat 11:00-6:00 ■ Maria and Acoris Andipa ■ Greek, French and Arabic spoken ■ Prices low to very high ■ Major credit cards ■ Trade discount ■ LAPADA

Icons, 18th and 19th century furniture, glass, jewellery and works of art. Restoration and research.

♟ MARK GALLERY

9 Porchester Place, Marble Arch, London W2 2BS ■ Tel: (0171) 262-4906 ■ Fax: (0171) 224-9416 ■ Mon-Fri 10:00-1:00/2:00-6:00, Sat 11:00-1:00, other times by appointment ■ BADA

Russian icons, from the 16th to the 19th century. Russian works of art.

RICHARDSON AND KAILAS

65 Rivermead Court, Ranelagh Gardens, London SW6 8RY ■ Tel: (0171) 371-0491 ■ By appointment ■ Chris Richardson ■ Major credit cards ■ BADA, LAPADA

Icons, frescoes and carvings. Restorations.

MARC ANTOINE DURY MEDIEVAL ART

31 Wimpole Street, London W1M 7AE ■ Telfax: (0171) 224-1259 ■ Sat 9:00-3:00 or by appointment ■ Marc Antoine Dury ■ French, Italian and Dutch spoken ■ Visa and MC accepted ■ Trade discount

Early and medievel works of art in bronze and stone. Specialist in illuminated manuscripts and miniatures on parchment.

SAM FOGG RARE BOOKS

35 St George Street, London W1R 9FA ■ Tel: (0171) 495-2333 ■ Fax: (0171) 409-3326 ■ Mon-Fri 9:30-5:30 ■ Sam Fogg ■ Prices medium to very high

Medieval manuscripts, miniatures, Oriental manuscripts and miniatures. Manuscripts and individual leaves.

LUGGAGE

BENTLEY'S

190 Walton Street, London SW3 2JL ■ Tel: (0171) 584-7770 ■ Fax: (0171) 584-8182 ■ Mon-Sat 10:00-6:00 ■ Tim Bent and Julian Hard-wicke ■ Prices medium to high ■ Major credit cards ■ Trade discount

Exceptional choice of antique luggage.

HILARY PROCTOR

Admiral Vernon Antique Market, 141 Portobello Road and Bourbon-Hanby Antiques Centre, 151 Sydney Street, London ■ Tel: (0171) 376-5921 ■ Mobile: 0956 876428 ■ Portobello, Sat 8:00-4:30 ■ Bourbon-Hanby: Mon-Sat 10:00-6:00, Sun 11:00-5:00 ■ Hilary Proctor ■ French spoken and some Italian and Portuguese ■ Prices low to high ■ Major credit cards ■ Professional discount

Antique luggage and antique and vintage handbags, petit-point handbags, crocodile luggage and accessories.

XS BAGGAGE CO.

Antiquarius Antiques Centre, 131-141 King's Road, Chelsea, London SW3 4PW ■ Telfax: (0171) 376-8781 ■ Mon-Sat 10:00-6:00 ■ Mr. & Mrs. Lehane ■ Prices medium to high ■ Major credit cards ■ Trade discount

Louis Vuitton trunks and suitcases, travel requisites, tea caddies, silver, enamels, decorative objects, crocodile photo frames and fitted cases. Quite a collection.

COLLECTORS TREASURES LTD

46 Kensington Church Street, London W8 4DA ■ Tel: (0171) 937-5317 ■ Mon-Sat 11:30-5:00 ■ Mrs. Paessler ■ Prices low to very high ■ Major credit cards ■ Trade discount

Antique maps of Great Britain and all parts of the world from 1550-1900. Antique prints on all subjects.

HARRODS OLD MAP & PRINT DEPARTMENT

Brompton Road, Knightsbridge, London SW1 ■ Tel: (0171) 730-1234 (Ext. 2124) ■ Mon, Tue, Sat 10:00-8:00, Wed, Thu, Fri 10:00-7:00 ■ Rolf Pressler ■ German spoken ■ Prices low to very high ■ Major credit cards ■ Trade discount

Antique maps of all parts of the world from 1550 to 1900. Antique prints on all subjects. Framing.

INTERCOL LONDON

114 Islington High Street, The Camden Passage, London N1 ■ Tel: (0181) 349-2207 ■ Fax: (0181) 346-9539 ■ Tue-Sat 10:00-6:00 ■ Yasha Beresiner ■ Several languages spoken ■ Prices medium ■ Major credit cards ■ Trade discount

Old maps, playing cards, fiscal documents, Freemasonry, erotica. Restoration of paper items.

LEE JACKSON

2 Southampton Street, London WC2E 7HA ■ Tel: (0171) 240-1970 ■ Mon-Fri 10:00-5:30 ■ Lee Jackson ■ Spanish and Danish spoken ■ Prices low to very high ■ Major credit cards

Antique maps and views. Flower prints.

THE MAP HOUSE OF LONDON

54 Beauchamp Place, Knightsbridge, London SW3 1NY ■ Tel: (0171) 584-4325 ■ Fax: (0171) 589-1041 ■ E-mail: mapa@themap-house.com ■ Mon-Fri 9:45-5:45, Sat 10:30-5:00 ■ Philip Curtis ■ Prices low to very high ■ Major credit cards

Antique maps, globes and prints.

OLD CHURCH GALLERIES

320 King's Road, Chelsea, London SW3 5UH ■ Tel: (0171) 351-4649 ■ Fax: (0171) 351-4449 ■ Mon-Sat 10:00-6:00 ■ Mati Harrington ■ Italian, Spanish and French spoken ■ Prices medium to high ■ Major credit cards ■ Trade discount

Antique maps and prints, sporting art and decorative picture frames.

THE O'SHEA GALLERY

120A Mount Street, London W1Y 5HB ■ Tel: (0171) 629-1122 ■ Fax: (0171) 629-1116 ■ Mon-Fri 9:30-6:00 ■ Raymond O'Shea ■ French spoken ■ Prices medium ■ Major credit cards ■ Professional discount ■ BADA

Antiquarian prints and maps. Framing and restoration.

JONATHAN POTTER LTD

125 New Bond Street, London W1Y 9AF ■ Tel: (0171) 491-3520 ■ Fax: (0171) 491-9754 ■ Mon-Fri 10:00-6:00 ■ Jonathan Potter ■ Prices low to very high ■ Most credit cards ■ Trade discount

Original antique maps, charts and plates of the world dating from the 16th to the 19th century. Mounting, framing and search service.

♛ TROWBRIDGE GALLERY

555 King's Road, London SW6 2EB ■ Tel: (0171) 371-8733 ■ Fax: (0171) 371-8138 ■ Mon-Fri 9:30-5:30 ■ Sat by appointment ■ Christopher W.R. Wilcox ■ Prices medium to very high ■ Trade discount ■ Major credit cards ■ LAPADA

Excellent choice of old prints and maps. Custom framing service.

MARINE MODELS

♛ LANGFORDS MARINE ANTIQUES

The Plaza, 535 King's Road, London SW10 0SZ ■ Tel: (0171) 351-4881 ■ Fax: (0171) 352-0763 ■ E-mail: langsford@dircon.co.uk ■ Mon-Fri 10:00-5:30, Sat by appointment ■ Trade discount ■ Major credit cards ■ BADA

Ships models, nautical artefacts and steam engines.

THE PARKER GALLERY

28 Pimlico Road, London SW1W 8LJ ■ Tel: (0171) 730-6768 ■ Fax: (0171) 259-9180 ■ Mon-Fri 9:30-5:30 ■ Adrian Newbury ■ Prices medium ■ Major credit cards ■ Trade discount

Naval, military, topographical, sporting prints and oils. Ship models of the 18th and 19th century. Catalogue available.

TREVOR PHILIP & SONS LTD

75A Jermyn Street, London SW1Y 6NP ■ Tel: (0171) 930-2954 ■ Fax: (0171) 321-0212 ■ Mon-Fri 9:00-6:00, Sat 10:00-4:00 ■ Prices medium to high ■ Trade discount ■ Major credit cards ■ BADA

Early instruments of science and natural philosophy and in particular globes; model ships.

MICHAEL YOUNG

22 The Mall, Camden Passage, 359 Upper Street, London N1 ■ Tel: (0171) 359-7477 ■ Wed & Sat 9:00-4:00 ■ Michael Young ■ Prices medium ■ Major credit cards ■ Professional discount

Antique marine models, boys' toys, pond boats.

MUSICAL INSTRUMENTS

J. & A. BEARE LTD

7 Broadwick Street, London W1V 1FJ ■ Tel: (0171) 437-1449 ■ Fax: (0171) 439-4520 ■ Mon-Fri 9:00-12:15/1:30-5:00, appointment advisable ■ BADA

Musical instruments of the violin family.

TONY BINGHAM

11 Pond Street, London NW3 2PN ■ Tel: (0171) 794-1596 ■ Fax: (0171) 433-3662 ■ By appointment ■ LAPADA

Musical instruments of the 17th to the early 20th century.

PERFUME AND SCENT BOTTLES

TERESA CLAYTON - TRIO

Grays Mews Antiques Market, 1-7 Davies Mews, London W1Y 1AR ■ Tel: (0171) 829-1184 ■ Fax: (0171) 493-9344 ■ Mon-Wed & Fri 10:30-5:30 ■ Teresa Clayton ■ Polish spoken ■ Prices medium to high ■ Visa accepted ■ Trade discount

Perfume bottles of the Georgian and Victorian periods. Art Nouveau and Art Deco Bohemian glass. Large selection of decorative glass of the 18th to the 20th century.

ACCENT (SCENT BOTTLES)

Admiral Vernon Antique Market, 141 Portobello Road, London SW1V 3XU ■ Tel: (0370) 851136 ■ Sat 7:00-4:00 ■ Vanessa Billings ■ Minimal French and Italian ■ Prices low to high ■ Major credit cards ■ Trade discount

19th and 20th century scent bottles, including Bohemian, Georgian, Victorian and Edwardian. Also can provide and fit atomizers.

SHIRLEY BRUNNING

Geoffrey Van Arcade, Stand 14, 105-107 Portobello Road, London W11 2QB ■ No phone or fax ■ Sat 7:00-4:00 ■ Trade discount

Scent and cologne bottles. Small silver items.

PUB MEMORABILIA

THE PUB WITH NO BEER

Unit 30A, Jubilee Market Hall, Covent Garden, London ■ Tel: (0171) 379-9450 ■ Mon-Fri 9:00-6:00 ■ Tracy Gaylor ■ Prices low to high ■ Major credit cards

Pub memorabilia, beer pumps, glasses, towels, hand-made pub signs.

PUPPETS AND MASKS

HARLEQUIN HOUSE

3 Kensington Mall, London W8 4EB ■ Tel: (0171) 221-8629 ■ Tue, Fri, Sat 11:00-5:30 ■ Jennifer Raison ■ Prices low to high ■ Trade discount for puppeteers

Puppets, antique and contemporary. Glove and finger puppets. All types of masks: party masks, theatrical masks, decorative masks. Also puppet doctoring and tender care.

SCIENTIFIC INSTRUMENTS AND MEDICAL

SCIENTIFIC & MEDICAL ANTIQUES, OLD TECHNOLOGY & BOOKS

Stands 23-25 Lipka Gallery, 286 Westbourne Grove, London W11 ■ Tel: (0181) 946-1470 ■ Fax: (0181) 944-7961 ■ E-mail: dgs@scienceantiques.co, ■ Sat 6:30-3:00 or by appointment ■ Desmond and Elizabeth Squire ■ Prices low to high ■ Visa and MC accepted ■ Trade discount

They specialize in old instruments of science, technology and medicine. They also offer books relating to the items they sell.

SMOKING

COLLECTORS HAVEN
290 Westbourne Grove, Portobello Road, London W11 ■ Tel: (0171) 831-7210 ■ Sat 6:30-4:00 ■ Roy and Niala Gilbert ■ Prices low to high ■ Trade discount

Old tobacco tins and cigarette packets. Show cards and all kinds of tobacco advertising. Over 1,000 tins in stock from all over the world.

SPORTING

SEAN ARNOLD SPORTING ANTIQUES
21-22 Chepstow Corner, Westbourne Grove, London W2 4XE ■ Tel: (0171) 221-2267 ■ Fax: (0171) 221-5464 ■ Mon-Sat 10:00-6:00 ■ Sean Arnold ■ German spoken ■ Prices low to high ■ Major credit cards ■ Trade discounts

Antique sports equipment, prizes and sports memorabilia. Restoration.

TOYS AND TRAINS

ALVIN'S VINTAGE GAMES AND TOYS
Alfie's Antique Market, 13-25 Church Street, London NW8 8DT ■ Tel: (0171) 723-1513 ■ E-mail: hiddenvalley@virgin.net ■ Tue-Sat 10:30-5:00 ■ Alvin Ross ■ French spoken ■ Prices low to high ■ Major credit cards ■ Trade discount

Vintage games, jigsaws, Pelham puppets, toys, dolls, teddy bears, Dinky, Lesney, Corgi, etc.

PETER & JOAN DUNK
288 Westbourne Grove, B. Lipka & Sons Ltd., London W11 2PS ■ Tel: (0181) 940-0576 ■ Sat ■ Prices low to high ■ Trade discount

Toy trains (pre-war only), tin toys, early spectacles, safety razors, irons, food moulds.

BENJAMIN POLLOCK'S TOY SHOP
44 The Market, Covent Garden, London WC2E 8RF ■ Tel: (0171) 379-7866 ■ Fax: (0171) 636-0559 ■ Mon-Sat 10:30-6:00, Sun 12:00-5:00 ■ P.F. and C.J. Baldwin ■ French and German spoken ■ Prices medium to high ■ Major credit cards

Toy theatres in paper or wood, miniature stages for producing plays, from the 19th to the 20th century. Traditional wood toys, teddy bears, paper dolls. Toy theatres have a long history in England.

THE ANTIQUE CLOTHING SHOP

282 Portobello Road, London W10 ■ Tel: (0181) 964-4830 ■ Fri & Sat 9:00-6:00 or by appointment ■ Sandy Stagg ■ Prices low to high ■ Visa and MC accepted ■ Trade discount

A large collection of women's, men's and children's vintage clothing of the period pre-1960. Some fabrics, trimmings, lace and needlepoint.

LUNN ANTIQUES LTD

22 Cucumber Alley, (off Neal Street), London WC ■ Tel: (0171) 379-1974 ■ Mon-Sat 10:30-6:30, Sun 1:00-6:00 ■ Stephen Lunn ■ Prices low to high ■ Major credit cards ■ Trade prices

Antique textiles. Victorian to 20s, 30s and 60s clothing. Accessories. All available for photo sessions.

RADIO DAYS

87 Lower Marsh, Waterloo, London SE1 7AB ■ Telfax: (0171) 928-0800 ■ Mon-Sat 11:00-5:00 or by appointment ■ Nik Sutherland and Christina Layzell ■ Prices low to medium ■ Visa and MC accepted ■ Trade discount

Vintage clothing of the 1920s to the 1970s. Other memorabilia. Prop hire.

See also: Portobello Road Antique Market.

Architectural Antiques

ARCHITECTURAL ANTIQUES

351 King Street, London W6 9NM ■ Tel: (0181) 741-7883 ■ Fax: (0181) 741-1109 ■ Mon-Sat 9:00-5:00 ■ Gervais Duc ■ French spoken ■ Prices medium ■ Trade discount

Antique marble and stone fireplaces, gilt mirrors and antique French furniture.

H & D FIREPLACE COMPANY

Arch 385, Mentmore Terrace, London Fields, London E8 3PN ■ Mon-Sat 10:00-5:30 ■ Mick Davies ■ German and Spanish spoken ■ Prices low to medium ■ Trade discounts

Flooring, stained glass, fireplaces in slate, granite, marble, gas and coal effect fires, ironwork, stone objects and antique furniture.

THE LONDON ARCHITECTURAL SALVAGE & SUPPLY CO LTD

St. Michael's Church, Mark Street, London EC2A 4ER ■ Tel: (0171) 739-0448 ■ Fax: (0171) 729-6853 ■ E-mail: lassco@zetnet.co.uk ■ Mon-Sun 10:00-5:00 ■ Anthony Reeve ■ French spoken ■ Prices low to very high ■ All major credit cards ■ Trade discount

London's largest specialist in architectural antiques, panelled rooms, door hardware, fireplaces, garden ornaments. Their catalogue is excellent.

WESTLAND & COMPANY

The Clergy House, Mark Street, London EC2A ■ Tel: (0171) 739-8094 ■ Fax: (0171) 729-3620 ■ E-mail: westland@westland.co.uk. ■ Mon-Fri 9:00-6:00, Sat-Sun 10:00-5:00 ■ Geoffrey Westland ■ German and French spoken ■ Prices low to very high ■ All credit cards ■ Trade discount

Period and contemporary fireplaces, antique panelling, statuary, garden ornaments, grills, gates, furniture, fountains and paintings.

Asian Antiques and Art

♛ GREGG BAKER ORIENTAL ART
132 Kensington Church Street, London W8 4BH ■ Tel: (0171) 221-3533 ■ Fax: (0171) 221-4410 ■ Mon-Fri 10:00-6:00 and by appointment ■ Gregg Baker ■ French and Japanese spoken ■ Prices medium to high ■ Visa, Amex ■ BADA, LAPADA

Japanese and Chinese works of art, specializing in metalwork and screens. Bronzes, cloisonne, lacquer and wood Chinese works of art, vases, figures, boxes.

♛ BERWALD ORIENTAL ART
101 Kensington Church Street, London W8 7LN ■ Tel: (0171) 229-0800 ■ Fax: (0171) 229-1101 ■ E-mail: berwald@aapi.co.uk ■ Website: www.berwald-oriental.com ■ Mon-Fri 10:00-6:00 ■ John Berwald ■ Prices medium to very high ■ Major credit cards ■ Trade discount ■ BADA

Fine antique Chinese porcelain, pottery and works of art.

BRANDT ORIENTAL ANTIQUES
29 New Bond Street, First floor, London W1Y 9HD ■ Telfax: (0171) 499-8835 ■ By appointment only ■ BADA

Japanese and Chinese works of art. Textiles.

PAUL CHAMPKINS
41 Dover Street, London W1X 3RB ■ Tel: (0171) 495-4600 ■ Fax: (01235) 751658 ■ By appointment only ■ BADA

Chinese, Japanese and Korean art.

COHEN & COHEN
101B Kensington Church Street, London W8 7LN ■ Tel: (0171) 727-7677 ■ Fax: (0171) 229-9653 ■ Mon-Fri 10:00-6:00, Sat 10:00-4:00 ■ Michael Cohen ■ French spoken ■ Prices medium to very high ■ Major credit cards ■ BADA

Chinese export porcelain: in particular armorials, services, European subjects and forms, famille verte, tobacco leaf, unusual blue and white pieces dating from circa 1650-1800 and Chinese works of art.

COHEN & PEARCE (ANTIQUE PORCELAIN)
84 Portobello Road, London W11 2QD ■ Tel: (0171) 229-9458 ■ Fax: (0171) 229-9653 ■ Fri 10:00-4:00, Sat 8:00-4:00 and by appointment ■ BADA

Oriental ceramics and works of art, specializing in Chinese export porcelain of the 17th and 18th centuries.

BARRY DAVIES ORIENTAL ART LTD

1 Davies Street, London W1Y 1LL ■ Tel: (0171) 408-0207 ■ Fax: (0171) 493-3422 ■ Mon-Fri 10:00-6:00 ■ BADA

All areas of Japanese art: netsuke, inro, ojime, lacquerware, enamels, metalwork, screens, swords, swordfittings, okimono, satsuma and early porcelains.

SHIRLEY DAY LTD

91B Jermyn Street, London SW1Y 6JB ■ Tel: (0171) 839-2804 ■ Fax: (0171) 839-3334 ■ Mon-Fri 10:00-5:00 ■ BADA

Hindu and Buddhist art from India and Southeast Asia. Asian antiquities, tribal textiles, Japanese paintings and screens.

ADELE DE HAVILLAND

The Bond Street Antique Centre, 124 New Bond Street, London W1X 9AE ■ Tel: (0171) 499-7127 ■ Mon-Fri 10:00-5:00 ■ Adele de Havilland ■ French and Italian spoken ■ Prices medium to high ■ Major credit cards ■ Trade discount

Oriental porcelain, fine jade, bronze figures, ivory netsukes and carvings. Art Deco and Art Nouveau jewellery.

JOHN ESKENAZI LTD

15 Old Bond Street, Lndon W1X 4JL ■ Tel: (0171) 409-3001 ■ Fax: (0171)629-2146 ■ E-mail: johneskenazi@john-eskenazi.com ■ Mon-Fri 9:00-6:00 ■ John Eskenazi, Kate Cook ■ Italian, French, Arabic and German spoken ■ Prices medium to high ■ BADA

Oriental antiques and Oriental rugs and textiles. Himalayan, Southeast Asian and Indian sculptures.

MICHAEL GOEDHUIS

116 Mount Street, London W1Y 5HD ■ Tel: (0171) 629-2228 ■ Fax: (0171) 409-3338 ■ Mon-Fri 9:30-6:00 ■ Prices high ■ Trade discount ■ BADA

Chinese and Japanese ancient and contemporary art including archaic and later bronzes and 20th century and contemporary Chinese paintings.

ALEXANDER GOTZ

35 Connaught Square, London W2 2HL ■ Tel: (0171) 724-4435 ■ Fax: (0171) 262-9891 ■ E-mail: agoetz@dircom.co.uk ■ Mon-Fri 10:00-6:00 ■ Alexander Gotz ■ German and some French and Italian spoken ■ Prices medium to very high

Ancient art from South and South East Asia. Sculptures in stone and bronze. Some gold and jewellery.

ANITA GRAY

Grays Antiques Market, 58 Davies Street, London W1Y 2LP ■ Tel: (0171) 408-1638 ■ Fax: (0171) 495-0707 ■ E-mail: info@chinese-porcelain.com ■ Mon-Fri 10:00-6:00 ■ French and Swedish spoken ■ Prices high ■ Major credit cards

Oriental porcelain and works of art, 14th to 18th century.

MARTYN GREGORY GALLERY

34 Bury Street, London SW1Y 6AU ■ Tel: (0171) 839-3731 ■ Fax: (0171) 930-0812 ■ Mon-Fri 10:00-6:00 ■ BADA

China trade (export) paintings, pictures related to South East Asia and British watercolours and paintings.

NICHOLAS GRINDLEY

13 Old Burlington Street, London W1X 1LA ■ Tel: (0171) 437-5449 ■ Fax: (0171) 494-2446 ■ Mon-Fri 2:00-5:00 and by appointment ■ BADA

Chinese furniture and works of art.

ROBERT HALL

15C Clifford Street, Mayfair, London W1X 1RF ■ Tel: (0171) 734-4008 ■ Fax: (0171) 734-4408 ■ Mon-Fri 10:00-5:30 ■ Robert Hall ■ German and some French spoken ■ Prices medium to very high nAmex, Visa ■ BADA

Antique Chinese snuff bottles and Chinese works of art.

GERARD HAWTHORN LTD

104 Mount Street, London W1Y 5HE ■ Tel: (0171) 409-2888 ■ Fax: (0171) 409-2777 ■ Mon-Fri 9:30-6:00 ■ BADA

Chinese and Japanese works of art and ceramics.

MILNE HENDERSON

15 Greville Place, London NW6 5JE ■ Tel: (0171) 328-2171 ■ Fax: (0171) 624-7274 ■ By appointment ■ BADA

Japanese and Chinese paintings, drawings and screens; 12th to 19th century Korean paintings and drawings.

OLIVER HOARE

7 Onslow Gardens, London SW7 3LY ■ Tel: (0171) 835-1600 ■ Fax: (0171) 373-5187 ■ By appointment

Fine antiques from the Middle East and Asia.

JAPAN PRINT GALLERY

43 Pembridge Road, London W11 3HG ■ Tel: (0171) 221-0927 ■ Fax: (0171) 792-8901 ■ Mon-Sat 11:00-10:00 ■ William O'Rorke ■ Japanese spoken ■ Prices medium to high ■ Major credit cards ■ Trade discount

Japanese wood block prints of the 18th to the 20th century.

KATIE JONES

195 Westbourne Grove, London W11 2SB ■ Tel: (0171) 243-5600 ■ Fax: (0171) 243-4653 ■ Tue-Fri 10:30-6:00, Sat 10:30-3:00 ■ Katie Jones ■ Japanese spoken ■ Prices low to very high ■ Major credit cards ■ Trade discount

Japanese antiques and some complementary contemporary works.

PETER KEMP ANTIQUES

170 Kensington Church Street, London W8 4BN ■ Telfax: (0171) 229-2988 ■ Mon-Fri 10:00-5:00 ■ P. Kemp ■ Prices medium ■ Trade discount

Porcelain and Oriental works of art.

ROGER KEVERNE

120 Mount Street, London W1Y 5HB ■ Tel: (0171) 355-1711 ■ Fax: (0171) 409-7717 ■ Mon-Fri 9:30-5:30 ■ Prices high ■ Trade discount ■ BADA

Chinese, Japanese and Oriental works of art.

KITE

15 Langton Street, Chelsea, London SW10 0JL ■ Tel: (0171) 351-2108 ■ Fax: (0171) 376-5867 ■ Mon-Fri 10:00-6:00, Sat 10:00-5:00 ■ John Willis ■ Prices medium ■ Visa and MC ■ Trade discount

17th to 19th century Chinese vernacular furniture and decorative objects.

ROBERT KLEINER & CO LTD

30 Old Bond Street, London W1X 4HN ■ Tel: (0171) 629-1814/(0171) 622-5462 ■ Fax: (0171) 629-1239 ■ Mon-Fri 9:30-5:30 ■ Prices high ■ Trade discount ■ BADA

Chinese works of art, jades, porcelains and snuff bottles.

👑 S. MARCHANT & SON
120 Kensington Church Street, London W8 4BH ■ Tel: (0171) 229-5319 ■ Fax: (0171) 792-8979 ■ E-mail: marchant@dircon.co.uk ■ Mon-Fri 9:30-6:00 ■ Richard Marchant ■ Spanish, French and German spoken ■ Major credit cards

Superb Chinese and Japanese porcelain and works of art. Their specialty is porcelain, especially Imperial, famille verte and 16th and 17th century blue and white wares, of the finest quality.

MALLETT
141 New Bond Street, London W1Y 0BS ■ Tel: (0171) 499-7411 ■ Fax: (0171) 495-3179 ■ Mon-Fri 9:30-5:30, Sat 11:00-4:00 ■ Prices high ■ Amex, Visa ■ Trade discount ■ BADA

Chinese export porcelain, lacquer, paper, paintings and furniture and other works of art.

👑 MALLETT AT BOURDON HOUSE LTD
2 Davies Street, London W1Y 1LJ ■ Tel: (0171) 629-2444 ■ Fax: (0171) 499-2670 E-mail: antiques@mallett.co.uk ■ Mon-Fri 9:00-6:00, Sat 11:00-4:00 ■ French and Spanish spoken ■ Prices high ■ Amex, Visa ■ Trade discount ■ BADA

Since 1865, highly unusual and rare Chinese export furniture, porcelain and works of art.

SYDNEY L. MOSS LTD
51 Brook Street, London W1Y 1AU ■ Tel: (0171) 629-4670 ■ Fax: (0171) 491-9278 ■ Mon-Fri 10:00-5:00 and by appointment ■ Prices high ■ Trade discount ■ BADA

Chinese and Japanese paintings and calligraphy. Chinese literati works of art, Japanese netsuke and lacquer.

ORIENTAL BRONZES LTD
Ryland House, 24A Ryland Road, London NW5 3EH ■ Telfax: (0171) 267-0828 ■ By appointment only ■ BADA

Chinese archaeology.

PHOENIX ORIENTAL ART
No. 6, The Lower Mall, 359 Upper Street, Islington, London N1 0PD ■ Tel: (0171) 226-4474 ■ Fax: (0181) 521-8846 ■ Wed-Sat 10:00-4:30 and by appointment ■ E-mail: elena18344@aol.com ■ Elena Edwards ■ Prices medium ■ Visa, Amex ■ Trade discount ■ LAPADA

Chinese and Japanese bronzes, snuff bottles, jades, carvings, netsuke.

PRIESTLEY & FERRARO

17 King Street, St James's, London SW1Y 6QU ■ Tel: (0171) 930-6228 ■ Fax: (0171) 930-6226 ■ E-mail: david_priestley@msn.com ■ Mon-Fri 9:30-5:30 ■ David Priestley ■ Prices high ■ Trade discount

Early Chinese ceramics and works of art.

SAINSBURY AND MASON

145 Ebury Street, London SW1 ■ Tel: (0171) 730-3393 ■ Fax: (0171) 730-8334 ■ Mon-Fri 10:00-1:00 by appointment ■ Barry Sainsbury and Jeremy Mason ■ French spoken ■ Prices low to high ■ Trade discount

Oriental works of art.

A.V. SANTOS

1 Campden Street, London W8 7EP ■ Tel: (0171) 727-4872 ■ Fax: (0171) 229-4801 ■ Mon-Fri 10:00-1:00/2:00-6:00 ■ BADA

Chinese export porcelain.

JACQUELINE SIMCOX LTD

54 Linton Street, Islington, London N1 7AS ■ Telfax: (0171) 359-8939 ■ Mobile: 0777 5566388 ■ Mon-Fri by appointment only

Asian textiles and works of art.

A & J SPEELMAN LTD ORIENTAL ART

129 Mount Street, London W1Y 5HA ■ Tel: (0171) 499-5126 ■ Fax: (0171) 355-3391 ■ Mon-Fri 9:00-5:30 ■ BADA

Oriental ceramics and works of art.

SPINK & SON LTD

5 King Street, St. James, London SW1Y 6QS ■ Tel: (0171) 930-7888 ■ Fax: (0171) 839-4853 ■ E-mail: spink@btinternet.com ■ Mon-Fri 9:00-5:30 ■ Christopher Knapton ■ French, Spanish and Mandarin spoken ■ Prices high to very high ■ Major credit cards ■ Trade discount

Chinese, Japanese, Korean, Himalayan, Indian and Southeast Asian works of art.

JAN VAN PEERS

34 Davies Street, London W1Y 1LG ■ Tel: (0171) 408-0434 ■ Fax: (0171) 355-1397 ■ Mon-Fri 10:00-6:00 ■ BADA

Buddhist art. Chinese, Japanese and Southeast Asian art.

LINDA WIGGLESWORTH LTD

34 Brook Street, Ground floor suite, London W1Y 1YA ■ Tel: (0171) 408-0177 ■ Fax: (0171) 491-9812 ■ Mon-Sat 10:00-6:00 and by appointment ■ BADA, LAPADA

Antique Chinese Ming and Qing dynasty costumes. Korean and Tibetan textiles.

Antique Fairs

The major antique and fine art fairs in London usually occur in the Spring and the Fall. The most important in London are The Grosvenor House Art and Antiques Fair, The Olympia, and The International Ceramics Fair & Seminar. Check on the dates.

THE GROSVENOR HOUSE ART & ANTIQUES FAIR

Grosvenor House, Park Lane, London W1 ■ Tel: (0171) 495-6406 ■ Fax: (0171) 495-8747 ■ E-mail: grosvenor-antiquesfair@msn.com ■ Website: www.grosvenor-antiquesfair.co.uk n

This is one of the best of the Fairs with a gathering of the best of the antique and art dealers from all over the world.

OLYMPIA FINE ART AND ANTIQUES FAIR

Hammersmith Road, London W14 ■ Tel: (0171) 370-8188 ■ Fax: (0171) 370-8221 ■ E-mail: olympia-antiques@eco.co.uk ■ Website: www.olympia-antiques.co.uk ■

A remarkable exhibition of some of the best art and antiques treasures in the world including carpets, porcelain and the unusual collectible. Spring: last week of February. Summer: first two weeks of June. Winter: third week of November.

THE INTERNATIONAL CERAMICS FAIR AND SEMINAR

The Park Lane Hotel, Ballroom Annex, Piccadilly, London W1 ■ Tel: (0171) 734-5491 ■ Fax: (0171) 494-4604 ■ E-mail: info@haughton.com ■ Brian and Anna Haughton ■ French spoken

Antique and contemporary pottery, porcelain and fine glass from 8,000 BC to the present.
NOTE: Brian and Anna Haughton are also the organizers of the excellent fairs in New York: The International Asian Art Fair, The International Fine Art Fair, and The International Fine Art & Antique Dealers Show.

THE ANTIQUES TRADE GAZETTE

17 Whitcomb Street, London WC2H 7PL ■ Tel: (0171) 930-9955 ■ Fax: (0171) 930-6391 ■ E-mail: editorial@atg-online.com ■ Subscription: subscriptions@atg-online.com ■ Editor, Mark Bridge

London's antiques trade weekly is recognized as the authoritative professional source of information on what is happening in the world of antiques, both in the UK and overseas.

ARCHITECTURAL ELEMENTS

Blast Cleaning

CAPITAL STONE
York Way, London N1 0AZ ■ Tel: (0171) 837-2421 ■ Mon-Fri 9:00-5:00
Shot blasters, stone, wood, brick, metal. Both pressure and chemical cleaning.

J & W RENOVATION CO LTD
4-8 Whites Grounds, London SE1 3LA ■ Tel: (0171) 740-1199 ■ Mon-Fri 9:00-5:00
Grit blasting anywhere in the London area.

Blinds, Awnings and Shutters

AMERICAN SHUTTERS
72 Station Road, London SW13 0LS ■ Tel: (0181) 876-5905 ■ Fax: (0181) 878-9548 ■ Mon-Fri 9:00-5:00 ■ Trade discount
American made shutters in all styles and all sizes of louvres. Also Shoji window screens to order in synthetic ricepaper

APPLIED BLINDS
5 Stanstead Road, London SE23 114G ■ Tel: (0181) 291-0777 ■ Mon-Fri 9:00-5:00 ■ Trade discount
Vertical, louvre, Venetian and conservatory blinds. Custom awnings, canopies, insect screens and window film.

ASPECT CONTRACT BLINDS
34 Lancaster Road, Edmonton, London N18 1HP ■ Tel: (0181) 372-0859/807-7404 ■ Fax: (0181) 482-9604 ■ Mon-Fri 9:00-5:00, Sat 10:00-1:00 ■ Major credit cards ■ Trade discount
Manufacturer and supplier of all types of blinds, awnings and curtains: Venetian, vertical, wood slats. Rooflight blinds. Electrical and mechanical controls. Blackout curtains.

BLACKWOOD BLINDS
66 Princess Road, Kilburn, London NW6 ■ Tel: (0171) 328-4490 ■ Mon-Fri 9:00-5:30, Sat 10:00-1:00 ■ Trade discount

Roller blinds, Roman blinds wooden and metal. Venetian, vertical blinds. Reeded wood, pleated blinds, Holland blinds, Lyverscreen. Awnings and canopies. Conservatory blinds a specialty.

CAPITAL
4 Brettenham Avenue, London E17 5DG ■ Telfax: (0181) 527-7144 ■ Mon-Fri 9:00-5:00 ■ Trade discount ■ Major credit cards

Commercial and residential. vertical and pleated blinds, roller blinds and blinds for conservatories. Free measure and fit service.

CAPITAL SUNBLINDS
Rear of 117A Anerly Road, London SE20 BAJ ■ Tel: (0181) 676-0239 ■ Mon-Fri 9:00-5:00 ■ Trade discount ■ Credit cards

All types of blinds, supplied and installed. Cleaning and repair of Venetian blinds and vertical blinds

CONCEPT BLINDS
162 Kensington Road, London SE11 6QR ■ Tel: (0171) 582-6030 ■ Mon-Fri 9:00-5:00 ■ Trade discount ■ Major credit cards

Venetian and vertical blinds. Roller blinds, pleated blinds. Free installation.

SILENT GLISS LIMITED – LONDON TRADE SHOWROOM
The Business Design Centre, Suite 325/6, 52 Upper Street, Islington, London N1 0QH ■ Tel: (0171) 288-6100 ■ Fax: (0171) 288-6103 ■ E-mail: info@silent-gliss.co.uk. ■ Mon-Fri 9:00-5:30 ■ Georgina Michael ■ Prices high ■ Professional discount

High quality curtain fitments, electric systems, decorative window blinds for all interiors. Fitting and expert measuring.

Ceilings

ACOUSTI-CEILING SERVICES LTD
138 Brompton Road, Knightsbridge, London SW3 1HY ■ Tel: (0171) 581-9510/4393 ■ Fax: (0171) 838-0914 ■ Mon-Fri 9:00-5:00 ■ Trade discount

Suspended ceilings, installations and repairs. Specialists in cleaning walls and ceilings. Also lighting supplied and installed.

S.J. BYFORD & SONS LTD
Unit 2a, Canterbury Court, 6 Camberwell New Road, London SE5 OTG ■ Tel: (0171) 793-0777 ■ Fax: (0171) 793-0377 ■ Mon-Fri 9:00-5:00 ■ Trade discount

Suspended ceilings, raised floors, partitions and integral lighting.

CEILINGS DISTRIBUTION
Unit 10, Highams Park Industrial Estate, Jubilee Avenue, London E4 6NJ ■ Tel: (0181) 523-2167 ■ Fax: (0181) 527-0606 ■ Mon-Fri 9:00-5:00 ■ Trade discount

Suspended ceilings and lighting.

CRAFTWORK INTERIORS
98 Lower Richmond Road, Putney, London SW15 1LN ■ Tel: (0181) 780-1798 ■ Fax: (0181) 780-1861 ■ Mon-Fri 9:00-5:00 ■ Trade discount

Suspended ceilings, partitions, lighting.

H. FINN LTD
176 Royal College Street, London NW1 ■ Tel: (0171) 485-5540 ■ Fax: (0171) 284-3278 ■ Mon-Fri 9:00-5:00 ■ Trade discount

Suspended ceilings, recessed lighting. Maintenance and repairs.

INTEGRA CONTRACTS LTD
Unit 21, Hackford Walk, 119-123 Hackford Road, London SW9 ■ Tel: (0171) 820-1800 ■ Mon-Fri 9:00-5:00 ■ Trade discount

Suspended ceilings, laser levelling and light settings.

Doors

COTSWOOD
5 Hampden Way, Southgate, London N14 5DJ ∎ Tel: (0181) 368-1664 ∎ Fax: (0181) 368-9635 ∎ Mon-Fri 9:00-5:00
63a Park Road, King'ston-on-Thames, Surrey ∎ Tel: (0181) 546-3621 ∎ Mon-Fri 9:00-5:00

Back, front, sliding and folding doors. Room dividers. Hardwood period doors, architraves, frames and screens custom made.

DARWIN BESPOKE FURNITURE MAKERS
38A Darwin Road, London W5 4BD ∎ Tel: (0181) 560-0424 ∎ Mon-Fri 9:00-5:00

Custom-made antique reproduction doors in hardwoods: mahogany and oak.

JOHN RUSSELL ARCHITECTURAL CARPENTRY & JOINERY
Unit 7, Rosemary Works, Branch Place, London N1 ∎ Tel: (0171) 739-2241 ∎ Mon-Fri 9:00-5:00

Custom Doors

THE LONDON DOOR COMPANY
153 St John's Hill, London SW11 1TQ ∎ Tel: (0171) 801-0877 ∎ Fax: (0171) 223-7296 ∎ Mon-Sat 9:30-5:00 ∎ John Williamson, Kerry Waters ∎ German and French spoken ∎ Prices medium to high ∎ Visa, MC ∎ Trade discount

Front and interior doors: traditional and contemporary. Room dividers, French doors. Bevelled, stained and etched glass. Expert fitting service.

OLD DOOR & FIREPLACE COMPANY
67-69 Essex Road, London N1 2SF ∎ Tel: (0171) 226-0910 ∎ Mon-Fri 9:00-5:00

Doors, shutters, stained glass windows, plain stripped down doors, old parquet flooring.

ORIGINAL DOOR SPECIALISTS
298 Brockley Road, London SE4 2RA ∎ Tel: (0181) 252-8109 ∎ Mon-Fri 9:00-5:00

Reclaimed doors, hundreds in stock. Stained glass windows, shutters, room dividers and cupboards for kitchens and bathrooms.

RENAISSANCE LONDON LTD
193-195 City Road, London EC1 ■ 3-11 Westland Place, London N1
The Old Door and Fireplace Co., 67-69 Essex Road, London N1 2SF
■ Tel: (0171) 251-8844 ■ Telfax: (0171) 226-0910 ■ Mon-Sat 8:00-6:00
■ Owen Pacey ■ Prices low to high

A very large stock of original doors and shutters as well as old fireplaces, old radiators and decorative objects.

Flooring

BELLE DESIGNS
414 King's Road, London SW10 OLJ ■ Tel: (0171) 795-0095 ■ Mon-Fri by appointment ■ Trade discount

Hardwood flooring specialists and Amtico tile.

CAMPBELL MARSON & COMPANY LTD
573 King's Road, London SW6 2EB ■ Tel: (0171) 371-5001 ■ Fax: (0181) 946-9395 ■ Mon-Sat 10:00-5:30 ■ Trade discount

High quality parquet and borders, wood mosaic, block and strip.

DESIGNER FLOORING LTD
69 Abingdon Road, London W8 ■ Tel: (0171) 460-0260 ■ Fax: (0171) 460-0294 ■ Mon-Sat 9:00-6:00 ■ B. Meftah ■ French and German spoken ■ Prices medium ■ Major credit cards ■ Professional discount

Parquet flooring, wood strip and all soft flooring. Supply and fitting services.

FLOORING CENTRE
2 Avenue Parade, Ridge Avenue, London N21 ■ Tel: (0181) 360-4242 ■ Mon-Fri 9:00-5:00 ■ Trade discount

New and reclaimed hardwoods for flooring in a variety of timbers and designs for parquet, woodblock and planking.

GALACROFT HARDWOOD FLOORING
19 Colindale Avenue, Colindale, London NW9 5DS ■ Tel: (0181) 358-6222 ■ Fax: (0181) 358-6223 ■ Mon-Sat 9:00-5:00 ■ Amir Adar ■ Hindi and Hebrew spoken ■ Prices low to high ■ Major credit cards ■ Professional discount

Pre-finished solid and laminate flooring and accessories. Fitting services.

NATURAL FLOORING DIRECT LTD
Tower Bridge Business Complex, Clements Road, London SE16 ■
Tel: (0181) 293-7122 ■ Fax: (0181) 293-7123 ■ Mon-Fri 9:00-5:00 ■
Major credit cards ■ Trade discount

Sisal, seagrass, coir, jute, wool and wood floor covering. Supply and installation.

TUDOR FLOORING CO LTD
2A Avenue Parade, Ridge Avenue, London N21 2AX ■ Tel: (0181)
360-4242 ■ Fax: (0181) 360-6881 ■ Mon-Sat 9:00-5:00 ■ Prices low to
high ■ Trade discount

All parquet and hardwoods. Resurfacing and renovation. Amtico and Forbo. Fitting and laying all floor products.

WOODROW
92 Battersea Rise, London SW11 ■ Telfax: (0171) 228-5106 ■ Mon-Fri
9:00-5:00 ■ Trade discount

All types of hardwood flooring supplied and fitted: woodstrips, woodblock, parquet design, wide oak boards. Natural floorcoverings: jute, coir, seagrass, sisal. Resurfacing, sanding and sealing of existing floors.

Gates & Railings

JAMES HOYLE & SON
50 Andrews Road, London E8 4RL ■ Tel: (0181) 551-6764 ■ Fax:
(0181) 550-0931 ■ Mon-Fri 7:00-4:00 ■ Alan Hoyle ■ Prices medium
to high

Architectural iron founder. Cast iron balustrades for staircases, railings, fireplaces. Reproduction of period pieces made to design. He refurbished the railings at the National Portrait Gallery.

J.H. PORTER & SON LTD
13 Cranleigh Mews, Cabul Road, Battersea, London SW11 2QL ■
Tel: (0171) 978-5576 ■ Fax: (0171) 924-7081 ■ Mon-Fri 8:00-5:00 ■
Fred Hodgins ■ Prices low ■ Trade discount

They make anything in decorative iron: gates, grilles, railings, staircases and balustrades, indoor and outdoor furniture. They restore antique iron work.

THE LONDON RAILING CO LTD

32 Sunderland Road, London ■ Tel: (0181) 871-4848 ■ Mon-Fri 8:00-5:00 ■ Trade discount

Specialists in spiral staircases balustrades and gates.

METALCRAFT (TOTTENHAM) LTD

6-40 Durnford Street, London N15 5NQ ■ Tel: (0181) 802-1715 ■ Fax: (0181) 802-1258 ■ Mon-Fri 8:00-9:00 ■ Trade discount

Design, maufacture and installation of spiral staircases, fire escapes, grilles, gates and railings.

TRESCHER FABRICATIONS LTD

R-A 1&2 Bermondsey Trading Estate, Rotherhithe New Road, London SE16 3LL ■ Tel: (0171) 231-8692 ■ Fax: (0171) 252-3303 ■ Mon-Fri 7:30-5:00 ■ C.A. Mee and J. Nobourn ■ Prices medium ■ Trade discounts

Design, fabrication and installation of gates, staircases, balustrades, railings, fencing, fire escapes.

WESTLAND & COMPANY

Saint Michael's Church, Leonard Street, London EC2A 4ER ■ Tel: (0171) 739-8094 ■ Fax: (0171) 729-3620 ■ E-mail: westland@westland.co.uk ■ Website: www.westland.co.uk ■ Mon-Fri 9:00-6:00, Sat-Sun 10:00-5:00 ■ Geoffrey Westland ■ German and French spoken ■ Prices low to very high ■ All credit cards ■ Trade discount

Antique architectural elements: grilles, gates and fountains.

Marble and Stone

FRANCIS BUCHANAN LTD

Masons Yard, 42 Magdalen Road, London SW18 3NP ■ Tel: (0181) 874-8363 ■ Fax: (0181) 871-1342 ■ Mon-Fri 8:00-6:00 ■ Roger Francis

Design and execution of projects in marble, granite and stone, including kitchens, bathrooms, firplaces, flooring, plaques, bases, memorials. Restoration and re-polishing a specialty. They also cut bricks, terra cotta, paving slabs and earthenware.

CLASSIQUE CO. TRADING LTD

39-69 Westmoor Street, London SE7 8NR ■ Tel: (0181) 853-1954 ■ Fax: (0181) 853-1955 ■ Mon-Fri 8:00-6:00 ■ A. Shandalou and M. Saedi ■ Farsi spoken ■ Prices medium ■ Trade discount

Marble and granite tiles, vanity tops, kitchen worktops. They supply and restore.

PAUL DAVIES DESIGN

King'ston, Kent ■ Tel: (0181) 541-0838 ■ Fax: (0181) 541-1962 ■ Mon-Fri 8:00-6:00 by appointment ■ Professional discount

English stone, limestone and sandstone, decorative concrete and terrazzo. Supply and fix.

GUNN MARBLE LIMITED

Unit One, 100-102 Woodhouse Road, Leytonstone, London E11 JNA ■ Tel: (0181) 536-1313 ■ Fax: (0181) 925-8153 ■ Mon-Sat 8:00-6:00 ■ John Main ■ Prices medium ■ Trade discount

Marble, granite, stone and slate for all applications. Supply, manufacture install and restore. Kitchen worktops a specialty.

HAYCAR RENOVATIONS & MAINTENANCE SERVICES LIMITED

1 Highcliffe Close, Wickford, Essex SS11 8JZ ■ Telfax: (01268) 768510 ■ Mon-Sat 8:00-6:00 and by appointment ■ Mr. B.J. Carew ■ Professional discount

Architectural renovation to buildings: marble, granite, terrazzo, stonework, brickwork, bronze, stainless steel, aluminum, brass. Renovation and maintenance by highly qualified craftsmen.

MARBLE ARCH LTD

431-432 Gordon Grove, Camberwell, London SE5 9DU ■ Tel: (0171) 738-7212 ■ Fax: (0171) 738-7613 ■ E-mail: robertmerry@mar-blearch.com ■ Mon-Fri 8:00-5:30 ■ Robert Merry ■ Portuguese spoken ■ Prices medium ■ Professional discount

Marble, granite, limestone. Supply, manufacture, installation. Work references include: Kensington Palace Gardens, Tower of Lethendy, Perth, The Boltons and Harrods in London and many more.

STONE IMAGE

3 Queensland Crescent, Chelmsford, Essex ■ Head Office Tel: (01245) 359794 ■ Mobile: 0585 370678 ■ Mon-Fri 8:00-5:00 ■ Trade discount

Installation, repair, renovation and maintenance specialists. Terrazzo & marble renovation. Marble, terrazzo, granite, limestone.

Mouldings

BUTCHER PLASTERING SPECIALISTS LTD
8 Fitzroy Road, Primrose Hill, London NW1 8TX ■ Tel: (0171) 722-9771 ■ Fax: (0171) 586-2953 ■ Mon-Fri 8:00-2:30 ■ R.W. Butcher ■ Prices low to very high

Fibrous plaster mouldings, cornices, ceiling centres, columns pilasters. Supply and restore.

CHARACTER MOULDINGS
Unit5, 39 Brighton Road, South Croydon, Surrey CR2 6EB ■ Tel: (0181) 688-2242 ■ Fax: (0181) 760-0230 ■ Mon-Sat 8:00-5:00 ■ J. Thompson ■ Trade discount

All aspects of decorative plaster. Cornices, friezes, dadoes, panel mouldings, corbels, centrepieces, plain or enriched cornices, wall niches, columns, pilasters and arches. They have worked at Windsor Castle, Buckingham Palace, RAF Club.

ANDREW LELLIOT
6 Tetbury Hill, Avening, Tetbury, Gloucestershire GL8 8LT ■ Tel: (01453) 835783 ■ E-mail: alellff@aol.com ■ Mon-Sat 9:00-6:00 ■ Andrew Lelliott ■ Prices medium

Matching mouldings service. Bespoke wood mouldings. Also furniture restoration and conservation.

LONDON PLASTERCRAFT
314 Wandsworth Bridge Road, Fulham, London SW6 2UF ■ Tel: (0171) 736-5146 ■ Fax: (0171) 736-7190 ■ Mon-Sat 9:00-5:00 ■ Mark McKeever ■ Prices medium ■ Trade discounts possible

Fibrous plasters, cornices, columns, surrounds and ceiling roses. Supply or supply and fix. Also restoration.

Panelling

DEACON & SANDYS
Apple Pie Farm, Cranbrook Road, Benenden, Kent TN17 4EU ■ Tel: (01580) 243331 ■ Fax: (01580) 243301 ■ E-mail: jonathan-deacon@msr.com ■ Mon-Fri 8:00-5:30, Sat 8:00-1:00 ■ Jonathan Deacon ■ Prices very high ■ Professional discount

Designers and manufacturers of 17th century oak interiors: wall panelling and staircases. Design, supply and fit. Also oak furniture. References: Oak panelling at the Lensbury Club in the Shell Building; furniture and oak floor in The Old Hall, Lincoln's Inn.

LASSCO (The London Architectural Salvage & Supply Co Ltd)
Saint Michael's, Mark Street, off Paul Street, London EC2A 4ER ■ Tel: (0171) 739-0448 ■ Fax: (0171) 729-6853 ■ E-mail: lassco@zetnet.co.uk ■ 7 days, 10:00-5:00 ■ Anthony Reeve ■ French spoken ■ Prices low to very high ■ Major credit cards ■ Professional discount

London's largest and best known dealer in architectural antiques, panelled rooms, fireplaces, decorative door hardware and garden ornaments.

LONDON'S GEORGIAN HOUSES
291 Goswell Road, London EC1V 7LA ■ Telfax: (0171) 833-8217 ■ Mon-Fri 9:00-5:30 ■ Mr. R.S. Wheeler

Re-instatement of English 18th and 19th century style common woodwork. Shutters, windows, doors, panelling. The woodwork originally found in ordinary Georgian and Victorian houses.

Tiles

CASTLENAU TILES
175 Church Road, London SW13 9HR ■ Tel: (0181) 741-2452 ■ Fax: (0181) 741-5316 ■ Mon-Fri 9:00-5:30, Sat 9:30-4:00 ■ French and Spanish spoken ■ Prices high to very high ■ Visa, MC ■ Trade discount

English Victorian style floor tiles. Natural stone, marble, slate and sandstone.

CHELSEA CERAMICS
100 New Bond Street, London W1 ■ Telfax: (0171) 351-0153 ■ By appointment ■ French, Spanish Italian and German spoken ■ Prices medium

Ceramic sculpture, ceramic tile murals.

MOSAIK
10 Kensington Square, London W8 5EP ■ Tel: (0171) 795-6253 ■ Fax: (0171) 376-9495 ■ Tue-Sat 12:00-6:30, Mornings by appointment ■ Pierrre Mesguich and Ann Hughes ■ French spoken ■ Prices medium to high ■ Trade discount

Hand-cut mosaic friezes and panels for walls and floors. Mosaic tiling supplied. Glass and ceramic. Design service, drawings and samples provided. Advice on bathoom design in use of mosaic. They have done private houses and swimming pools, palaces, showrooms of the great couturiers, hotels and restaurants all over the world.

WALTON CERAMICS
21 Walton Street, London SW3 2HX ■ Tel: (0171) 589-7386 ■ Fax: (0171) 581-3957 ■ Mon-Fri 9:30-5:30, Sat 10:00-4:00 ■ Italian spoken ■ Prices medium to very high ■ Major credit cards ■ Trade discount

Delft and Victorian tiles, stone and ceramic tile. Reproductions of old hand-painted tiles.

WORLDS END TILES
9 Langton Street, London SW10 0TL ■ Tel: (0171) 351-0279 ■ Fax: (0171) 376-5533 ■ Mon-Fri 9:00-5:00 ■ Melissa Mackenzie ■ Prices medium to high ■ Major credit cards ■ Professional discount

Specialist in design and hand-crafted wall and floor tiles in ceramic, glass, stone, mosaics and marble.

Windows and Doors

APEX DOUBLE GLAZING LIMITED
67 Pound Lane, London NW10 2HH ■ Tel: (0181) 459-5161 ■ Fax: (0181) 459-0023 ■ Mon-Fri 5:00-5:00 ■ Ed Gibson ■ Polish and French spoken ■ Prices medium ■ Trade discount

Conservatories, windows and doors. Secondary glazing for hotels, schools and domestic use. Hardwood PVCU and aluminium.

THE LONDON DOOR COMPANY
153 St. John's Hill, London SW11 1TQ ■ Tel: (0171) 801-0877 ■ Fax: (0171) 223-7296 ■ Mon-Sat 9:30-5:00 ■ John Williamson and Kerry Walters ■ French and German spoken ■ Prices medium to high ■ Trade discount ■ Visa, MC

Made-to-order doors: traditional and contemporary. Decorative, etched, stained and bevelled glass.

LONDON'S GEORGIAN HOUSES
291 Goswell Road, London EC1V 7LA ■ Telfax: (0171) 833-8217 ■ Mon-Fri 9:00-5:30 ■ Mr. R.S. Wheeler

Re-instatement of English 18th and 19th century style common woodwork. Shutters, windows, doors, panelling. The woodwork originally found in ordinary Georgian and Victorian houses.

N.S.B. CASEMENTS LTD
3 Steele Road, Park Royal, London NW10 7AR ■ Tel: (0181) 961-3090 ■ Fax: (0181) 961-3050 ■ Mon-Sat 8:00-4:30 ■ Mr. D.R. Northam ■ Some Spanish spoken ■ Prices medium

Specialist in steel windows and doors.

THE ORIGINAL DOUBLE GLAZED SASH WINDOW REPLACE- MENT COMPANY
58 Mill Lane, London NW6 1NJ ■ Telfax: (0171) 435-0367 ■ Mobile: 0956 293882 ■ Mon-Fri 8:00-5:00 ■ Trade discount.

Replacement of timber windows, double glazed.

RENAISSANCE LONDON LTD
193-195 City Road, London EC1 ■ Telfax: (0171) 251-8844 ■ Mon-Sat 8:00-6:00 ■ Owen Pacey ■ Prices low to high ■ Trade discount

A large stock of original doors and shutters, radiators and dec- orative objects. Antique and reproduction fireplaces and radia- tors.

RESTORATION WINDOWS AND CONSERVATORIES
25 Marlborough Crescent, London W4 1HE ■ Tel: (0181) 747-4619 ■ Fax: (0181) 995-7490 ■ Mon-Fri 8:00-5:00 ■ Trade discount

Windows made to listed-building regulations. Quality hard and soft-wood frames. French windows. Single or double glazed.

GEOFF JACKSON – CARPENTER'S WORKSHOP
Cobden Mill, Square Street, Ramsbottom, Bury BL0 9AZ ■ Tel: (01706) 825033 ■ Mon-Fri 7:30-4:30 ■ Prices medium

Architectural carpenters and joiners. Specialists in period doors and staircases for listed buildings and houses. Georgian windows with box sashes and circular windows also their specialty.

ANDREW JOHN SMITH
31 Northumberland Road, Walthamstow C17 8JC ■ Tel: (0181) 539-6362 ■ Fax: (0181) 923-9817 ■ Mon-Sat 9:00-7:00 ■ Prices medium

Secondary glazing for sound-proofing. Member of The Guild of Master Craftsmen.

VICTORIAN WINDOWS
Unit 23 IBC House, South Way, Wembley, Middlesex HA9 OTJ ■ Tel: (0181) 974-5223 ■ Mon-Fri 7:30-4:30 ■ Trade discount

Repair and renewal of sash windows. Complete renovation. Single or double glazing. Draughtproofing. Quality pine or hardwood. Member of The Guild of Master Craftsmen.

WOODLAND
St Peter's House, 6 Cambridge Road, King'ston-upon-Thames, Surrey KTI 3JY ■ Tel: (0181) 547-2171 ■ Fax: (0181) 547-1722 ■ E-mail: boxsash.demon.co.uk. ■ Mon-Fri 9:00-5:00 ■ John West ■ Portuguese spoken ■ Prices medium ■ Possible trade discount

Manufacturing traditional box windows and French doors. Good craftsmen.

ART GALLERIES

London has become one of the great fine art trading centres of the world. Of course, it has great museums and stunning private collections in its stately homes and palaces, but it is in the art galleries and the auction rooms of London where the real action takes place.

Fortunately, London is like Paris or New York where art dealers tend to cluster in one part or another of their own city. With this guide, the art lover or collector will discover that London, in spite of it vast size, is quite manageable.

There is, however, one thing the cautious shopper should watch for, the symbol SLAD on the door or front window of an art gallery. The symbol identifies the dealer as a member of The Society of London Art Dealers. Membership is limited to those who have been in business for at least three years and are located within 15 miles of Hyde Park Corner. Members must sign an undertaking to be bound by the rules of The Society and abide by and observe the provisions of "The Code of Fair Practice for Fair and Honest Dealing".

The current commercial interest in fine art makes it necessary for the buyer to have as much knowledge as possible and complete confidence in the art dealer with whom he is dealing. With SLAD there is always a recourse should something go wrong. Many art dealers are also members of BADA and LAPADA.

ARTHUR ACKERMAN & PETER JOHNSON LTD
27 Lowndes Street, London SW1X 9HY ■ Tel: (0171) 235-6464 ■ Fax: (0171) 823-1057 ■ Mon-Fri 9:00-5:00, Sat 10:00-12:00 by appointment ■ BADA

Paintings, drawings and watercolours.

♕ AGNEW'S
43 Old Bond Street, London W1X 4BA ■ Tel: (0171) 629-6176 ■ Fax: (0171) 629-4359 ■ E-mail: art@agnewsgallery.com ■ Internet: http://www.agnewsgallery.com ■ Mon-Fri 9:30-5:30, Thu until 6:30 ■ M.H. Julian Agnew, Chairman ■ BADA

Speciality, Old Master pictures, Old Master drawings, English pictures and English watercolours. 20th century British paintings, drawings, prints.

GIACOMO ALGRANTI LTD
33 Davies Street, London W1Y 1FN ■ Tel: (0171) 495-8865 ■ Fax: (0171) 499-3906 ■ By appointment

Old Master paintings.

SUSANNA ALLEN FINE ART
13 Masons Yard, London SW1 Y6BU ■ Tel: (0171) 321-0495 ■ Fax: (0171) 321-0496 ■ Mon-Fri 10:30-5:00, appointment preferable ■ Marco Gambino and Susanna Allen ■ Prices high to very high ■ Professional discount

19th century European paintings and Old Masters.

THE ANDIPA GALLERY
162 Walton Street, Knightsbridge, London SW3 2JL ■ Tel: (0171) 589-2371 ■ Fax: (0171) 225-0305 ■ E-mail: art@andipa.com. ■ Tue-Sat 11:00-6:00 ■ Maria and Acoris Andipa ■ Greek, French and Arabic spoken ■ Prices low to very high ■ Professional discount ■ Major credit cards

Icons, Old Master paintings and Old Master drawings. 14th to 19th century. Restoration and research.

ARTEMIS FINE ARTS LTD
15 Duke Street, St. James's, London SW1Y 6DB ■ Tel: (0171) 930-8733 ■ Fax: (0171) 839-5009 ■ Mon-Fri 10:00-5:30 ■ Timothy Bathurst

Old Master and Modern paintings, drawings and prints, sculpture and antiquities.

AUSTIN/DESMOND FINE ART LTD

Pied Bull Yard, 68/69 Great Russell Street, London WC1B 3BN ■ Tel: (0171) 242-4443 ■ Fax: (0171) 404-4480 ■ Mon-Fri 10:30-6:00, Sat by appointment and 11:30-2:30 during exhibitions ■ John Austin

Modern and 20th century British paintings, drawings, prints and sculpture.

JULIAN BARRAN LTD

42 Old Bond Street, London W1X 3AF ■ Tel: (0171) 495-0499 ■ Fax: (0171) 493-0745 ■ Mon-Fri 9:30-5:30 ■ Julian Barran

19th and 20th century paintings, drawings, watercolours and sculpture, including Russian paintings and watercolours, and works related to the theatre and ballet.

JOHN BENNETT FINE PAINTINGS

206 Walton Street, London SW3 2JL ■ Tel: (0171) 225-2227 ■ Fax: (0171) 581-3629 ■ Mon-Fri 10:00-6:00, Sat 11:00-4:00 ■ John Bennett ■ Polish, Italian and French spoken ■ Prices low to high ■ Major credit cards ■ Trade discount

17th to 19th century British and European oil paintings, including landscapes, still life and portraits. Animal and sporting subjects.

BERGGRUEN ET ZEVI LTD

33 Davies Street, London W1Y 1FN ■ Tel: (0171) 495-8867 ■ Fax: (0171) 499-3906 ■ By appointment ■ Olivier Berggruen, Mark H. Getty, Aroldo Zevi

20thcentury and contemporary works of art.

BERKELEY SQUARE GALLERY

23A Bruton Street, London W1X 8JJ ■ Tel: (0171) 493-7939 ■ Fax: (0171) 493-7798 ■ E-mail: art@berkeley-square-gallery.co.uk ■ Mon-Fri 10:00-6:00, Sat 10:00-2:00 ■ Peter Osborne ■ French, German, Italian and Spanish spoken ■ Visa, Amex

20th century Modern Masters. Sculpture and works on paper. Moore, Chadwick, Picasso, Miro, Chagall. Hockney, Warhol, Sophie Ryder, Robert MacLaurin, Ian Phillips and Philip Sutton.

♔ KONRAD O. BERNHEIMER LTD

1 Mount Street, London W1Y 5AA ■ Tel: (0171) 495-7028 ■ Fax: (0171) 495-7027 ■ By appointment ■ Konrad O. Bernheimer ■ BADA

Old Master paintings and drawings, 18th century Continental furniture, Chinese ceramics and works of art.

GALERIE BESSON

15 Royal Arcade, 28 Old Bond Street, London W1X 3HB ■ Tel: (0171) 491-1706 ■ Fax: (0171) 495-3203 ■ Mon 1:00-5:30, Tue-Fri 10:00-5:30 ■ Anita Besson

International contemporary ceramic art.

THE BLOXHAM GALLERIES

4 & 5 The Parade, St. John's Hill, London SW11 1TG ■ Tel: (0171) 924-7500 ■ Fax: (0171) 585-3901 ■ Mon-Sat 10:00-6:00 ■ Cathy Dickinson and John Bloxham ■ Some French spoken ■ Prices low to high ■ Professional discount ■ Major credit cards

London's first gallery devoted to contemporary erotic art of quality. Artists from the U.S., France, Germany and Australia. Framing service.

IVOR BRAKA LTD

63 Cadogan Square, London SW1X 0DY ■ Tel: (0171) 235 0266 ■ Fax: (0171) 235-8064 ■ By appointment ■ Ivor Braka, Graham Moss

Impressionist and Modern paintings.

♛ BROWSE & DARBY LTD

19 Cork Street, London W1X 2LP ■ Tel: (0171) 734-7984/5 ■ Fax: (0171) 437-0750 ■ E-mail: browse@slad.org ■ Website: www.slad.org/browse_and_darby ■ 10:00-5:30, Sat 10:30-1:00 ■ William Darby, Laetitia Darby

19th and 20th century French and British paintings, drawings and sculpture.

CARLT GALLERY

182 Westbourne Grove, London W11 2RH ■ Tel: (0171) 229-9309 ■ Fax: (0171) 727-8746 ■ 7 Days 9:30-6:00 ■ Edward and Zoe Crawshaw ■ Spanish and French spoken ■ Prices low to medium ■ Major credit cards ■ Trade prices

Dealer to the trade in period oil paintings. Strong in undervalued Impressionists.

♛ P & D COLNAGHI & CO LTD

15 Old Bond Street, London W1X 4JL ■ Tel: (0171) 491-7408 ■ Fax: (0171) 491-8851 ■ Mon-Fri 9:30-6:00, Sat only during special exhibitions ■ Jean-Luc Baroni, Stephen Rudge ■ BADA

Old Master paintings and drawings.

CONNAUGHT BROWN

2 Albemarle Street, London W1X 4JL ■ Tel: (0171) 408-0362 ■ Fax: (0171) 495-3137 ■ E-mail: cb@anc2000.co.uk ■ Internet http://www.connaught-brown.co.uk ■ Mon-Fri 9:30-6:00, Sat 10:00-12:30 ■ Anthony Brown

Post Impressionist, Scandinavian and Modern paintings, drawings and prints.

CRANE KALMAN GALLERY LTD

178 Brompton Road, London SW3 1HQ ■ Tel: (0171) 584-7566/(0171) 225-1931 ■ Fax: (0171) 584-3843 ■ E-mail: 100711.336@compuserve.com ■ Mon-Fri 10:00-6:00, Sat 10:00-4:00 ■ A. Kalman, Sally Kalman

Late 19th and 20th century Modern British and European paintings and sculpture. American art from 1920-1960.

ANTHONY D'OFFAY GALLERY

9,21,23 & 24 Dering Street, London W1R 9AA ■ Tel: (0171) 499-4100 ■ Fax: (0171) 493-4443 ■ E-mail: doffay@compuserve.com ■ Mon-Fri 10:00-5:30, Sat 10:00-1:00 ■ Anthony d'Offay, Anne d'Offay

International contemporary art.

SIMON DICKINSON LTD

58 Jermyn Street, London SW1Y 6LX ■ Tel: (0171) 493-0340 ■ Fax: (0171) 493-0796 ■ Mon-Fri 10:00-6:00 or by appointment ■ Simon Dickinson

Old and Modern Master paintings.

♕ DOUWES FINE ART LTD

38 Duke Street, London SW1Y 6DF ■ Tel: (0171) 839-5795 ■ Fax: (0171) 839-5904 ■ Mon-Fri 10:00-5:00, Sat by appointment ■ Evert J.M. Douwes, Jr., Evert J. M. Douwes, Sr.

16th and 17th century Old Master paintings and drawings, 19th to 20th century Modern paintings, drawings and watercolours. Restoration.

DOVER STREET GALLERY

13 Dover Street, London W1X 3PH ■ Tel: (0171) 409-1540 ■ Fax: (0171) 409-1565 ■ E-mail: doverstreet@netmattes.co.uk ■ Mon-Fri 10:00-6:00 ■ Richard Nagy, Edmondo di Robilant ■ Italian, French and German spoken ■ Prices very high ■ Occasional discounts

Italian and French 15th to 19th century paintings and drawings and German Expressionist, Viennosse Successionist paintings.

WILLIAM DRUMMOND

8 St. James's Chambers, 2-10 Ryder Street, St. James's, London SW1Y 6QA ■ Telfax: (0171) 930-9696 ■ By appointment ■ William Drummond ■ BADA

English oil paintings, watercolours and drawings of the 18th and 19th centuries.

EATON GALLERY

34 Duke Street, St. James's, London SW1Y 6DF ■ Tel: (0171) 930-5950 ■ Fax: (0171) 839-8076 ■ E-mail: eatongallery@rtinternet.com ■ and 9 Princes Arcade, Jermyn Street, London SW1Y 6DS ■ Mon-Sat 10:00-5:30 ■ Dr. J. Douglas George ■ French spoken ■ Prices low to high ■ Major credit cards ■ LAPADA

19th and early 20th century English, Irish and European paintings.

ANNE FAGGIONATO

20 Dering Street, 4th floor, London W1R 9AA ■ Tel: (0171) 493-6732 ■ Fax: (0171) 493-9693 ■ Mon-Fri 10:00-5:30 ■ Anne Faggionato, Irene Faggionato

Impressionist, Modern and contemporary art.

THE FINE ART SOCIETY PLC

148 New Bond Street, London W1Y 0JT ■ Tel: (0171) 629-516 ■ Fax: (0171) 491-9454 ■ E-mail: art@the fineartsociety.co.uk ■ Internet http://www.the-fine-art-society.co.uk ■ Mon-Fri 9:30-17:30, Sat 10:00-1:00 ■ Lord Macfarlane of Bearsden, Chairman

Oil paintings, watercolours, drawings, prints, sculpture, 19th and 20th century designer furniture, ceramics, glass and textiles.

FLEUR DE LYS GALLERY

227A Westbourne Grove, London W11 2SE ■ Telfax: (0171) 727-8595 ■ E-mail: henrifdel@panther.netmania.co.uk ■ Website: www.fleurdelys.com ■ Mon-Sat 10:30-5:30 ■ Henri S. Coronel ■ Dutch and Spanish spoken ■ Prices medium to high ■ Major credit cards ■ Trade discount

19th century oil paintings.

ANGELA FLOWERS GALLERY PLC

Flowers East, 199-205 Richmond Road, London E8 3NJ ■ Tel: (0181) 985-3333 ■ Fax: (0181) 985-0067

Flowers East, London Dields, 282 Richmond Road, London E8 3QS ■ Tel: (0181) 533-5554 ■ Tue-Sat 10:00-6:00 ■ Angela Flowers ■ E-mail: 100672.1003@compuserve.com

Contemporary art.

HILDEGARD FRITZ-DENNEVILLE

Fine Arts Ltd, New Bond Street, London W1Y 9HD ■ Tel: (0171) 629-2466 ■ Fax: (0171) 408-0804 ■ Mon-Fri 2:00-5:00 ■ Miss Hildegard Fritz-Denneville

British Old Masters (1500-1850), 19th century European Impressionist and Modern, German Expressionist. Old Master prints. Contemporary.

👑 FROST & REED

2-4 King Street, St. James's, London SW1Y 6QP ■ Tel: (0171) 839-4645 ■ Fax: (0171) 839-1166 ■ E-mail: frost&reed@btinternet.com ■ Mon-Fri 9:00-5:30 ■ A.G. Nevill, M. Rose, J. Johnson, C. Kingzett ■ French and Italian spoken ■ Prices low to high ■ Major credit cards ■ Trade discount ■ BADA

British and European paintings of the 19th and 20th centuries. Marine and sporting paintings by Sir Alfred Munnings and Montague Dawson. French Impressionist drawings and watercolours, selected contemporary British artists.

THOMAS GIBSON FINE ART LTD

44 Old Bond Street, London W1X 4HQ ■ Tel: (0171) 499-8572 ■ Fax: (0171) 495-1924 ■ Mon-Fri 10:00-5:00 ■ Anthea F.C. Gibson

19th and 20th century paintings, contemporary art, drawings, sculptures and selected Old Masters.

GIMPEL FILS LTD

30 Davies Street, London W1Y 1LG ■ Tel: (0171) 493-2488 ■ Fax: (0171) 629-5732 ■ E-mail: gimpel@compuserve.com ■ Websiste: www.slad.org/gimpel_fils ■ Mon-Fri 10:00-5:30, Sat 10:00-1:00 ■ Peter Gimpel, Rene Gimpel

Modern and contemporary American, European and British paintings, drawings and sculpture.

FRANCIS GRAHAM-DIXON GALLERY LTD

17-18 Great Sutton Street, London EC1V 0DN ■ Tel: (0171) 250-1962 ■ Fax: (0171) 490-1069 ■ Tue-Sat 11:00-6:00 ■ Francis Graham-Dixon

Contemporary British and European paintings and works on paper.

♔ RICHARD GREEN (FINE PAINTINGS)

147 New Bond Street, London W1Y 9FE & 39 Dover Street, London W1X 3RB
33 New Bond Street, London W1Y 9HD ■ Tel: (0171) 493-3939 ■ Fax: (0171) 629-2609 ■ E-mail: pictures@rgreen.ftech.com ■ Mon-Fri 10:00-6:00, Sat 10:00-12:30 ■ Richard Green, Jennifer Green, Jonathan Green ■ BADA

Fine Old Master paintings, Victorian and European paintings, British sporting and marine paintings, French Impressionist and Modern British paintings.

MARTYN GREGORY

34 Bury Street, London SW1Y 6AU ■ Tel: (0171) 839-3731 ■ Fax: (0171) 930-0812 ■ Mon-Fri 10:00-6:00, Sat 10:00-1:00 during exhibitions ■ BADA

British watercolours and paintings and pictures related to China and the Far East.

HALL AND KNIGHT LTD

15 Duke Street, St. James's, London SW1Y 6DB ■ Tel: (0171) 839-4090 ■ Fax: (0171) 839-4091 ■ Mon-Fri 9:30-5:30 ■ Nicholas Hall, Richard Knight

Specialists in Old Master and 19th century paintings.

LAURENCE HALLETT

London SW1 ■ Tel: (0171) 798-8977 ■ By appointment ■ LAPADA

Paintings, watercolours and drawings.

♔ JULIAN HARTNOLL

14 Masons Yard, 71 Duke Street, St. James's, London SW1Y 6BU ■ Tel: (0171) 839-3842 ■ Fax: (0171) 930-8234 ■ Mon-Fri by appointment ■ Julian Hartnoll ■ French spoken ■ Prices low to very high ■ Trade discount

Pre-Raphaelite and British pictures of the 1950s, especially the "Kitchen Sink" school. Paintings, prints and drawings.

HAZLITT GOODEN & FOX LTD

38 Bury Street, St. James's, London SW1Y 6BB ■ Tel: (0171) 930-6422 ■ Fax: (0171) 839-5984 ■ Mon-Fri 9:30-5:30 ■ Colin Hunter

Paintings, drawings and sculpture.

HOBHOUSE

67-68 Jermyn Street, London SW1Y 6NY ■ Tel: (0171) 839-6371 ■ Fax: (0171) 839-6378 ■ By appointment ■ Niall A. Hobhouse

Old Masters and 19th century paintings and drawings.

HOULDSWORTH FINE ART

Pall Mall Deposit, 124-128 Barlby Road, London W10 6BL ■ Tel: (0181) 969-8197 ■ Fax: (0181) 964-3595 ■ Mon-Fri 11:00-6:00, Sat 11:00-2:00 during exhibitions, or by appointment ■ Pippy Houldsworth

Contemporary art.

JOHN HUNT

15 King Street, St. James's, London SW1Y 6QU ■ Telfax: (0171) 839-2643 ■ By appointment only ■ LAPADA

Paintings, watercolours, drawings, sculpture and bronze.

MANYA IGEL FINE ARTS LTD.

21-22 Peters Court, Porchester Road, London W2 5DS ■ Tel: (0171) 229-1669 ■ By appointment ■ LAPADA

Paintings, water colours and drawings.

MALCOLM INNES GALLERY LTD

7 Bury Street, London SW1Y 6AL ■ Tel: (0171) 839-8083/8084 ■ Fax: (0171) 839-8085 ■ E-mail: malcolm-innes@slad.org ■ Website: www.slad.org/malcolm_innes_gallery ■ Mon-Fri 9:30-6:00, Sat 10:00-2:00 during exhibitions, or by appointment ■ Malcolm Innes

19th and 20th century Scottish landscape, sporting and military pictures.

WILLIAM JACKSON GALLERY

16 Gillingham Road, London NW2 1RT ■ Telfax: (0181) 450-1867 ■ By appointment ■ Andrew Railton, William Jackson

Modern and contemporary British art.

BERNARD JACOBSON GALLERY

14A Clifford Street, London W1X 1RF ■ Tel: (0171) 495-8575 ■ Fax: (0171) 495-6210 ■ E-mail: bernard-jacobson@slad.org ■ Website: www.slad.org/bernard_jacobson_gallery ■ Mon-Fri 10:00-6:00, Sat 10:00-1:00 ■ Bernard Jacobson

Modern and contemporary British art.

JASON & RHODES

4 New Burlington Place, London W1X 1FB ■ Tel: (0171) 434-1768 ■ Fax: (0171) 287-8841 ■ E-mail: art@jason-and-rhodes.com ■ Internet http://www.jason-and-rhodes.som ■ Mon-Fri 10:00-6:00, Sat 10:00-1:30 ■ Gillian Jason, Benjamin Rhodes

Modern and contemporary British art.

JILL GEORGE GALLERY

38 Lexington Street, London W1R 3HR ■ Tel: (0171) 439-7319 ■ Fax: (0171) 287-0478 ■ Internet: http://www.194.73.81.13/banca/geojils ■ Mon-Fri 10:00-6:00, Sat 11:00-5:00 ■ Jill George

British contemporary art: paintings, drawings, watercolours, limited edition prints.

DEREK JOHNS LTD

12 Duke Street, St. James's, London SW1Y 6BN ■ Tel: (0171) 839-7671/2 ■ Fax: (0171) 930-0986 ■ 9:00-5:30 ■ Derek Johns, Daphne Johns

Old Master paintings, drawings and sculpture.

ANNELY JUDA FINE ART

23 Dering Street, London W1R 9AA ■ Tel: (0171) 629-7578 ■ Fax: (0171) 491-2139 ■ Mon-Fri 10:00-6:00, Sat 10:00-1:00 and by appointment ■ Annely Juda, David Juda

Contemporary painting and sculpture, Russian constructivists, Bauhaus and early 20th century art.

DANIEL KATZ LTD

59 Jermyn Street, London SW1Y 6LX ■ Tel: (0171) 493-0688 ■ Fax: (0171) 499-7493 ■ E-mail: danny@katz.co.uk ■ Internet: http://www.katz.co.uk ■ Mon-Fri 9:00-6:00 ■ Daniel Katz

European works of art and sculpture. Old Master paintings.

PATRICIA KLEINMAN

The Mall Antiques Arcade (G3), Camden Passage, 359 Upper Street, London N1 OPD ■ Tel: (0171) 704 0798 ■ Wed & Sat 10:00-4:00, Fri 11:30-3:00 and by appointment ■ LAPADA

Paintings, watercolours and drawings.

ENID LAWSON GALLERY

36A Kensington Church Street, London W8 4BX ■ Tel: (0171) 937-8444 ■ Fax: (0171) 938-4786 ■ Mon-Sat 10:00-6:00 ■ Enid Lawson ■ Prices low to very high ■ MC and Visa accepted ■ Trade discount

Contemporary fine art, paintings, prints and studio ceramics.

THE LEFEVRE GALLERY
(Alex Reid & Lefèvre Ltd)

30 Bruton Street, London W1X 8JD ■ Tel: (0171) 493-2107 ■ Fax: (0171) 499-9088 ■ E-mail: reidlefevre@btinternet.com ■ Internet: http://www.slad.org/lefevre_gallery ■ Mon-Fri 10:00-5:00 ■ Gerald Stuart Corcoran, Desmond Leon Corcoran, Phyllis Ruth Corcoran

Impressionist and Post Impressionist paintings. Modern British and contemporary art.

LISSON GALLERY LONDON LTD

67 Lisson Street, London NW1 5DA ■ Tel: (0171) 724-2739 ■ Fax: (0171) 724-7124 ■ Mon-Fri 10:00-6:00, Sat 10:00-5:00 ■ Nicholas Logsdail

British painting and sculpture, European and American contemporary art from 1960 to present.

LUMLEY CAZALET LTD

33 Davies Street, London W1Y 1FN ■ Tel: (0171) 491-4767 ■ Fax: (0171) 493-8644 ■ E-mail: lumleycaz@slad.org ■ Internet: http://www.slad.org/lumley_cazalet_ltd ■ Mon-Fri 10:00-6:00 ■ Caroline Lumley, Camilla Cazalet

Late 19th and 20th century original prints, drawings and sculpture. Works by Henri Matisse and Elisabeth Frink.

THE MAAS GALLERY LTD

15A Clifford Street, London W1X 1RF ■ Tel: (0171) 734-2302 ■ Fax: (0171) 287-4836 ■ E-mail: maas@slad.org ■ Internet: http://www.slad.org/maas_gallery ■ Mon-Fri 10:00-5:30 ■ R.N. Maas

British paintings, drawings and watercolours, sculptures and prints 1840-1940.

JAMES MACKINNON

5 Holland Villas Road, London W14 8BP ■ Tel: (0171) 603-7439 ■ Fax: (0171) 603-5872 ■ By appointment only ■ James Mackinnon

Old Masters, 19th century paintings, watercolours and drawings.

♔ THE MALLETT GALLERY

141 New Bond Street, London W1Y 0BS ■ Tel: (0171) 499-7411 ■ Fax: (0171) 495-3179 ■ Mon-Fri 9:30-5:30, Sat 11:00-4:00 ■ Lanto M. Synge ■ French and Spanish spoken ■ Prices high ■ Trade discount ■ Amex, Visa ■ BADA

Fine paintings, watercolours, drawings, sculpture and works of art.

MARLBOROUGH FINE ART (LONDON) LTD

6 Albemarle Street, London W1X 4BY ■ Tel: (0171) 629-5161 ■ Fax: (0171) 629-6338 ■ E-mail: marlborough@sla.org ■ Internet: http://www.slad.org/marlborough ■ Mon-Fri 10:00-5:30, Sat 10:00-12:30 ■ Duke of Beaufort, Chairman

Impressionists and Post Impressionists. 20th century paintings, drawings and sculpture. Original graphics and photographs by leading 20th century artists.

MATHAF GALLERY LTD

24 Motcomb Street, London SW1X 8JU ■ Tel: (0171) 235-0010 ■ Fax: (0171) 823-1378 ■ E-mail: art@mathafgallery.demon.co.uk ■ Website: www.slad.org/mathaf ■ Mon-Fri 9:30-5:30, Sat by appointment ■ Brian MacDermot, Chairman and Georgina MacDermot ■ Prices high ■ Professional discount ■ Major credit cards ■ LAPADA

19th century Orientalist paintings, oils and watercolours, of Arabia.

♔ MATTHIESEN FINE ART LTD

7-8 Masons Yard, Duke Street, St. James's, London SW1Y 5BU ■ Tel: (0171) 930-2437 ■ Fax: (0171) 930-1387 ■ E-mail: oldmaterslondon@compuserve.com ■ Mon-Fri 10:00-5:30 ■ Patrick D. Matthiesen ■ Italian and French spoken ■ Prices medium to very high

Finest Italian Old Master paintings from 1300 to 1800. Spanish painting from 1600 to 1800. French painting from 1600 to 1860.

THE MAYOR GALLERY

22A Cork Street, London W1X 1HB ■ Tel: (0171) 734-3558 ■ Fax: (0171) 494-1377 ■ Mon-Fri 10:00-5:30, Sat 10:00-1:00 ■ James Mayor

Modern and contemporary American, European and British paintings, drawings and sculpture.

MERCURY GALLERY LTD

26 Cork Street, London W1X 1HB ■ Tel: (0171) 734-7800 ■ Fax: (0171) 287-9809 ■ E-mail: mercury@netcomuk.co.uk ■ Internet: http://www.mercury-gallery.co.uk ■ Mon-Fri 10:00-5:30; Sat 10:00-12:30 ■ Gillian Raffles

20th century Modern British and European paintings, watercolours, drawings, sculpture, prints. Specialists in the work of Henri Gaudier-Brzeska. Contemporary British artists.

DAVID MESSUM FINE ART

8 Cork Street, London W1X 1PB ■ Tel: (0171) 437 5545 ■ Fax: (0171) 734 7018 ■ Mon-Fri 10:00-6:00, Sat 10:00-4:00 ■ BADA, LAPADA

British Impressionist paintings, watercolours and drawings. Contemporary art.

DUNCAN R. MILLER FINE ARTS

17 Flask Walk, London NW3 1HJ ■ Tel: (0171) 435-5462 ■ Fax: (0171) 431-5352 ■ Tue-Fri 11:00-6:00, Sat 11:00-5:00, Sun 2:00-5:00 ■ Duncan R. Miller ■ French spoken

20th century British artists, specializing in the Scottish colourists.

MILNE & MOLLER

35 Colville Terrace, London W11 2BU ■ Tel: (0171) 727-1679 ■ By appointment ■ LAPADA

Paintings, watercolours and drawings.

JOHN MITCHELL & SON

160 New Bond Street, London W1Y 9PA ■ Tel: (0171) 493-7567 ■ Fax: (0171) 493-5537 ■ Mon-Fri 9:30-5:30, Sat by appointment ■ Peter Mitchell ■ BADA

17th century Dutch and Flemish paintings. 18th century English and 19th century French paintings and watercolours, specializing in flower paintings.

MORETON STREET GALLERY

40 Moreton Street, London SW1V 2PB ■ Tel: (0171) 834-7775 ■ Fax: (0171) 834-7834 ■ Mon-Fri 9:00-6:00 ■ W.M. Pearson ■ French and German spoken ■ Prices low to high

Georgian art of the 18th and 19th century. Italian Renaissance drawings. Engravings of Westminster, Pimlico and London.

GUY MORRISON

91A Jermyn Street, London SW1Y 6JB ■ Tel: (0171) 839-1454 ■ Fax: (0171) 321-0685 ■ E-mail: 106175.113@compuserve.com ■ Mon-Fri 9:30-5:30 ■ G.M.J. Morrison

19th and 20th century British paintings and watercolours.

ANTHONY MOULD LTD

173 New Bond Street, London W1Y 9PB ■ Tel: (0171) 491-4627 ■ Fax: (0171) 355-3865 ■ Mon-Fri 9:30-6:00 ■ A.S.W. Mould, A.M. Mould

18th century English pictures.

NEFFE-DEGANDT

32A St. George Street, London W1R 9FA ■ Tel: (0171) 493-2630/(0171) 629-9788 ■ Fax: (0171) 493-1379 ■ E-mail: neffede-gandt@slad.org ■ Internet: http://www.slad.org/neffe_degandt_gallery ■ Tue-Fri 10:00-5:30 and by appointment ■ Christian Neffe, Lana Neffe

French Impressionist and Post Impressionist paintings, water-colours and drawings, 19th and 20th century French sculpture.

NEVILL-KEATING PICTURES LTD

7 Durham Place, London SW3 4ET ■ Tel: (0171) 352-0989 ■ Fax: (0171) 376-5243 ■ By appointment ■ Angela Nevill, William Keating

19th and 20th century European and Australian paintings, draw-ings and sculptures.

NOORTMAN (LONDON) LTD

40-41 Old Bond Street, London W1X 4HP ■ Tel: (0171) 491-7284 ■ Fax: (0171) 493-1570 ■ E-mail: 1017402720@compuserve.com ■ Mon-Fri 9:30-5:30, Sat by appointment ■ Robert Noortman

Old Masters and Impressionist paintings.

N. R. OMELL GALLERY

6 Duke Street, St. James's, London SW1Y 6BN ■ Tel: (0171) 839-6223/4 ■ Fax: (0171) 930-1625 ■ Mon-Fri 9:30-6:00, Sat by appoint-ment ■ N.R. Omell, G.A. Omell, C.N.P. Omell

English and European marine and landscape paintings of the 18th ,19th and 20th century.

FLAVIA ORMOND FINE ARTS LTD

Flat 3, 24 Brechin Place, London SW7 4QA ■ Tel: (0171) 244-7883 ■ Fax: (0171) 373-8139 ■ Mobile: 0468-730546 ■ By appointment ■ Flavia Ormond, J.F. Ormond, Jocelyn Ormond

Old Master drawings and 19th century European drawings.

THE O'SHEA GALLERY

120A Mount Street, London W1Y 5HB ■ Tel: (0171) 629-1122 ■ Fax: (0171) 629-1116 ■ Mon-Fri 9:30-6:00 ■ Raymond O'Shea ■ French spoken ■ Prices medium ■ Major credit cards ■ Professional discount ■ BADA

Antiquarian prints and maps. Framing and restoration.

PAISNEL GALLERY

22 Mason's Yard, Duke Street, St. James's, London SW1Y 6BU ■ Tel: (0171) 930-9293 ■ Fax: (0171) 930-7282 ■ E-mail: paisnelgallery@slad.org ■ Internet: http://www.slad.org/paisnel ■ Mon-Fri 10:00-6:00 ■ Stephen Paisnel, Sylvia Paisnel ■ French spoken ■ Prices medium to high ■ Amex accepted ■ Trade discount

Late 19th and early 20th century British and Continental paintings. Specialty: Modern British paintings, especially Newlyn and St. Ives Schools of 1900-1970. Some works on paper.

THE PARKER GALLERY (Est 1750)

28 Pimlico Road, London SW1W 8LJ ■ Tel: (0171) 730-6768 ■ Fax: (0171) 259-9180 ■ Mon-Fri 9:30-5:30, Sat by appointment ■ Brian J. Newbury, Managing Director ■ Prices medium to high ■ Professional discount ■ Major credit cards ■ BADA

Good collection of old prints, oils and watercolours, paintings of the English School, marine and military subjects and topographical and sporting. Ship models and curios.

PARTRIDGE FINE ARTS PLC

144-146 New Bond Street, London W1Y 0LY ■ Tel: (0171) 629-0834 ■ Fax: (0171) 495-6266 ■ Mon-Fri 9:00-5:30 ■ John A. Partridge, Chairman; Mrs. R.F. Partridge

18th century French and English furniture, works of art, sporting pictures. Old Master paintings. Silver.

W.H. PATTERSON FINE ARTS LTD

19 Albemarle Street, London W1X 4LA ■ Tel: (0171) 629-4119 ■ Fax; (0171) 499-0119 ■ E-mail: whpatterson@slad.org ■ Internet: http://www.slad.org/w_h_patterson_fine_arts_ltd ■ Mon-Fri 9:30-6:00, Sat by appointment ■ W.H. Patterson, P.M. Patterson

European Masters of the 19th century. The contemporary works of senior Royal Academicians and other leading contemporary British artists are always on view.

PAWSEY & PAYNE

PO Box 11830, London SW10 9FE ■ Tel: (0171) 930-4221 ■ Fax: (0171) 370-0959 ■ By appointment ■ The Hon. Nicholas Wallop, Mrs. Lavinia Wallop

18th and 19th century fine British paintings and drawings.

RICHARD PHILP

59 Ledbury Road, London W11 2AA ■ Tel: (017) 727-7915 ■ Fax: (0171) 792-9073 ■ Mon-Sat by appointment ■ Richard Philp, Claire Brown ■ Prices medium to high ■ Trade discount

Old Masters, 20th century drawings, early portraiture. Medieval and Renaissance sculpture and antiquities.

THE PICCADILLY GALLERY LTD.

16 Cork Street, London W1X 1PF ■ Tel: (0171) 629-2875 ■ Fax: (0171) 499-0431 ■ E-mail: piccadilly@slad.org ■ Internet: http://www.slad.org/piccadilly_gallery ■ Mon-Fri 10:00-5:30, Sat 10:30-1:00 during exhibitions ■ Godfrey Pilkington, Eve Pilkington

Important 20th century drawings and watercolours, Symbolist and Art Nouveau paintings and drawings, contemporary British figurative painters.

POLAK GALLERY

21 King Street, St. James's, London SW1Y 6QY ■ Tel: (0171) 839-2871 ■ Fax: (0171) 930-3467 ■ E-mail: polak@btinternet.com ■ Mon-Fri 9:30-5:30 ■ Stephen Jack ■ German, Greek and French spoken ■ Prices medium to high ■ Visa and MC ■ Trade discount

19th century English and Continental paintings and sculpture. Contemporary paintings and some watercolours.

PORTLAND GALLERY

9 Bury Street, London SW1Y 6AB ■ Tel: (0171) 321-0422 ■ Fax: (0171) 321-0230 ■ E-mail: art@portland-gallery.com ■ Internet: http://www.portland-gallery.com ■ Mon-Fri 10:00-5:00 and by appointment ■ Tom Hewlett

20th century British and European paintings, drawings and sculpture. British contemporary paintings and Scottish colourists.

PYMS GALLERY

9 Mount Street, London W1Y 5AD ■ Tel: (0171) 629-2020 ■ Fax: (0171) 629-2060 ■ Mon-Fri 9:30-6:00 and by appointment ■ A. Hobart, M. Hobart

Speciality: 18th, 19th and 20th century British, French and Irish paintings and drawings.

RAAB BOUKAMEL GALLERIES LTD

9 Cork Street, London W1X 1PD ■ Tel: (0171) 734-6444 ■ Fax: (0171) 287-1740 ■ E-mail: raabboukamel@slad.org ■ Internet: http://www.slad.org/raab_boukamel ■ Mon-Fri 10:00-6:00, Sat 10:00-2:00 ■ Bassam Boukamel, Ingrid Raab

Contemporary art.

THE REDFERN GALLERY LTD

20 Cork Street, London W1X 2HL ■ Tel: (0171) 734-1732/0578 ■ Fax: (0171) 494-2908 ■ Mon-Fri 10:00-5:30, Sat 10:00-1:00 ■ David Gault, Chairman

Modern and contemporary paintings, watercolours, sculpture drawings and prints.

MICHAEL & STEVEN RICH

39 Duke Street, London SW1Y 6DF ■ Tel: (0171) 930-9308 ■ Fax: (0171) 930-2088 ■ E-mail: rich@slad.org ■ Internet: http://www.slad.org/rich ■ Mon-Fri 10:00-6:00 or by appointment ■ Michael Rich, Steven Rich

Old Master paintings. 19th and 20th century paintings and works of art.

JULIAN SIMON FINE ART LTD

70 Pimlico Road, London SW1W 8LS ■ Tel: (0171) 730-8673 ■ Fax: (0171) 823-6116 ■ E-mail: juliansimon@compuserve.co.uk ■ Mon-Fri 10:00-6:00, Sat 10:00-4:00 ■ Michael and Julian Brookstone ■ Afrikaans and French spoken ■ Prices medium to high ■ Trade discount

18th and 19th century English and European paintings.

KATE DE ROTHSCHILD

C/O Natwest Bank plc, 186 Brompton Road, London SW3 1XJ ■ Tel: (0171) 589-9440 ■ Fax: (0171) 584-5253 ■ E-mail: 106505,377@compuserve.com ■ By appointment only ■ Kate de Rothschild

Old Master drawings and decorative drawings.

SABIN GALLERIES LTD

Camden Lodge, 82 Camden Hill Road, London W8 7AA ■ Tel: (0171) 937-0471 ■ By appointment ■ Sidney Frederick and Peregrine Gabriel Sabin ■ Prices medium to very high ■ Professional export discount ■ BADA

British paintings and watercolours, mostly of the 18th century.

THE SLADMORE GALLERY LTD.

32 Bruton Place, Off Berkely Square, London W1X 7AA ■ Tel: (0171) 499-0365 ■ Fax: (0171) 409-1381 ■ E-mail: art@sladmore-sculpture.com ■ Internet: http://www.sladmore-sculpture.com ■ Mon-Fri 10:00-6:00, Sat 10:00-1:00 during exhibitions only ■ Edward Horswell

Fine 19th and 20th century art and contemporary bronze sculpture.

STEPHEN SOMERVILLE LTD

14 Old Bond Street, London W1X 3DB ■ Tel: (0171) 493-8363 ■ Fax: (0171) 738-5995 ■ By appointment ■ Stephen Somerville

Old Master paintings, drawings and prints. English drawings, watercolours and paintings.

EDWARD SPEELMAN LTD

Empire House, 175 Piccadilly, London W1V 0NP ■ Tel: (0171) 493-0657 ■ Fax: (0171) 493-6642 ■ Mon-Fri 10:00-5:00 ■ A.A. Speelman

Old Master paintings.

👑 SPINK-LEGER PICTURES

13 Old Bond Street, London W1X 4HU ■ Tel: (0171) 629-3538 ■ Fax: (0171) 493-8681 ■ Mon-Fri 9:00-5:30 ■ Lowell Libson, Director ■ Prices high ■ BADA

Old Master paintings and drawings. British paintings, watercolours and drawings of the 17th to the 20th century.

STERN ART DEALERS

46 Ledbury Road, London W11 2AB ■ tel: (0171) 229-6187 ■ Fax: (0171) 229-7016 ■ E-mail: pisaro@globalnet.co.uk ■ Mon-Sat 10:00-6:00 ■ David Stern ■ French, Spanish, Dutch and German spoken ■ Prices low to very high ■ Major credit cards

19th and 20th century English and European oil paintings, Impressionist and Post Impressionist paintings. Restoration and framing.

STOPPENBACH & DELESTRE LTD

25 Cork Street, London W1X 1HB ■ Tel: (0171) 734-3534 ■ Fax: (0171) 494-3578 ■ E-mail: stoppenbach_and delestre@slad.org ■ Internet: http://www.slad.org/stoppenbach_and_delestre ■ Mon-Fri 10:00-5:30, Sat 10:00-1:00 ■ Robert Stoppenbach, Francois Delestre

19th and 20th century paintings, drawings and sculpture.

THACKERAY RANKIN GALLERY

18 Thackeray Street, London W8 5ET ■ Tel: (071) 937-5883 ■ Fax: (0171) 937-6965 ■ E-mail: thackeray-rankin@slad.org ■ Internet: http://www.slad.org/thackeray_rankin_gallery ■ Tue-Fri 10:00-6:00, Sat 10:00-4:00 ■ Anne Thomson

Modern British paintings and sculpture.

WILLIAM THUILLIER

14 Old Bond Street, London W1X 3DB ■ Tel: (0171) 499-0106 ■ Fax: (0171) 233-8965 ■ E-mail: thuillart@aol.com ■ Mon-Fri 10:00-6:00 by appointment ■ William Thuillier ■ French, Italian and German spoken ■ Prices medium ■ Trade discount

Old Master paintings and drawings.

MICHAEL TOLLEMACHE LTD

43 Duke Street, St. James's, London SW1Y 6DD ■ Tel: (0171) 930-9883 ■ Fax: (0171) 930-7080 ■ E-mail: oldmasters@tollemache.co.uk ■ Internet: http://www.tollemache.co.uk ■ Mon-Fri 9:00-5:30, Sat by appointment ■ The Hon Michael Tollemache, Therese Tollemache

Old Masters and British 18th and 19th century paintings, drawings, watercolours, prints and sculpture.

TRAFALGAR GALLERIES / B. COHEN & SONS

35 Bury Street, St. James's, London SW1Y 6AY ■ Tel: (0171) 839-6466/7 ■ Fax: (0171) 976-1838 ■ Mon-Fri 9:30-5:30, appointment advisable ■ Prices high to very high ■ BADA

Old Master paintings.

♔ RAFAEL VALLS LTD

11 Duke Street, St. James's, London SW1Y 6BN ■ Tel: (0171) 930-1144 ■ Fax: (0171) 976-1596 ■ Mon-Fri 9:30-6:00 ■ Rafael Valls, Caroline Valls ■ Spanish, Italian and French spoken ■ Prices very high

Dutch and Flemish 17th century Old Masters. European oil paintings from the 17th to the 19th century.

♔ JOHNNY VAN HAEFTEN LTD

13 Duke Street, St. James's, London SW1Y 6DB ■ Tel: (0171) 930-3062 ■ Fax: (0171) 839-6303 ■ Mon-Fri 10:00-6:00, Sat by appointment ■ Johnny Van Haeften, Sarah Van Haeften ■ French spoken

Dutch and Flemish 17th century paintings.

VERNER AMELL LTD
4 Ryder Street, St. James's, London SW1Y 6QB ■ Tel: (0171) 925-2759 ■ Fax: (0171) 321-0210 ■ Mon-Fri 10:00-5:30 ■ Verner Amell

Old Master paintings.

THEO WADDINGTON FINE ART LTD
5A Cork Street, London W1X 1PB ■ Tel: (0171) 494-1584 ■ Fax: (0171) 287-0926 ■ Tue-Fri 11:00-6:00, Sat 11:00-5:00, closed Mon ■ Theo Waddington

Impressionist, Modern and Contemporary paintings, sculpture, works on paper and prints.

WADDINGTON GALLERIES LTD.
11, 12 & 34 Cork Street, London W1X 2LT ■ Tel: (0171) 437-8611/(0171) 439-6262 ■ Fax: (0171) 734-4146 ■ E-mail: art@waddington-galleries.com ■ Internet: http://www.waddington-galleries.com ■ Mon-Fri 10:00-5:30, Sat 10:00-2:00 ■ Leslie Waddington

20th century paintings, drawings, watercolours, sculptures by British, American and European artists.

WALPOLE GALLERY
38 Dover Street, London W1X 3RB ■ Tel: (0171) 499-6626 ■ Fax: (0171) 493-4122 ■ Mon-Fri 9:30-5:30 ■ David Alessandrini

Italian Old Master paintings and works of art.

WALTON CONTEMPORARY ART
188 Walton Street, London SW3 2JL ■ Tel: (0171) 581-9011 ■ Fax: (0171) 581-0585 ■ Mon-Fri 9:30-5:30, Sat 12:00-6:00 ■ Michael Potter ■ French spoken ■ Prices low to medium ■ Major credit cards ■ Trade discount

Contemporary "gentle" Abstract art and sculpture, predominantly British. Framing.

WILLIAM WESTON GALLERY
7 Royal Arcade, Albemarle Street, London W1X 4JN ■ Tel: (0171) 493-0722 ■ Fax: (0171) 491-9240 ■ Mon-Fri 9:30-5:30, Sat 11:00-3:30 ■ William Weston, Managing Director: The Hon. Mrs. Weston

19th and 20th century European prints, British prints from 1780 to 1940. European Master drawings 1800 to 1950.

WHITFIELD FINE ART LTD

180 New Bond Street, London W1Y 9PD ■ Tel: (0171) 499-3592 ■ Fax: (0171) 495-6488 ■ E-mail: fineart@whitfield.prestel.co.uk ■ Website: www.whitfieldfineart.com ■ Mon-Fri 9:30-5:30 ■ Clovis Whitfield, Dr. Irene Cioffi (Whitfield) ■ French, Italian and Spanish spoken ■ Prices low to very high

Italian and Northern Old Master paintings from the 14th to the 19th century.

WILDENSTEIN & CO LTD

46 St. James's Place, London SW1A 1NS ■ Tel: (0171) 629-0602 ■ Fax: (0171) 493-3924 ■ By appointment only ■ Alec Wildenstein, Guy Wildenstein ■ French spoken

Impressionist and Old Master paintings and drawings.

WILKINS & WILKINS

1 Barrett Street, London W1M 6DN ■ Tel: (0171) 935-9613 ■ Fax: (0171) 935-4696 ■ Mon-Fri 9:15-5:00 ■ Maryanne Wilkins ■ French spoken ■ Prices medium ■ Trade discount

British portraits and 17th and 18th century decorative paintings.

♔ CAMPBELL WILSON

17 West Square, London SE11 4SN ■ Mobile tel: 0973 800158 ■ Fax: (01256) 389040 ■ E-mail: neilwilson@campbell.wilson.demon.co.uk ■ By appointment only ■ Prices low to high ■ MC and Visa

Victorian and Modern British paintings, drawings and watercolours specializing in the Pre-Raphaelite school. Paintings offered for sale in a beautiful private house in a Georgian Square in South London.

CHRISTOPHER WOOD

20 Georgian House, 10 Bury Street, London SW1Y 6AA ■ Tel: (0171) 839-3963 ■ Fax: (0171) 839-3963 ■ By appointment ■ Christopher Wood ■ BADA

Fine Victorian and Edwardian paintings, drawings and watercolours, sculpture and works of art, ceramics, Gothic furniture.

Special Categories of Art

AFRICAN TRIBAL ART

L. & R. ENTWISTLE & CO LTD
6 Cork Street, London W1X 2EE ■ Tel: (0171) 734-6440 ■ Fax: (0171) 734-7966 ■ Mon-Sat 10:00-5:30 ■ L. Entwistle, R. Entwistle

Tribal art, Modern Masters and contemporary art.

ANTHONY JACK
Antique Arcade, 293 Westbourne Grove, London W11 2QA ■ Telfax: (0171) 272-4982 ■ Saturdays 8:00-4:00 ■ French spoken ■ Prices medium ■ Trade discount ■ Visa, MC

Ethnographic antiques, with special emphasis on tribal weaponry and artifacts of Islamic Africa.

DAVID LEWIN
Geoffrey Van Arcade, 105-107 Portobello Road, London W11 ■ Mobile tel: 0413 19809 ■ Fax: (0181) 673-0692 ■ E-mail: schneeky@atlas.co.uk ■ Sat 8:00-4:00 ■ Prices medium

Personal and domestic objects largely dating from the 19th century, from a tribal and folk art background, aimed at the enthusiast, collector and eclectic decorator.

BRYAN REEVES GALLERY OF AFRICAN TRIBAL ART
1 Westbourne Grove Mews, London W11 2RU ■ Telfax: (0171) 221-6650 ■ Tue, Fri, Sat 10:30-6:00 or by appointment ■ Bryan Reeves ■ Prices low to very high ■ Trade discount

African tribal art, tribal furniture, masks, stools, headresses.

MICHAEL TELFER-SMOLLETT
88 Portobello Road, W11 ■ Tel: (0171) 727-0117 ■ Wed, Fri 10:00-4:00, Sat 7:30-5:00

Specialist in Islamic furniture and tribal art.

AARON GALLERY
34 Bruton Street, London, W1X 7DD ■ Tel: (0171) 499-9434/5 ■ Fax: (0171) 499-0072 ■ Mon-Fri 9:30-6:00, Sat by appointment ■ Prices high ■ Trade discount ■ Major credit cards
Islamic and ancient art.

ATTIC ART LTD
Flat 11, 16 Bina Gardens, London SW5 0LA ■ Tel: (0171) 370-2830 ■ Fax: (0171) 373-8583 ■ By appointment
Antiquities.

COINCRAFT
45 Great Russell Street, London WC1B 3LU ■ Tel: (0171) 636-1188 ■ Fax: (0171) 323-2860 ■ Barry Clayden
Greek, Roman, Egyptian antiquities and coins.

CHARLES EDE LTD
20 Brook Street, London W1Y 1AD ■ Tel: (0171) 493-4944 ■ Fax: (0171) 491-2548 ■ Mon-Fri 9:30-5:30 ■ James Ede ■ Prices medium to high ■ Trade discount ■ Major credit cards
Classical and pre-Classical antiquities.

FAUSTUS ANCIENT ART & JEWELLERY
41 Dover Street, London W1X 3RB ■ Tel: (0171) 930-1864 ■ Fax: (0171) 495-2882 ■ Mrs. Susan Hadida ■ Mon-Fri 10:00-6:00 ■ Prices medium to high ■ Trade discount ■ Major credit cards
Ancient gold jewellery and general antiquities.

VANESSA FERRY ANCIENT ART
The Country Seat, Huntercombe, Manor Barn, Henley-on-Thames, Oxfordshire RG9 5RY ■ Tel: (01491) 641349 ■ Fax: (01491) 641533 ■ Mon-Sat 9:00-5:00 and by appointment ■ BADA
Classical Greek, Roman and Egyptian antiquities and other ancient cultures. Exhibits at 30 national fairs annually.

BRUCE MCALPINE
McAlpine Ancient Art Ltd ■ Flat 3, 61 Cadogan Gardens, London SW3 2RA ■ Tel: (0171) 823-9505 ■ Fax: (0171) 823-9503 ■ By appointment only
Greek, Roman and Egyptian antiquities.

MANSOUR GALLERY

46-48 Davies Street, London W1Y 1LD ■ Tel: (0171) 491-7444 ■ Fax: (0171) 629-0682 ■ Mon-Fri 9:30-5:30 ■ M. and N. Mokhtarzadeh ■ Persian spoken

Greek, Roman, Egyptian and Islamic art. Pottery, bronze, marble and glass.

J. MARTIN (COINS) LTD

85 The Vale, Southgate, London N14 6AT ■ Tel: (0181) 882-1509 ■ Fax: (0181) 886-5235 ■ By appointment only

Greek, Roman, Byzantine coins and artefacts. Retail and wholesale.

SEABY ANTIQUITIES

14 Old Bond Street, London W1X 4JL ■ Tel: (0171) 495-2590 ■ Fax: (0171) 491-1595 ■ Mon-Fri 10:00-5:30 and by appointment ■ Peter A. Clayton ■ Prices high ■ Trade discount ■ Major credit cards

Egyptian, Greek and Roman antiquities.

♛ SPINK & SON LTD

5 King Street, St. James's London SW1Y 6QS ■ Tel: (0171) 930-7888 ■ Fax: (0171) 925-0037 ■ Mon-Fri 9:00-5:30 ■ Christopher Knapton ■ Most languages spoken ■ Prices high to very high ■ Major credit cards ■ Trade discount

Good collection of Near and Far Eastern ancient art.

♛ RUPERT WACE ANCIENT ART LTD

14 Old Bond Street, London W1X 3DB ■ Tel: (0171) 495-1623 ■ Fax: (0171) 495-8495 ■ E-mail: rupert.wace@btinternet.com ■ Mon-Fri 10:00-5:00 or by appointment ■ Rupert Wace ■ Prices low to high ■ Professional discount ■ Major credit cards

Egyptian, Classical Greek and Roman, Near Eastern and Dark Age European antiquities.

ANIMAL ART

♛ IONA ANTIQUES

PO Box 285, London W8 6HZ ■ Tel: (0171) 602-1193 ■ Fax: (0171) 371-2843 ■ E-mail: iona@iona-antiques.demon.co.uk ■ By appointment only and at the major shows ■ Stephen and Iona Joseph ■ Italian, French and Spanish spoken ■ Prices medium to very high ■ Major credit cards ■ Trade discount

Wonderful collection of 19th century English paintings of animals. Unique in the art field and charming people.

SLADMORE SCULPTURE GALLERY LTD

32 Bruton Place, Berkeley Square, London W1X 7AA ■ Tel: (0171) 499-0365 ■ Fax: (0171) 409-1381 ■ E-mail: art@sladmore-sculpture.com ■ Website: www.sladmore-sculpture.com ■ Mon-Fri 10:00-6:00, Sat by appointment ■ Prices high ■ Professional discount ■ Major credit cards ■ BADA

Fine 19th and 20th century sporting and animal bronze sculptures.

ARCHITECTURAL ART

RACHEL AND DAVID BLISSETT

C/O Coutts Co., PO Box 1EE, 16 Cavendish Square, London W1A 1EE ■ Tel: (01264) 771768 ■ Fax: (01264) 771769 ■ Rachel and David Blissett ■ French and Italian spoken ■ Prices medium to very high ■ Trade discount

A remarkable collection of 16th to 20th century architectural drawings from Britain, France, Italy, Austria. Note: these are original drawings and not prints.

PETER JACKSON

146 Portobello Road, London W11 2DZ ■ Tel: (01923) 829079 ■ Sat only 9:00-4:00 ■ Peter Jackson

Old London reconstructed. Reproductions of paintings of historical London by Peter Jackson. Available as well at The Guildhall Library Book Shop or ordered direct from Quadrille, 146 Portobello Road, London W11 2DZ.

CHILDREN'S ART

JEREMIAH FINE ART

G12, Alfie's Antique Market, 13-25 Church Street, London NWB 6DT ■ Tel: (0181) 426-9099 ■ Fax: (0181) 968-9737 ■ Tue-Sat 10:30-5:30 ■ Jeremy Sewell ■ Prices low to high ■ Major credit cards ■ Trade discount

Prints from 1850 to 1950 for children and children's rooms.

ROBERT YOUNG ANTIQUES

68 Battersea Bridge Road, London SW11 3AG ■ Tel: (0171) 228-7847 ■ Fax: (0171) 585-0489 ■ Tue-Fri 10:00-6:00, Sat 10:00-5:00 ■ Robert and Josyane Young ■ French spoken ■ Prices medium to high ■ Major credit cards ■ Trade discount

Folk art of all kinds and country furniture.

PAUL MASON GALLERY

149E Sloane Street, London SW1X 9BZ ■ Tel: (0171) 730-3683/7359 ■ Fax: (0171) 581-9084 ■ Internet: http://www.desiderata.com/pmason ■ Mon-Fri 9:00-6:00, Wed 9:00-7:00, Sat 9:00-1:00, other times by appointment ■ BADA

18th and 19th century marine, sporting and decorative paintings and prints. Ship models, portfolio stands, picture easels and glass pictures.

N. R. OMELL GALLERY

6 Duke Street, St. James's, London SW1Y 6BN ■ Tel: (0171) 839-6223/4 ■ Fax: (0171) 930-1625 ■ Mon-Fri 9:30-6:00, Sat by appointment ■ N.R. Omell, G.A. Omell, C.N.P. Omell

English and European marine and landscape paintings of the 18th, 19th and 20th century.

THE PARKER GALLERY (Est 1750)

28 Pimlico Road, London SW1W 8LJ ■ Tel: (0171) 730-6768 ■ Fax: (0171) 259-9180 ■ Mon-Fri 9:30-5:30, Sat by appointment ■ Brian J. Newbury, Managing Director ■ Prices medium to high ■ Professional discount ■ Major credit cards ■ BADA

Good collection of old prints, oils and watercolours, paintings of the English School, marine and military subjects and topographical and sporting. Ship models and curios.

ROYAL EXCHANGE ART GALLERY

14 Royal Exchange, London EC3V 3LL ■ Tel: (0171) 283-4400 ■ Fax: (0171) 623-1833 ■ Mon-Fri 10:30-5:15 & Roger and Jill Hadlee ■ Prices low to high ■ Major credit cards

18th, 19th and 20th century marine paintings.

PORTRAIT MINIATURES

JUDY AND BRIAN HARDEN

Bourton On The Water, Gloucestershire ■ Telfax: (01451) 810684 ■
By appointment only ■ Judy and Brian Harden ■ French, Spanish
and some German spoken ■ Prices medium to very high ■ Visa and
MC ■ Trade discount

**Portrait miniatures. An extraordinary collection. They also have
some objets de vertu, some French clocks and English and
Meissen porcelain.**

D. S. LAVENDER ANTIQUES LTD

26 Conduit Street, London W1R 9TA ■ Tel: (0171) 629-1782 ■ Fax:
(0171) 629-3106 ■ E-mail: dslavender@clara.uk● Mon-Fri 9:30-5:30
■ David Lavender ■ French and German spoken ■ Major credit cards
■ Professional discount ■ BADA

**16th to early 19th century portrait miniatures, snuff boxes, fine
jewels, objets d'art. Repair.**

S.J. PHILLIPS LTD

139 New Bond Street, London W1A 3DL ■ Tel: (0171) 629-6261 ■
Fax: (0171) 495-6180 ■ Mon-Fri 10:00-5:00 ■ Prices high ■ Major
credit cards ■ BADA

**Some lovely portrait miniatures and snuff boxes. Antique jew-
ellery.**

POSTERS

BARCLAY SAMSON LIMITED

65 Finlay Street, London SW6 6HF GB ■ Tel: (0171) 731-8012 ■ Fax:
(0171) 731-8013 ■ E-mail: rb@bsltd.demon.co.uk ■ By appointment
■ Richard Barclay ■ French spoken ■ Amex and Visa accepted

**Vintage lithographic posters from France, Britain, America and
Germany. Posters by Lautrec, Mucha, Purvis, Cuneo, Fries.**

LIZ FARROW "DODO"

Alfie's Antique Market, F073-83, 13-25 Church Street, London NW8
8DT ■ Tel: (0171) 706-1545 ■ Tue-Sat 10:30-5:30 ■ Liz Farrow ■ Prices
medium to high ■ Trade discount ■ Visa, MC
Admiral Vernon Antique Market, 141-149 Portobello Road, London
■ Sat 9:00-4:00

Antique posters, signs, showcards, labels, tins. Est.1960.

ONSLOW'S

The Old Depot, 2 Michael Road, London SW6 2AD ■ Tel: (0171) 371-0505 ■ Fax: (0171) 384-2682 ■ Mon-Fri 9:30-5:00 ■ Patrick Bogue ■ Prices low to very high ■ Visa, MC

Posters, especially travel, 1920s through 1930s. Advertising, war propaganda, transport, HMS Titanic, motoring, railway, maritime, aeronautical. Collectors' items. Catalogue available upon subscription. Full mail order facilities.

THE POSTER SHOP

28 James Street, Covent Garden, London WC2E 9PP ■ Tel: (0171) 240-2526 ■ Fax: (0171) 376-0867 ■ Mon-Sat 10:00-8:00, Sun 12:00-6:00 ■ Mr. Minesh ■ Prices low to very high ■ Major credit cards ■ Trade discount

Original limited editions, fine art imagery, framing services.

PRINTS AND ENGRAVINGS

LUCY B. CAMPBELL

123 Kensington Church Street, London W8 7LP ■ Tel: (0171) 727-2205 ■ Fax: (0171) 229-4252 ■ E-mail: lucy.b.campbell@dial.pipes.co ■ Mon-Fri 10:00-6:00, Sat 10:00-4:00 ■ Mrs. Lucy Campbell ■ Prices low to medium ■ Visa and MC

Fine antiquarian prints and paintings. Contemporary naïve art.

MICHAEL FINNEY BOOKS & PRINTS

37 Museum Street, London WC1A 1LP ■ Tel: (0171) 430-0202 ■ Fax: (0171) 430-0404 ■ Mon-Sat 10:00-6:00 ■ Michael Finney ■ Spanish and some Italian spoken ■ Prices low to very high ■ Major credit cards ■ Professional discount

Antique decorative prints: particularly David Roberts, Piranesi, Bartolozzi. Mainly 17th to 19th century.

THE O'SHEA GALLERY

120a Mount Street, London W1Y 5HB ■ Tel: (0171) 629-1122 ■ Fax: (0171) 629-1116 ■ Mon-Fri 9:30-6:00n Raymond O'Shea ■ French spoken ■ Prices medium ■ Major credit cards ■ Professional discount ■ BADA

Antiquarian prints and maps.

PHILLIPS–WOOD FINE ART LTD

104 Lower Marsh, Waterloo, London SE1 7AB ■ Tel: (0171) 928-4928 ■ Fax: (0171) 928-4944 ■ Mon-Sat 10:00-5:30 or by appointment ■ Kevin and Sheila Phillips ■ Prices low to high ■ Major credit cards ■ Trade discount

Limited open edition fine art prints. Washington Green images, de Montfort fine art. Fine art conservation and museum quality framing.

FRANK T. SABIN

13 The Royal Arcade, Old Bond Street, London W1X 3HB ■ Tel: (0171) 493-3288 ■ Fax: (0171) 499-3593 ■ Mon-Fri 9:30-5:30, Sat 10:00-1:00 ■ John and Mark Sabin ■ Prices medium to high ■ Major credit cards ■ Trade discount

18th and 19th century engravings, sporting, caricature, marine and genre.

HENRY SOTHERAN LTD

2-5 Sackville Street, Piccadilly, London W1X 2DP ■ Tel: (0171) 439-6151 ■ Fax: (0171) 434-2019 ■ Mon-Fri 9:30-6:00, Sat 10:00-4:00 ■ Andrew McGeachin ■ French and Italian spoken ■ Prices high to very high ■ Major credit cards ■ Trade discounts

Prints in the areas of travel, literature, architecture, children's illustrated, natural history.

STAGE DOOR PRINTS

9 Cecil Court, St. Martins Lane, London WC2N 4EZ ■ Tel: (0171) 240-1083 ■ Fax: (0171) 379-5598 ■ Mon-Sat 11:00-6:00 ■ Al Reynold ■ Prices low to very high ■ Visa and MC ■ Trade discount

Autographs from the performing arts. Antique prints and film posters and memorabilia.

TROWBRIDGE GALLERY

555 King's Road, London SW6 2EB ■ Tel: (0171) 371-8733 ■ Fax: (0171) 371-8138 ■ Mon-Fri 9:30-5:30 ■ Sat by appointment ■ Christopher W.R. Wilcox ■ Prices medium to very high ■ Trade discount ■ Major credit cards ■ LAPADA

Extensive collection of framed 17th and 18th century decorative antique and reproduction prints. Large selection of unframed antique prints. Choice includes flowers, fruit, natural history, architecturals and more.

JOHN BENNETT FINE PAINTINGS

206 Walton Street, London SW3 2JL ■ Tel: (0171) 225-2227 ■ Fax: (0171) 581-3629 ■ Mon-Fri 10:00-6:00, Sat 11:00-4:00 ■ John Bennett ■ Sat: Polish, Italian and French spoken ■ Prices low to high ■ Major credit cards ■ Trade discount

17th to 19th century British and European oil paintings, including landscapes, still life and portraits. Animal and sporting subjects.

MALCOLM INNES GALLERY LTD

7 Bury Street, London SW1Y 6AL ■ Tel: (0171) 839-8083/8084 ■ Fax: (0171) 839-8085 ■ E-mail: malcolm-innes@slad.org ■ Website: www.slad.org/malcolm_innes_gallery ■ Mon-Fri 9:30-6:00, Sat 10:00-2:00 during exhibitions, or by appointment ■ Malcolm Innes

19th and 20th century Scottish landscape, sporting and military pictures.

THE PARKER GALLERY

28 Pimlico Road, London SW1W 8LJ ■ Tel: (0171) 730-6768 ■ Fax: (0171) 259-9180 ■ Mon-Fri 9:30-5:30 ■ Adrian Newbury ■ Prices medium ■ Major credit cards ■ Trade discount

Naval, military, topographical, sporting prints and oils. Ship models of the 18th and 19th century. Catalogue available.

TYRON & SWANN GALLERY

23-24 Cork Street, London W1X 1HB ■ Tel: (0171) 734-6961/2256 ■ Fax: (0171) 287-2480 ■ E-mail: tyron-and swann@slad.org ■ Internet http://www.slad.org/tyron_and_swann ■ Mon-Fri 9:30-5:30 ■ The Hon D.E.H. Bigham, C. de P. Berry, O. Swann

Sporting, wildlife and marine paintings, prints, bronzes and books.

ART NOUVEAU, ART DECO

ABSTRACT

58-60 Kensington Church Street, London W8 4DB ■ Tel: (0171) 376-2652 ■ Fax: (0171) 937-3400 ■ Mon-Sat 11:00-5:00 ■ Juliette Bogaers and Galya Aytac ■ French, Dutch, German and Turkish spoken ■ Prices medium to high ■ Trade discount ■ Major credit cards ■ LAPADA

Art Deco and Art Nouveau glass, ceramics, sculpture, metalware and perfume bottles.

AESTHETICS

Stand V2, Antiquarius, 131-141 King's Road, London SW3 4PW ■ Tel: (0171) 352-0395 ■ Fax: (0171) 376-4057 ■ Mon-Sat 10:00-6:00 ■ BADA, LAPADA

Art Nouveau and Art Deco, decorative objects, porcelain, pottery and silver.

ART NOUVEAU ORIGINALS

4/5 Pierrepont Row Arcade, Camden Passage, London N1 8EF ■ Tel: (0171) 359-4127 ■ Mobile 0374 718096 ■ Wed 8:00-3:30, Sat 9:00-4:00 ■ Cathy Turner ■ Trade discount ■ Major credit cards ■ LAPADA

Art Nouveau small items of furniture, glass, porcelain and bronzes. In the other part of their shop Studio 2000 sells British studio pottery.

BARCLAY SAMSON LIMITED

65 Finlay Street, London SW6 6HF GB ■ Tel: (0171) 731-8012 ■ Fax: (0171) 731-8013 ■ E-mail: rb@bsltd.demon.co.uk ■ By appointment ■ Richard Barclay ■ French spoken ■ Amex and Visa accepted

Vintage lithographic posters from France, Britain, America and Germany. Posters by Lautrec, Mucha, Purvis, Cuneo, Fries.

NIGEL BENSON

Unit 7, The Antiques Centre, 58-60 Kensington Church Street, London W8 4DB ■ Telfax: (0171) 729-9875 ■ Mon-Sat 11:00-5:00 ■ Prices medium to high ■ Trade discount

Art Deco and 20th century glass.

BIZARRE ART DECO

24 Church Street, Marylebone, London NW8 8EP ■ Tel: (0171) 724-1305 ■ Fax: (0171) 724-1316 ■ Mobile 0374 607253 ■ Mon-Fri 9:30-5:30 ■ Professional discount

Quality Art Deco furniture and objects.

N. BLOOM & SON

The Bond Street Antiques Centre, 124 New Bond Street, London W1Y 9AE ■ Tel: (0171) 629-5060 ■ Fax: (0171) 493-2528 ■ Mobile: 0973 149363 ■ E-mail: nbloom@nbloom.co.uk ■ Internet: http://www.nbloom.co.uk ■ LAPADA

Art Nouveau and Art Deco jewellery.

CAMEO GALLERY

38 Kensington Church Street, London W8 4BX ■ Tel: (0171) 938-4114 ■ Fax: (0171) 938-4112 ■ Mon-Fri 10:00-5:00 ■ Prices medium to high ■ LAPADA

Art Nouveau and Art Deco glass, lighting, sculpture and bronzes.

CIANCIMINO LTD

99 Pimlico Road, London SW1W 8PH ■ Tel: (0171) 730-9950 ■ Fax: (0171) 730-5365 ■ Mon-Fri 10:00-6:00 ■ French, German and Spanish spoken ■ Trade discount

Art Deco furniture.

DIDIER

58-60 Kensington Church Street, London W8 4DB ■ Telfax: (0171) 938-2537 ■ Mobile: 0973 800415 ■ Mon-Sat 11:00-5:00 ■ Trade discount

Art Deco and Art Nouveau furniture and objects.

EDITIONS GRAPHIQUES LTD

3 Clifford Street, London W1X 1RA ■ Tel: (0171) 734-3944 ■ Fax: (0171) 487-1859 ■ Mon-Fri 11:00-6:00, Sat 11:00-9:00 ■ French spoken ■ Prices low to high ■ Professional discount ■ Major credit cards

Art Nouveau and Art Deco 1880-1930 paintings, drawings, graphics, sculpture, art glass, jewellery, furniture, ceramics, books, silver.

FREEFORMS

Unit 6, The Antiques Centre, 58-60 Kensington Church Street, London W8 4DB ■ Mobile 0966 219520 ■ Mon-Sat 11:00-4:00

Scandinavian and Czech glass.

THE GILDED LILY

Grays Antiques Market, 58 Davies Street, London W1Y 2LP ■ Tel: (0171) 499-6260 ■ Wed-Sat 9:00-5:00 ■ LAPADA

Art Nouveau and Art Deco objects, jewellery.

DAVID GILL

60 Fulham Road, London SW3 6HH ■ Tel: (0171) 589-5946 ■ Mon-Fri 10:00-6:00 ■ Trade discount ■ LAPADA

Art Nouveau and Art Deco, early 20th century furniture, glass, porcelain, oil paintings, silver.

SERGIO FERNANDO GUAZZELLI

Unit B7, Camden Stables Market, Chalk Farm Road, London NW1 8AH ■ Mobile tel: 0956 645492 ■ Fax: (0171) 221-9003 ■ Sat-Sun 9:00-6:00 and by appointment ■ Italian, French, Spanish and Portuguese spoken ■ Prices low to high ■ All credit cards ■ Professional discount

Furniture and lighting from 1880 to the present. Liberty, Art Deco, Modern.

JOHN JESSE

160 Kensington Church Street, London W8 4BN ■ Tel: (0171) 229-0312 ■ Fax: (0171) 229-4732 ■ Mon-Fri 10:00-6:00, Sat 11:00-4:00 ■ John Jesse ■ French and Italian spoken ■ Prices medium ■ Professional discount ■ Major credit cards

20th century decorative arts, Art Nouveau, Art Deco, Bauhaus and Post War. Glass, ceramics, bronzes, furniture, jewellery, silver, posters and paintings.

JHG DECORATIVE ARTS

58-60 Kensington Church Street, London W8 4DB ■ Tel: (0171) 938-4404 ■ Fax: (0171) ■ Mon-Sat 11:00-6:00 ■ C.A. Warner, G. Morgan, G. Strickland ■ Prices medium to high ■ Trade discount ■ Major credit cards

Art Nouveau and Arts and Crafts.

STEVE JOHNSON DECORATIVE ARTS

The Antique Centre, 58 Kensington Church Street, London W8 4DB ■ Tel: (0171) 937-8318 ■ Fax: (0171) 937-3400 ■ Mon-Sat 11:00-5:30 ■ French spoken ■ Prices low to high ■ Professional discount

19th and 20th century decorative arts: pewter, cameo glass, ceramics, sculpture, Art Nouveau, Art Deco and Secession.

LA CLOCHE FRERES
1 Three King's Yard, London W1Y 1FL ■ Tel: (0171) 355-3471 ■ Fax: (0171) 355-3473 ■ LAPADA

Art Deco and Art Nouveau decorative objects, glass, jewellery, sculpture and bronzes.

♔ FAY LUCAS GALLERY
50 Kensington Church Street, London W8 4DA ■ Tel: (0171) 938-3763 ■ Fax: (0171) 376-1055 ■ E-mail: faylucasgallery@btinternet.w ■ Mon-Sat 10:30-6:00 ■ Fay Lucas and Ben Walker ■ French, Spanish, Italian and Persian spoken ■ Prices medium to very high ■ Professional discount ■ Major credit cards ■ BADA, LAPADA

Fine English and Continental Arts and Crafts, Art Nouveau, Art Deco silver. The best of 20th century design in sterling silver and sport jewellery.

PIETER OOSTHUIZEN
Bourbon-Hanby Antiques Centre, 151 Sydney Street, London SW3 6NT ■ Tel: (0171) 352-6071/460-3078 ■ Mon-Sun 10:00-5:00 ■ Dutch and German spoken ■ Prices medium to high ■ Trade discount ■ Major credit cards

Dutch Art Nouveau pottery and Boer War memorabilia.

ROBERT W. PETERSON
58-60 Kensington Church Street, London W8 4DB ■ Tel: (0171) 937-8318 ■ Fax: (0171) 287-9739 ■ Mon-Sat 10:00-6:00 ■ Prices low to very high ■ Trade discount ■ Amex

Late 19th and 20th century applied arts including paintings and sculpture. 1850-1960.

MADELEINE C. POPPER
PO Box 19024, London N7 6WS ■ Mobile: 0850 942880 ■ Fax: (0171) 272-4226 ■ E-mail: madeleine.popper@tugland.com ■ By appointment only ■ French and some German spoken ■ Prices medium ■ Professional discount ■ Major credit cards ■ LAPADA, FGA

Art Nouveau, Art Deco, and antique jewellery. Will search for specific items.

SYLVIA POWELL DECORATIVE ARTS
The Mall, Camden Passage, London N1 OPD ■ Tel: (0171) 354-2977 ■ Fax: (0181) 458 4543 ■ Wed, Sat 9:30- 5:00 ■ LAPADA

Art Nouveau, Art Deco, porcelain, sculpture and bronze.

THE TARGET GALLERY
7 Windmill Street, London W1 1HF ■ Telfax: (0171) 636-6295 ■ Mon-Sat 10:00-6:00 ■ Prices medium to high ■ Trade discount ■ Major credit cards
Unusual 20th century decorative objects.

TADEMA GALLERY
10 Charlton Place, Camden Passage, London N1 8AJ ■ Tel: (0171) 359-1055 ■ Fax: (0171) 359-1055 ■ Wed, Sat 10:00-5:00, other times by appointment ■ BADA
Art Nouveau, Art Deco, Arts and Crafts, jewellery.

TITUS OMEGA
Shop 18, Georgian Village, Camden Passage, London N1 8EF ■ Tel: (0171) 688-1295 ■ Wed, Sat 9:00-4:00 ■ Prices medium ■ Trade discount ■ Visa, MC
Art Nouveau, Liberty, Gallé, Daum.

TWO ZERO C APPLIED ART
56 Abbey Business Centre, Ingate Place, off Queenstown Rd., Battersea, London SW8 3NS ■ Tel: (0171) 720-2021 ■ Fax: (0171) 720-1015 ■ E-mail: appliedart@twozeroc.co.uk ■ Website: www.twozeroc.co.uk ■ By appointment ■ Michael Playford ■ French, Italian and Japanese spoken ■ Trade discount ■ LAPADA
All 20th century applied art including Wiener Werkstatte, Loetz glass, Art Deco, Modernist: furniture, ceramics and glass.

VAN DEN BOSCH DECORATIVE ARTS
Georgian Village, Camden Passage, Islington N1 8AE ■ Tel: (0171) 359-4560 ■ Wed, Sat 9:30-5:00 ■ LAPADA
Art Nouveau and Art Deco objects, jewellery and silver.

GORDON WATSON LTD
50 Fulham Road, London SW3 6HH ■ Tel: (0171) 589-3108 ■ Mon-Sat 11:00-6:00 ■ LAPADA
Art Nouveau, Art Deco, early 20th century furniture, glass, porcelain, silver and jewellery.

MIKE WEEDON GALLERY
7 Camden Passage, Islington, London N1 8EA ■ Tel: (0171) 226-5319/(0171) 609-6826 ■ Wed, Sat 9:30-5:00 ■ LAPADA
Art Nouveau, Art Deco. Paintings.

ROBERT WHITFIELD ANTIQUES

Tunnel Avenue Antique Warehouse, Trading Estate, Greenwich SE10 OQH ■ Tel: (0181) 305-2230 ■ Call first ■ LAPADA

Art Deco and Art Nouveau, 19th and 20th century furniture.

ARTISANS AND CRAFTSMEN

The artisans and craftsmen are the guardians of man's patrimony. They are the key to the preservation of the great works of art and craftsmanship which are part of our heritage. They are citizens of the world of art which goes beyond nationality and language. The magic in their hands and their devotion to their profession should be cherished by all of us. They deserve our admiration and respect.

Through the ages the system of The Guilds has helped preserve the mementos and treasures of the past and put them into the context of the present. Fortunately, in England, The Guilds remain strong. They are unequivocal. Those who do not meet the standards cannot become members and if they fail to maintain those standards they will be dropped.

Art Foundries

B.A.C. CASTINGS
62 Britton Street, London EC1M ■ Tel: (0171) 253-3856 ■ Mon-Fri 8:00-6:00 by appointment

Lost wax casting for the metal parts of antique furniture: claw feet, keyhole escutcheons, etc. Restoration and replacement of cabinet hardware for antique furniture, chandelier parts and candelabra in silver and bronze.

BRONZE AGE SCULPTURE CASTING FOUNDRY
Island Row, Limehouse Docklands, London E14 7HY ■ Tel: (0171) 538-1388 ■ Fax: (0171) 538-9723 ■ Mon-Fri 8:00-6:00, Sat 10:00-4:00 ■ Mark Kennedy and Duncan Heather ■ French, Spanish and German spoken ■ Prices medium

Fine art casting. Lost wax ceramic shell process. Exclusively for sculpture of medium size. They work for many of the world's best sculptors.

M. S. MERIDIAN FOUNDRY

The Arches 840-842, Consort Road, London SE15 2PH■ Tel: (0171) 639-2553 ■ Fax: (0171) 277-9486 ■ Mon-Fri 9:00-6:00 by appointment ■ William Pye, Ivor Roberts Jones ■ Prices medium

Sculpture founders. Lost wax, ceramic shell and sand casting processes for casting fine sculpture. From small to monumental, in bronze and precious metals. Since 1967. Sculptors include Henry Moore, Elisabeth Frink, John Mills, Anthony Gormly and many others.

QUALITY CASTINGS UK LTD

7 Canalside Studios, 2-4 Orsman Road, London N1 5QJ ■ Tel: (0171) 729-3041 ■ Fax: (0171) 729-4684 ■ Mon-Thu 9:00-5:00, Fri 9:00-1:00 ■ Alan Factor ■ German, Polish and Spanish spoken ■ Prices medium

Lost wax casters for the jewellery trade, silversmiths, musical instrument manufacturers. Repair and restoration of small antique brass and bronze objects.

THE SCULPTURE FACTORY

21 Perseverence Works, 38 Kingsland Road, London E2 8DA ■ Tel: (0171) 739-7876 ■ Fax: (0171) 739-8095 ■ Mon-Fri 8:30-5:30 ■ John Crisfield ■ French spoken ■ Prices medium to high

Fine art fabrication in bronze and steel: sculpture, fountains, gates, screens, etc. Top references from many of Britain's leading sculptors.

WHITECHAPEL BELL FOUNDRY LTD

32-34 Whitechapel Road, London E1 1DY ■ Tel: (0171) 247-2599 ■ Fax: (0171) 375-1979 ■ Alan Hughes, Kathryn Hughes ■ Prices as you would expect for the best ■ Marvellous catalogues available

These are the folks who cast The Liberty Bell in 1752 and London's BIG BEN as well as the Bicentennial Bell given as a gift from Britain to the US in 1976. Handbells are their specialty. Fine casting.

BURLEIGHFIELD ARTS LTD
Loudwater, High Wycombe, Bucks. HP10 9RF ■ Tel: (01494) 521341 ■ Fax: (01494) 461953 ■ By appointment ■ Paul Dimishky

Art and architectural casting in bronze and precious metals. From small objects to major pieces such as their recent project of a 13-meter sword for the new Sports Stadium in Kuala Lumpur. Clients are mainly artists as well as institutions.

COLLIER CASTINGS LTD
Raybar Hooe Battle, East Sussex TN33 9EU ■ Telfax: (01424) 892248 ■ Mon-Fri 7:30-5:30 ■ Mr. L. Collier ■ Prices medium

Ormolu brass casting. Lost wax process and sand casting for fine art. Custom door and window decorative hardware and lamps. Restoration and gilding. Very good references.

NAUTILUS FINE ART FOUNDRY
Swinborne Drive, Springwood Indust. Est., Braintree, Essex CM7 2YP ■ Tel: (01376) 343222 ■ Fax: (01376) 348480 ■ Mon-Fri by appointment ■ Paul Joyce, Rod Seaman

Fine casting by expert craftsmen. Lost wax process of casting sculpture for small medals and figurines up to 16-foot horses. Top references.

Art Quilters

HENRY CLIVE
46 Ledbury Road, London W11 2AB ■ Tel: (0171) 229-8376 ■ Fax: (0171) 229-2928 ■ Mon-Fri 9:00-6:00

Outline quilts, appliqué, made to order. Any form of quilting to a geometric outline. Seems to be the only quilter in London. Not surprising, since quilting is mostly an American tradition.

Basket Makers

HENRY GROSS LTD
74 Maidstone Buildings, Borough High Street, London SE1 1XE ■ Tel: (0171) 407-0942 ■ Fax: (0171) 407-5942 ■

Specialists in basketware and basketware supplies.

🏭 THE SOMERSET WILLOW CO
Unit 10-12 Wireworks Trading Est., Bristol Road, Bridgewater, Somerset TA6 4AP ■ Tel: (01278) 424003 ■ Fax: (01278) 446415 ■ Mon-Fri 8:30-5:00 ■ Aubrey and Darrell Hill ■ Prices medium to high ■ Trade discount ■ Major credit cards

Everything woven in willow: traditional English basketware, hot air balloon baskets, conservatory furniture, willow coffins.

WYCOMBE CANE & RUSH WORKS
Victoria Street, High Wycombe, Buckinghamshire HP11 2QR ■ Tel: (01494) 442429 ■ Mon-Fri 9:00-5:00, Sat by appointment ■ Peter Gilbert

Established 100 years. Makers of baskets of any kind to order. Restorers of antique cane furniture. Also work in rush and willow.

Cabinet Makers

ADZE CRAFTSMEN
24 Heriot Avenue, Chingford, London E4 8AP ■ Tel: (0181) 529-4151 ■ By appointment only ■ M.A. Carnell ■ Polish spoken ■ Prices medium to high

Hand-made furniture to any design.

HOWDLE LTD
9 Marylebone High street, London W1M 3PB ■ Tel: (0171) 224-6453 ■ Fax: (0171) 224-1516 ■ Mon 12:00-5:00, Tue-Thu 10:00-5:00, Fri 10:00-4:00 ■ C. Howdle ■ Prices high ■ Major credit cards

Kitchens, bathrooms, bookcases, bedroom furniture. Joinery items such as staircases, panelling, desks, tables. Design, manufacture and fitting.

PEGRAM BIANCO
183 Royal College Street, London NW1 0SG■ Tel: (0171) 267-1115
■ Fax: (0171) 267-9894 ■ Mon-Fri 8:30-5:00 ■ Andrew J. Pegram ■
French and Italian spoken ■ Prices high

Cabinet making, joinery. Store fittings a specialty.

YOUNG & HEASMAN
501 Old York Road, London SW18 1TF ■ Tel: (0181) 870-3151 ■ By
appointment

Specialists in custom-designed and custom-made free-standing furniture. Design service available.

OUTSIDE LONDON

BREWERY ANTIQUES
2 Cirencester Workshops, Brewery Court, Cirencester, Glos. GL7
1JH ■ Tel: (01285) 658817 ■ Fax: (01285) 644060 ■ Mobile: 0976
722028 ■ Mon-Fri ■ 8:00-5:30, Sat: 8:30-1:00 ■ Stephen Hill ■ Prices
medium

Cabinet making and fine furniture restoration and conservation. They have a good collection of antique furniture, prints and pictures as well as upholstered chairs.

▓ DEACON & SANDYS
Apple Pie Farm, Cranbrook Road, Benenden, Kent TN17 4EV ■ Tel:
(01580) 243351 ■ Fax: (01580) 243301 ■ E-mail: jonathan_deacon@msr.com ■ Mon-Fri 8:00-5:30, Sat 8:00-1:00 ■ Jonathan Deacon ■ Prices very high ■ Professional discount

Designer and manufacturers of 17th century oak interiors. Oak furniture, wall panelling and staircases. Design, supply and fit. Some work references include Shell–Lensbury Club: oak panelling, Lincoln's Inn: furniture and oak floor in the Old Hall.

GEOFF JACKSON – CARPENTER'S WORKSHOP
Cobden Mill, Square Street, Ramsbottom, Bury BL0 9AZ ■ Tel:
(01706) 825033 ■ Mon-Fri 7:30-4:30 ■ Prices medium

Hand-made tables and four poster-beds. Architectural carpenters and joiners. Specialists in period doors and staircases for listed buildings and houses, Georgian windows with box sashes and circular windows.

Caning and
Cane Restoration

THE CANE STORE
207 Blackstock Road, London N5 ■ Telfax: (0171) 354-4210 ■ Mon-Thu 10:00-7:00, Fri 10:00-1:00, Sat 10:00-6:00

Caning and cane restoration.

TITIAN STUDIO
318 Kensal Road, Kensington, London W10 5BN ■ Tel: (0181) 960-6247 ■ Fax: (0181) 969-6126 ■ Mon-Fri 8:00-5:30 ■ Rodrigo and Rosaria Titian ■ Italian, French and German spoken ■ Prices low to high ■ Some trade discounts ■ Visa, Access, MC

Caning and rushing. Total restoration workshop. Projects: Queen House Greenwich, Kensington Palace. Work for top West End dealers. BAFRA.

OUTSIDE LONDON

ANTIQUE & MODERN CANERS
10 Croxden Walk, Morden, Surrey SM4 6JY ■ Tel: (0181) 648-2499 ■ Mon-Fri by appointment

Traditional caning and restoration of cane. Seagrass and rush-cord repairs. Pick-up and delivery in London.

CANE & RUSH RESTORATION CO.
14 High Street, West Wycombe, Bucks. ■ Telfax: (01494) 452453 ■ Mon-Fri 9:00-5:00, Sat 10:00-5:00

Repairs on cane and rush chairs. Lloyd Loom specialists. Restorer for the National Trust.

WYCOMBE CANE & RUSH WORKS
Victoria Street, High Wycombe, Buckinghamshire HP11 2QR ■ Tel: (01494) 442429 ■ Mon-Fri 9:00-5:00, Sat by appointment ■ Peter Gilbert

Established 100 years. Restorers of antique cane furniture. Also rush and willow. Makers of baskets of any kind to order.

Carvers and Gilders

BEN BACON

30-34 Woodfield Place, London W9 2BJ ■ Tel: (0171) 289-5481 ■ By appointment ■ Ben Bacon ■ German spoken ■ Prices low to medium

Carving and gilding. Restoration of carved and gilded furniture, mirrors and picture frames.

RUPERT BEVAN

40 Fulham High Street, London SW6 3LQ ■ Telfax: (0171) 731-1919 ■ E-mail: rupert@workshop.enta.net ■ Mon-Fri 9:00-6:00 ■ Prices medium to high

The restoration and reproduction of fine painted, gilded antique furniture.

♕ CAMPBELL'S OF WALTON STREET

164 Walton Street, London SW3 2JL ■ Tel: (0171) 584-9268 ■ Fax: (0171) 581-3499 ■ Mon-Fri 9:30-5:30, Sat 10:00-5:00 ■ Roy Hogben ■ Some French spoken ■ Prices medium to high ■ Major credit cards ■ Trade discount

Carvers and gilders. Hand-crafted picture frames, restoration and conservation. Member of The Guild of Master Craftsmen and the Fine Art Trade Guild.

CARVERS & GILDERS

9 Charterhouse Works, Eltringham Street, London SW18 1TD ■ Tel: (0181) 870-7047 ■ Fax: (0181) 874-0470 ■ Mon-Fri by appointment ■ William McCombe, Aasha Tyrrell, Christine Palmer ■ Some Spanish and French spoken ■ Prices medium to high

Fine wood carvers and gilders. Carve to commission frames, mirrors, furniture, as well as free carving. Work for museums, royal palaces and private clients. Holders of a Royal Warrant.

COMPTON HALL RESTORATION

A133 Riverside Business Centre, Haldane Place, London SW18 4UQ
■ Mon-Fri 9:00-5:00 ■ Lucinda Compton and Karen Haslewood ■ Italian and Spanish spoken ■ Prices medium to high ■ Trade discount

Antique furniture restoration. Gilding, painting, Oriental lacquering, papier maché and tôle. Top references.

DÉCOR ARTS

7 Graces Mews, London SE5 8JF ■ Tel: (0171) 252-7364 ■ Fax: (0171) 252-5467 ■ Mon-Fri 9:00-5:00 ■ Elena Vinylomb and Philip Westerdale ■ Italian spoken ■ Prices low to very high ■ Trade discounts

Fine applied and gilded decoration. Oil and water gilding in gold, silver and other metal leaves. Wood graining and all painted finishes, including murals. Special varnishing techniques. Clients include royal palaces, hotels, department stores, exclusive boutiques and private clients.

THE PAUL FERGUSON WORKSHOP

Workshop 20, 21 Wren Street, London WC1X 0HF ■ Telfax: (0171) 278-8759 ■ E-mail: ferguson@cw.com ■ Mon-Fri 8:30-5:00 ■ Paul Ferguson ■ Prices low to very high

Wood carving and gilding. New work and conservation and restoration. One-off commissions. Member of the Master Carvers' Association and UKIC.

♛ CHRISTIAN GEORGET

6 Longyard, Lamb's Conduit Street, London WC1N 3LU ■ Telfax: (0171) 405-9585 ■ By appointment ■ French spoken ■ Trade discount

Fine art gilding of picture frames and furniture. Restoration of any type of gilding. Wide selection of English picture frames of the late 18th to 19th century. Reproduction frames made to suit any picture. Work references include The Courtauld Institute and many top London art dealers. 25 years experience.

GILTWOOD RESTORATIONS

7 Addington Square, London SE5 7JZ ■ Tel: (0171) 703-4351 ■ Fax: (0171) 703- 1047 ■ Mon-Fri 9:00-6:00 ■ Martin Body ■ Prices medium

Carving and gilding. Conservation and restoration of period gilt furniture, lighting and objects. Architectural gilding. Small stock of fine English looking glasses. References upon request.

SUE HAYNES
Unit 121, Aberdeen House, 22 Highbury Grove, London N5 2DQ ■ Tel: (0171) 226-4082 ■ Fax: (0171) 359-5016 ■ Mon-Fri 10:00-6:00 by appointment only ■ Prices medium to high

One off pieces designed in consultation with client. Large scope of individually designed pieces carved in wood: free carved sculpture, heraldry, frames and much more. Excellent references.

PHILIP JOYCE
Unit 2, Sunbury Workshops, London E2 7LF ■ Tel: (0171) 739-3240 ■ Fax: (0181) 878-8619 ■ Mon-Fri 10:00-6:00 appointment suggested

High quality carving and gilding. Restoration of moulding, mirrors and furniture. References upon request.

ALEXANDER GEORGE LEY & SONS
13 Brecknock Road, London N7 0BL ■ Tel: (0171) 267-3645 ■ Fax: (0171) 267-4462 ■ Mon-Fri 8:00-6:30 by appointment ■ Prices high

Expert carvers and gilders. Restoration of fine giltwood furniture. Also makers of fine giltwood furniture and mirrors. Stock of mirrors, furniture and fine frames.

TITIAN STUDIO
318 Kensal Road, Kensington, London W10 5BN ■ Tel: (0181) 960-6247 ■ Fax: (0181) 969-6126 ■ Mon-Fri 8:00-5:30 ■ Rodrigo and Rosaria Titian ■ Italian, French and German spoken ■ Prices low to high ■ Some trade discounts ■ Visa, Access, MC

Gilding, lacquering, carving, French polishing, painted and decorated furniture. Restoration of marquetry and parquetry. Leather and marble conservation. Caning and rushing. Projects: Queen House Greenwich, Kensington Palace. Work for top West End dealers. BAFRA.

W. THOMAS RESTORATIONS LTD
12 Warwick Place, London W9 2PX ■ Tel: (0171) 286-1945 ■ Fax: (0171) 266-2521 Mon-Fri 8:00-5:30 ■ Partridge Fine Arts/Raymond Dudman ■ Prices medium

Carving and gilding restoration. Reproductions. BAFRA.

BERNARD BLACKBURN

8C Stoney Brow, Roby Mill, Upholland, Lancashire WN8 0QE ■ Tel: (01695) 633146 ■ Mon-Fri by appointment

Wood carver–turner. Bespoke woodwork. Extraordinary and unique pieces. Architectural carving, friezes, all types of intricate mouldings, statuary and objects. Plaque work and miniature furniture. His work travels to many parts of the world.

♛ DICK REID

23 Fishergate, York YO10 4AE ■ Tel: (01904) 659121 ■ Fax: (01904) 640018 ■ E-mail: dick.reid.carver@virgin.net ■ Mon-Fri 8:30-5:30 ■ Prices medium to high

High quality architectural wood, stone and furniture carving. Historic restoration, modelling for sculpture and plasterwork. Work is principally for architects, interior designers and private clients. 40 years experience working in royal palaces, stately homes and cathedrals.

Decorative Painting and Trompe l'Oeil

BELINDA CANOSA

38 St. Mary's Grove, London W4 3LN ■ Tel: (0181) 747-0436 ■ Fax: (0181) 995-1099 ■ By appointment only ■ French and Spanish spoken ■ Prices medium to high

Agent for artists working to commission for murals, trompe l'oeil, fresco, portraits, fine copies of paintings and pastiches. Works internationally for museums, palaces, ocean liners, hotels and private clients.

DAVID CARTER

109 Mile End Road, London E1 4UJ ■ Telfax: (0171) 790-0259 ■ By appointment ■ French spoken

Decorative paint effects, bespoke furniture. Full service decoration and project management.

THE CURTAIN COUTURIER

285 New King's Road, London SW6 4RD ■ Tel: (0171) 371-9255 ■ Fax: (0171) 371-9266 ■ Mon-Sat 9:30-5:30 ■ Anne Thompson ■ French spoken ■ Prices low to very high ■ Major credit cards ■ Trade discount

Planned murals, trompe l'oeil, skies, stonework and blocking. Stencilling and prints, stripes and frottage. References upon request.

DECOR ARTS

7 Graces Mews, London SE5 8JF ■ Tel: (0171) 252-7364 ■ Fax: (0171) 252-5467 ■ Mon-Fri 9:00-5:00 ■ Elena Vinylomb and Philip Westerdale ■ Italian spoken ■ Prices low to very high ■ Trade discounts

Decorative painting and faux finishes, marbling, wood graining and all painted finishes. Murals and wide experience in high performance and other paint systems together with an interesting range of varnishing techniques.
Fine gilded decoration. Oil and water gilding in gold, silver and other metal leaves. Impressive client list: royal palaces all over the world, hotels, department stores, banks and private clients.

HANNERLE DEHN

4 Southam Street, London W10 5PP ■ Tel: (0181) 964-0599 ■ Fax: (0171) 602-1192 ■ Mon-Fri 8:00-6:00, Sat by appointment ■ German and some French spoken

Decorative painter. Specialty: authentic 18th and 19th century finishes, painted or gilded. Painting on fabric, faux bois finishes. Paper, silk and leather screens. Any gilding, mostly water. Works for interior decorators, antique dealers and private clients. Excellent references upon request.

DKT (DAVIES KEELING TROWBRIDGE LTD)

3 Charterhouse Works, Eltringham Street, London SW18 1TD ■ Tel: (0181) 874-3565 ■ Fax: (0181) 874-2058 ■ E-mail: info@dkt.co.uk ■ Web: www.dkt.co.uk ■ Mon-Fri 8:30-5:30 ■ Stephen Keeling and Sean Trowbridge ■ Spanish and French spoken ■ Prices medium to very high

Paint finishes, murals, gilding, decorative design, mosaics, special plasterwork. References upon request.

DIANA FINCH

12 Glebe Place, Chelsea, London SW3 5LB■ Tel: (0171) 352-0131 ■
Fax: (0171) 376-7140 ■ By appointment 9:00-5:00 ■ Diana Finch ■
French, Italian and Spanish spoken ■ Prices medium

Muralist, gilder, specialist painter. Good references.

STONOR & STONOR - FANTASTIC FINISHES

Flat 4, 31 Powis Square, Nottinghill Gate, London W11 2AY ■ Tel:
(0171) 229-0854 ■ Fax: (01865) 512346 ■ Everyday by appointment
■ Giles and Jeremy Stonor ■ Some French spoken

**Specialists in paint finishes: marbling, woodgraining, distress-
ing, ragging, colour washing, etc. Murals and trompe l'oeil. Traditional gilding. References on request.**

SEBASTIAN WAKEFIELD

Cam Laithe, Far Lane, Kettlewell, Skipton, N. Yorks, BD23 5QY ■ Tel:
(01756) 760809 ■ Fax: (01756) 760209 ■ E-mail: seb@sebastian-
w.demon.co.uk ■ By appointment

**Twenty-two years of experience in painting murals, trompe l'oeil
and faux finishes. Oil and water gilding. Works directly onto
walls on site or paints on to canvas in the studio and then glues
up and finishes on site. Top references from all over the world.**

French Polishers

CREST FRENCH POLISHING

31 Lessingham Avenue, Tooting SW17 8L2 ■ Tel: (0181) 682-0225 ■
Mobile: 0966 185461 ■ By appointment ■ Clive Roberts ■ Trade discount

**All types of French polishing, stripping, refinishing, liming,
colour matching. Bar top specialists. Staircases also a specialty. Mostly work for building trade, offices, banks, restaurants,
pubs. Work references include the P&O Shipping line, Lloyds
Bank and McDonalds.**

GREENHAM & SON

43 Hillside Gardens, London E17 3RH ■ Telfax: (0181) 520-7122 ■
By appointment ■ Bryan Greenham ■ Prices low to medium

**Master French Polishers: high quality wood finishing. French
polishing, liming, waxing, cellulose lacquering for commercial
use. Wood finishing: ebonizing, pickling and fuming.**

J. S. POLISHING

366 City Road, London EC1V 2PY ■ Tel: (0171) 278-6803 ■ Fax: (0171) 837-9802 ■ Mon-Fri 9:00-5:00 ■ John White, Steve Brady

Polishing contractors. French polishing, wax polishing, lacquering, antique restoration. Large contracts and small.

ROJEH ANTIQUES

Alfie's Units 22-35, 13 Church Street, London NW8 8ET ■ Tel: (0171) 724-6960 ■ Telfax: (0181) 964-5959 ■ Mobile: 0860 156390 ■ Mon-Sat 8:00-6:00 ■ Sam Rojeh or Tony

Traditional French polishing and restoration of veneers. Upholstery. Work for dealers and private clients.

STOKER

53-55 Lisson Grove, London NW1 6UH ■ Tel: (0171) 258-0778 ■ Mon-Fri 8:00-5:00, Sat 8:00-1:00

French polishing for the antique trade. Leather polishing of any leather, especially upholstery. Restoration and revival of leather desk tops.

TERRY WATERS

82 Great Eastern Street, Shoreditch, London EC2A 3JL ■ Tel: (0171) 359-3833 ■ Fax: (01675) 481894 ■ Mon-Sat by appointment ■ Trade discount

Fine craftsman. All wood finishes, domestic and commercial. Panelling, boardroom furniture. Work references: Restoration of woodwork at Windsor Castle and re-furbishing of hardwood flooring at Hampton Court.

Glass Artists

FUSION GLASS DESIGNS

365 Clapham Road, London SW9BT ■ Tel: (0171) 938-5888 ■ Fax: (0171) 738-4888 ■ Mon-Fri 9:00-6:00. Sat 10:00-5:00 ■ A. Clemson, R. Robertson, F. Ellington ■ Prices low to very high ■ Trade discount

Decorative glass, sandblasting. Kiln forming, laminating for architectural interiors.

THE LONDON GLASSBLOWING WORKSHOP

7 The Leathermarket, Weston Street, London SE1 3ER ■ Tel: (0171) 403-2800 ■ Fax: (0171) 403-7778 ■ Mon-Fri 10:00-5:00 ■ Peter Layton ■ French, German, Swedish and Danish spoken ■ Prices low to high ■ Major credit cards ■ Trade discount

Free blown studio glass in any texture or form. Tableware, architectural glass, Unique decorative items. Author of "Glass Art".

NOSTALGIC GLASS

Unit 2, Union Road, Union Court, Clapham, London SW4 6JH ■ Telfax: (0171) 720-5876 ■ Mon-Fri 9:00-6:00 ■ Mehmet Kuzu ■ German and Turkish spoken ■ Prices medium ■ Trade discount

Bespoke glass making in any size, shape, colour and design. Specialists in antique glass replacements. Engraving, cutting, restoration. Parts for chandeliers, wall lights, candelabra, liners, decanters, mirrors, shades. Work references: Buckingham Palace, Asprey, Mallet, Garrard and Harrods.

Mosaic Artists

DKT (DAVIES KEELING TROWBRIDGE LTD)

3 Charterhouse Works, Eltringham Street, London SW18 1TD ■ Tel: (0181) 874-3565 ■ Fax: (0181) 874-2058 ■ E-mail: info@dkt.co.uk ■ Web: www.dkt.co.uk ■ Mon-Fri 8:30-5:30 ■ Stephen Keeling and Sean Trowbridge ■ Spanish and French spoken ■ Prices medium to high

Mosaics, special plasterwork, paint finishes, murals, gilding, decorative design, mosaics, special plasterwork. References upon request.

♛ MOSAIK

10 Kensington Square, London W8 5EP ■ Tel: (0171) 795-6253 ■ Fax: (0171) 376-9495 ■ Tue-Sat 12:00-6:30, mornings by appointment ■ Pierrre Mesguich and Ann Hughes ■ French spoken ■ Prices medium to high ■ Trade discount

Hand-cut mosaic friezes and panels for walls and floors. Mosaic tiling supplied: glass and ceramic. Design service: drawings and samples provided. Advice on bathroom and swimming pool design in use of mosaic. Clients are: royal palaces, international hotels, great restaurants, private houses, haute couture showrooms, the world over.

CATHERINE PARKINSON

6 Dalgarno Gardens, London W10 6AD ■ Tel: (0171) 964-1945 ■
Mon-Fri 9:30-3:30 ■ Catherine Parkinson ■ Prices high

Hand-chopped marble mosaic to commission. One-off designs. Excellent and durable surface for interior and exterior walls, ceilings and floors. Especially beautiful when combined with moving water.

Ornamental Metal Craftsmen

ARKILL & HILL LTD

Mortlake Court Business Centre, 28 Sheen Lane, London SW14 8LW ■ Tel: (0181) 878-4096 ■ Fax: (0181) 392-9495 ■ Mon-Fri 9:00-5:00

Specialists in bronze: restoration and maintenance. Very well established firm who undertake major projects.

■ BJS COMPANY LTD

65 Bideford Avenue, Perivale, Greenford, Middlesex UB6 7PP ■ Tel: (0181) 810-5779 ■ Fax: (0181) 810-5883 ■ E-mail: bjs.co.ltd@dial.pipex.com ■ Mon-Thu 8:00-5:30, Fri 8:00-5:00, Sat 8:00-12:00 ■ Richard Lewis ■ Prices medium ■ Trade discount ■ Visa, MC

Finishing and restoration of interior and exterior design metal components. Electroplating, polishing, bronzing. Interior designed components made to order: door and window hardware, bathroom fittings, chandeliers and all types of lighting. Holder of a Royal Warrant and ISO 9002. They work for royal palaces, ministries, private homes, private aircraft and yachts.

MICHAEL BROOK

192 Camberwell Grove, London SE5 8RJ■ Telfax: (0171) 708-0467 ■ Mon-Fri 9:00-6:00 and by appointment ■ Prices medium

Specialist in 17th, 18th and 19th century English and French ormolu and bronze. All repairs, cleaning, casting, chasing and gilding of mounts. Patination, bronzing and metal finishes. Metal gilding.

JAMES HOYLE & SON

50 Andrews Road, London E8 4RL ■ Tel: (0181) 551-6764 ■ Fax: (0181) 550-0931 ■ Mon-Fri 7:00-4:00 ■ Prices medium to high

Architectural iron founder. Cast iron balustrades for staircases, fireplaces, railings, period firebacks for open fires. Reproductions of pieces from 1540 made to drawings. Work references include: the cast iron lamp posts along the Chelsea Embankment; roof crenellation and underfloor grilles at the Natural History Museum; refurbishment of all the railings at the National Portrait Gallery, Trafalgar Square.

J.H. PORTER & SON LTD

13 Cranleigh Mews, Cabul Road, London SW11 2QL ■ Tel: (0171) 978-5576 ■ Fax: (0171) 924-7081 ■ Mon-Fri 8:00-5:00 ■ Fred Hodgins ■ Prices low

They make anything in decorative iron: gates, staircases, railings, furniture (indoor and out), grilles, balustrates. Made-to-measure iron work. Restoration of antique iron work.

TRESCHER FABRICATIONS

R-A 1&2 Bermorodes Trading Estate, Rotherhithe New Road, London SE16 3LL ■ Tel: (0171) 231-8692 ■ Fax: (0171) 252-3303 ■ Mon-Fri 7:30-5:00 ■ C.A. Mee and J. Nobourn ■ Prices medium ■ Trade discounts

All types of fabrication, large and small, in mild steel, aluminum and stainless steel. Design, fabrication and full site installation. References upon request.

VERDIGRIS

Arch 290 Crown Street, London SE5 0UR■ Tel: (0171) 703-8373 ■ Fax: (0171) 703-9120 ■ Mon-Fri 9:00-5:00 ■ Gerard Bacon ■ Spanish spoken

Pewter bartops, metalwork and antique restoration. Metal colouration and patination. Specialist etchers, artistic metalwork makers. Work references include: restoration and re-gilding of the Speaker's Staircase at the Palace of Westminster, pewter and copper etched wall panels for Young & Rubicam Greater London House.

BRONZE RESTORATIONS
Unit A, Rear of 137-165 Hook Road, Surbiton, Surrey ■ Tel: (0181) 391-9116 ■ Mon-Fri 9:00-5:00

Specialists in architectural and monumental bronze refurbishing and maintenance. Monumental projects undertaken. Top references.

BRONZEWOOD RESTORATION
7 Millwood Road, Orpington, Kent BR5 3LG ■ Telfax: (01689) 813080 ■ By appointment

Specialists in metal restoration, bronze toning, brass lacquering, sprayed finishes. Top references.

HAYCAR RENOVATIONS & MAINTENANCE SERVICES LIMITED
1 Highcliffe Close, Wickford, Essex SS11 8JZ ■ Telfax: (01268) 768510 ■ Mon-Sat 8:00-6:00 and by appointment ■ Mr. B.J. Carew ■ Professional discount

Architectural renovation to buildings: marble, granite, terrazzo, stonework, brickwork, bronze, stainless steel, aluminium, brass. Renovation and maintenance by highly qualified craftsmen.

Porcelain Artists

STEPHANIE FERNALD CERAMIC DESIGNS
10 Longley Road, Rochester, Kent ME1 2HD ■ Telfax: (01634) 401427 ■ E-mail: stephfernald@hotmail.com ■ 7 days by appointment ■ Trade discount

Hand-decorated English bone china. Complete range of bone china tableware. Commissions undertaken, either from design to completion or using customer's own artwork. Classical designs, sporting, fossils and bugs. Catalogue available.

CAROLINE WHYMAN

21 Iliffe Yard, Crampton Street, London SA17 3QA ■ Telfax: (0171) 708-5904 ■ By appointment only ■ Caroline Whyman ■ Prices medium to high ■ Trade discounts

Hand-made porcelain ceramics inlaid in geometric patterns with gold. Vases, bowls, plates. Special commissions undertaken.

Sculptors

CATHY BURKEMAN (FIRES)

Studio 24, Great Western Studios, Great Western Road, London W9 3NY ■ Tel: (0171) 289-0545 ■ Mobile: 0956 324006 ■ Mon-Fri 9:30-5:30 approx. ■ French, Italian and some Spanish spoken ■ Prices high

Unique sculptures around a bonfire theme with differing size and shaped rods. These provide excellent heat conductors and create wonderful effects in the midst of a fire. Each piece is made to commission.

JULIAN MELGRAVE - PORTRAIT SCULPTOR

Studio 4, Fleming Close, Chelsea, London SW10 0AH ■ Telfax: (0171) 351-0153 ■ By appointment ■ French, German, Spanish and Italian spoken ■ Prices medium

Small portrait sculptures on commission.

THE SCULPTURE COMPANY

108 Old Brompton Road, London SW7 3RA ■ Tel: (0171) 373-8615 ■ Fax: (0171) 370-3721■ Mon-Fri 9:30-5:30 ■ Philomena Davidson Davis ■ Prices high ■ MC and Visa accepted

Unique sculpture on commisssion. Database of contemporary sculpture.

OUTSIDE LONDON

BARRY DAVIES

Pendomen, Llanrhaeadr-Ym-Mochnant, Oswestry, SY10 0DS ■ Telfax: (01691) 780295 ■ By appointment

Sculptor of classic marble statues and busts in figurative form. For interior and exterior.

Stained Glass Window
Artists & Makers

♕ RAY BRADLEY ARCA

3 Orchard Studios, Brook Green, London W6 7BU■ Tel: (0171) 602-1840 ■ By appointment ■ Some French and Italian

Artist designer. Specialty: architectural glass designed, produced and installed as site specific commissions for religious and secular buildings on any scale in the UK and abroad. Windows, walls, ceilings and screens of stained glass and combined techniques of enamelling, silvering, sand blasting and acid embossing to float and toughened glass as single, double or laminated units to fit any situation. Many private and public commissions in UK and also Europe, Africa, Middle East and Australasia.

GILBERT & MCCARTY

30A Borwick Avenue, Walthamstowe E17 GRA ■ Tel: (0181) 509-1894 ■ By appointment

Specialists in the design and manufacture of leaded and stained glass windows. Repairs to church windows, leaded lights and manufacturers of copper light windows.

♕ GODDARD & GIBBS STUDIOS LTD

41-49 Kingsland Road, London E2 ■ Tel: (0171) 739-6563 ■ Fax: (0171) 739-1979 ■ Mon-Fri 9:00-5:30 ■ Christopher Borst ■ Russian, French and Italian spoken

Designers and craftsmen in stained and decorative glass. Traditional to contemporary. Restoration and conservation. Work on historic buildings as well as new stained glass work. They make stained glass for artists. Their work is world wide: Churches in the U.S., mosques, synagogues, institutions and banks as well as private clients.

♕ GRAHAM JONES

58 First Avenue, London SW14 8SR ■ Telfax: (0181) 876-6930 ■ E-mail: graham@asgd.demon.co.uk ■ By appointment ■ ARCA

Stained glass artist. Everything from traditional techniques to present day high tech. Work references include: The Memorial Window over Chaucer's Tomb in Poet's Corner of Westminster Abbey, Temples in Brazil, Alaska, Ecuador and Shanghai. Churches throughout Germany, the new airport in Hong Kong, Shell Oil, ICI, BAT, Coca Cola.

LEAD & LIGHT

35A Hartland Road, London NW1 4DB ■ Tel: (0171) 485-0997 ■ Fax: (0171) 284-2660 ■ Mon-Sat 9:00-5:00 ■ Marc Garstel ■ French and Italian spoken ■ Prices medium ■ Major credit cards

Antique-style stained glass, coloured glass and stained glass supplies. Stained glass panels a specialty.

MCMILLAN GLASS COMPANY

Unit 1, Studio D, Clapham North Business Centre, Voltaire Road, London SW4 6DH ■ Tel: (0171) 498-0100 ■ Fax: (0171) 622-0805 ■ E-mail: mcmglass@aol.com ■ Mon-Fri 9:00-5:30, Sat 10:00-2:00

Stained glass windows and leaded lights. Coloured glass, sandblasted glass. Design and installation.

♕ ANDREW MOOR ASSOCIATES

14 Chamberlain Street, London NW1 8XB ■ Tel: (0171) 586-8181 ■ Fax: (0171) 586-8484 ■ By appointment ■ Andrew Moor ■ Prices high ■ Trade discoount

Stained glass, etched-glass screens, doors, design and fabrications. Has reproduced the works of well-known painters in the Tate Gallery, the 30-foot tall windows in Westminster Abbey and many other highly visible examples. One of the best in the UK.

NEIL PHILLIPS STAINED GLASS LTD

99 Portobello Road, London ■ Tel: (0171) 229-2213 ■ Fax: (0171) 229-1963 ■ Mon-Fri 9:00-5:00, Sat 7:00-4:00 ■ Neil Phillips ■ German spoken ■ Prices medium to very high ■ Trade discount

Stained glass windows and panels. Ecclesiastical antiques. Work on commission as well as restoration of stained glass.

STAINED GLASS CONSTRUCTION

62 Fairfield Street, London SW18 1DY ■ Tel: (0181) 874-8822 ■ Fax: (0181) 870-0643 ■ E-mail: enquiries@stainedglassguild.co.uk ■ Mon-Fri 8:00-5:00, Sat 9:00-1:00 ■ David Meakin ■ Spanish and some French spoken

Making and repairing of painted or decorative glass in the traditional manner. Work references: Church of Saint John Fisher at Morden, London, Kensington Museums, Sir Robert McAlpine Ltd. They have a school for serious amateurs.

Restorers

Antique Conservation and Restoration Workshops

ANTIQUE RESTORATIONS

45 Windmill Road, Brentford, Middlesex, London TW7 7HJ ■ Tel: (0181) 568-5249 ■ Mon-Fri 8:30-5:30 ■ Alun and Ann Smith

Restoration of polychrome surfaces including japanning, Oriental lacquer and gilding.

COMPTON HALL RESTORATION

A133 Riverside Business Centre, Haldane Place, London SW18 4UQ ■ Mon-Fri 9:00-5:00 Lucinda Compton and Karen Haslewood ■ Italian and Spanish spoken ■ prices medium to high ■ Trade discount

Antique and contemporary furniture restoration. Painting, gilding, lacquering, papier maché and tôle.

THE CONSERVATION STUDIO

77 Troutbeck, Albany Street, London NW1 4EJ ■ Tel: (0171) 387-4994 ■ Mon-Fri 9:00-5:00 ■ Florence Hayward ■ French, Spanish and Italian spoken ■ Prices high

Conservation and restoration of ceramics, glass and related objects in marble, malachite, jade, ivory, enamels.

COUTTS GALLERIES

75 Blythe Road, London W14 0HP ■ Telfax: (0171) 602-3980 ■ Mon-Fri 9:00-5:00, Sat by appointment ■ Seabury Coutts and Joan Coutts (Framing) ■ Prices medium ■ Trade discount

Gilders. Fine antique restoration, wood carving, lacquer work and everything to do with good quality furniture, including upholstery, leatherwork. They have a stock of over-mantel mirrors for sale, mostly with original glass and these need restoration. Framing and restoration of oils and watercolours.

COX

Unit 2A, Block 13, Long Street, Shoreditch, London E2 8HJ ■ Tel: (0171) 739-1814 ■ Mon-Fri by appointment

All types of furniture restoration. Staircases, panelling, floors and French polishing. Works for dealers, museums and private clients. References upon request.

CRAWLEY STUDIOS

39 Woodvale, London SE23 3DS ■ Telfax: (0181) 516-0002 ■ Mon-Fri 9:00-6:00 ■ Marie Louise Crawley ■ French spoken

Conservation of painted or gilded furniture, lacquer work and papier maché. Painting for special effects. BAFRA, UKIC, Conservation Register.

A.J. FREEMAN FRENCH POLISHERS

Unit 4B, 39 Autumn Street, London E3 2TT ■ Tel: (0181) 980-4155 ■ Mobile: 0956 369763 ■ Fax: (0181) 301-3497 ■ Mon-Fri 9:00-5:00, Sat 8:00-1:00 by appointment ■ John Freeman

Antique restoration and gilding. Specialists in French polishing, using traditional and modern techniques. Will also upholster furniture. On-site and off-site refurbishment. Clients include The Sultan of Brunei and the Lanesborough Hotel.

HOPE & PIAGET

12-13 Burmarsh Workshops, Marsden Street, London NW5 3JA ■ Telfax: (0171) 267-6040 ■ Mon-Fri 9:30-6:00 ■ Brian A. Duffy ■ French and German spoken ■ Prices high ■ BAFRA

Conservation and restoration of fine quality furniture. Gilding, lacquering, ivory, mother of pearl and bone, japanning and carving. BAFRA.

♔ TITIAN STUDIO

318 Kensal Road, Kensington, London W10 5BN ■ Tel: (0181) 960-6247 ■ Fax: (0181) 969-6126 ■ Mon-Fri 8:00-5:30 ■ Rodrigo and Rosaria Titian ■ Italian, French and German spoken ■ Prices low to high ■ Some trade discounts ■ Visa, MC

Gilding, lacquering, carving, French polishing, painted and decorated furniture. Restoration of marquetry and parquetry. Leather and marble conservation. Caning and rushing. Projects: Queen House Greenwich, Kensington Palace. Work for top West End dealers. BAFRA.

VOLTEK CONSERVATION OF WORKS OF ART

9 Whitehorse Mews, Westminster Bridge Road, London SE1 7QD ■ Telfax: (0171) 928-6094 ■ Mon-Fri 9:00-7:00 ■ Voltek and Elizabeth Sobczynski ■ Polish spoken ■ Prices medium to high

Conservation and restoration of works of art on paper: prints, watercolours. Restoration of sculpture, marble, terra cotta, wood and scagliola.

Restoration Workshops
Outside London

♔ ANTIQUE RESTORATIONS

The Old Wheelwright's Shop, Brasted Forge, Brasted, Kent TN16 1JL ■ Tel: (01959) 563863 ■ Fax: (01959) 561262 ■ By appointment ■ Raymond Konyn

Restoration of antique furniture. Has worked for the Victoria and Albert Museum, Apsley House, Mansion House and Guild Hall.

BOXWOOD ANTIQUE RESTORERS

67 High Street, Wincanton, Somerset BA9 8JZ ■ Tel: (01963) 33988 ■ Fax: (01963) 32555 ■ Alan Stacey

Boulle work, ivory, mother of pearl and bone, marine antiques. Good references.

CZAJKOWSKI AND SON

96 Tor-o-Moor Road, Woodhall Spa, Lincolnshire LN10 6SB ■ Tel: (01526) 352895 ■ Fax: (01526) 352845 ■ Michael Czajkowski

Barographs, barometers, boulle work, clock dials, clock movements, gilding, ivory, mother of pearl and bone, japanning, keyboard instrument cases, lacquer work, musical boxes and their movements, painted furniture.

REGINALD W. DUDMAN

Old Vicarage, Blakemore, Herefordshire HR2 9PY ■ Tel: (01981) 500413

Clock dials, gilding, ivory, mother of pearl and bone, japanning, keyboard instrument cases, marine antiques, organ case and pipework, painted furniture.

JOHN HARTLEY

The Old Forge, Village Street, Sheet, Petersfield, Hampshire GU32 2AQ ■ Tel: (01730) 233792 ■ Fax: (01730) 233922 ■ Mobile: (0850) 331956

Boulle work, gilding, japanning, lacquer work.

MICHAEL HEDGECOE

21 Burrow Hill Green, Chobham, Woking, Surrey GU24 8QS ■ Telfax: (01276) 858206 ■ Mobile: (0831) 493620

Boulle work, ivory, mother of pearl and bone.

RICHARD HIGGINS (CONSERVATION)

The Old School, Longnor, Shrewsbury, Shropshire SY5 7PP ■ Tel: (01743) 718162 ■ Fax: (01743) 718022 ■ Mobile: (0802) 660584 ■ Richard A. Higgins

Barographs, barometers, boulle work, clock dials, clock movements, foundrywork, gilding, ivory, mother of pearl and bone, japanning, keyboard instrument cases, keyboard instrument actions, lacquer work, marble conservation, musical boxes and their movements, ormolu, including chasing and plating, painted furniture.

ANDREW LELLIOT

6 Tetbury Hill, Avening, Tetbury, Gloucestershire GL8 8LT ■ Tel: (01453) 835783 ■ E-mail: alellff@aol.com ■ Mon-Sat 9:00-6:00 ■ Andrew Lelliott ■ Prices medium

Furniture restoration and conservation. Barometers and keyboard instrument cases. Matching mouldings service.

MALVERN STUDIOS

56 Cowleigh Road, Malvern, Worcestershire WR14 1QD ■ Tel: (01684) 574913 ■ Fax: (01684) 569475 ■ Jeffrey Hall

Boulle work, gilding, ivory, mother of pearl and bone.

CHARLES PERRY RESTORATIONS LTD

Praewood Farm, Hemelhempstead Road, St. Albans, Hertfordshire AL3 6AA ■ Tel: (01727) 853487 ■ Fax: (01727) 846668 ■ John B. Carr

Barometers, boulle, work, clock dials, clock movements, gilding, ivory, mother of pearl and bone, japanning, keyboard instrument cases, lacquer work, leather conservation, marble conservation, marine antiques, musical boxes and their movements, ormolu, including chasing and plating, painted furniture, papier maché.

ALUN & ANN SMITH

45 Windmill Road, Brentford, Middlesex TW8 0QQ ■ Tel: (0181) 568-5249 ■ Fax: (0181) 560-4017 Mon-Fri 9:00-5:00 and by appointment ■ French spoken

Restoration and conservation of: Oriental lacquer, japanning, gilding, any painted surface. Work for top London dealers and auction houses. BAFRA.

SOTHEBY'S RESTORATION WORKSHOPS

Summers Place, Billinghurst, West Surrey RH14 9AD ■ Tel: (0141) 383-3626 ■ Fax: (0140) 383-3697 ■ Mon-Fri 9:00-5:00 ■Roddy McViltie ■ Prices low to very high ■ Visa and MC accepted

Restoration of furniture and related objects. First class references.

THE TANKERDALE WORKSHOP

Johnson's Barns, Waterworks Road, Petersfield, Hampshire GU32 2BY ■ Tel: (01730) 233792 ■ Fax: (01730) 233922 ■ E-mail: tankerdale@aol.com ■ Mon-Fri 8:00-5:30 ■ John Hartley and Hugh Routh ■ Prices medium to high

Restoration and conservation of antique furniture and fine joinery. Cabinet work, polishing, marquetry, carving and gilding of furniture and frames. Highest standard of craftsmanship. Most of their work is for The National Trust, English Heritage, museums and international private clients.

♔ Restorers of Antique Furniture

"BRITISH ANTIQUE FURNITURE RESTORERS' ASSOCIATION, BAFRA, was founded in 1979 to safeguard the interests of owners and buyers of antique furniture and the antique trade, as well as safeguarding the reputations of qualified and experienced furniture conservator-restorers. Membership of BAFRA is only open to artist-craftsmen who have been engaged in full-time restoration for a minimum of five years. Candidates for BAFRA Membership are required to provide satisfactory references and are then assessed by an Examiner appointed by the Executive Committee. Candidates are assessed on the levels and diversity of their skills, their knowledge of antique furniture and its history and also their integrity as conservators. Their studio-workshops are assessed and they must satisfy the highest levels of professional standards. A large number of BAFRA Members are listed on the Conservation Register of the Museums and Galleries Commission together with their many and diverse specialties."

DAVID BATTLE
PHOENIX ANTIQUE FURNITURE RESTORATION LTD
96 Webber Street, London SE1 0QN ■ Tel: (0171) 928-3624 ■ By appointment

Specialists in restoring 17th to 19th century English and Continental furniture and clock cases. Restoration and conservation: polishing, woodturning, veneer and marquetry. BAFRA

ANTIQUE RESTORATIONS
Brasted Forge, Brasted, Westerham, Kent TN16 1JL ■ Telfax: (01959) 563-3863 ■ E-mail: ar@gemint.com.uk ■ Mon-Fri 9:30-4:30 ■ Raymon Konyn ■ Dutch spoken ■ Prices high

Restoration of antique furniture. Also long case clock restoration.

ANTIQUES & PIANO RESTORATION
90 Lots Road, London SW10 ■ Tel: (0171) 352-9876 ■ By appointment

Restoration of antiques, specialists in piano restoration.

BALLANTYNE BOOTH LTD

Cadogan House, Hythe Road, London NW10 6RS ■ Tel: (0181) 960 3255 ■ Fax: (0181) 960-4567 ■ Mon-Fri 9:00-6:00 ■ Helen Mark ■ Prices medium ■ Possible credit card facility ■ Member of UKIC/Conservation register

All aspects of antique and furniture restoration. Cabinet making, polishing.

BARNET-ON-WHEELS & RESTORATION SERVICES

The Old Marble Works, Glenhaven Avenue, Borehamwood, Herts. WD6 1BB ■ Tel: (0181) 207-6792 ■ Fax: (0171) 376- 2817 ■ Mon-Fri 8:00-5:00 ■ Richard J. Gerry ■ A little German spoken ■ Prices medium ■ Major credit cards

Quality antique furniture restoration. All periods, all services.

LAWRENCE BRASS

154 Sutherland Avenue, Maida Vale, London W9 ■ Tel: (0122) 585-2222 ■ By appointment

Restoration and conservation of antiques, gilding and upholstery. Approved by the Museum and Galleries Commission.

AUBREY BROCKLEHURST

124 Cromwell Road, South Kensington, London SW7 4ET ■ Tel: (0171) 373-0319 ■ Fax: (0171) 373-7612 ■ Mon-Fri 9:00-1:00, 2:00-5:30, Sat 10:00-1:00 ■ Aubrey Brocklehurst ■ French and some German spoken ■ Major credit cards ■ Professional discount ■ BADA

Antique clocks and barometers. Repairs of clocks and barometers. Furniture restoration.

WILLIAM COOK

167 Battersea High Street, London SW11 3JS ■ Tel: (0171) 736-5329 ■ By appointment ■ BAFRA

Museum quality furniture restoration of 18th century furniture and period English furniture.

CHRISTOPHER COOKE

Taybridge House, 3 Taybridge Road, London SW11 5PR ■ Tel: (0171) 350-0504 ■ Fax: (0171) 978-5461 ■ E-mail: cooke@mcmail.com ■ Mon-Fri 10:00-5:00 ■ Prices high

This restoration and conservation workshop specializes in antique Chinese and other Asian furniture. Twenty-five years of experience and the important projects on which he has worked make him one of the finest of the craftsmen. Projects include royal palaces, museums and work for private individuals. There is also a sales gallery.

W.R. HARVEY & CO
70 Chalk Farm Road, London NW1 ■ Tel: (01993) 706501 ■ Fax: (01993) 706601 ■ By appointment only ■ BADA

Restoration and conservation of antique furniture. Traditional cabinet making, marquetry, caning, French polishing, desk leathering, upholstering. BADA. The Guild of Master Craftsmen.

HERITAGE RESTORATIONS
96 Webber Street, Waterloo, London SE1 OQN ■ Tel: (0171) 476-2017 ■ (0171) 928 3624 ■ By appointment

Restoration and conservation of English and Continental furniture. Cabinet makers and French polishers. Free estimates. Collection and delivery.

MICHAEL MARRIOTT
588 Fulham Road, London SW6 5NT ■ Tel: (0171) 736-3110 ■ Mon-Fri 10:00-6:00, Sat 10:00-1:00 ■ Prices medium ■ Major credit cards

Restoration of furniture and traditional upholstery. Also sells English furniture and antique prints.

MICHAEL PARFETT
Unit 407, Clerkenwell Workshops, 31 Clerkenwell Close, London EC1R OAT ■ Tel: (0171) 490-8768 ■ Fax: (0171) 490-0063 ■ Mon-Fri 9:30-6:00, Sat 10:00-2:00 Michael Parfett L.C.G ■ Prices medium to high

Repair, restoration and conservation of antique furniture and antique musical instruments: harps, pianos and harpsichords. Gilding and conservation of mirrors and frames. Piano tuning. Works for museums and galleries. References upon request.

MIMI SANSONE
24A Bartholomew Villas, London NW5 2LL ■ Tel: (0171) 424-0298 ■ E-mail: mimisansone@yahoo.com ■ Mon-Fri 9:00-5:00 Mimi Sansone ■ Italian and French spoken ■ Prices medium

Furniture restoration using traditional methods and materials. Works all over the world. Excellent references.

CLIFFORD J. TRACY
6-40 Durnford Street, off Seven Sisters Road, London N15 5NQ ■ Tel: (0181) 800-4773 ■ Fax: (0181) 800-4351 ■ Mon-Fri 7:00-4:00 ■ Prices medium to very high ■ BAFRA

Antique furniture restoration, leather-top desks, polishing and high quality cabinet making. Restoration and polishing of fine antique furniture. BAFRA.

MICHAEL BARRINGTON

The Old Rectory, Warmwell, Dorchester, Dorset DT2 8HQ ■ Telfax: (01395) 852-604 ■ Mon-Sat 9:00-6:00 ■ Michael Barrington ■ German spoken ■ Prices medium ■ BAFRA and Conservation Register

Antique furniture restoration including clocks, barometers, music boxes and upholstered furniture.

Restorers of Art

GRAHAM BIGNELL PAPER CONSERVATION & RESTORATION

Standpoint Studios, 45 Coronet Street, Shoreditch, London N1 6HD ■ Telfax: (0171) 729-8161 ■ Mon-Fri 9:00-6:00 ■ Graham Bignell ■ Prices medium

Paper conservation and print restoration. Restoration of posters.

SEBASTIAN D'ORSAI (A.B.) LTD

8 Kensington Mall, London W8 4EA ■ Tel: (0171) 229-3888 ■ Fax: (0171) 221-0746 ■ Mon-Sat 10:00-5:00 ■ G.W. Taylor ■ Prices low to high ■ Major credit cards ■ Trade discount

Restoration of oils, watercolours, prints, engravings, Also frame restoration.

SIMON R. GILLESPIE STUDIO

16 Albemarle Street, London W1X 3HA ■ Tel: (0171) 493-0988 ■ Fax: (0171) 493-0955 ■ E-mail: simon.r.gillespic@binternet.com ■ By appointment

Conservation of early English, Old Master paintings and portraits. Restoration of oil paintings on panel or canvas, as well as some works on paper. References include museums and major galleries, English Heritage and the Palace of Westminster.

HAHN & SON LTD

47 Albemarle Street, London W1X 3FE ■ Tel: (0171) 493-9196 ■ Fax: (0171) 495-4497 ■ Mon-Fri 9:45-5:30 ■ Paul Hahn ■ Prices high ■ Trade discount

Restoration of paintings, especially English 18th and 19th century paintings.

P. KONECNZY

11 Stanley Gardens, London W11 2N ■ Tel: (0171) 229-7529 ■ Fax: (0171) 313-9674 ■ By appointment

Restoration of Old and Modern Masters. Oil paintings principally. Works for museums and major art galleries.

LEES FINE ART RESTORERS

11 Wellington Close, Ledbury Road, London W11 2AN ■ Telfax: (0171) 229-3521 ■ Mon-Sat 10:00-6:00 ■ Adrian Lees ■ Spanish, French Italian and Portuguese spoken ■ Prices low to very high

Conservation and restoration of paintings and gilt frames.

MARGUERITE MARR

403 Elm Tree Court, St. John's Wood, London NW8 9JJ ■ Tel: (0171) 289-0877 ■ Mon-Fri 9:30-5:00

Cleaning and restoration of oil paintings. From Old Masters to 20th century art.

CLAUDIO MOSCATELLI OIL PAINTING

46 Cambridge Street, London SW1V 4QH ■ Tel: (0171) 828-1304 ■ By appointment

Oil paintings cleaned, relined, retouched and varnished.

THOMAS M. SCHNEIDER

9 Old Bond Street, London W1X 3TA ■ Tel: (0171) 629-2985 ■ Fax: (0171) 499-8935 ■ Mon-Fri 9:00-5:00 ■ By appointment ■ German and Italian spoken

Restoration of antique paintings.

Restorers of Carpets and Tapestries

HAROUT BARIN
57A New King's Road, London SW6 4SE ■ Tel: (0171) 731-0546 ■ Fax: (0171) 384-1620 ■ Mon-Sat 9:00-6:00 ■ Harout Barin ■ Prices low to medium

Specialist in the repair and cleaning of fine carpets, tapestries, Aubussons. Also appraisals and counsel.

ALEXANDER JURAN & CO
74 New Bond Street, London W1Y 9DD ■ Tel: (0171) 629-2550 ■ Telfax: (0171) 493-4484 ■ Mon-Fri 9:30-5:00 ■ Alexander Juran ■ German, French, Russian and other languages spoken ■ Prices medium to very high ■ Professional discount ■ BADA

Antique Oriental rugs and textiles from the 18th century. Specially fine old Caucasian, Persian and Turkish. Repairs done in their own workshop.

KENSINGTON CARPETS
Oriental Carpet Centre, 105 Eade Road, London N4 1TJ ■ Tel: (0181) 800-4455 ■ Fax: (0181) 800-4466 ■ Mon-Fri 9:30-6:00 ■ Vivien Eder ■ Prices low to very high ■ Major credit cards ■ Trade discount

Made-to-order hand-made rugs. Carpet and tapestry restoration and cleaning.

THE ORIENTALIST
152 Walton Street, London SW3 2JJ ■ Tel: (0171) 581-2332 ■ Fax: (0171) 589-0760 ■ Mon-Sat 10:25-5:15 ■ Persian and French spoken ■ Prices medium to very high ■ Major credit cards ■ Trade discount

Repairing and cleaning of Oriental rugs, Aubussons and tapestries.

PILGRIM PAYNE & CO LTD
290-294 Latimer Road, London W10 6QU ■ Tel: (0181) 960-5656 ■ Mon-Fri 9:00-5:00 ■ Prices medium to high

Experts, since 1850, in the restoration and cleaning of fine carpets, rugs and tapestries.

THE RESTORATION STUDIO
Unit 11 Kolbe House, 63 Jeddo Road, London W12 9EE ■ Telfax: (0181) 740-4977 ■ Mon-Fri 8:30-4:00 ■ Ela Sosnowska ■ Prices medium ■ Trade discounts

Restoration, cleaning, lining and mounting of tapestries. Aubusson carpets, kilims, embroidery and other kinds of needlework. Top references.

THAMES CARPET CLEANERS LTD
48-56 Reading Road, Henley-On-Thames RG9 1AG ■ Tel: (01491) 574576 ■ Fax: (01491) 577877 ■ C. Aigin, D. Bernardout ■ French spoken ■ Prices medium ■ Major credit cards ■ Trade discount

Cleaning and restoration of Oriental carpets, wall-to-wall carpeting. Standard carpet cleaning service.

Restorers & Repairers of Clocks

ACB CLOCK RESTORERS
Metropolitan College of Craftsmen
Enfield Road, London N1 ■ Tel: (0171) 254-8919 ■ Mon-Fri 9:00-5:00 ■ Prices medium

Restoration and repair of fine clocks.

ALLEN & WAINWRIGHT
33A Burn Ash Hill, Lee, London SE12 ■ Tel: (0181) 831-3749 ■ Mon-Fri 9:00-5:00

Restoration and repair of antique clocks and music boxes. Long case clocks a specialty.

AUBREY BROCKLEHURST
124 Cromwell Road, London SW7 4ET ■ Tel: (0171) 373-0319 ■ Fax: (0171) 373-7612 ■ Mon-Fri 9:00-1:00, 2:00-5:30, Sat 10:00-1:00 ■ Aubrey Brocklehurst ■ French and German spoken ■ Prices medium ■ Major credit cards ■ Tade discount

Fellow of the British Horological Institute. Repairs and restorations of fine antique clocks, both French and English. Grandfather, carriage and bracket clocks.

THE CLOCK CLINIC LTD.

85 Lower Richmond Road, Putney, London SW15 1EU ■ Tel: (0181) 788-1407 ■ Fax: (0181) 780-2838 ■ Tue-Fri 9:00-6:00, Sat 9:00-1:00 ■ Robert S. Pedler ■ Prices medium ■ Major credit cards ■ LAPADA

Repair and restoration of antique barometers and clocks.

EOS CLOCKS

Stall 4, Portwine Galleries, 175 Portobello Road, London W11 ■ Tel: (0171) 856-0817 ■ Sat 8:00-4:30 ■ German spoken ■ Prices low to medium ■ Trade discount

Clocks and barometers repaired.

GUTLIN CLOCKS

616 King's Road, London SW6 2DU ■ Telfax: (0171) 384-2439 ■ Mon-Fri 9:30-5:00 ■ Prices medium ■ Trade discount

All types of antique clocks and barometers repaired and restored.

E. HOLLANDER

1 Bennetts Castle, 89 The Street, Capel, Dorking, Surrey, RH5 5JX ■ Tel: (01306) 713377 ■ Fax: (01306) 712013 ■ Mon-Fri 8:00-4:30, Sat 8:30-12:00 ■ David Pay ■ French spoken ■ Prices medium ■ Occasional professional discounts ■ B.H.I., BADA

Restoration and repair of clocks of all descriptions and ages: movements, cases and dials; and all forms of barometers. Member of the Worshipful Company of Clockmakers.

JILLINGS

17 Croft House, Church Street, Newent, Gloucestershire GL181YN ■ Tel.: (01531) 822100 ■ Fax: (01531) 822666 ■ Mon-Fri 9:00-6:00 ■ Prices medium ■ Trade discount

Antique clocks and barometers restored and sold.

WILLIAM MANSELL

24 Connaught Street, Marble Arch, London W2 2AF ■ Tel: (0171) 723-4154 ■ Fax: (0171) 724-2273 ■ Mon-Fri 9:00-6:00, Sat 10:30-12:00 ■ William Salisbury ■ Prices medium ■ Major credit cards

Repair and sale of fine antique clocks, chronographs, grandfathers, barometers.

NEWCOMBE & SON

89 Maple Road, London SE20 8UL ■ Telfax: (0171) 778-0816 ■ Mike Newcombe ■ Prices medium ■ Trade discount

Specialist in the making, repair and restoration of long case, bracket and wall clocks. Barometers repaired. Silvering and gilding. Clock faces, including enamel restored and repainted. Member of the Registry of Museums and Galleries Commission.

JOHN WALKER

64 South Molton Street, London W1Y 1HH ■ Tel: (0171) 629-3487 ■ Mon-Fri 9:00-5:00 ■ Prices medium

Specialists in the repair of antique clocks. Member of The Guild of Master Craftsmen.

PETER K. WEISS

18 London Silver Vaults, London WC2A 1QS ■ Tel: (0171) 242-8100 ■ Mon-Fri 9:00-5:00, Sat 9:00-12:30 ■ Prices medium ■ Trade discount

Antique clock and watch repair.

Restorers of Enamels

ISTVAN MARKOVITS – ENAMELLER

11 Mallard Place, Strawberry Vale, Twickenham, Middlesex TW1 3SW ■ Tel: (0181) 891-1743 ■ Mobile: 0421 622791

Badgemakers. Restorers of enamel jewellery. Restorers of clock faces and ceramics.

KEMPSON & MAUGER LTD

Unit 26, 63 Clerkenwell Road, London EC1M 5NP ■ Tel: (0171) 251-0578 ■ Fax: (0171) 251-5678 ■ Mon-Fri 8:15-5:00 ■ Graham Hamilton ■ Prices medium to high ■ Trade discout

Enamelling of objets d'art and jewellery. Restoration of antique enamelled watches. Engraving and painting. Member of The Goldsmiths Company.

Restorers of Glass

NOSTALGIC GLASS
Unit 2, Union Road, Union Court, Clapham, London SW4 6JH ■
Telfax: (0171) 720-5876 ■ Mon-Fri 9:00-6:00 ■ Mehmet Kuzu ■ German and Turkish spoken ■ Prices medium ■ Trade discount

Specialists in antique glass replacements. Engraving, cutting, restoration. Any glass item can be made in any size, shape, colour or design. Parts for chandeliers, wall lights, candelabra, liners, decanters, mirrors, shades. Work references: Buckingham Palace, Asprey, Mallet, Garrard and Harrods.

CHRISTINE BRIDGE ANTIQUES
78 Castelnau Barnes, London SW13 9EX ■ Telfax: (0181) 741-5501
■ Mobile: 0831 126668 ■ By appointment ■ Christine Bridge and
Darryl Bowles ■ Prices medium to high ■ Major credit cards ■ Trade
discount ■ LAPADA

Glass restoration service and glass de-clouding, chips reduced, enamels repaired and silver re-plating. They sell 18th century collectors' glass, 19th century coloured glass samplers and small antiques and needlework.

Restorers of Icons

RICHARDSON & KAILAS
65 Rivermead Court, Ranelagh Gardens, London SW6 8RY ■ Tel:
(0171) 371-0491 ■ By appointment ■ Chris Richardson ■ Visa and
MC accepted ■ BADA

Restoration of icons, valuations.

MARIA ANDIPA & SON ICON GALLERY
162 Walton Street, Knightsbridge, London SW3 2JL ■ Tel: (0171)
589-2371 ■ Fax: (0171) 225-0305 ■ E-mail: art@andipa.com ■ Tue-
Sat 11:00-6:00 ■ Maria and Acoris Andipa ■ Greek, French and Arabic spoken ■ Prices low to very high ■ Major credit cards ■ Trade
discount ■ LAPADA

Icons, 18th and 19th century furniture, glass, jewellery and works of art. Restoration, research and valuations.

Restorers of Leather

CLIFFORD J. TRACY
6-40 Durnford Street, off Seven Sisters Road, London N15 5NQ ■ Tel: (0181) 800-4773 ■ Fax: (0181) 800-4351 ■ Mon-Fri 7:00-4:00 ■ Clifford Tracy ■ Prices medium to very high

Restoration of leather top desks. Restoration of antique furniture. BAFRA.

STOKER
53-55 Lisson Grove, London NW1 6UH ■ Tel: (0171) 258-0778 ■ Mon-Fri 8:00-5:00, Sat 8:00-1:00

French polishing for the antique trade. Leather polishing of any leather, especially upholstery. Restoration and revival of leather desk tops.

TITIAN STUDIO
318 Kensal Road, Kensington, London W10 5BN ■ Tel: (0181) 960-6247 ■ Fax: (0181) 969-6126 ■ Mon-Fri 8:00-5:30 ■ Rodrigo and Rosaria Titian ■ Italian, French and German spoken ■ Prices low to high ■ Some trade discounts ■ Visa, MC

Gilding, lacquering, carving, French polishing, painted and decorated furniture. Restoration of marquetry and parquetry. Leather and marble conservation. Caning and rushing. Projects: Queen House Greenwich, Kensington Palace. Work for top West End dealers. BAFRA.

Restorers of Metal

MICHAEL BROOK
192 Camberwell Grove, London SE5 8RJ■ Telfax: (0171) 708-0467 ■ Mon-Fri 9:00-6:00 and by appointment ■ Prices medium

Specialist in 17th, 18th and 19th century English and French ormolu and bronze. All repairs, cleaning, casting, chasing and gilding of mounts. Patination, bronzing and metal finishes. Metal gilding. Will work on site. Collection and delivery service.

DANICO BRASS LIMITED

31 Winchester Road, Swiss Cottage, London NW3 3NR ■ Tel: (0171) 483-4477 ■ Fax: (0171) 722-7992 ■ E-mail: Danico@compuserve.com ■ Mon-Fri 9:30-6:00, Thu until 8:00 ■ Ashok Dani ■ French and German spoken ■ Prices medium to very high ■ Visa, MC accepted ■ Trade discount

Refurbishing and repolishing of brass bathroom fittings and door hardware. Plating in gold, chrome and other finishes.

DAVID TURNER ANTIQUES RESTORATION

24 Tottenham Road, London N1 4BZ Tel: (0171) 241-5488 ■ Fax: (0171) 349-2379 ■ Mon-Fri 9:30-6:00 ■ David Turner ■ French and Italian spoken ■ Prices medium

Restoration of antique metalwork, mostly brass and bronze, some wrought iron. They also have a few antique reproductions of small lamps.

♕ VERDIGRIS

Arch 290, Crown Street, London SE5 0UR ■ Tel: (0171) 703-8373 ■ Fax: (0171) 703-9120 ■ Mon-Thu 9:00-5:00, Fri 9:00-100 ■ Mr. Gerard Bacon ■ Spanish spoken

Antique metalwork restorers. Restoration and regilding of metal items including patination, etching, polishing. Architectural interior and exterior metal etched walls and partitions. Specialist short runs in pewter, brass, copper and "one offs". Restored and gilded the Speaker's Staircase at the Palace of Westminster. Many excellent references.

Restorer of Musical Instruments

MICHAEL PARFETT

Unit 407, Clerkenwell Workshops, 31 Clerkenwell Close, London EC1R 0AT ■ Tel: (0171) 490-8768 ■ Fax: (0171) 490-0063■ Mon-Fri 9:30-6:00, Sat 10:00-2:00 ■ Michael Parfett L.C.G ■ Prices medium to high

Repair, restoration and conservation of antique furniture and antique musical instruments: harps, pianos and harpsichords. Piano tuning. Gilding and conservation of mirrors and frames. Piano tuning. Works for museums and galleries. References upon request.

Restorers of Porcelain, Ceramics and Pottery

CHINA REPAIRERS
64 Charles Lane, London NW8 7SB ■ Tel: (0171) 722-8407 ■ Mon-Thu 10:00-1:00/2:15-5:00, Fri 10:00-12:30 ■ Virginia Baron ■ French spoken ■ Prices medium to high ■ Professional discount

All sorts of ceramic restoration: porcelain and pottery, antique and modern. Invisible repairs and museum repairs. Glass grinding. Gives restoration courses. Clients include professionals and the general public.

FINE CHINA RESTORATION
15 Heathfield Gardens, Chiswick, London W4 4JU ■ Tel: (0181) 994-8990 ■ Fax: (0181) 994-9406 ■ Mon-Sun 9:30-6:00 ■ Madonna Elliott ■ Prices medium

Specialists in repair of fine china and glassware. Invisible restorations.

LION WITCH & LAMPSHADE
C/O Muriel Michalos Ltd, 57 Elizabeth Street, London SW1W 9PP ■ Tel: (0171) 730-1774 ■ By appointment ■ Nick and Nicky Dixon ■ German spoken ■ Prices medium to high ■ Professional discount ■ MC, Visa

Expert restorers of china and glassware. Classes given.

ROSEMARY HAMILTON CHINA REPAIRS
44 Moreton Street, London SW1V 2PB ■ Tel: (0171) 828-5018 ■ Fax: (0171) 828-1325 ■ Mon-Fri 9:30-5:30 ■ Rosemary Hamilton ■ French spoken ■ Prices medium ■ Visa and MC accepted ■ Trade discount

Restoration of fine china. Not large items and not every-day things.

ARTIST AND ARTISAN SUPPLIES

ATLANTIS EUROPEAN LTD
146 Brick Lane, London E1 6RU ■ Tel: (0171) 377-8855 ■ Fax: (0171) 377-8850 ■ Mon-Sat 9:00-6:00, Sun 10:00-5:00 ■ Mark and Genie Winthrop ■ French, Italian and Spanish spoken ■ Prices low ■ All major credit cards

Artists painting materials, gilding, papers, brushes, paints. Archival and conservation projects. Mail order service available.

BIRD & DAVIS LTD
45 Holmes Road, Kentish Town, London NW5 3AN ■ Tel: (0171) 485-3797 ■ Fax: (0171) 284-0509 Mon-Fri 8:00-5:30, Sat 8:00-11:00 ■ Roberto Orsi ■ Greek and Italian spoken ■ Prices low to medium ■ Major credit cards ■ 10% discount to students

Canvases, easels, stretcher frames, paints and brushes.

CASS ARTS & CRAFTS
13 Charing Cross Road, London WC2H ■ Tel: (0171) 930-9940 ■ Fax: (0171) 930-1982 ■ Mon-Sat (9:45-6:15) ■ Simon Pownall ■ Student discount ■ Major credit cards

Fine art materials and frames. Some graphic supplies.

CANONBURY ART SHOP
266 Upper Street, Islington, London N1 2UQ ■ Tel: (0171) 226-4652 ■ Fax: (0171) 704-1781 ■ Mon-Sat 9:30-6:00 ■ Maggie Hall ■ French spoken ■ Prices medium ■ Discount for quantity ■ Major credit cards

Art materials, paints, pads and over 700 different papers. Lascaux, Turner paints and acrylics and gouaches.

L. CORNELISSEN & SON LTD
105 Great Russell Street, London WC1B 3RY ■ Tel: (0171) 636-1045 ■ Mon-Sat 9:30-5:00 ■ Prices medium ■ Trade discount ■ Major credit cards

Materials and equipment for painters, gilders, pastellists, printmakers, specialist decorators, canvas stretching and easel hire. Worldwide mail order service available.

COWLING & WILCOX LTD

26-28 Broadwick Street, London W1V ■ Tel: (0171) 734-9557 ■ Fax: (0171) 434-4513 ■ Mon-Fri 9:00-6:00, Sat 10:00-5:00 ■ J. Millen, Jane Goodwin ■ Prices low to high ■ 10% discount available to full-time students ■ Major credit and debit cards

Portfolios and display books. Fine art, craft and graphic artists materials. Local delivery and mail order available.

DALER-ROWNEY LTD

12 Percy Street, London W1A 2BP ■ Tel: (0171) 636-8241 ■ Fax: (0171) 580-7534 ■ Mon-Fri 9:00-5:30, Sat 10:00-5:00 ■ Prices medium ■ Student and trade discount

Everything for the artist. Daler-Rowney's own products as well as Windsor and Newton and Liquitex acrylics. Mail order and framing services available.

FALKINER FINE PAPERS

76 Southampton Row, London WC1B 4AR ■ Tel: (0171) 831-1151 ■ Fax: (0171) 430-1248 ■ Mon-Sat 9:30-5:30 ■ Gabrielle Falkiner ■ Dutch, French and German spoken ■ Prices medium ■ Visa and MC ■ Quantity discounts

Paper for all artists, designers, craftsmen and photographers. European hand-made papers. Also books and some bookbinding. Member of The Guild of Master Craftsmen.

4D MODELSHOP

151 City Road, London EC1V 1JH ■ Tel: (0171) 253-1996 ■ Fax: (0171) 253-1998 ■ Mon-Sat 9:30-6:00 ■ E-mail: info@modelshop.demon.co.uk ■ Spanish spoken ■ Visa, MC

Creative materials and model making. Design accessories for all 3D projects. Raw materials, wood, plastic, metal. Acid etching, white metal casting and dry transfers.

GREEN & STONE OF CHELSEA LTD

259 King's Road, Chelsea, London SW3 5EL ■ Tel: (0171) 352-0837 ■ Fax: (0171) 351-1098 ■ Mon-Fri 9:00-6:00, Wed 9:00-7:00, Sat 9:30-6:00, Sun 12:00-5:00 ■ Rodney Baldwin ■ Professional discount negotiable ■ Major credit cards

Framing and canvas stretching to order. Art and craft materials including stretchers, canvases, easels, pigments, gifts, cards and antiques.

A.S. HANDOVER LTD

37H Mildmay Grove, London N1 4RH ■ Tel: (0171) 359-4696 ■ Fax: (0171) 354-3658 ■ Mon-Fri 8:30-5:00 ■ Michael Venus ■ French and Spanish spoken ■ Prices low to high ■ Major credit cards ■ Trade discounts

Artists brushes made to order. Glazes, sign-writing paints, gold leaf and gilding materials. All artists materials. Next day mail-order service.

INTAGLIO PRINTMAKER

62 Southwark Bridge Road, London SE1 OAS ■ Tel: (0171) 928-2633 ■ Fax: (0171) 928-2711 ■ Mon-Fri 10:00-6:00, Sat 11:00-4:00 ■ Karyn White, Jill Watton, Christine Munton ■ Prices low to medium ■ Visa, MC, Switch

Materials for printmakers a specialty. Materials for etching, lithography, technical advice. Wide selection of presses and studio rollers. Mail order.

THE JOHN JONES ART CENTRE

4 Morris Place, Stroud Green Road, Finsbury Park, London N4 3JG ■ Tel: (0171) 281-5439 ■ Fax: (0171) 281-5956 ■ Mon-Fri 8:00-6:00, Sat-Sun 10:00-5:00 ■ John Jones ■ Spanish spoken ■ Prices medium ■ Visa, MC accepted ■ Some member discounts

Artists materials and stretchers. They claim to be the biggest art materials shop in the U.K.

SEAN KELLY GALLERY

21 London Road, London SE1 6JX ■ Tel: (0171) 928-9722 ■ Fax: (0171) 793-1306 ■ Mon-Sat 9:00-5:30 ■ Carol Greengrass ■ Prices medium ■ MC, Euro and Visa ■ Trade discount

Art materials, gilding and specialty finishes, boards, papers and frames.

T. N. LAWRENCE & SON LTD

117-119 Clerkenwell Road, London EC1R 5BY ■ Tel: (0171) 242-3534 ■ Fax: (0171) 405-4225 ■ E-mail: artbox@lawrence.co.uk ■ Mon-Sat 9:00-5:00 ■ Philip Coombs ■ Prices low to medium ■ Major credit cards

Painting and printmaking supplies including a wide range of papers. Golden acrylics, graining tools. Mail order and catalogue service available.

LONDON GRAPHIC CENTRE

16-18 Shelton Street, Covent Garden, London WC2H 9JJ ■ Tel: (0171) 240-0095
13 Tottenham Street, LondonW1P 3PB ■ Tel: (0171) 637-2199
254 Upper Richmond Road, Putney, London SW15 6TQ ■ Tel: (0171) 785-9797

Graphic art supplies. Mail order and delivery service available.

THE PAINT LIBRARY

5 Elyston Street, London SW3 3NT ■ Tel: (0171) 823-7755 ■ Fax: (0171) 823-7766 ■ Mon-Fri 9:00-5:30 ■ David Oliver, Georgina Lewis ■ Spanish spoken ■ Prices medium ■ Visa and MC accepted

Quality paint without vinyl, unique colours, contemporary wallpapers, paints and papers.

PAINT MAGIC

5 Elgin Crescent, London W11 2JA ■ Tel: (0171) 792-8012 ■ Fax: (0171) 727-0207 ■ Mon-Sat 10:00-6:00 ■ Mark Weston ■ Prices low to medium ■ All major credit cards ■ Trade discounts

Specialized paint finishes, sample boards, stencil cutting, painting, interior and exterior. They hold workshop sessions on everything from painting mosaics to oil gilding.

PAINTWORKS LTD

99-101 Kingsland Road, London E2 8AG ■ Tel: (0171) 729-7451 ■ Fax: (0171) 739-0439 ■ Mon-Sat 9:30-5:30, Fri until 7:00 ■ Dorothy Wood ■ Prices low ■ Visa, MC ■ Quantity discounts

Artist materials and picture frames. Paints, papers, canvas, craft materials.

PAPERS AND PAINTS LTD

4 Park Walk, London SW10 0AD ■ Tel: (0171) 352-8626 ■ Fax: (0171) 352-1017 ■ E-mail: sales@papers-paints.co.uk ■ Mon-Fri 8:00-5:30 ■ Patrick Baty ■ French, Spanish and Swedish spoken ■ Prices high ■ Visa and MC ■ Trade discount

Paint, colour matching, architectural use of colour in the 18th century, paint brushes, tools, accessories and books.

PLOTON (SUNDRIES) LTD

273 Archway Road, London N6 5AA ■ Tel: (0181) 348-0315 ■ Fax: (0171) 348-3141 ■ E-mail: ploton@ploton.co.uk ■ Mon-Sat 10:00-3:45 ■ Spanish spoken ■ Major credit cards ■ Trade discount

Supplier of gold and silver leaf. Specialist in decorative brushes and paints from Italy, France, Germany. Canvases made to measure. Gilding equipment.

THE PRINT GALLERY

22 Pembridge Road, London W11 3HL ■ Tel: (0171) 221-8885 ■ Fax: (0171) 221-2449 ■ Mon-Fri 9:00-6:00, Sat 10:00-7:00 ■ Mr. Khan ■ Many languages spoken ■ Prices medium ■ All major credit cards ■ Trade discounts

A comprehensive range of art, craft, graphic and restoration supplies.

REEVES

128 Kensington High Street, London W8 7NX ■ Tel: (0171) 937-5370 ■ Mon-Fri 9:00-5:30, Sat 9:30-5:30, Sun 12:00-5:00 ■ Major credit cards

Full range of artists supplies, Windsor and Newton paints, and a craft centre.

RUSSELL & CHAPPLE LTD

23 Monmouth Street, London WC2H 9DE ■ Tel: (0171) 836-7521 ■ Fax: (0171) 497-0554 ■ Mon-Fri 8:30-5:00, Sat 10:00-5:00 ■ R.W. Boyd ■ Prices low to high ■ Most major credit cards

Full range of artists materials. Hessians, muslins, dyed cotton canvas. Stretched canvases to order.

D & J SIMONS AND SONS LTD

122-150 Hackney Road, London E2 7QS ■ Tel: (0171) 739-3744 ■ Fax: (0171) 739-4452 ■ Mon-Thu 8:30-5:30, Fri 8:30-4:45, Sat 8:30-11:45 ■ Stephen Simons, Howard Simons, Brian Simons ■ Prices low

Manufacturers and distributors of fine art supllies. Picture frame mouldings, artists materials.

STUART R. STEVENSON

68 Clerkenwell Road, London EC1M 5QA ■ Tel: (0171) 253-1693 ■ Fax: (0171) 490-0451 ■ Mon-Fri 9:00-5:30 ■ Stuart Stevenson ■ Prices medium ■ Visa and MC

Artist and gilding materials, gold leaf, metal leaf, powder and paillons.

ALEC TIRANTI LTD

27 Warren Street, London W1P 5DG ■ Telfax: (0171) 636-8565 ■ E-mail: sales@tiranti.co.uk ■ Mon-Fri 9:00-5:30 ■ Sat 9:30-1:00 ■ Prices low ■ Visa and MC

Sculptors tools, materials and studio equipment. Everything for modelling, carving, casting. Clays, plasters, resins, tin alloys, gold leaf. Carving stands. Catalogue available.

Needlecraft Retailers

THE W.H.I. TAPESTRY SHOP LTD

85 Pimlico Road at Lower Sloane Street, London SW1W 8PH ■ Tel: (0171) 730-5366 ■ Mon-Fri 9:30-5:00 ■ Mrs. Frances Salter ■ Prices medium ■ Visa or MC accepted

Needlepoint designs, hand-painted canvases, large stock of Appleton wools, canvas. Can create any design to order. Books. Blocking and finishing of any needlepoint.

SEW-KNIT LTD

40 Nunhead Green, London SE15 3QF ■ Tel: (0171) 639-6130 ■ Mon-Sat 9:00-5:30 ■ Patrick Edward Maloney ■ French spoken ■ Prices low

Haberdashery, knitting wool, needlecraft, curtain material and accessories.

AUCTION HOUSES

ACADEMY AUCTIONEERS & VALUERS
Northcote House, Northcote Avenue, London W5 3UR ■ Tel: (0181) 579-7466 ■ Fax: (0181) 519-0511 ■ Mon-Fri 9:00-5:00 ■ Polish spoken ■ Most credit cards

Auctions of antiques, fine art and collectibles, valuations for sale, probate, insurance, family division.

BLOOMSBURY BOOK AUCTIONS
3&4 Hardwick Street, London EC1R 4RY ■ Tel: (0171) 833-2636 ■ Fax: (0171) 833-3954 ■ Mon-Fri 9:30-5:30 ■ Rupert Powell ■ French and German spoken ■ Prices low to high

Printed books, manuscripts, prints, photographs, maps, drawings, atlases, ephemera. Valuations for auctions, insurance, probate.

BONHAMS
Montpelier Street, London SW7 1HH ■ Tel: (0171) 393-3900 ■ Fax: (0171) 393-3905 ■ E-mail: info@bonhams.com ■ Mon-Fri 9:00-4:30, Sun 11:00-4:00 ■ Visa, Amex, MC

Fine art auctions, furniture, paintings, silver, ceramics, jewellery, musical instruments, antique clocks, antiquities. A huge range. Free auction valuations. Probate and insurance valuations.

CHRISTIE'S
8 King Street, St. James's, London SW1Y 6QT ■ Tel: (0171) 839-9060 ■ Fax: (0171) 839-1611 ■ Mon-Fri 9:00-5:00
85 Old Brompton Road, London SW7 3LD ■ Tel: (0171) 581-7611 ■ Fax: (0171) 321-3321 ■ Mon-Fri 9:00-5:00

One of the world's big hitters in the auction field. Always in the news. Major sales of everything in the fine art, antiques or collectibles fields.

CHRISTIE'S IMAGES
1 Langley Lane, London SW8 ■ Tel: (0171) 582-1282 ■ Fax: (0171) 582-5632 ■ Mon-Fri 9:00-5:00

Old sales catalogues including interior design sales. Sales of items by individual designers such as dresses.

CRITERION AUCTIONEERS

53-55 Essex Road, Islington London N1 2BN ■ Tel: (0171) 359-5707 ■ Fax: (0171) 354-9843 ■ E-mail: www.criterion.auctioneers.co.uk ■ Mon 10:00-6:00, Fri 4:00-8:00, Sat-Sun 11:00-3:00 ■ Prices medium to very high ■ Major credit cards accepted with a 2% charge

Auctions of antique and decorative furnishings. Weekly general antique sales.

GLENDINING'S

101 New Bond Street, London W1Y 9LG ■ Telfax: (0171) 493-2445 ■ Mon-Fri 8:30-5:00 ■ A. Litherland ■ French spoken ■ Prices medium ■ Visa,MC

International auctioneers & valuers of coins and medals. Insurance and probate valuations.

HARMERS OF LONDON STAMP AUCTIONEERS LTD

91 New Bond Street, London W1A 4EH ■ Tel: (0171) 629-0218 ■ Fax: (0171) 495-0260 ■ Mon-Fri 9:15-5:15 ■ Mrs. Caron de Vico ■ French, Italian and Spanish spoken ■ Prices medium to very high ■ Major credit cards

Collectible stamp auctioneers.

LLOYDS INTERNATIONAL AUCTION GALLERIES LTD

118 Putney Bridge Road, London SW15 2NQ ■ Tel: (0181) 788-7777 ■ Fax: (0181) 874-5390 ■ Sales every two weeks ■ Prices low ■ Major credit cards

Victorian and Edwardian furniture, lighting. Valuations. Furniture, china and collectibles sold fortnightly on Saturdays. Lost property sold fortnightly on Thursdays. Call for schedule.

LOTS ROAD GALLERIES

71 Lots Road, Chelsea, London SW10 0RN ■ Tel: (0171) 351-7771 ■ Fax: (0171) 376-8349 ■ Mon 9:00-9:30, Tue-Wed 9:00-6:00, Fri 9:00-4:00, Sat-Sun 10:00-4:00 ■ Roger Ross ■ Many languages spoken ■ Prices low to very high ■ All major credit cards

General auctions of furniture and works of art. Auctions every Monday. Call for schedule. Auctioneers and valuers of antiques and modern furnishings. Collection and delivery service available.

ONSLOW'S COLLECTORS AUCTIONS

The Old Depot, The Gasworks, 2 Michael Road, London SW6 2AD■ Tel: (0171) 371-0505 ■ Fax: (0171) 384-2682 ■ Mon-Fri 9:30-5:00 ■ Prices low to very high ■ Visa and MC accepted

Auctions of posters and advertising art, war propaganda, transport memorabilia (especially The Titanic), collectors items. Full mail order facilities.

ROSEBERY'S

74-76 Knights Hill, West Norwood, London SE27 0JD ■ Tel: (0181) 761-2522 ■ Fax: (0181) 761-2524 ■ Mon-Fri 9:30-5:00 ■ Mr. J. Cadzow ■ Prices low to high ■ Major credit cards

Antique and general auctions held fortnightly. Call for schedule. Valuations. Collection and delivery service available.

SOTHEBY'S

34-35 New Bond Street, London W1A 2AA ■ Tel: (0171) 293-5000 ■ Fax: (0171) 293-5989 ■ Website: www.sothebys.com.uk ■

One of the world's best-known auction houses. Famous for auctions of rare antiques, incredible works of art at incredible prices, porcelain, jewellery, collectibles. Call or visit. It will be worth the trip.

SOTHEBY'S INSTITUTE

30 Oxford Street, London W1N 9FL■ Tel: (0171) 462-3232 ■ Fax: (0171) 580-8160 ■ Mon-Fri 9:00-5:00

Undergraduate, postgraduate and extramural courses in fine and decorative art.

SOTHEBY'S PICTURE LIBRARY

34-35 New Bond Street, London W1A ■ Tel: (0171) 408-5383 ■ Mon-Fri 9:00-5:00

Catalogues of sales and items dating from the 8th century to the 1930s.

SPINK & SON LTD

5 King Street, St. James's, London SW1Y 6QS ■ Tel: (0171) 930-7888 ■ Fax: (0171) 839-4853 ■ E-mail: spink@btinternet.com ■ Mon-Fri 9:00-5:30 ■ Christopher Knapton ■ Most languages spoken ■ Prices high to very high ■ Major credit cards

Auctions of coins, banknotes, medals and stamps. Call for schedule.

BATHROOMS

ABACUS INTERNATIONAL
681-689 Holloway Road, London N18 5SE ■ Tel: (0171) 281-4136 ■ Fax: (0171) 272-5081 ■ Mon-Sat 9:00-5:30, Sun 10:30-1:00 ■ Victor or David Bloom ■ Prices low to very high ■ Major credit cards ■ Trade discount

Bathrooms, showers, kitchens, appliances supplied and installed. Ceramic and marble tiles.

A&H BRASS
201-203 Edgeware Road, London W2 1ES ■ Tel: (0171) 402-1854 ■ Fax: (0171) 402-0110 ■ Mon-Sat 9:00-6:00 ■ Prices medium to high ■ Major credit cards ■ Trade discount

Bathroom accessories. All types of brass accessories. Repolishing and engraving.

ARCHITECTURAL COMPONENTS
4-8 Exhibition Road, London SW7 2HF ■ Tel: (0171) 581-2401 ■ Fax: (0171) 589-4928 ■ Mon-Sat 9:00-5:00 ■ G.J. Pearson-Wright ■ Prices low to very high ■ Major credit cards ■ Trade discount

British brass bathroom accessories and fittings. Also hardware for doors and windows

ASTON-MATTHEWS LTD
141-147 Essex Road, Islington, London N1 2SN ■ Tel: (0171) 226-7220 ■ Fax: (0171) 354-5951 ■ Mon-Fri 8:30-5:00, Sat 9:30-2:00 ■ Howard Birch ■ Prices medium to high ■ Visa and MC

Bathroom specialists since 1823. The largest range from stock of bathroom equipment from all over the world: baths, sanitaryware, taps, showers, cast iron baths, ceramic shower trays, double Belfast-style sinks, high quality taps and mixers in nickel, chrome, Inca brass and astonite. More than 100 styles of wash basins and WCs. In-house design and free delivery in and around London.

BATHING BEAUTIES
43 Muswell Hill Road, London N10 3JB ■ Tel: (0181) 365-2794 ■ Fax: (0181) 444-2383 ■ Mon-Fri 9:00-5:30, Sat 9:30-4:00 ■ Ron Phillips ■ Prices high ■ Major credit cards ■ Trade discount

Roll top baths and a selection of Victorian stands and taps. They will also re-enamel baths in your own home. Traditional showers.

BATHS ' N ' TILES PLUS

384 Finchley Road, Chields Hill, London NW2 ■ Tel: (0171) 435-3141 ■ Fax: (0171) 435-6397 ■ 170 Ballards Lane, London N3 ■ Tel: (0181) 346-4643 1103-1107 Finchley Road, Temple Fortune, London NW11 ■ Tel: (0181) 458-1437 ■ 1115 Finchley Road, London NW11 ■ Tel: (0181) 731-9026 ■ Mon-Sat 9:00-5:00 ■ Prices medium to high ■ Professional discount ■ Major credit cards

Luxury bath and shower rooms. Jacuzzis and whirlpools. Cast iron and steel baths. Power and steam showers, mirrors, tiles and accessories. Design and installations.

BODYWASH LTD

433 High Road, Ilford, Essex WG1 1TR ■ Tel: (0181) 478-1617 ■ Fax: (0181) 478-3347 ■ Mon-Sat 9:00-5:30, Wed 9:00-7:30 ■ J. Healy ■ Prices medium to high ■ Major credit cards ■ Trade discount

London's largest showroom of bathroom and shower equipment. Bathrooms, showers, jacuzzis, airbaths, shower cubicles.

CHELSEA INTERIORS (TRADING AS TSUNAMI)

27 Wigmore Street, London W1H 9LD ■ Tel: (0171) 408-2230 ■ Fax: (0171) 408-2210 ■ Mon-Sat 9:30-5:30 ■ David Knights ■ Prices high to very high

High quality bathroom designs and installations. Many branded fixtures and appliances. Great Tsunami baths.

COLOURWASH

165 Chamberlayne Road, London NW10 3NV ■ Tel: (0171) 459-8918 ■ Fax: (0171) 459-4280 ■ Mon-Sat 9:30-5:30 ■ David Jones ■ Prices medium ■ Major credit cards ■ Trade discount

Bathrooms and bathroom accessories in all styles from leading popular brands to the classics.

♛ CZECH & SPEAKE LTD

39C Jermyn Street, London SW1Y 6DN ■ Tel: (0171) 439-0216 ■ Fax: (0171) 734-8587 ■ Mon-Fri 9:00-5:00 ■ Prices high ■ Trade discount ■ Major credit cards
125 Fulham Road, London SW3 6RT ■ Tel: (0171) 225-3667 ■ Fax: (0171) 225-3407 ■ Mon-Sat 9:00-5:00 ■ Prices high ■ Trade discount ■ Major credit cards

Highest quality custom bathrooms and accessories. The accessories, especially their mirrors and heated towel racks, are of unique and beautiful design. Their other smaller accessories, such as their bath racks, soap holders and towel rails are the most stunning you will find anywhere.

DANICO BRASS LIMITED

31 Winchester Road, Swiss Cottage, London NW3 3NR ■ Tel: (0171) 483-4477 ■ Fax: (0171) 722-7992 ■ Mon-Fri 9:30-6:00, Thu 9:00-8:00 ■ Ashor Dani ■ Prices medium to very high ■ Visa and MC ■ Trade discount

Large range of bathroom accessories as well as door and window hardware. They refurbish and re-polish brass, as well as plate in gold and chrome. Special items to order.

DURANTE INTERNATIONAL & THE JACUZZI CENTRE

266 Brompton Road, London SW3 2AS ■ Tel: (0171) 589-9990 ■ Fax: (0171) 589-9955 ■ E-mail: durante@biconnect.com ■ Mon-Fri 9:30-5:30, Sat 10:30-5:00 ■ Aubrey and Paula Durante ■ Prices medium to very high ■ Major credit cards ■ Trade discount

Design and installation of bathrooms and showers. Jacuzzis a specialty. Also specialists in design and installations in marble and granite. Specialists in installations of jacuzzi whirlpool baths.

EDWINS BATHROOM CENTRE

19 All Saints Road, London SW6 3QR ■ Tel: (0171) 221-9340 ■ Fax: (0171) 243-0206 ■ Mon-Fri 8:00-5:00 ■ Bill Wood, Matt David ■ Spanish spoken ■ Prices low to high ■ Major credit cards ■ Trade discount

Modern minimalist and traditional bathroom installations and fittings.

C.P. HART & SONS LIMITED

Newnham Terrace, Hercules Road, London SE1 7DR ■ Tel: (0171) 902-1000 ■ Fax: (0171) 902-1001 ■ Mon-Sat 9:00-5:30 ■ Mr. Stephen Maguire ■ Italian spoken ■ Prices medium to high ■ Trade discount ■ Major credit cards

London's leading bathroom company with designer traditional and contemporary products. Cast iron baths, taps, ceramics, accessories.

INTERIORS

4-6 Exhibition Road, South Kensington, London SW7 2HF ■ Tel: (0171) 581-3869 ■ Fax: (0171) 589-4928 ■ Mon-Sat 9:00-5:00 ■ G.T. Wright ■ Prices low to very high ■ Major credit cards ■ Trade discount

Bathroom accessories.

JACUZZI (U.K.) LTD

17 Mount Street. London W1Y 5RA ■ Tel: (0171) 409-1776 ■ Fax: (0171) 495-2353 ■ Mon-Fri 10:00-5:00 ■ Prices high to very high ■ Trade discount

Jacuzzis. Need we say more.

MAX PIKE BATHROOMS
4 Eccleston Street, London SW1W ■ Tel: (0171) 730-7216 ■ Fax: (0171) 730-3789 ■ E-mail: max_pike@compuserve.com ■ Mon-Fri 10:00-6:00 ■ Prices high to very high ■ Trade discount

Mostly their own products: taps, hydro-massage, vitrite tubs, traditional and modern design. Unusual and worth a visit.

PIPE DREAMS
70-72 Gloucester Road, London SW7 4QT ■ Tel: (0171) 225-3978 ■ Fax: (0171) 589-8841 ■ Mon-Fri 9:30-5:30, Sat 10:00-5:00 ■ Robert Brown ■ Major credit cards

Complete design, supply and installation of bathrooms. He's one of the best and exports worldwide.

SACHELLE STUDIOS
1 Colindale Avenue, Edgware Road, London NW9 5DS ■ Tel: (0181) 200-6697 ■ Fax: (0181) 200-7726 ■ Mon-Fri 9:30-5:30, Sun 10:00-1:00 ■ Mr. Ezekiel ■ French and Hebrew spoken

Design and supply of luxury bathrooms. Cast iron and steel baths, marble, granite and Corian construction. Power shower systems and shower doors. All the leading brands. Work references: Heathrow Airport, Hilton Hotel, Mayfair House, Buckingham Palace and Windsor Castle.

Bath Renovation

BATH RENOVATION LTD
Ashland House, 20 Moxon Street, London W1M 3JE ■ Tel: (0171) 935-6590 ■ Fax: (0171) 486-7636 ■ Mon-Fri 8:00-5:00 ■ Terry Ash, Keith Morris ■ Prices medium ■ Trade discount

Re-enameling cast iron bathtubs. Repairs and re-finishing.

HARRY HEWETSON T/A INTERBATH RESTORATION SERVICES
10 Barley Mow Passage, London W4 4PH ■ Telfax: (0181) 995-6552 ■ Mon-Fri 9:00-7:00 ■ Harry Hewetson ■ Prices medium ■ Trade discount

On-site bath renovation.

RENUBATH SERVICES
248 Little Road, London SW6 7QA ■ Tel: (0171) 381-8337 ■ Fax: (0171) 381-8907 ■ E-mail: renubath@aol.com ■ Mon-Fri 9:00-5:30 ■ Ross Jones ■ Prices medium to high ■ Visa and MC ■ Trade discount

Re-surfacing and re-polishing of baths and sanitary ware. Repairs to chips and cracks. Roll top antique baths sold.

BILLIARDS & SNOOKER

THURSTON

110 High Street, Edgware Road, London HA8 7HF ■ Tel: (0181) 952-2002 ■ Fax: (0181) 952-0222 ■ E-mail: eaclare@compuserve.com ■ Mon-Fri 8:30-5:30, Sat 8:30-1:00 ■ Peter E. Crail ■ Prices low to very high ■ Visa and MC ■

New and restored billiard and snooker tables and accessories. Bowling Green equipment, indoor club games. Oldest snooker table makers in the world. Established, believe it or not, in 1799!

OUTSIDE LONDON

ACADEMY BILLIARD COMPANY

5 Camphill Industrial Estate, West Byfleet, Surrey KT14 6EW ■ Tel: (01932) 352067 ■ Fax: (01932) 353904 ■ Mobile: 0860 523757 ■ Mon-Sat by appointment ■ Robert Donnachie ■ French spoken ■ Prices low to very high ■ Visa, MC

Billiard, snooker and pool tables, especially antiques. All sizes from combination billiard/dining tables to extremely elegant and elaborate full size antique tables. Accessories, light fittings, racks and room games. Repairs, removals, valuations and full export service available. Member of The Guild of Master Craftsmen. Member of World Pool Billiard Association. Member of European Pool Association.

HUBBLE & FREEMAN

Invicta Works, Teston, Maidstone, Kent ME18 5AW ■ Tel: (01622) 814191 ■ Fax: (01622) 817086 ■ E-mail: peter@alfredreader.co.uk ■ Mon-Sat 8:30-6:00 ■ Peter Ludgate ■ French spoken ■ Prices low to very high ■ Major credit cards ■ Trade discount

A major sports equipment retailer for billiards, pool, bagatelle, bar-billiards, table tennis, croquet, football, cricket, hockey, golf, tennis, all the Sunday sports. French polishing, joinery carving. Manufacture of new and renovation of antique billiards and snooker tables. Removal, export, service and maintenance available.

BOOKS

The English and especially Londoners are "book people". Their love of language and the work of their
writers and poets is just about the greatest in the
world. The list, beginning with Beowulf and on down
through Shakespeare, Hardy, Shaw, Blake, Thackeray, Dickens, Wordsworth, Beatrix Potter and Oscar
Wilde, outranks in volume and quality the literary
work of any other nation on earth: and we are not
forgetting the Irish. The classic neighborhood-style
book shop in London has survived the onslaught of
the supermarkets and the internet. Londoners still
believe that books are made to be held, fondled,
enjoyed and cherished. The ALL LONDON authors
have selected their favourites for location, conve-
nience and the pure pleasure of the surroundings.

Bookbinding

BOOKWORKS
19 Hollywell Row, London EC2A 4JB ■ Tel: (0171) 247-2536 ■ Mon-
Fri 9:00-5:00
**Specialist in hand bookbinding, boxmaking and letterpressing.
Leather bindings, one-offs, presentation books, display albums,
portfolios and limited editions. Gold tooling and lettering.**

FALKINER FINE PAPERS
76 Southampton Row, London WC1B 4AR ■ Tel: (0171) 831-1151 ■ Fax:
(0171) 430-1248 ■ Mon-Sat 9:30-5:30 ■ Gabrielle Falkiner ■ French and
German spoken ■ Visa and MC accepted ■ Trade discounts
**Bookbinding. Fine Japanese and European hand-made papers
for artists, designers, craftsmen, photographers. Member of
The Guild of Master Craftsmen.**

THE RODE BINDERY
13 Crescent Place, London SW3 2EA ■ Telfax: (0171) 823-9930 ■
Mon-Fri 9:00-5:00 ■ Randle Baker Wilbraham ■ Prices medium
**Fine binding on commission. Blank books, personal record
books. Restoration of books and bindings. Member of The London Crafts Council.**

CATHY ROBERT

Studio 409, 31 Clerkenwell Close, London EC1R 0AT ■ Tel: (0171) 250-1803 ■ Fax: (0171) 490-3231 ■ Mon-Fri 9:00-6:00 ■ French spoken ■ Prices low to very high

Personalized portfolios. Hand-made portfolios, boxes, menus. Fine binding of limited editions.

SHEPHERDS BOOKBINDERS LTD

76 Rochester Row, London SW1P 1JU ■ Tel: (0171) 630-1184 ■ Fax: (0171) 931-0541 ■ Mon-Fri 9:00-5:30, Sat 10:30-5:00 ■ Bob Shephard ■ Visa and MC

Fine binding, paper conservation, fine stationery and bookbinding materials. Paper conservation, book restoration and some framing.

HENRY SOTHERAN LTD

2-5 Sackville Street, Piccadilly, London W1X 2DP ■ Tel: (0171) 439-6151 ■ Fax: (0171) 434-2019 ■ Mon-Fri 9:30-6:00, Sat 10:00-4:00 ■ Andrew McGeachin ■ French and Italian spoken ■ Prices low to very high ■ Trade discount ■ Major credit cards

Book search, book restoration and book binding.

Faux Books and Books by the Yard

ANY AMOUNT OF BOOKS

56 & 62 Charing Cross Road, London WC2H 0BB ■ Tel: (0171) 836-3697 ■ Fax: (0171) 240-1769 ■ Seven days 10:30-9:30 ■ Nigel Burwood ■ Prices low to high ■ ■ Trade discount ■ Visa and MC

Books, especially "by the yard". Large quantities, leather-bound and cloth.

THE MANOR BINDERY LIMITED

Calshot Road, Fawley, Southampton SO45 1BB ■ Tel: (01703) 894488 ■ Fax: (01713) 899418 ■ E-mail: manorbindery@btinternet.com ■ Mon-Fri 8:30-5:00 ■ Philip Bradburn ■ Visa, MC

Hand-made leather false books, replica book panels, library shelf edging. Designs for false book layouts.

J. SHINER & SONS LTD

8 Windmill Street, London W1P 1HF ■ Tel: (0171) 636-0740 ■ Fax: (0171) 580-0740 ■ Mon-Fri 6:45-3:00 ■ Major credit cards

Dummy books and faux doors as well as door handles, locks and restorations.

Booksellers

ANTIQUARIAN BOOKS & PRINTS
Chelsea Gallery, 535 King's Road, London SW10 OSZ ■ Tel: (0171)
823-3248 ■ LAPADA
Fine rare books and antique and reproduction prints.

ATLAS RARE BOOKS
2 Dunstable Mews, London W1N 1RQ ■ Tel: (0171) 486-4403 ■ Fax:
(0171) 487-5036 ■ Mon-Fri 9:30-5:30 ■ Prices medium to high
Specialist dealers in rare travel books, topographical art and photographs.

DENISE AUTMAN
W. Jones Arcade, 291 Westbourne Grove, London W11 2JL ■ Telfax:
(01280) 850437 ■ Saturdays only 8:15-3:30 ■ Denise Autman and
Gabriel Byrne ■ French and Italian spoken ■ Prices low to medium
■ Trade discount ■ Visa and MC
Antiquarian books, maps, leather-bound sets, botanicals and decorative items.

CHELSEA GALLERY
The Plaza, G5, 535 King's Road, London SW10 052 ■ Tel: (0171)
823-3248 ■ Fax: (0171) 352-1579 ■ Mon-Sat 10:00-7:00 ■ G. Toscani
■ Italian and German spoken ■ Prices medium to very high ■ Major
credit cards ■ Trade discount
Illustrated books, natural history, travel, history. Fine bindings, maps, decorative prints and framing.

CHRISTOPHER EDWARDS
63 Jermyn Street, London SW1Y 6LX ■ Tel: (0171) 495-4263 Fax: (0171)
495-4264 ■ Mon-Fri 10:00-6:00 ■ Christopher Edwards, Margaret Ersk-
ine ■ French spoken ■ Prices medium ■ Trade discount ■ Visa and MC
Antiquarian books, specializing in English and Continental history to 1850.

♕ SAM FOGG RARE BOOKS
35 St George Street, London W1R 9FA ■ Tel: (0171) 495-2333 ■ Fax:
(0171) 409-3326 ■ E-mail: samfogg@demon.co.uk ■ Mon-Fri 9:30-
5:30 ■ Sam Fogg ■ French, Italian, German and Dutch spoken ■
Prices medium to very high ■ Professional discount
Medieval manuscripts and miniatures. Oriental manuscripts and miniatures. Manuscripts and individual leaves.

GLOUCESTER ROAD BOOKSHOP

Dennys Sanders & Green, Ltd. ■ 123 Gloucester Road, London SW7 4TE ■ Tel: (0171) 370-3503 ■ Fax: (0171) 373-0610 ■ Mon-Fri 8:30-10:30, Sat-Sun 10:30-6:30 ■ Nicholas Dennys and Sarah Rogers ■ French spoken ■ Prices medium to high ■ Major credit cards

Secondhand and antiquarian books. First editions, history, biography, art, literature and books by the yard.

NICHOLAS GOODYER

15 Calabria Road, Highbury Fields, London N5 1JB ■ Tel: (0171) 226-5682 ■ Fax: (0171) 354-4716 ■ Mon-Fri 9:30-5:00 by appointment ■ Nicholas Goodyer ■ French, Italian and Portuguese spoken ■ Prices high to very high ■ Major credit cards

Illustrated natural history books, colour-plate books, plate books of all kinds, costume, architecture, art history. Antiquarian books only.

HARRINGTON BROS.

The Chelsea Antique Market, 253 King's Road, Chelsea, London SW3 5EL ■ Tel: (0171) 352-5689 ■ Fax: (0171) 823-3449

Antiquarian books bought and sold, including English literature, voyages, travel, maps and atlases, colour plates, natural history, children's books, leather bound sets, first editions, fine bindings.

HARRISON'S BOOKS

Grays Antiques Market, 1-7 Davies Mews, London W1Y 2LP ■ Tel: (0171) 629-1374 ■ Fax: (0171) 493-9344 ■ Mon-Fri 10:00-6:00 ■ Leo Harrison ■ Prices low to very high ■ Trade discount ■ Major credit cards

Antiquarian books. Books on angling, children's illustrated books. Fine leather bindings. Bookbinding.

MAGGS BROTHERS LTD

50 Berkeley Square, London W1X 6EL ■ Tel: (0171) 493-7160 ■ Fax: (0171) 499-2007 ■ Website: www.maggs.com ■ Mon-Fri 9:30-5:00 ■ John Magg ■ Many languages spoken ■ Prices low to very high ■ Visa and MC

Rare books and manuscripts in a wide range of fields.

MARLBOROUGH RARE BOOKS LTD

144-146 New Bond Street, London W1Y 9FD ■ Tel: (0171) 493-6993 ■ Fax: (0171) 499-2479 ■ Website: sales@mrb-books.com.uk ■ Mon-Fri 9:30-5:30 ■ Jonathan Gestetner ■ French and German spoken ■ Prices medium ■ Trade discount ■ Major credit cards

Rare books on art, architecture, travel, topography, English literature.

♛ BERNARD QUARITCH LTD

5-8 Lower John Street, Golden Square, London W1R 4AU ■ Tel: (0171) 734-2983 ■ Fax: (0171) 437-0967 ■ E-mail: rarebooks@quaritch.com ■ Website: www.quaritch.com ■ Mon-Fri 9:30-5:30 ■ Lord Parmoor ■ Many languages spoken ■ Prices medium to very high ■ Trade discount

Rare books and manuscripts. Early books on art and architecture, bibliography, English and Continental literature, human sciences, science and medicine, travel. BADA.

BERNARD J. SHAPERO

32 St George Street, London W1R 0EA ■ Tel: (0171) 493-0876 ■ Fax: (0171) 229-7860 ■ Mon-Sat 9:30-6:30 ■ Bernard Shapero ■ French and German spoken ■ Prices low to very high ■ Major credit cards

Rare books, antique prints and photographs. Books on natural history, illustrated children's books, books on travel. First editions.

NIGEL WILLIAMS RARE BOOKS

22 & 25 Cecil Court, off Charing Cross Road, London WC2N 4HE ■ Tel: (0171) 836-7757 ■ Fax: (0171) 379-5918 ■ E-mail: nwrarebook@tcp.co.uk ■ Mon-Sat 10:00-6:00 ■ Nigel Williams ■ Major credit cards

Fine and rare books. First editions of literature, detective fiction and children's books. Mail order available.

Architecture, Fine Arts and Decoration

THE BOOK WAREHOUSE

120 Southampton Row, London WC1 ■ 72-74 Notting Hill Gate, London W11 ■ Tel: (0171) 242-1119 ■ Fax: (0171) 404-5636 ■ Open 7 days 8:30-10:00 ■ Prices low ■ All credit cards

Large selection of books on art, architecture, design and cookery.

THE BUILDING BOOKSHOP

At The Building Centre, 26 Store Street, London WC1E 7BT ■ Tel: (0171) 692-4040 ■ Fax: (0171) 636-3628 ■ E-mail: bookshop@buildingbookshop.co.uk ■ Website: www.buildingbookshop.co.uk ■ Mon-Fri 9:30-5:15, Sat 10:00-1:00 ■ Roshnikara ■ MC and Amex accepted

Britain's largest selection of titles relating to the construction industry. Everything is covered, from minor works to building homes and large-scale civil engineering projects, maintenance and restoration. This bookshop is the most comprehensive supplier of publications on do-it-yourself home improvement and decoration.

THE CAMBERWELL BOOKSHOP

28 Camberwell Grove, London SE5 8RE ■ Tel: (0171) 701-1839 ■ Fax: (0171) 703-7255 ■ Open 7 days 11:00-7:00 ■ Paul Claydon ■ Prices medium ■ Professional discount

Books on fine and applied art, architecture and interior design.

THE COUNTRYSIDE BOOKSHOP

39 Goodge Street, London W1P 1FD ■ Tel: (0171) 636-3156 ■ Fax: (0171) 323-6879 ■ Mon-Fri 10:00-6:00, Sat 11:00-5:00 ■ Marion Hills ■ All major credit cards

Books on interiors, crafts, cookery and general.

DILLONS BOOKSTORE

82 Grove Street, London WC1E 6EQ ■ Tel: (0171) 636-1577 ■ Fax: (0171) 580-7680 ■ E-mail: arts@dillons.org.uk ■ Mon-Fri 9:00-7:00, Sat 9:30-6:00, Sun 12:00-6:00 ■ John Thwaites ■ Major credit cards

Extensive range of books on architecture, art, interior design sources and interior design. Books on art, ethnic art and fine and applied art. Catalogue available.

THE DOVER BOOKSHOP

18 Earlham Street, London WC2H 9LN ■ Tel: (0171) 836-2111 ■ Fax: (0171) 836-1603 ■ Mon-Wed 10:00-6:00, Thu- Sat 10:00-7:00 ■ M.S. Oddie and Tim Matthews ■ French spoken ■ Prices low to high ■ Trade discount on large orders ■ Major credit cards

The world's largest collection of public domain design resources, plus a large collection of books on the fine and applied arts and art history.

FALKINER FINE PAPERS

76 Southampton Row, London WC1B 4AR ■ Tel: (0171) 831-1151 ■ Fax: (0171) 430-1248 ■ Mon-Sat 9:30-5:30 ■ Gabrielle Falkiner ■ Dutch, French and German spoken ■ Prices medium ■ Visa and MC ■ Quantity discounts

Books for artists, designers, typographers, calligraphers. Beautiful papers.

STEPHEN FOSTER

95 Bell Street, London NW1 6TL ■ Telfax: (0171) 724-0876 ■ E-mail: stephen.foster@sfbooks.com ■ Mon-Sat 10:30-6:00 ■ Stephen Foster ■ Prices medium ■ Trade discount for large orders ■ Major credit cards.

Books on the arts, decoration, architecture. Old and rare books.

FRENCH BOOKSELLERS – LIBRAIRIE LA PAGE

7 Harrington Road, South Kensington, London SW7 3ES ■ Tel: (0171) 589-5991 ■ Fax: (0171) 225-2662 ■ Mon-Fri 8:30-6:15 ■ Sat 10:00-5:00 ■ R. Shepping ■ French spoken ■ Prices low to medium ■ Trade discount ■ Major credit cards

Books in French on the arts, architecture, design, languages. Also French magazines and children's books.

♔ THOMAS HENEAGE ART BOOKS

42 Duke Street, St. James's, London SW1Y 6DS ■ Tel: (0171) 930-9223 ■ Fax: (0171) 839-9223 ■ E-mail: artbooks@heneage.com ■ Mon-Fri 9:00-6:00 ■ Prices low to very high ■ Major credit cards

Reference books on fine and decorative arts. One of the best resources in London for books on interior decoration, architecture, the fine and applied arts, art history and gardens.

HENRY PORDES BOOKS LTD

58-60 Charing Cross Road, London WC2H 0BB ■ Tel: (0171) 836-9031 ■ Fax: (0171) 886-2201 ■ E-mail: henrypordes@clara.net ■ Mon-Sat 10:00-7:00 ■ Gino della Ragione ■ Italian spoken ■ Prices medium ■ Trade discount ■ Major credit cards

Art, literature, the performing arts, antiquarian and military.

SERPENTINE GALLERY BOOKSHOP

Kensington Gardens, London W2 3XA ■ Tel: (0171) 298-1503 ■ Fax: (0171) 402-4103 ■ E-mail: bookshop@serpentinegallery.org ■ Mon-Sun 10:00-6:00 ■ Prices medium ■ Major credit cards

Books on art criticism, aesthetic and cultural theory, philosophy, contemporary art, videos, CDs, magazines and cards. Very nice pause on a weekend walk in the park.

SHIPLEY SPECIALIST ART BOOKSELLERS

70 Charing Cross Road, London WC2H 0BB ■ Tel: (0171) 836-4872 ■ Fax: (0171) 379-4358 ■ E-mail: artbook@compuserve.com ■ Mon-Sat 10:00-6:00 ■ Ian Shipley ■ French and German spoken ■ Prices medium to high ■ Major credit cards

In- and out-of-print books on art, architecture, fashion, fine and applied arts, planning and urban design, rugs and carpets, textiles, furniture, ceramics, horology. Advertising and artists books, photography, graphic design, interiors, monographs, catalogues. Book search services.

THE TRIANGLE BOOKSHOP

36 Bedford Square, London WC1B 3EC ■ Tel: (0171) 631-1381 ■ Fax: (0171) 436-4373 ■ E-mail: info@trianglebookshop.com ■ Mon-Fri 10:00-6:30 ■ Major credit cards

Books on architecture, landscape and philosophy. Magazines and CDROMs. Mail order service.

WALDEN BOOKS

38 Harmood Street, London NW1 8DP ■ Tel: (0171) 267-8146 ■ Thu-Sun 10:30-6:30 ■ Prices low to medium ■ Trade discount ■ Major credit cards

Books on art and architecture and quality non-fiction books. Rare, hard-to-find volumes. Book search available.

ZWEMMER ART BOOKSHOP

24 Litchfield Street, London WC2 9NJ ■ Tel: (0171) 240-4158 ■ Fax: (0171) 836-7049 ■ E-mail: zwemmer-co@btinternet.com ■ Mon-Fri 10:00-6:30, Sat 10:00-6:00 ■ Denise Dean ■ French and German spoken ■ Prices low to very high ■ Major credit cards ■ Possible volume discount

Books and journals on art, architecture. Magazines. Mail order service. They also have a shop in the New York D&D Building at 979 Third Avenue.

Arms and Military

HANDSWORTH BOOKS

The Basement, 148 Charing Cross Road, London WC2H 0LB ■ Tel: (0171) 240-3566 ■ Mobile: 0976 329042 ■ Mon-Sat 19:00-8:00, Sun 12:00-6:00 ■ Stephen Glover ■ Prices medium ■ Trade discount ■ Major credit cards

Scholarly books in the humanities, especially military, history, literature and the arts.

MILITARY HISTORY BOOKSHOP

Lower Ground, 77-81 Bell Street, London NW1 6TA ■ Tel: (0171) 723-2095 ■ Fax: (0171) 723-4665 ■ Mon-Fri 10:00-6:00, Sat 10:00-2:00 ■ Kelvin Barber ■ Prices low to high ■ Major credit cards

Specialist in books on military history, mainly our of print and hard-to-find books.

CHILDREN'S BOOK CENTRE

237 Kensington High Street, London W8 6SA ■ Tel: (0171) 937-7497 ■ Fax: (0171) 938-4968 ■ Mon, Wed, Fri, Sat 9:30-6:30, Tue 9:30-6:00, Thu 9:30-7:00 ■ Liz Gee ■ French spoken ■ Prices low to medium ■ Major credit cards ■ Trade discount

Books for children, tapes, videos, CDs, toys.

INDEX BOOKSTORE

10-12 Atlantic Road, London SW9 8HY ■ Telfax: (0171) 274-8342 ■ Mon-Sat 10:00-6:00 ■ M.P. Daly ■ Prices low to medium ■ Major credit cards

This is a bookstore which specializes in children's books, black writers and African history.

Foreign Language

THE FRENCH BOOKSHOP

28 Bute Street, South Kensington, London SW7 3EX ■ Tel: (0171) 584-2840 ■ Fax: (0171) 823-9259 ■ E-mail: info@frenchbookshop.com ■ Mon-Fri 8:30-6:00, Sat 10:00-7:00 ■ Mr. and Mrs. Zaigue ■ French, Spanish and Arabic spoken ■ Prices low to high ■ Visa accepted

Books in the French language.

GRANT & CUTLER LTD

55-57 Great Marlborough Street, London W1V 2AY ■ Tel: (0171) 734-2012 ■ Fax: (0171) 734-9272 ■ E-mail: postmaster@grant-c.demon.co.uk ■ Mon-Sat 9:00-5:30, Thu 9:00-7:00 ■ Stephen Cooper ■ Many languages spoken ■ Prices medium ■ Major credit cards

Foreign language books a specialty. Catalogues and mail service available.

THE ITALIAN BOOKSHOP

7 Cecil Court, London WC2N 4EZ ■ Tel: (0171) 240-1634 ■ Mon-Sat 9:00-5:00 ■ Prices medium to high ■ Major credit cards
Specialists in books on Italy and Italian language.

JAPAN CENTRE

212 Piccadilly, London W1V ■ Tel: (0171) 439-8035 ■ Mon-Sat 9:00-5:30 ■ Prices medium ■ Major credit cards
Books in the Japanese language.

THE MULTILINGUAL GALLERY

228A St. Paul's Road, Islington, London N1 21J ■ Tel: (0171) 359-1200 ■ Mon-Thu 12:00-7:00, Fri 12:00-5:00 ■ Prices medium ■ Major credit cards

Specialist in secondhand French, Russian, Spanish and Italian books, as well as children's titles in Asian and African languages.

Gastronomy and Oenology

BOOKS FOR COOKS

4 Blenhein Crescent, London W11 ■ Tel: (0171) 221-1992 ■ Fax: (0171) 221-1517 ■ E-mail: info@booksforcooks.com.uk ■ Mon-Sat 9:30-6:00 ■ Heidi Lascelles ■ French, German and Italian spoken ■ Major credit cards

International cookbooks and books on wine. Taste kitchen open for lunch!

History

INDEX BOOK CENTRE

10-12 Atlantic Road, London SW9 8HY ■ Telfax: (0171) 274-8342 ■ Mon-Sat 10:00-6:00 ■ M. P. Daly ■ Prices low to medium ■ Major credit cards

Bookstore specializing in African history, children's books and media studies.

THE MUSEUM BOOKSHOP

36 Great Russell Street, London WC1B 3PP ■ Tel: (0171) 580-4086 ■ Fax: (0171) 436-4364 ■ Mon-Sat 10:00-5:30 ■ Ashley Jones ■ Prices low to high ■ Major credit cards

Books on history, archaeology, ancient history, especially Egyptology and the Middle East. Catalogues available and book search service.

UNSWORTH BOOKSELLERS LTD

12 Bloomsbury Street, London WC1B 3QA ■ Tel: (0171) 820-7709/ (0171) 436-9836 ■ Fax: (0171) 637-7334 ■ Mon-Sat 10:00-8:00 ■ Sun 12:00-8:00

37 York Road, London SE1 ■ Tel: (0171) 928-0966

Secondhand, antiquarian and remainders on history, the arts and social sciences.

WOBURN BOOKSHOP

10 Woburn Walk, London WC1H 0JI ■ Tel: (0171) 388-7278 ■ Fax: (0171) 263-5196 ■ E-mail: andrew@burgin.freeser.co.uk ■ Mon-Fri 11:00-6:00, Sat 11:00-5:00 ■ Andrew Burgin ■ French spoken ■ Prices medium ■ Major credit cards ■ Trade discount

Books on history, cultural studies, Judaica, philosophy, art and photography.

--- Science ---

DILLONS AT THE SCIENCE MUSEUM

Exhibition Road, London SW7 2DD ■ Tel: (0171) 938-8255 ■ Fax: (0171) 581-2899 ■ Open 7 days 10:00-6:00 ■ Noel Rasmussen ■ Danish and Hebrew spoken ■ Prices medium ■ Major credit cards ■ Student discounts
Books on science, CDs. Basically for schools and institutions.

SKOOB BOOKS LTD

15 Sicilian Avenue, London WC1A 2QH ■ Tel: (0171) 404-3063 ■ Fax: (0171) 404-4398 ■ E-mail: books@skoob.com ■ Mon-Sat 10:30-6:30 ■ I.K. Ong ■ German and Chinese spoken ■ Prices medium to high ■ Major credit cards ■ Trade and student discounts
Books on science, mathematics, computing, psychology, history, literature, art and architecture.

--- Theatre & Film ---

THE CINEMA BOOKSHOP

13-14 Great Russell Street, London WC1B 3N ■ Tel: (0171) 637-0206 ■ Fax: (0171) 436-9979 ■ Mon-Sat 10:30-5:30 ■ Fred Zentner ■ German spoken ■ Prices medium ■ Major credit cards
Books on film, old and new. Magazines, old and new. Posters, pressbooks and stills.

THE CINEMA STORE

48/4C Orion House, Upper St Martins Lane, London WC2H 9EJ ■ Tel: (0171) 379-7838 ■ Fax: (0171) 240-7689 ■ 7 days 10:00-6:00 ■ Paul McEvoy, Neil Palmer ■ Prices low to high ■ Major credit cards
Movie, TV memorabilia. Magazines, books, posters, video, DVD. Mail order.

DANCE BOOKS LTD

15 Cecil Court, London WC2N ■ Tel: (0171) 836-2314 ■ Mon-Sat 9:00-5:00 ■ Prices medium ■ Major credit cards
Books on dance and the dance world.

⚜ OFFSTAGE THEATRE AND FILM BOOKSHOP

37 Chalk Farm Road, London NW1 8AJ ■ Tel: (0171) 485-4996 ■ Fax: (0171) 916-8046 ■ Mon-Sun 10:00-6:00 ■ Brian Schwartz, Linda Reitsis ■ Greek and French spoken ■ Prices low to high ■ Major credit cards ■ Discounts for teachers and institutions

Books on theatre, directing, performance art, avant-garde, physical theatre, drama in education, writing for theatre, cinema and television.

SAMUEL FRENCH LTD

52 Fitzroy Street, London W1P ■ Tel: (0171) 387-9373 ■ Mon-Fri 9:00-5:00 ■ Prices medium to high

A huge collection of play texts

ROYAL NATIONAL THEATRE BOOKSHOP

Royal National Theatre, Upper Ground, South Bank, London SE1 9PX ■ Tel: (0171) 452-3456 ■ Fax: (0171) 452-3457 ■ E-mail: ntbooks@dircon.co.uk ■ Mon-Sat 10:00-10:45pm ■ Toby Radford ■ Prices low to high ■ Major credit cards

Playtexts. Texts for most of the National, RSC and West End repertories. Books on the theatre, criticism, acting, directing, technical. Also videos and CDROMs. Theatre posters and engravings.

Travel and Voyages of Discovery

EUROBOOKS LTD

2 Woodstock Street, London WC1 1HD ■ Telfax: (0171) 491-0223 ■ Mon-Fri 10:00-6:00, Sat 11:00-4:00 ■ French spoken ■ Prices medium ■ Major credit cards ■ Trade discount

Illustrated travel books: Americana a specialty. Books, maps, prints and pictures.

GRENVILLE BOOKS

40A Museum Street, London WC1A 1LT ■ Telfax: (0171) 404-2872 ■ Mon-Sat 11:00-6:30, Sun by appointment ■ Margaret Johnson ■ French, Spanish and some Italian and Portuguese spoken ■ Prices medium ■ Trade discount

All aspects of Spain, Portugal, Latin America, the Caribbean including literature, art, language, history, politics, travel. Secondhand and antiquarian books. Book search service available.

THE NATIONAL MAP CENTRE
22-24 Caxton Street, London SW1H 0QU ■ Tel: (0171) 222-2466 ■ Fax: (0171) 222-2619 ■ E-mail: info@mapsnmc.com ■ Mon-Fri 9:00-6:00 ■ Keith Ferries ■ Prices medium ■ Professional discount ■ Major credit cards

Maps, travel guides, electronic mapping.

REG & PHILIP REMINGTON
18 Cecil Court, London WC2N 4HE ■ Tel: (0171) 836-9771 ■ Fax: (0171) 497-2526 ■ Mon-Fri 9:00-5:00 ■ Reg and Philip Remington ■ Prices low to high ■ Visa and MC accepted ■ Trade discount

Voyages and travel books. Catalogues available.

THE TRAVEL BOOKSHOP
13 Blenheim Crescent, London W11 2EG ■ Tel: (0171) 229-5260 ■ Fax: (0171) 243-1552 ■ E-mail: post@thetravelbookshop.co.uk ■ Mon-Sat 10:00-6:00 ■ Sean Swallow ■ Prices medium ■ Major credit cards ■ Trade discount

Travel books a specialty. Mail order.

General

BELL, BOOK & RADHALL
4 Cecil Court, London WC2N 4HE ■ Tel: (0171) 240-2161 ■ Fax: (0171) 379-1062 ■ Mon-Fri 10:00-5:30, Sat 11:00-4:00 ■ J. Bell, J. Tindley ■ Prices medium ■ Major credit cards ■ Trade discount

20th century literature.

BLACKWELL'S
100 Charing Cross Road, London WC 2H ■ Tel: (0171) 292-5100
11 Copthall Avenue, London EC2R * Tel: (0171) 638-1991

Fiction, non-fiction, the sciences, history, biography, cooking, the arts and design.

THE BOOK WAREHOUSE
296 High Holborn, London WC1V ■ Tel: (0171) 404-1708
72-74 Notting Hill Gate, London W11 ■ Tel: (0171) 727-4149
46 Shaftesbury Avenue, London W1V ■ Tel: (0171) 287-2414
120 Southampton Row, London WC1B ■ Tel: (0171) 242-1119
209-210 Tottenham Court Road, London W1P ■ Tel: (0171) 323-0166

A chain that sells all the books in-print on all subjects.

BOOKS ETC. LTD
120 Charing Cross Road, London WC2H ■ Tel: (0171) 379-6838
30 Broadgate Circle, London EC2M ■ Tel: (0171) 628-8944
70 Cheapside, London EC2V ■ Tel: (0171) 236-0398
60 Fenchurch Street, London EC3M ■ Tel: (0171) 481-4425
176 Fleet Street, London EC4A ■ Tel: (0171) 353-5939
263 High Holborn, London WC1V ■ Tel: (0171) 404-0261
26 James Street, Covent Garden, London WC2E ■ Tel: (0171) 379-6947
54 London Wall, London EC2M ■ Tel: (0171) 628-9708
163 Oxford Street, London W1R ■ Tel: (0171) 734-8287
South Bank Centre, Belvedere Road, London SE1 ■ Tel: (0171) 620-0403
Unit 19, Ground Floor, Whiteley Centre, Bayswater, London W2 ■ Tel: (0171) 229- 3865 ■ Check for opening hours

The great chain of stores that offers all recent publications in just about every subject area.

THE COUNTRYSIDE BOOKSHOP
39 Goodge Street, London W1P 1FD ■ Tel: (0171) 636-3156 ■ Mon-Fri 9:00-5:00

Gardening, cookery, crafts and guides.

CRIME IN STORE
14 Bedford Street, Covent Garden, London WC2E 9HE ■ Tel: (0171) 379-3795 ■ Fax: (0171) 319-8988 ■ E-mail: www.ndirect.co.uk/-ecorrigan/cis/crimeinstore.htm ■ Mon-Sat 10:30-6:30 ■ Geoffrey Bailey ■ Prices medium ■ Major credit cards ■ Trade discount

Crime and mystery fiction, true crime, adventure. Also audio tapes and second- hand paperbacks.

DILLON'S MAP SHOP
58 Ludgate Hill, London EC4M ■ Tel: (0171) 248-3554

Maps, charts and travel.

DILLON'S, THE BOOKSTORE

82 Gower Street, London WC1E ■ Tel: (0171) 636-1577
Barbican Centre, Silk Street, EC2Y ■ Tel: (0171) 382-7007
Calcutta House, Old Castle Street, London E1 ■ Tel: (0171) 247-0727
10-12 James Street, London W1M ■ Tel: (0171) 629-8206
150 King's Road, London SW3 ■ Tel: (0171) 351-2023
28 Margaret Street, London W1N ■ Tel: (0171) 580-2812
10 Northampton Square, London EC1V ■ Tel: (0171) 608-0706
19-23 Oxford Street, London W1R ■ Tel: (0171) 434-9759
213 Piccadilly, London W1V ■ Tel: (0171) 434-9617
Unit B&C, Grand Buildings, Trafalgar Square, London WC2N ■ Tel: (0171) 839-4411
Science Museum, Exhibition Road, South Kensington SW7 ■ Tel: (0171) 938-8255

A chain of bookstores offering recent publications in almost every general subject area.

FANTASY CENTRE

157 Holloway Road, London N7 8LX ■ Telfax: (0171) 607-9433 ■ Mon-Sat 10:00-6:00 ■ Ted Bak, Eric Arthur ■ Prices medium to high ■ Major credit cards ■ Trade discount

Science fiction, fantasy, horror, magazines, reference and works on art. Catalogues available.

FARRINGDON BOOKS

27 Exmouth Market, London EC1R 4QL ■ Tel: (0171) 278-0776 ■ Mon-Sat 11:30-6:00 ■ Alan Austin ■ Prices medium ■ Professional discount

General second hand and some antiquarian books.

W. & G. FOYLE

119 Charing Cross Road, London WC2H ■ Tel: (0171) 437-5660 ■ Mon-Sat 9:00-5:00 ■ Major credit cards

One of the largest in London. Huge collection of new and some used books. A bit of a sprawl. Has a great reputation for finding everything you could want.

HAMMICK'S BOOKSHOPS LTD

191-192 Fleet Street, London EC4A 2NJ ■ Tel: (0171) 405-5711 ■ Fax: (0171) 831-9849 ■ Mon-Sat 9:00-6:00 ■ Tony Newson ■ Italian, Spanish, Dutch and German spoken ■ Prices medium ■ Trade discount if purchase is over 2,000 pounds sterling ■ Major credit cards

Law books from all publishers. Books, looseleafs, law reports, CDs. Essential if you want to know something of British law.

♛ HATCHARDS

187 Piccadilly, London W1V 0LE ■ Tel: (0171) 439-9921 ■ Fax: (0171) 494-1313 ■ E-mail: books@hatchards.co.uk ■ Mon, Wed, Fri 9:00-6:00, Tue, Sat 9:30-6:00, Sun 12:00-6:00 ■ Roger Katz ■ Prices low to very high ■ All major credit cards

London's best. This is what one always imagines a great London bookstore should be. A full range of literature, books on art, architecture, design, gardens, collectibles, music, biography, history. It is all here. Enjoy yourself.

THE HORSEMAN'S BOOKSHOP

1&4 Lower Grosvenor Place, London SW1W ■ Tel: (0171) 834-5606/(0171) 828-8855/(0171)630-7686 ■ Mon-Fri 9:00-5:30, Sat morning

If you love horses and anything to do with horses, this is the place.

IN FOCUS

8, 9 & 10 Royal Opera Arcade, Pall Mall, London SW1Y ■ Tel: (0171) 839-188 ■ Mon-Fri 10:30-5:30, Sat 10:00-4:00

Specialists in books on birds and bird watching. Spyglasses.

MIDHEAVEN BOOKSHOP

Astrology Trading Centre, 396 Caledonian Road, London N1 ■ Tel: (0171) 607-4133 ■ Telephone for hours

The astrology bookshop.

MURDER ONE

71-73 Charing Cross Road, London WC2H 0AA ■ Tel: (0171) 734-3483 ■ Fax: (0171) 734-3429 ■ E-mail: 106562.2021@compuserve.com ■ Mon, Wed 10:00-7:00, Thu, Sat 10:00-8:00 ■ Maxim Jakubowski ■ Major credit cards

Special crime, science fiction and romance bookshop. A large Sherlock Holmes collection. Also magazines that deal with the subject.

♛ ROYAL NATIONAL THEATRE BOOKSHOP, NT

Royal National Theatre, South Bank, London SE1 9PX ■ Tel: (0171) 928-2033 ■ Fax: (0171) 401-2684

They call it the most impressive theatre-based bookshop in Britain. Probably right.

W.H. SMITH LTD

Block D, New London Bridge Station, London SE1 ■ Tel: (0171) 403-3288
Charing Cross Station Forecourt, The Strand, London WC2N ■ Tel: (0171) 839-4200
Elephant & Castle Shopping Centre, London SE1 ■ Tel: (0171) 703-8525
Finchley Road, Hampstead, London NW3 ■ Tel: (0171) 722-4441
Kings Cross Station, London N1 ■ Tel: (0171) 837-5580
92 Notting Hill Gate, London W11 ■ Tel: (0171) 727-9261
36 Sloane Square, London SW1W ■ Tel: (0171) 730-0351
The Mall, Broadgate, London EC2M ■ Tel: (0171) 628-1617
120 The Plaza, Oxford Street, London W1N ■ Tel: (0171) 436-6282
Victoria Central, Victoria Station, London SW1V ■ Tel: (0171) 630-9677
Victoria East Terminal, Victoria Station, London SW1V ■ Tel: (0171) 828-2853

One of England's best known bookstore chains with large collections of everything from contemporary fiction to design and decoration, travel, biography. You name it and you will very likely find it.

HENRY SOTHERAN LTD

2-5 Sackville Street, Piccadilly, London W18 2DP ■ Tel: (0171) 439-6151 ■ Fax: (0171) 434-2019 ■ Mon-Fri 9:30-6:00, Sat 10:00-4:00 ■ Andrew McGeachin ■ French and Italian spoken ■ Prices low to very high ■ Trade discount ■ Major credit cards ■

Fine books and prints, in literature, travel, architecture, children's illustrated and natural history.

SPORTSPAGES

94-96 Charing Cross Road, London WC2H 0JG ■ Tel: (0171) 240-9604 ■ Fax: (0171) 836-0104 ■ Prices medium ■ Major credit cards

As the name implies, a bookstore that takes sport seriously.

ULYSSES

40 Museum Street, London WC1A 1LT ■ Tel: (0171) 831-1600 ■ Fax: (0171) 419-0070 ■ E-mail: ulyssesbooks@compuserve.com ■ Mon-Sat 10:30-6:00, Sun 10:00-6:00 ■ Joanna Harold ■ French spoken ■ Prices high ■ Major credit cards

20th century literature, first editions, illustrated books.

♕ WATERSTONE'S BOOKSELLERS

99-101 Old Brompton Road, South Kensington, London SW7 ■ Tel: (0171) 581- 8522

128 Camden High Street, London NW1 ■ Tel: (0171) 284-4948

121-125 Charing Cross Road, London WC2H ■ Tel: (0171) 434-4291

266 Earls Court Road, London SW5 ■ Tel: (0171) 370-1616

9-13 Garrick Street, London WC2E ■ Tel: (0171) 836-6757

11 Islington Green, London N1 ■ Tel: (0171) 704-2280

193 Kensington High Street, London W8 ■ Tel: (0171) 937-8432

39-41 Notting Hill Gate, London W11 ■ Tel: (0171) 229-9444

1-7 Whittington Avenue, Leadenhall Market, London EC3V ■ Tel: (0171) 220-7882

Marvellous layout of books in all categories. A pleasure to visit and have a leisurely browse.

CARPETS & TAPESTRIES

A.D. CARPETS
227 Westbourne Grove, London W11 2SB ■ Telfax: (0171) 243-2264 ■ Mon-Sat 10:00-5:00 ■ Prices medium to high ■ Trade discount ■ LAPADA

Oriental carpets, some from the 18th and 19th century.

ATLANTIC BAY GALLERY
5 Sedley Place, London W1R 1HH ■ Tel: (0171) 355-3301 ■ Fax: (0171) 355-3760 ■ E-mail: atlanticgallery@btinternet.com ■ Mon-Fri 9:00-5:30 ■ W. Grodzinski ■ Polish spoken ■ Prices medium ■ Major credit cards ■ Trade discount ■ BADA

Antique Oriental and European carpets and textiles. Islamic and Indian art.

JENNY HICKS BEACH
London SW11 ■ Telfax: (0171) 228-6900 ■ By appointment only ■ LAPADA

19th to mid-20th century textiles and flat-weave kilims, mostly from Southern Russia. She specializes in Karabagh decorative animal and floral weaves. Some rugs and carpets.

♛ BENARDOUT & BENARDOUT
7 Thurloe Place, London SW7 2RG ■ Tel: (0171) 409-1234 ■ Telfax: (0171) 584-7658 ■ Mon-Fri 10:00-6:00,Sat 11:00-4:00 ■ Mr. & Mrs. E. Kayvan ■ French and Spanish spoken ■ Prices low to medium ■ Major credit cards ■ Trade discount

Oriental and European antique carpets, hangings and cushions. They also provide custom-made carpets to measure and have a conservation, repair and cleaning service.

DAVID BLACK ORIENTAL CARPETS
96 Portland Road, Holland Park, London W11 4LN ■ Tel: (0171) 727-2566 ■ Fax: (0171) 229-4599 ■ Mon-Fri 10:00-6:00, Sat 11:00-5:00 and by appointment ■ David Black ■ French and German spoken ■ Prices low to very high ■ Major credit cards ■ Trade discount ■ BADA

Antique and new vegetable-dyed carpets and rugs; tapestry, needlework and fabrics. Cleaning, restoration and valuation.

BLENHEIM CARPET CO LTD

41 Pimlico Road, London SW1W 8NE ■ Tel: (0171) 823-5215 ■ Fax: (0171) 823-5210 ■ Mon-Fri 9:00-5:00 ■ Steven Foster ■ Prices high to very high ■ Visa and MC accepted ■ Trade discount

Custom-made carpets. Any quantity. Wilton 100% flat weaves, manufacture through to installation.

JULIA BOSTON

London W11 ■ Tel: (0171) 727-2166 ■ Mobile: 0836 226423 ■ Fax: (0171) 792- 0924 ■ By appointment only ■ LAPADA

Aubusson carpets and tapestries, antiquities and art objects.

CHELSEA HANDMADE CARPETS

331 King's Road, Chelsea, London SW3 5ES■ Tel: (0171) 795-0122 ■ Fax: (0171) 795-0144 ■ Mon-Sat 10:00-6:00 ■ Richard Ringrose ■ French and German spoken ■ Prices medium to high ■ Major credit cards ■ Trade discount

Contemporary hand-knotted carpets. Carpets from Nepal, Iran, Afghanistan. Carpets made to clients' choice of colour, design and size.

COATS ORIENTAL CARPETS & CO LTD

4 Kensington Church Walk, London W8 4NB ■ Tel: (0171) 937-0983 ■ Mon-Sat 11:00-6:00 ■ Alexander Coats ■ French and Spanish spoken ■ Prices low to very high ■ Visa ■ Trade discount

Antique Oriental rugs and carpets. Textiles mainly of Islamic origin. Cleaning and restoration.

ESSIE CARPETS

Albemarle House, 62 Piccadilly, London W1V 9HL ■ Tel: (0171) 493-7766 ■ Fax: (0171) 495-3456 ■ E-mail: essiesakhai@compuserve.com ■ Most languages spoken ■ Prices medium to very high ■ Professional discount

Fine Persian and decorative carpets, rugs and tapestries. She wrote a book on the subject.

JACK FAIRMAN (CARPETS) LTD

218 Westbourne Grove, London W11 2RH ■ Tel: (0171) 229-2262 ■ Fax: (0171) 229-2263 ■ Mon-Sat 10:00-6:00 ■ John and Serina Page, Harvey Page ■ Prices medium to high ■ Visa and MC ■ Trade discount

Contemporary nomadic carpets. Antique Tibetan rugs.

👑 S. FRANSES LTD

80 Jermyn Street, London SW1Y 6JD ■ Tel: (0171) 976-1234 ■ Fax: (0171) 930-8451 ■ Mon-Fri 9:00-5:00 ■ Prices high to very high

Great collection of antique Oriental and European carpets, tapestries and textiles.

M. HESKIA

C/O C. FASS Ltd., 42 Ponton Road, London SW8 5BA ■ Telfax: (0171) 373-4489 ■ M. Heskia ■ French and Persian spoken ■ By appointment ■ BADA

Mainly 19th century Oriental carpets, rugs and European tapestries.

👑 C. JOHN (RARE RUGS) LTD

70 South Audley Street, London W1Y 5FE ■ Tel: (0171) 493-5288 ■ Fax: (0171) 409-7030 ■ Mon-Fri 9:30-5:00, appointment advisable ■ BADA

Exceptional carpets and rugs, tapestries, needlework and fabrics.

ALEXANDER JURAN & CO

74 New Bond Street, London W1Y 9DD ■ Tel: (0171) 629-2550 ■ Telfax: (0171) 493-4484 ■ Mon-Fri 9:30-5:00 ■ Alexander Juran ■ German, French, Russian and other languages spoken ■ Prices medium to very high ■ Professional discount ■ BADA

Antique Oriental rugs and textiles from the 18th century. Specially fine old Caucasian, Persian and Turkish. Repairs done in their own workshop.

👑 KESHISHIAN

73 Pimlico Road, London SW1W 8NE ■ Tel: (0171) 730-8810 ■ Fax: (0171) 730-8803 ■ Mon-Fri 9:30-6:00, Sat 10:00-5:00 ■ Mr. Keshishian ■ French, Armenian and Turkish spoken ■ Prices medium to high ■ Trade discount ■ BADA

Antique carpets, European period tapestries and 16th to 18th century Aubussons. Arts and Crafts and Art Deco carpet specialists.

KENNEDY CARPETS

Oriental Carpet Centre, 105 Eade Road, London N4 1TJ ■ Tel: (0181) 800-4455 ■ Fax: (0181) 800-4466 ■ Mon-Fri 9:30-6:00 ■ Michael Kennedy ■ French German and Italian spoken ■ Prices medium to very high ■ Visa and Amex accepted ■ Trade discount ■ LAPADA

Large sized antique and decorative rugs. New rugs woven on demand to any size.

KENSINGTON CARPETS

Oriental Carpet Centre, Building G, 105 Eade Road, London N4 1TJ ■ Tel: (0181) 800-4455 ■ Fax: (0181) 800-4466 ■ Mon-Fri 9:30-6:00 ■ Vivien Eder ■ Prices low to very high ■ Major credit cards ■ Trade discount

Made-to-order large sized hand-made rugs and antique carpets including Aubussons, kilims. Restoration and cleaning.

THE KILIM WAREHOUSE LTD

28A Pickets Street, London SW12 8QB ■ Tel: (0181) 675-3122 ■ Fax: (0181) 675-8494 ■ Mon-Fri 10:00-5:30, Sat 10:00-4:00 ■ Jose Luczyo-Wyhowska ■ French, Spanish, Portuguese, Turkish spoken ■ Prices medium to high ■ Major credit cards ■ Trade discount

Specialty importers, wholesalers and retailers of kilims, and flat weave rugs from Turkey, Iran, Eastern Europe, Russia, Caucasus, Central Asia and Afghanistan. Antique and decorative kilims. Cleaning and restoration of kilims and carpets.

LIDA LAVENDER

15 Deane House, 27 Greenwood Place, Highgate Road, London NW5 1LB ■ Tel: (0171) 424-0600 ■ Fax: (0171) 424-0404 ■ E-mail: lida@dircon.lco.uk ■ Mon-Fri 10:00-6:00 ■ Lida and Paul Lavender ■ Persian spoken ■ Prices medium to high ■ Visa and MC

Antique carpets, textiles and tapestries for design and decoration.

J. LAVIAN

Oriental Carpet Centre, Building E, Ground Floor, 105 Eade Road, London N4 1TJ ■ Tel: (0181) 800-0707 ■ Fax: (0181) 800-0404 ■ Mon-Fri 9:30-6:00 ■ Prices medium to very high ■ Trade discount ■ LAPADA

Antique Oriental carpets and textiles.

CLIVE LOVELESS

54 St. Quintin Avenue, London W10 6PA ■ Tel: (0181) 969-5831 ■ Fax: (0181) 969-5292 ■ By appointment ■ BADA

18th and 19th century Oriental tribal rugs. 17th to 19th century Ottoman, Central Asian, African and Pre-Colombian textiles.

♛ MANSOUR

56 South Audley Street, London W1Y 5FA ■ Tel: (0171) 499-5601 ■ Fax: (0171) 355-3662 ■ Mon-Fri 9:30-6:00 ■ Benjamin Soleimani ■ Prices low to high ■ Major credit cards ■ Trade discount

Splendid selection Oriental and European carpets, Aubusson, Savonneries and tapestries. Both old and new.

MAYORCAS LTD

8 Duke Street, St. James's, London SW1Y 6BN ■ Tel: (0171) 839-3100 ■ Fax: (0171) 839-3223 ■ Mon-Fri 9:30-5:30, Sat by appointment ■ BADA

European tapestries, textiles and needlework, carpets and rugs.

PAUL NELS LTD.

6-8 Sedley Place, London W1R 1HG ■ Tel: (0171) 629-1909/(0171) 493-5902 ■ Fax: (0171) 629-3136 ■ Mon-Fri 9:00-5:00 ■ LAPADA

Needlework, Oriental items, rugs and carpets and textiles.

THE ORIENTALIST

152 Walton Street, London SW3 QJJ ■ Tel: (0171) 581-2332 ■ Fax: (0171) 589-0760 ■ Mon-Sat 11:00-5:00 ■ Persian and French spoken ■ Prices medium to very high ■ Major credit cards ■ Trade discount

Large stocks of hand-made antique Oriental and European carpets. Tapestries, Aubussons and lots of cushions. Textiles new and old. Repair and cleaning.

PEREZ

199 Brompton Road, London SW3 1LA ■ Tel: (0171) 589-2199 ■ Fax: (0171) 371-9620 ■ Mon-Sat 10:00-5:00 ■ LAPADA

Rugs, carpets and textiles.

SHAIKH & SON (ORIENTAL RUGS) LTD

16 Brook Street, London W1Y 1AA■ Tel: (0171) 629-3430 ■ Fax: (0171) 495-8864 ■ Mon-Sat 10:00-6:00 ■ M.A. Shaikh ■ Prices medium ■ Major credit cards ■ Trade discount

Unusual old rugs. Uzbek, Afghan, Persian, Turkish, Kashmiri and Caucasian. Some antiques.

SHARAFI & CO

53 Highgate Road, London NW5 ■ Tel: (0171) 284-2488 ■ Fax: (0171) 485-0193 ■ Mon-Fri 9:00-6:00 ■ Mehdi Sharafi ■ Persian and Urdu spoken ■ Prices low to very high

A large selection of Oriental carpets, old and new from Persia, Afghanistan, Pakistan, Turkey. Cleaning and repair.

SOVIET CARPET & ART CENTRE

303-305 Cricklewood Broadway, (off Temple Rd.), London NW2 6PG ■ Tel: (0181) 452-2445 ■ Fax: (0181) 450-2642 ■ Mon-Fri by appointment ■ Sun 10:30-5:30 ■ R. Rabi ■ Russian, Persian and Turkish spoken ■ Prices low to high ■ Trade prices ■ Major credit carpets

Oriental and Caucasian carpets. Some Russian art, oil paintings, prints, textiles, ceramics and crafts.

ROBERT STEPHENSON CARPETS

1 Elystan Street, Chelsea Green, London SW3 3NT ■ Telfax: (0171) 225-2343 ■ Mon-Fri 9:30-5:30, Sat 10:30-2:00 ■ Robert Stephenson, Giuseppe Giannini ■ French and Italian spoken ■ Prices medium to high ■ Visa and MC ■ Trade discount ■ LAPADA

Antique carpets, kilims and tapestries. Also contemporary carpets in old and modern designs. Cleaning and restoration.

STOCKWELL CARPETS LTD

24 Harcourt Street, London W1H 1DT ■ Tel: (0171) 224-8380 ■ Fax: (0171) 224-8381 ■ E-mail: stockwellcarpets@mcmail.com ■ Mon-Fri 9:30-5:30 ■ John Stockwell ■ Some French and German spoken ■ Prices medium to very high ■ Trade discount

Design and custom-made, hand-crafted, hand-tufted and hand-knotted carpets. Also tapestries woven. Work references include: The Royal Pavilion at Brighton, Chatsworth House, the British Embassies in Paris, Brussels, Vienna and Washington, the Governor's Mansion, Puerto Rico.

THE TEXTILE GALLERY, MICHAEL AND JACQUELINE FRANSES

12 Queen Street, Mayfair, London W1X 7PL ■ Tel: (0171) 499-7979 ■ Fax: (0171) 409-2596 ■ E-mail: post@textile-art.com ■ Internet http://www.textile-art.com ■ By appointment only ■ BADA

Textile art, including classical carpets.

JOYCE V'SOSKE - HANDMADE CARPETS OF IRELAND

The Clocktower Design Centre, Unit 16 Coda Centre, 189 Munster Road, London SW6 6AW ■ Tel: (0171) 386-7200 ■ Fax: (0171) 386-9220 ■ E-mail: vsoske@enterprise.net ■ Mon-Fri 9:00-5:30 ■ Marj Conlan ■ Italian spoken ■ Prices high to very high ■ Trade discount

Hand-tufted carpets and wall hangings made to order in 100% wool. Full design service. Member of The Guild of Master Craftsmen.

VIGO CARPET GALLERY

6A Vigo Street, London W1X 1AH ■ Tel: (0171) 439 6971■ Fax: (0171) 439-2353 ■ E-mail: vigo@btinternet.com ■ Mon-Sat 10:00-6:00 ■ Arif Siddique ■ Major credit cards ■ LAPADA

Hand-knotted carpets with re-created designs in vegetable dyes using hand-spun wool. Some antiques and textiles.

LUCY WASSELL

1408 New North Road, London N1 7BH ■ Tel: (0171) 226-5560 ■ Mon-Fri 9:00-5:00 by appointment ■ Prices medium

100% pure wool hand-tufted rugs on commission. One-off designs.

ALEXANDER D. WILKINS

27 Princess Road, Regents Park, London NW1 8JR ■ Tel: (0171) 722-7608 ■ Fax: (0171) 483-0423 ■ Mon-Fri 9:00-5:00 by appointment ■ Alexander D. Wilkins ■ Prices low to very high ■ Visa and MC ■ Trade discount

Brokers who supply all types of Oriental rugs and carpets both old and new. Hand-made Oriental rugs. Restorations.

GALLERY YACOU

127 Fullham Road, London SW3 6RT ■ Tel: (0171) 584-2929 ■ Fax: (0171) 584-3535 ■ Mon-Fri 10:30-6:00, Sun 12:00-5:00 ■ Robin Yacoubian ■ French spoken ■ Prices medium ■ Major credit cards ■ LAPADA

Antique and decorative Oriental and European carpets. A large selection of 19th century Aubusson carpets. Repairs.

ZADAH FINE ORIENTAL CARPETS

35 Bruton Place, London W1X 7AB ■ Tel: (0171) 493-2622 ■ Fax: (0171) 629-6682 ■ Mon-Fri 9:30-5:30 ■ Trade discount ■ LAPADA

Rugs, carpets and textiles.

Antique Pillows

PILLOWS OF BOND STREET

Grays Antiques Centre, Stand 301, 58 Davies Street, London W1Y 2LP ■ Tel: (0171) 495-8853 ■ Fax: (0171) 792-3158 ■ Sun-Fri 10:00-6:00 ■ Robin Kumar ■ Professional discount

17th to 19th century Aubusson tapestry pillows.

THE ORIENTALIST

152 Walton Street, London SW3 QJJ ■ Tel: (0171) 581-2332 ■ Fax: (0171) 589-0760 ■ Mon-Sat 11:00-5:00 ■ Persian and French spoken ■ Prices medium to very high ■ Major credit cards ■ Trade discount

Lots of pillows in Aubusson tapestry and antique textiles.

SUSSEX HOUSE & ENGLISH HOME COLLECTION

92 Wandsworth Bridge Road, London SW6 2TF ■ Tel: (0171) 371-5458 ■ Fax: (0171) 371-7590 ■ Mon-Fri 10:00-6:00, Sat 10:30-5:00 ■ Gaynor Churchward ■ French, Italian and Spanish spoken ■ Prices medium to high ■ Professional discount ■ Major credit cards

Aubusson tapestry pillows and a great selection of embroidered and woven decorative pillows.

Antique Textiles

SHEILA COOK TEXTILES
184 Westbourne Grove, London W11 2RH ■ Tel: (0171) 792-8001 ■ Fax: (0171) 229-3855 ■ E-mail: sheila.cook@dial.pipex.com ■ Website: www.sheilacook.co.uk ■ Tue-Sat 10:00-6:00 ■ Sheila Cook ■ Prices medium ■ Trade discount ■ Major credit cards

Antique costume, textiles and accessories from the mid-18th century to the 1970s. All stock is in very good condition and has an interesting design slant.

♔ THE GALLERY OF ANTIQUE COSTUME & TEXTILES
2 Church Street, Marylebone, London NW8 8ED ■ Telfax: (0171) 723-9981 ■ Lionel Segal ■ Mon-Sat 10-5:30 ■ French spoken ■ Prices medium to very high ■ Some trade discounts ■ Major credit cards

Antique textiles: period drapes from the 19th century and earlier, period pillows, bedspreads, wall hangings, quilts. Beautiful collection of period costume, mainly 1930s and earlier, accessories. Some rare pieces of the 16th century.

JOSS GRAHAM ORIENTAL TEXTILES
10 Eccleston Street, London SW1W 9LT ■ Telfax: (0171) 730-4370 ■ E-mail: joss.graham@btinternet.com ■ Mon-Sat 10:00-6:00 ■ Joss Graham ■ French spoken ■ Prices medium to high ■ Trade discount ■ Visa, MC

Asian and African costume and textiles, antique and contemporary. He also has rugs, kilims, embroideries and tribal art.

♔ LINDA GUMB
9 Camden Passage, London N1 8EA ■ Tel: (0171) 354-1184 ■ Fax: (0171) 359-0103
Chatsworth Interiors, 71D Chatsworth Road, London NW2 4BG ■ Tel: (0181) 451-2951 ■ Telephone for hours ■ She also does the major antique shows

Linda Gumb is an antique dealer and is one of England's leading specialists in 18th and 19th century European textiles. In Camden Passage she sells tapestries, cushions and some needlework, as well as some decorative furniture and art objects.

DAVID IRELAND

283 Westbourne Grove, London W11 ■ Telfax: (0181) 968-8887 ■ E-mail:
david.i@virgin.net ■ Saturdays only 9:00-4:30 ■ French and Japanese
spoken ■ Prices low to very high ■ Trade discount ■ Major credit cards

Antique costume and textiles from Europe and Asia.

KATHERINE POLE

30 Hamilton Gardens, London NW8 9PU ■ Tel: (0171) 286-5630 ■
Mon-Fri by appointment ■ Prices low to high ■ Trade discount

French and English antique textiles of the 18th to the 20th century.

BRYONY THOMASSON

19 Ackmar Road, London SW6 4UP ■ Tel: (0171) 731-3693 ■ By
appointment only ■ 283 Westbourne Grove, Portobello Road, London
W11 ■ Sat only 8:00-4:00 ■ Mon-Fri by appointment ■ French spoken
■ Prices low to medium ■ Trade discount ■ Major credit cards

**Antique hand-woven rustic textiles. Agricultural working
clothes, jeans with patches, holes and darns. Also some agricultural accessories.**

RHONA VALENTINE

Admiral Vernon Arcade, 141 Portobello Road, W11 ■ Tel: (01372)
726931 ■ By appointment ■ Prices medium to high ■ Trade discount
■ Visa, MC

**European decorative textiles of the 17th to the 19th century.
Cushions.**

♔ CHELSEA HARBOUR DESIGN CENTRE

Chelsea Harbour Design Centre, Lots Road, Chelsea Harbour, London SW10 0XE ■ Tel: (0171) 351-4433 ■ Fax: (0171) 352-7868 ■ Mon-Fri 9:30-5:00.

Chelsea Harbour Design Centre is the London centre for the Interior Design Industry. Situated just off King's Road, the Design Centre provides one-stop service for the interior design industry. Professionals and their clients will find a wide range of furniture, fabrics, trimmings and accessories beautifully displayed. Skilled professional staff are always on hand to help. There is a nice café open throughout the day. Most showrooms accept the major credit cards.

Carpets

AFIA CARPETS
G11 ■ Tel: (0171) 351-5858 ■ Fax: (0171) 351-9677

Sole distributors in the UK for Stark Carpets, Van Besouw, Flipo and Marc, Inc. They offer both rugs and patterned and plain carpets with borders.

CARPET DESIGN STUDIO
3/13 ■ Telfax: (0171) 349-8835

A comprehensive carpeting service. Many stock ranges from coir and sisal to plain velvets and textured carpets. Also custom-made carpets and expert fitting.

CHRISTINE VAN DER HURD
2/17 ■ Tel: (0171) 352-8300 ■ Fax: (0171) 376-3574

Christine Van der Hurd's own carpet and rug designs (hand-tufted in 100% wool). Also a full range of coordinating fabrics and cushions

Fabrics & Wallcoverings

ABBOTT & BOYD
G8 ■ Tel: (0171) 351-9985 ■ Fax: (0171) 823-3127

Fabrics: woven upholstery, printed cottons, sheers, voiles, linens, jutes, damasks. Also tiebacks, fringes and general furnishing trimmings.

ALEXANDER BEAUCHAMP
2/12 ■ Tel: (0171) 376-4556 ■ Fax: (0171) 376-3435
Hand-printed fabrics and wallpapers plus stock ranges. Historical advice. Extensive archives 1680-1950.

BORDERLINE
2/27 ■ Tel: (0171) 823-3567 ■ Fax: (0171) 351-7644 ■ E-mail: borderline@iddv.com.uk ■ Sally Baring
Printed paisleys, Portuguese and Classic Document prints. Throws.

BRUNSCHWIG & FILS
10 The Chambers ■ Tel: (0171) 351-5797 ■ Fax: (0171) 351-2280 ■ Bruno Garros ■ French spoken
Founded in France in 1900. Fabrics, wallpapers, trimmings, upholstered furniture, tables, lamps and mirrors.

COLONY
2/14 ■ Tel: (0171) 351-3232 ■ Fax: (0171) 351-2242
Italian fabrics: lampasses, brocades, damasks and silks.

COLE & SON
G9 ■ Tel: (0171) 376-4623 ■ Fax: (0171) 376-4631 ■ Mon-Fri 9:30-5:30 ■ Rick Ball ■ Prices medium to high
Hand-blocked wallpapers made to order as well as stock collections.

BELINDA COOTE
3/14 ■ Tel: (0171) 351-0404 ■ Fax: (0171) 352-4808 ■ Belinda Coote, Jeremy Loxton ■ French spoken
Quality tapestry fabrics, trimmed tapestry cushions, decorative wall hangings and bedspreads. All in Belinda Coote's refined and exclusive style.

CHASE ERWIN
G22 ■ Tel: (0171) 352-7271 ■ Fax: (0171) 352-7170
Upholstery and curtain-weight hand-woven Thai silks, heavy duty plain and animal print ultrasuede in 102 colours and hand-woven chenilles. Throws from Textillery Weavers, a collection of herringbone upholstery silks and cotton-weight checks.

HILL & KNOWLES
2/15 ■ Telfax: (0171) 376-4686
High quality fabrics and wallpapers: known for their voile collections. A wide range of co-ordinating fabrics, wallpapers and borders, predominantly traditional in style.

JAGTAR

3/11 ■ Tel: (0171) 351-4220 ■ Fax: (0171) 351-4404 ■ E-mail: jagtar.uk@virgin.net Henry Belloy, Marc Lefebvre ■ French spoken

High quality silks. Traditional and contemporary designs. Over 150 designs with an extensive colour palette. Curtain making.

JASON D'SOUZA

1/6 ■ Tel: (0171) 351-4440 ■ Fax: (0171) 351-4396

Classical collection of hand-printed linens, hand-woven trimmings made-to-order. Linens, silks, upholstery, upholstery weaves, tassel tie-backs. Fabric and trimmings colour-matched to order.

KRAVET LONDON

G17 ■ Tel: (0171) 795-0110 ■ Fax: (0171) 349-0678

Kravet is the USA's largest fabric house and Kravet London represents the best from this important collection. The emphasis is on textured weaves and chenilles.

LEE JOFA

G19 ■ Tel: (0171) 351-7760 ■ Fax: (0171) 351-7752 ■ Peter Hostler ■ French and German spoken

A large collection of hand-block printed linens and glazed cottons made in England. Printed and woven decorative upholstery fabrics. Exclusive distributor of Christopher Moore Toile de Jouy collections, and plaids and stripes from Weathervane Hill.

MARY FOX LINTON

1/8 ■ Tel: (0171) 351-9908 ■ Fax: (0171) 351-0907

A wide range of international fabrics including Italian prints, weaves, sheers, taffetas, textured fabrics and sheers.

MARVIC TEXTILES LTD

G26 ■ Tel: (0171) 352-3119 ■ Fax: (0171) 352-3135 ■ E-mail: sales@marvictextiles.co.uk ■ Peter Afia

A wide variety of upholstery weaves, chenilles, silks, damasks, moires, toiles de Jouy and printed linen. Wallpapers with complementary fabrics. Toiles de Jouy fabrics reproduced in matching papers.

ORNAMENTA

3/12 ■ Tel: (0171) 352-1824 ■ Fax: (0171) 376-3398

Original hand-printed wall papers. Trompe l'oeil papers, borders, hand-printed silks, created by designer Jane Gordon Clark. The papers have the look of antique panelling, stone block walls or carved architectural friezes or mouldings. 22 carat gold leaf and sterling silver leaf contemporary designs are also on display.

H.A. PERCHERON LTD

G6 ■ Tel: (0171) 376-5992 ■ Fax: (0171) 631-4720

Distributors of French and Italian textiles for nearly one hundred years, Percheron has added a London stock range. From plain cotton to printed silk, from hand-loomed silk velvet to linen voile.

SAHCO HESSLEIN

G24 ■ Tel: (0171) 352-6168 ■ Fax: (0171) 352-0767

Furnishing fabrics of the highest quality. From silks to the more avant-garde sheers and upholstery weaves.

IAN SANDERSON

G13 ■ Tel: (0171) 351-2481 ■ Fax: (0171) 351-7868 ■ Lynda Hindi

Furnishing fabrics and trimmings with coordinating colours. Original tickings, weaves, damasks, floral prints and chenilles. Chenille/bouclé trimmings.

J. ROBERT SCOTT

2/19 ■ Tel: (0171) 376-4705 ■ Fax: (0171) 376-4706

Designs by American designer Sally Sirkin Lewis. Textiles and leathers ranging from traditional and formal to contemporary minimalist.

THE SILK GALLERY

G25 ■ Tel: (0171) 351-1790 ■ Fax: (0171) 376-4693 ■ Kathryne Horbve ■ French spoken

Fabrics for interiors: silk blend and hand prints. All can be custom coloured.

JIM THOMPSON

G10 ■ Tel: (0171) 351-2829 ■ Fax: (0171) 351-0907

Largest manufacturer and distributor of Thai silk, producing an incredibly high-standard silk. More than 3,500 fabrics in a huge colour palette.

TISSUNIQUE

2/10 ■ Tel: (0171) 349-0096 ■ Fax: (0171) 349-0097 ■ E-mail: info@tissunique.demon.co.uk ■ Website: www.tissunique.com

Classical French designs from Provence, percales, toiles and upholstery weights as well as specially commissioned and edited lines from traditional sources. Also large-scale Italian silk damasks and a linen velvet.

TITLEY & MARR
1/7 ■ Tel: (0171) 351-2913 ■ Fax: (0171) 351-6318 ■ Ruth Harrison-Ward
Fine furnishing fabrics in classical designs. Chenille, cotton taffetas, toiles de Jouy, traditional damasks, and chintz.

BRUNO TRIPLET
G1 ■ Tel: (0171) 795-0395 ■ Fax: (0171) 376-3070 ■ Bruno Triplet ■ French spoken
Furnishing textiles and wallcoverings.

WARNER FABRICS
G9 ■ Tel: (0171) 376-7578 ■ Fax: (0171) 376-8277
A full range of fine fabrics in classical, traditional and contemporary designs. An extensive archive.

WATTS OF WESTMINSTER
2/9 ■ Tel: (0171) 376-4486 ■ Fax: (0171) 376-4636 ■ E-mail: wattsofwestminster@iddv.com ■ Website: www.watts of westminster.co.uk ■ Danuta Bildzuik ■ French spoken
Fabrics, wallpaper and trimmings. Period decoration from an important design archive.

BRIAN YATES
G27 ■ Tel: (0171) 352-0123 ■ Fax: (0171) 352-6060 ■
Fabrics and wallcoverings from Europe for both the residential and contract markets. Sole distributors for Arte, Pepe Penalver and Taco Edition.

ZIMMER + ROHDE (UK) LTD
G15 ■ Tel: (0171) 351-7115 ■ Fax: (0171) 351-5661 ■ Mr. C. Lee
Furnishing fabrics: plain, woven and sumptuous silks. Distributors of the Ardecora and Jack Lenor Larson lines.

ZOFFANY LTD
G11 ■ Tel: (0171) 349-0043 ■ Fax: (0171) 351-9677
Wallpaper and furnishing fabrics reproduced from period print documents in their own archives. They also offer carpets and trimmings.

Decorative Hardware

FRANCHI INTERNATIONAL
2/11 ■ Tel: (0171) 351-4554 ■ Fax: (0171) 351-2803 ■ Marco Franchi
Contemporary and traditional door handles.

Furniture

GREENGATE
2/23 ■ Tel: (0171) 349-0794 ■ Fax: (0171) 349-0795
Designers and manufacturers of an extensive range of traditional sofas, chairs, stools, and ottomans. An exclusive collection of hand-made replica pieces. All frames are of ash and beech.

MALIA LIMITED
C2/C3 ■ Tel: (0171) 352-6656 ■ Fax: (0171) 352-6616 ■ also Sat 10:00-1:00 ■ Osama Al-Sayed ■ Italian, German and Arabic spoken
Producers of a wide range of reproduction furniture in a variety of styles, from Art Deco to modern classics in mahogany, rattan, bamboo and banana wood with coconut inlay. Also decorative accessories.

DAVID SEYFRIED
1/5 ■ Tel: (0171) 823-3848 ■ Fax: (0171) 823-3221 ■ David Seyfried
Upholstered furniture: traditional style sofas.

SUTHERLAND (EUROPE)
2/20 ■ Tel: (0171) 823-3456 ■ Fax: (0171) 376-5758 ■ Patricia Stratford
Custom-made furniture: teak outdoor furniture and fabric.

TITCHMARSH & GOODWIN
2/23 ■ Tel: (0171) 376-7567 ■ Fax: (0171) 376-7658
A family firm of cabinet makers established for 80 years, comprising a gilder, a lacquer artist, carvers and turners and French polishers. Dining tables, desks, dining chairs, console tables in a variety of woods, including walnut and yew.

General

ALTFIELD
KG4 ■ Tel: (0171) 351-5893 ■ Fax: (0171) 376-5667
Chinoiserie. Porcelain, lamps, cushions, rosewood and lacquer furniture, mirror frames, water-colour artwork and Japanese screens. Scalamandré and Boris Kroll fabrics, Maya Romanoff and Blumenthal wallcoverings and Clockhouse furniture. Antique Chinese furniture.

JAB ANSTOETZ
1/15-16 ■ Tel: (0171) 349-9323 ■ Fax: (0171) 349-9282

An extensive collection of furnishing and upholstery fabrics. Wallcoverings from Jab and Club Creation and Design Edition rugs from leading European designers.

DONGHIA UK LTD
G23 ■ Tel: (0171) 823-3456 ■ Fax: (0171) 376-5758

Donghia's handcrafted furniture, textiles and accessories.

INTERDESIGN
G30 ■ Tel: (0171) 376-5272 ■ Fax: (0171) 376-3020

Suppliers of Mastro Raphael, Duralee, Designer's Fantasy and Bornat rugs. A full range of furniture, fabrics, rugs and objects. New furniture from Boffi and a line of screens by Fornasetti.

INTERIOR SUPPLY
2/16 ■ Tel: (0171) 352-0502 ■ Fax: (0171) 352-2026 ■ Jonathan Farrer

Classical furniture and accessories. Contemporary lighting, fabrics, wallpapers and sheers, rugs, cushions and throws, modern and traditional upholstery, bespoke and contract cabinet making.

RAMM, SON & CROCKER
G28 ■ Tel: (0171) 352-0931 ■ Fax: (0171) 352-0935

Quality furnishing fabrics, hand-block and hand-screen archive prints. Wallpapers, passementerie and a range of traditional furniture.

RBI INTERNATIONAL
G18 ■ Tel: (0171) 376-3766 ■ Fax: (0171) 376-3763

The George Franc collection of fabrics of rich chenilles and co-ordinating woven jacquards, toiles de Jouy, fabric collections from Vidivi, Atelia Casa Kawashima. Fabrics and rugs from Missoni, carpets from Fabrica and linens from TJ.

TURNELL & GIGON
G20 ■ Tel: (0171) 351-5142 ■ Fax: (0171) 376-7945

Fabrics, trimmings, wallpapers and furniture from: L'Abeille, Cesari, Decortex, Les Passementeries de L'Ile de France, SAT Creations, Schumacher and Turnell & Grigon.

Lighting

WOOLPIT INTERIORS
G13 ■ Tel: (0171) 351-2481 ■ Fax: (0171) 351-7868 ■ Lynda Hindi
Decorative lighting, lamps and shades.

Linen

PRATESI
1/2 ■ Tel: (0171) 349-0090 ■ Fax: (0171) 349-0035
The finest Egyptian cotton, percales, jacquards, linens, silks and Mongolian cashmere are used throughout their collection of bed, bath and table linens. A new range of custom-made upholstered headboards.

Trimmings

WENDY CUSHING TRIMMINGS
G7 ■ Tel: (0171) 351-5796 ■ Fax: (0171) 351-4246 ■ Mon-Fri 10:00-5:00 ■ Stella Joannidou ■ Greek spoken
Tie-backs, fringes, braids, cords and accessories made to order.

Upholstery & Soft Furnishings

GYPSY TABLES
3/6 ■ Tel: (0171) 351-0292 ■ Fax: (0171) 351-3034 ■ E-mail: gypsytables@design-online.co.uk ■ Website: www.design-online.co.uk
Soft furnishings including curtains, tablecloths, bedcovers, as well as upholstered bedheads and dressing-table stools. An internet directory for interior designers on their worldwide web.

Wallcoverings

COLE & SON (WALLPAPERS) LIMITED

G9 ■ Tel: (0171) 376-4623 ■ Fax: (0171) 376-4631 ■ Patrick Ball

Handblocked wallpapers made to order and stock collections.

NOBILIS FONTAN

G3 ■ Tel: (0171) 351-7878 ■ Fax: (0171) 376-3507 ■ Mrs. Gemma Allman

Wallcoverings, upholstery fabrics, silks, prints, weaves. Cotton prints, silk damasks, small weaves, textured wall coverings.

FABRICS

LAURA ASHLEY LTD
9 Harriet Street, London SW1X ■ Tel: (0171) 235-9797
193 Warwick Road, Kensington, London W14 ■ Tel: (0171) 603-2285
Mon-Sat 9:30-5:30 ■ Prices low to high ■ Major credit cards
The well-known line: traditional prints, stripes, checks. Table linens and a line of children's fabrics.

BEAUMONT & FLETCHER
261 Fulham Road, London SW3 6HY ■ Tel: (0171) 352-5594 ■ Fax: (0171) 352-3546 ■ Mon-Sat 9:30-5:30 ■ John Crowell, Brian Worthington ■ Prices high ■ Professional discount ■ Major credit cards
Document-based fabrics of their own design. Traditional hand-sprung upholstery, hand-woven carpets, mirrors, wall lights, copies of antique furniture.

👑 BENNISON FABRICS
16 Holbein Place, London SW1W 8NL ■ Tel: (0171) 730-8076 ■ Fax: (0171) 823-4997 ■ Mon-Fri 10:30-5:30 ■ Gillian Newberry ■ French and Spanish spoken ■ Prices very high ■ Trade discount ■ Major credit cards
Beautifully printed designs adapted from 18th and 19th century French and English documents. Screen-printed document designs on linen. Tie-back fringes and cord. Curtain making.

👑 BENTLEY & SPENS
1-2 Mornington Street, London NW1 7QD ■ Telfax: (0171) 387-7374 ■ Mon-Fri, Sat mornings ■ Telephone for hours ■ Kim Bentley, Sally Spens ■ Prices medium ■ Trade discount
Contemporary hand-printed linens and cottons. Printed and hand-printed cushions. Fabrics for upholstery and curtains. Blinds, throws and curtain poles. Upholstery services. Their designs have been added to the collection in the Victoria and Albert Museum.

THE BERWICK STREET CLOTH SHOP
14 Berwick Street, London W1V 3RG ■ Tel: (0171) 287-2881 ■ Fax: (0171) 734-3476 ■ Mon-Fri 9:00-6:00, Sat 9:00-5:00 ■ Spencer Harvey ■ French, Spanish, Turkish and Israeli spoken ■ Prices low to very high ■ Major credit cards
Silks, wools, linens, velvets, laces. Some unusual theatrical fabrics.

BROADWICK SILKS LTD

9-11 Broadwick Street, London W1V 1FN ■ Tel: (0171) 734-3320 ■ Fax: (0171) 734-3476 ■ Mon-Fri 9:00-6:00 ■ Spencer Harvey ■ French, Spanish, Turkish and spoken ■ Prices low to very high ■ Major credit cards

Silks, wools, linens, velvets, laces. Unusual theatrical fabrics.

BOURNE STREET LINEN

93 Pimlico Road, London SW1W 8PH ■ Telfax: (0171) 376-1113 ■ Mon-Fri 9:00-5:00, Sat 10:00-2:00 ■ Thynne and Howe ■ French and Chinese spoken ■ Prices high ■ Professional discount ■ Major credit cards

Linen fabrics.

♔ **MANUEL CANOVAS**

2 North Terrace, Brompton Road, London SW3 2BA ■ Tel: (0171) 225-2298 ■ Fax: (0171) 823-7848 ■ Mon-Fri 9:30-5:30 ■ Prices medium to very high ■ Trade discount ■ Major credit cards

Fine collection of cotton prints and woven stripes, as well as velvets, jacquards, damasks and plains.

CHANEE DUCROCQ DESCHEMAKER

168 New Cavendish Street, London W1M 7FJ ■ Tel: (0171) 631-5223 ■ Fax: (0171) 436-4657 ■ Mon-Fri 1:00-5:00 ■ French spoken ■ Prices medium to high

Woven furnishing fabrics: jacquards, velvets, silks, ottomans, prints.

CHELSEA TEXTILE DESIGN

7 Walton Street, London SW3 2JD ■ Tel: (0171) 594-0111 ■ Fax: (0171) 584-7170 ■ E-mail: info@chelsea-textiles.co.uk. ■ Mon-Sat 9:00-6:00 ■ Mona Perlingen ■ Prices high ■ Professional discount to shop accounts ■ Major credit cards

Hand-embroidered fabrics that can be made up into bedcovers, curtains, needlpoint cushions.

JANE CHURCHILL

151 Sloane Street, London SW1X 9BX ■ Tel: (0171) 730-9847 ■ Fax: (0171) 259-9189 ■ Mon-Sat 10:00-6:00, Wed until 7:00 ■ Annabel Holmes ■ French spoken ■ Prices medium to high ■ Major credit cards

Fabric, wallpapers, decorative accessories and furniture.

CLOTH HOUSE
98 Berwick Street, Soho, London W1V 3PP ■ Telfax: (0171) 287-1555 ■ Mon-Sat 9:30-6:00 ■ Jay Harley ■ Prices medium ■ Major credit cards
High-tech fabrics, stretch fabrics, brocades.

COLEFAX & FOWLER
39 Brook Street, London W1Y 2JE ■ Tel: (0171) 493-2231 ■ Fax: (0171) 355-4037
110 Fulham Road, London SW3 6RL ■ Tel: (0171) 244-7427 ■ Fax: (0171) 373-7916 ■ Mon-Fri 9:30-5:30 ■ Prices high ■ Trade discount ■ Major credit cards
Traditional English chintzes and woven fabrics.

THE DECORATIVE FABRICS GALLERY
278-280 Brompton Road, London SW3 ■ Tel: (0171) 589-4778 ■ Fax: (0171) 589-4781 ■ Mon-Fri 9:30-5:30, Sat 10:00-5:00 ■ Angela Fawcett ■ French, Greek and Finnish spoken ■ Prices medium to high ■ Major credit cards
Furnishing fabrics, accessories from Monkwell, G.P. & J. Baker, Knoll. Also wallpaper.

DESIGNERS GUILD
267-271 King's Road, London SW3 5EN ■ Tel: (0171) 243-7300 ■ Fax: (0171) 243-7710 ■ Showroom hours: Mon-Tue 9:30-5:30, Wed-Thu 9:30-6:00, Sat 10:00-6:00 ■ Tricia Guild ■Professional discount ■ Major credit cards
Wide selection of fabrics in neutrals and colourful patterns and a good choice of wallpapers. They also sell Ralph Lauren's fabrics.

DE WINTER LTD
223 Kensington Church Street, London W8 7LX ■ Tel: (0171) 229-4949 ■ Fax: (0171) 221-5635 ■ Mon-Fri 9:00-6:00, Sat 9:00-4:30 ■ H.S. Berger ■ French spoken ■ Prices low to high ■ Visa and MC
Curtain upholstery fabric, loose slip covers, tapestries, toiles, velvets. Cushions, poles, blinds, trimmings and tie backs, wall hangings and rugs.

FIRTH & MARSHALL FABRICS
31 Seward Street, London EC1V 3PA ■ Tel: (0171) 490-1404 ■ Fax: (0171) 490-1561 ■ Mon-Fri 9:00-5:30 ■ R.C. Thomas ■ French, Spanish and German spoken ■ Prices medium to high
A stock of fabrics from major manufacturers.

TIMNEY FOWLER LTD

388 King's Road, London SW3 5UZ ■ Tel: (0171) 352-2263 ■ Fax: (0171) 352-0351 ■ Mon-Sat 9:30-6:00 ■ Michael Flannigan ■ Prices medium to high ■ Trade discount ■ Major credit cards

Contemporary furnishing fabrics, particularly black and white prints, and accessories.

ANNA FRENCH LTD

343 King's Road, London SW3 5ES ■ Tel: (0171) 351-1126 ■ Fax: (0171) 351-0421 ■ E-mail: enquires@anna-french.demon.co.uk ■ Mon-Sat 9:30-5:30 ■ Prices medium ■ Professional discount ■ Visa, MC

Printed fabric, upholstery fabric, cotton lace. Wallpapers, borders and accessories.

♕ PIERRE FREY (UK) LTD

251-253 Fulham Road, London SW3 6HY ■ Tel: (0171) 376-5599 ■ Fax: (0171) 352-3024 ■ Mon-Fri 9:30-5:30 ■ Prices high ■ Trade discount ■ Major credit cards

Major fabric house from France. A full range of decorating fabrics. Great coordinates.

♕ THE GAINSBOROUGH SILK WEAVING CO LTD

16 The Coda Centre, 189 Munster Road, Fulham, London SW6 6AM ■ Tel: (0171) 386-7153 ■ Fax: (0171) 386-9220 ■ E-mail: sales@gainsborough.co.uk ■ Mon-Fri 9:00-5:30 ■ Anna-Maria Feniello ■ Italian spoken ■ Prices medium to very high ■ Trade discount ■ Major credit cards

Fine furnishing fabrics including damasks, chenilles and taffetas in 100% silk. Silk and cotton, cotton viscose and 100% cotton. Woven fabrics, trimmings and wallpapers. Can weave to order.

NICHOLAS HERBERT LTD

118 Lots Road, Chelsea, London SW10 0RJ ■ Tel: (0171) 376-5596 ■ Fax: (0171) 376-5572 ■ Website: www.I-I.net/nicholasherbertltd ■ Mon-Fri 9:30-5:30 ■ Nicholas Herbert ■ Major credit cards ■ Some trade discounts

French document-based florals, upholstery fabric, wallpapers, folding tables. Design and upholstery services.

♕ HODSOLL MCKENZIE

52 Pimlico Road, London SW1W 8LP ■ Tel: (0171) 730-2877 ■ Fax: (0171) 259-9292 ■ Mon-Fri 10:00-5:00 ■ Alex McKenzie and Mark Butcher ■ Prices high ■ Professional discount ■ Major credit cards

Great selection of fabrics and wallpapers. Small line of furniture.

KVADRAT

62 Princedale Road, London W11 4NL ■ Tel: (0171) 229-9969 ■ Fax: (0171) 229-1543 ■ Mon-Fri 8:30-5:30 ■ Jan Versholt ■ Danish, German and some French spoken ■ Prices high ■ Trade discount

High quality curtain and upholstery fabrics for the contract market.

☷ LELIEVRE (UK)

101 Cleveland Street, London W1P 5PN ■ Tel: (0171) 636-3461 ■ Fax: (0171) 637-5070 ■ Mon-Fri 9:30- 5:30 ■ Prices medium to high ■ Trade discount ■ Major credit cards

Upholstery fabrics in cotton viscose, silks, brocades, damasks, jacquards, velvets. One of the best French fabric houses with a wonderful choice of wide width fabric for wall upholstery.

LOUBI (UK) LTD

The Clocktower Workspace, Unit 10, 4 Shearling Way, London N7 9TH ■ Telfax: (0171) 609-3310 ■ Mon-Fri 9:30-6:30 ■ Sarah Maynard ■ Prices high ■ Professional discount

Printed silks, velvets, wallpapers. Furniture, lighting, soft furnishings.

IAN MANKIN NATURAL FABRICS LTD

109 Regents Park Road, London NW1 8UR ■ Tel: (0171) 722-0997 ■ Fax: (0171) 722-2159 ■ Mon-Fri 10:00-5:30, Sat 10:00-4:00 ■ Ian Mankin ■ Trade discount

Fabric: natural cotton or linen cotton mix in checks, stripes or plains.

OSBORNE & LITTLE

304 King's Road, London SW3 5UH ■ Tel: (0171) 352-1456 ■ (0171) 351-7813 ■ E-mail: osborneandlittle.co.uk ■ Mon-Fri 9:30-6:00, Sat 10:00-5:30 ■ Tim Walters ■ Prices medium to high ■ Major credit cards

Specialist fabrics and wallpapers, borders and trimmings. Also poles, finials and other drapery hardware.

CLAIRE O'SHEA

Ground floor, 102 Burrows Road, London NW10 5SH ■ Telfax: (0181) 964-3664 ■ Mon-Fri 9:00-6:00 ■ Claire O'Shea ■ Prices medium to high ■ Professional discount

Textile design. Printing onto fabric or paper. Cushions, throws, lampshades, silkscreen printing.

A. PENN FABRICS LTD

196 Kensington Park Road, London W11 2ES ■ Tel: (0171) 792-2457 ■ Fax: (0171) 727-4719 ■ Mon-Fri 9:30-5:30 ■ Bimbi Bellhouse ■ French, German and Italian spoken ■ Prices medium ■ Professional discount

Hand-printed fabrics taken from old documents for curtains and covers. Some fabric-covered accessories.

PONGEES LTD

28-30 Hoxton Square, London N1 6NN ■ Tel: (0171) 739-9130 ■ Fax: (0171) 739-9132 ■ E-mail: info@pongees.co.uk ■ Mon-Fri 9:00-4:30 ■ Caroline Banks ■ Prices medium to high ■ MC and Visa

Silk fabrics by the metre or the roll. Trade only and not for retail.

SEW FANTASTIC

107 Essex Road, London N1 2SL ■ Tel: (0171) 226-2725 ■ Mon-Wed, Fri-Sat 10:00-5:30 ■ Prices low to medium

Fake fur fabrics and stage and costume workers stock.

THE SILK SOCIETY

44 Berwick Street, London W1V 3RE ■ Tel: (0171) 287-1881 ■ Fax: (0171) 734-3476 ■ Mon-Fri 9:00-6:00 ■ Spencer Harvey ■ French, Spanish, Israeli and Turkish spoken ■ Prices low to very high ■ Major credit cards

Silks, wools, linens, velvets and laces. Some theatrical fabrics.

OTTILIE STEVENSON

4 Charlotte Road, London EC2A 3DH ■ Tel: (0171) 739-7321 ■ Fax: (0171) 739-7371 ■ Mon-Fri 9:00-5:30 ■ Ottilie Stevenson ■ French spoken ■ Professional discount

Traditional and contemporary furnishing fabrics, wallpapers and paints.

BERNARD THORP & CO LTD

6 Burnsall Street, London SW3 3ST ■ Tel: (0171) 352-5745 ■ Fax: (0171) 376-3640 ■ Mon-Fri 9:00-5:30 ■ Bernard Thorp ■ French and Italian spoken ■ Prices low to high ■ Trade discount

Custom-coloured, printed and woven fabrics and wallpapers.

TOP LAYER

5 Egerton Terrace, Knightsbridge, London SW3 2BX ■ Tel: (0171) 581-1019 ■ Fax: (0171) 589-9043 ■ Mon-Fri 9:30-5:00 ■ Barrie Coppin ■ Prices low to very high ■ Professional discount ■ Major credit cards

Fabrics, wallpapers, trimmings. They call themselves the best curtain makers in the UK.

TRADE EIGHTY

63-65 Riding House Street, London W1P 7PP ■ Tel: (0171) 637-5188 ■ Fax: (0171) 637-5187 ■ Mon-Fri 9:00-5:30 ■ Mr. Dev Khanna ■ Prices medium to high

100% silk fabrics. Numerous fabric varieties: woven and embroidered to order.

WOLFIN TEXTILES LTD

64 Great Titchfield Street, London W1P 7AE ■ Tel: (0171) 636-4949 ■ Fax ■ (0171) 580-4724 ■ E-mail: cotton@wolfintextiles.co.uk ■ Mon-Fri 8:45-5:15 ■ Howard Wolfin ■ Prices low ■ Major credit cards

Calico, muslin, natural unbleached and bleached cottons. Also fine linen for artists. Furnishings, blackout for theatres and photo studios. Cut lengths or in bulk. Has served The National Trust, The Royal Academy, BBC-TV and The Royal Opera House.

♕ ZOFFANY

63 South Audley Street, Mayfair, London W1Y 5BF ■ Tel: (0171) 495-2505 ■ Fax: (0171) 493-7257 ■ Mon-Fri 9:00-5:30 ■ Lydia Anikitou ■ Prices medium to high

Curtain and upholstery fabric. Wallpapers and carpets.

OUTSIDE LONDON

ANTIQUE LEATHERS

Unit 2, Bennetts Field Trading Estate, Wincanton, Somerset BA9 9DT ■ Tel: (01963) 33163 ■ Fax: (01963) 33164 ■ E-mail: info@antique-leathers.co.uk ■ Mon-Fri 9:30-5:00 ■ Roy Holliday and Jackie Crisp ■ A little French spoken ■ Prices medium to high ■ Trade discounts

Leathers for desk tops with gold tooling. Highest quality re-upholstery of antique chairs.

♛ CONTEXT WEAVERS

Park Mill, Holcombe Road, Helmshore, Rossendale, Lancs. BB4 4NP ■ Tel: (01706) 220917 ■ Mon-Fri 9:00-5:00 ■ Neil Warburton, Anna Benson ■ Prices medium

Weaving of historic reproduction fabrics and braids. Mainly wool worsted, cotton and linen fabrics and silk and wool braids. Typically 18th and 19th century fabrics. The National Trust and English Heritage are their main English customers.

SANDERSON DESIGN ARCHIVE

Arthur Anderson & Sons on 100 acres, Sanderson Road, Uxbridge, Middlesex UB8 ■ Tel: (01895) 238244 ■ By arrangement with the Archivist

Thousands of late 19th and early 20th century textiles and wallpaper designs by many of the greats, Jeffrey & Co, Morris & Co, Charles Knowles and Sanderson.

ASHLEY WILDE DESIGN GROUP

Emmanuel House, Travellers Close, Welham Green, Herts. AL9 7LD ■ Tel: (01707) 635201 ■ Fax: (01707) 635247 ■ Mon-Fri 8:30-5:30 ■ A.L. Brodin ■ Several languages spoken ■ Prices low to high ■ Trade discount ■ Major credit cards

Silk and cotton curtaining, voiles and upholstery ready made.

♛ THE WORKING SILK MUSEUM

New Mills, South Street, Braintree, Essex CM7 GB ■ Tel: (01376) 553393 ■ Fax: (01376) 330642 ■ Website: www.humphriesweaving.co.uk ■ Mon-Fri 10:00-12:30/1:30-5:00 ■ Factory tours: 12:00-4:00 ■ Mr. R.J. Humphries ■ Major credit cards

England's last remaining hand-loom silk weavers using 150 year-old looms. See how silk fabric is produced from the raw material to the finished cloth. Small gift items and embroidery threads.

See also: Chelsea Harbour Design Centre.

Children's Fabrics

THE NURSERY WINDOW
83 Walton Street, London SW3 2HP ■ Tel: (0171) 581-3358 ■ Fax: (0171) 823-8839 ■ Mon-Sat 10:00-5:30 ■ J. Hughes Hallett ■ French spoken ■ Prices medium ■ Major credit cards

Children's fabrics, wallpapers and borders. Nursery accessories and Teddy bears. Towels, duvets, changing bags, Moses baskets.

Trimmings

WENDY CUSHING TRIMMINGS
G7, Chelsea Harbour Design Centre, Chelsea Harbour, London SW10 0XE ■ Tel: (0171) 351-5796 ■ Fax: (0171) 351-4246 ■ Mon-Fri 10:00-5:00 ■ Stella Joannidou ■ Greek spoken ■ Prices high ■ Trade discount ■ Major credit cards

Tie-backs, fringes, braids, cords and accessories made to order.

FRIENDLY LINE
Unit 7, Silwex House, Quaker Street, London E1 6SN ■ Tel: (0171) 247-5201 ■ Fax: (0171) 377-5073 ■ Mon-Fri 9:30-5:30 ■ Mr. Steiner ■ Prices low to medium

All trimmings.

HENRY NEWBERY & COMPANY
18 Newman Street, London W1P 4AB ■ Tel: (0171) 636-2053 ■ Fax: (0171) 436-6406 ■ Mon-Fri 9:00-5:00 ■ Prices medium to high ■ Trade discount

Upholstery and curtain trimmings: bullion fringe, tiebacks and tassels.

CHRISTINA OJO

Studio 2, 90 Wandsworth Bridge Road, London SW6 2TF ■ Telfax: (0171) 371-9485 ■ By appointment only

Large choice of hand-made trimmings and tiebacks. Fringes in linen, wool and chenille.

V.V. ROULEAUX

54 Sloane Square, Clivedon Place, London SW1W 8AX ■ Tel: (0171) 730-3125 ■ Fax: (0171) 730-3468 ■ Mon-Sat 9:30-6:00, Wed 9:30-6:30 ■ Prices medium to high ■ Major credit cards

Large selection of all kinds of trimmings: fringes, braids, cords in cotton, linen, wool and chenille, tassels, bullions, tiebacks. Excellent choice.

TEMPTATION ALLEY

361 Portobello Road, London W11 5SA ■ Tel: (0181) 964-2004 ■ Fax: (0171) 727-4432 ■ Prices low to medium ■ Trade discount

Large collection of inexpensive trimmings including tassels, fringes and ribbons.

♕ G. J. TURNER TRIMMINGS

Fitzroy House, Abbott Street, London E8 3DP ■ Tel: (0171) 254-8187 ■ Fax: (0171) 254-8471 ■ Mon-Fri 9:00-5:30 ■ Charles Courtier-Dutton ■ Prices high ■ Trade only

Bespoke hand-made furniture trimmings: braids, fringes, tassels, and superb tiebacks in silk, linen, wool and cotton.

♕ WEMYSS HOULES LTD

40 Newman Street, London W1P 3PA■ Tel: (0171) 255-3305 ■ Fax: (0171) 580-9420 ■ Mon-Fri 9:00-4:30 ■ Prices medium to very high ■ Trade discount ■ Major credit cards

Specialists in the superb trimmings from Houlès in Paris. Very elegant and one of the world's best known. Difficult to find a colour tone they do not have.

See also: Chelsea Harbour Design Centre.

FIREPLACES

ACQUISITIONS FIREPLACES LTD

24-26 Holmes Road, Kentish Town, London NW5 3AB ■ Tel: (0171) 482-2949 ■ Fax: (0171) 267-4361 ■ E-mail: sales@acquisitions.co.uk ■ Mon-Sat 9:00-5:00 ■ Ken Kennedy ■ Prices medium ■ All credit cards

Victorian and Edwardian cast iron fireplaces. Surrounds, tiles, hearths. Installations.

♛ AMAZING GRATES LTD

61-63 High Road, East Finchley, London N2 8AB ■ Tel: (0181) 883-9590 ■ Fax: (0181) 365-2053 ■ Website: www.amazinggrates.co.uk. ■ Mon-Sat 10:00-5:30 ■ Tabitha Tew ■ Prices low to very high ■ Trade discount ■ All credit cards

Reproduction stone and marble fire surrounds. Antique originals in cast iron, stone, marble and wood. Grates and accessories.

ARCHITECTURAL ANTIQUES

351 King Street, London W6 9NM ■ Tel: (0181) 741-7883 ■ Fax: (0181) 741-1109 ■ Mon-Sat 9:00-5:00 ■ Gervais Duc ■ French spoken ■ Prices medium ■ Trade discount

Antique marble and stone fireplaces, gilt mirrors and antique French furniture.

♛ THE BETTER HEARTH

109 Holloway Road, Islington, London N7 8LT■ Tel: (0171) 609 3245 ■ Fax: (0171) 226-2257 ■ E-mail: kevin.owen@mcmail.com ■ Mon-Sat 9:00-5:30 ■ Kevin Owen ■ Prices medium ■ Trade discount ■ Major credit cards

Very likely the largest display of fireplaces and mantels in North London. Victorian fireplaces in marble and stone their specialty. Restorations and installations.

CHESNEY'S ANTIQUE FIREPLACE WAREHOUSE

194-202 Battersea Park Road, London SW11 4ND ■ 734-736 Holloway Road, London N19 3JF ■ Tel: (0171) 627 1410 ■ Fax: (0171) 622-1078 ■ E-mail: sales@antiquefireplace.co.uk ■ Mon-Fri 9:00-5:30, Sat 10:00-5:00 ■ Paul Chesney ■ French, Spanish and German spoken ■ Prices medium to very high ■ Trade discount ■ Major credit cards ■

Antique and reproduction marble and stone chimneypieces. Cast iron chimneypieces and associated products.

THE CHISWICK FIREPLACE COMPANY

68 Southfield Road, Chiswick, London W4 1BD ■ 360 Lower Richmond Road, Richmond, Surrey TW9 4LE ■ Tel: (0181) 392-9299 ■ Fax: (0181) 392-9992 ■ Mon-Sat 9:30-5:30 ■ Paul Balogh ■ French spoken ■ Prices medium ■ Trade discount ■ Most credit cards

Specialists in original cast iron registers from Victorian to Art Nouveau. Gas and coal fires made to measure. Installations.

THE FIREPLACE SHOP

108-116 Glenthorne Road, Hammersmith, London W6 OLP ■ Telfax: (0181) 741-5013 ■ Mon-Sat 10:00-6:00, Closed Thu ■ Jim Gannon ■ Spanish, French and Italian spoken ■ Prices medium ■ Trade discount ■ All credit cards

Old and contemporary mantelpieces, fireplaces, chimneypieces. Fire grates, gas, log and coal effect fires. Installations and accessories.

FIREPLACE COMPANY

Arch 385 Mentmore Terrace, London Fields, London E8 3PN ■ Tel: (0181) 985-4830 ■ Fax: (0181) 533-7799 ■ Mon-Sat 10:00-5:30 ■ Mick Davies ■ German and Spanish spoken ■ Prices low to medium ■ Trade discount

Irish and Georgian fireplaces, flooring, stained glass, lots of architectural salvage of interest.

HOLLINGSHEAD & CO

247 Munster Road, Fulham, London SW6 6BS ■ Tel: (0171) 385-0843 ■ Fax: (0181) 346-4333 ■ Mon-Fri 9:00-4:00, Sat 9:00-12:00 ■ Douglas Hollingshead ■ Prices medium ■ Trade discount ■ Most credit cards

Antique and reproduction marble fireplaces in marble or wood. Hearths and accessories.

LASSCO (LONDON ARCHITECTURAL SALVAGE & SUPPLY CO LTD)

St. Michael's Church, Mark Street, London EC2A 4ER ■ Tel: (0171) 739-0448 ■ Fax: (0171) 729-6853 ■ E-mail: lassco@zetnet.co.uk ■ Mon-Sun 10:00-5:00 ■ Anthony Reeve ■ French spoken ■ Prices medium to very high Trade discount ■ All credit cards

London's largest and best-known specialist in architectural antiques. A large selection of fireplaces and garden ornaments. Everything from panelled rooms to doorknobs.

REAL FLAME

80 New King's Road, London SW6 4LT ■ Tel: (0171) 731-2704 ■ Fax: (0171) 736-4625 ■ Website: www.realflame.co.uk ■ Mon-Sat 9:00-6:00 ■ Prices low

Gas, log and coal-effect fires. Marble and wooden mantelpieces. Fire grates and accessories. Fenders and fire screens.

RENAISSANCE LONDON LTD

193-195 City Road, London EC1V ■ Telfax: (0171) 251-8844 ■ Mon-Sat 8:00-6:00 ■ Owen Pacey ■ Prices low to high ■ Trade discount

Antique and reproduction fireplaces in marble, stone and wood. Full installations. They also stock original doors, shutters, radiators and decorative objects.

SEERS ANTIQUES

213 Trafalgar Road, Greenwich, London ■ Tel: (0181) 293-0273 ■ Fax: (0181) 305-2305 ■ Tue-Sat 10:00-6:00, Sun 10:00-4:00 ■ Sue Seers ■ Italian and French spoken ■ Prices low ■ Trade discount ■ Major credit cards

Antique and reproduction fireplaces in marble and wood. Tiled and cast iron inserts. Restoration of fireplaces in situ. Member of The Guild of Master Craftsmen.

GHISLAINE STEWART

110 Fentiman Road, London SW8 1QA ■ Telfax: (0171) 820-9440 ■ By appointment only ■ Dutch, German and French spoken ■ Prices high to very high ■ Trade discount ■ Visa and MC

Special design in fireplace surround and implements. Metal can be finished in patina of choice.

♔WESTLAND & COMPANY

St. Michael's Church, Leonard Street, London EC2A 4ER ■ Tel: (0171) 739-8094 ■ Fax: (0171) 729-3620 ■ Mon-Fri 9:00-6:00, Sat-Sun 10:00-5:00 ■ E-mail: westland@westland.co.uk ■ Website: www.westland.co.uk ■ Geoffrey Westland ■ French and German spoken ■ Prices medium to very high ■ Trade discount ■ All credit cards

A stunning collection of antique fireplaces in marble, stone and wood, from the 17th, 18th and 19th century.

HALLIDAYS

The Old College, Dorchester on Thames, Oxfordshire OX10 7HL ■ Tel: (01865) 340028 ■ Fax: (01865) 341149 ■ Mon-Fri 9:00-5:00, Sat 10:00-4:00 ■ E. Reily-Collins ■ Prices medium to high ■ Professional discount ■ Major credit cards

Carved pine mantlepiees, room panelling, bookcases.

FRAMES AND FRAMING

ACADEMY FRAMING
Burlington House, Piccadilly, London W1V 0DS ■ Tel: (0171) 494-5646 ■ Fax: (0171) 434-0837

This frame shop is affiliated with The Royal Academy. It offers high quality framing and reasonable prices. Also provides restoration and conservation services.

ART CONTACT
2 Rickett Street, London SW6 1RU ■ Tel: (0171) 381-8655 ■ Fax: (0171) 386-9015 ■ Mon-Fri 9:00-5:00 ■ To the trade only

Framing and installation service. Specialists in commercial installation. Also paintings, prints, engravings, posters and mirrors.

ARTEFACT
36 Windmill Street, London W1P 1HF ■ Tel: (0171) 580-4878 ■ Fax: (0171) 580-0987 ■ Mon-Fri 10:00-5:30, Sat 11:00-6:00 ■ Minda Dowling, Director, Amanda Nightingale, Manager ■ Prices low to high ■ Trade discount ■ Major credit cards

Custom framing. Framed pictures, intaglio seals, silhouettes and miniatures, decorative accesssories for the wall. Member of The Fine Art Trade Guild and The Guild of Master Craftsmen.

BELGRAVIA FRAMEWORKS
9 Kinnerton Street, Belgravia, London SW1X 8EA ■ Tel: (0171) 245-1112 ■ Fax: (0171) 245-1156 ■ E-mail: framewks@aol.com ■ Mon-Fri 9:30-6:00, Sat 9:30-1:00 ■ Andrew McCann ■ Prices medium ■ Trade discount ■ Major credit cards

Hand-made gilt swept frames a specialty. Bespoke framing of pictures. Restoration, stretching, wash mounts, conservation framing. Fine Art Trade Guild, Exemplary Framer Top Award.

BOURLET FINE ART FRAME MAKERS
32 Connaught Street, London W2 2AX ■ Telfax: (0171) 724-4837 ■ Mon-Fri 11:00-5:30, Sat 11:00-2:00 ■ Gabrielle Rendell ■ French and Persian spoken ■ Prices medium ■ Trade discount ■ MC and Barclaycard

Hand-made frames, period and contemporary. Carving and gilding. Restoration services.

LUCY B. CAMPBELL GALLERY

123 Kensington Church Street, London W8 7LP ■ Tel: (0171) 727-2205 ■ Fax: (0171) 229-4252 ■ E-mail: lucy.b.campbell@dial.pipex.uk ■ Mon-Fri 10:00-6:00, Sat 10:00-4:00 ■ Lucy B. Campbell ■ Prices low to medium ■ Visa, MC

Framing and restoration. Antiquarian prints, paintings, contemporary naïve art.

CAMPBELL'S OF WALTON STREET

164 Walton Street, London SW3 2JL ■ Tel: (0171) 584-9268 ■ Fax: (0171) 581-3499 ■ Mon-Fri 9:30-5:30, Sat 10:00-5:00 ■ Roy Hogben ■ Poor French spoken ■ Prices medium to high ■ Trade discount ■ Most credit cards

Hand-crafted picture frames, carvers and gilders. Restoration and conservation. Impressionist style paintings. Member of The Guild of Master Craftsmen and The Fine Art Trade Guild.

COURT FRAMES (MAYFAIR)

10 Sedley Place, London W1R 1HG ■ Telfax: (0171) 493-3265 ■ Mon-Fri 9:30-5:30 ■ Mark Fisher ■ Prices low to very high ■ Some trade discounts

The design and creation of hand-built frames and mirrors. References include the leading auction houses and members of the Royal Family.

DAGGETT GALLERY

153 Portobello Road, 1st and 2nd floors, London W11 ■ Tel: (0171) 229-2248 ■ Mon-Fri 10:00-4:00, Sat 9:00-3:30 ■ Prices medium to high ■ Major credit cards

18th to 20th century frames. Restoration of frames, gilding. Picture plaques.

JOHN DAVIES FRAMING LTD

8 Bury Street, St. James's, London SW1Y 6AB ■ Tel: (0171) 930-7977 ■ Fax: (0171) 976-1518 ■ Mon-Fri 9:00-5:30 ■ John Davies ■ French spoken ■ Prices medium to high ■ Trade only

Custom-made reproduction frames in ebony, fruitwood or carved giltwood.

SEBASTIAN D'ORSAI (A.B.) LTD

8 Kensington Mall, Kensington, London W8 4EA ■ Tel: (0171) 229-3888 ■ Fax: (0171) 221-0746 ■ E-mail: sebsbel@msn.com ■ Mon-Sat 10:00-5:00 ■ G.W. Taylor ■ French spoken ■ Prices low to very high ■ Trade discount ■ All credit cards

A marvellous collection of picture frames and mouldings, both machine and hand made. A complete service of framing, restoration and re-gilding of antique frames. They have mirrors and fan cases.

ALEC DREW PICTURE FRAMES LTD

7 Cale Street, London SW3 3QT ■ Telfax: (0171) 352-8716 ■ Mon-Fri 9:00-5:00, Sat 9:30-1:00 ■ David Hughes ■ Prices medium ■ Trade discount ■ Major credit cards

Traditional and contemporary English-style framing and mounting. Hand-made and factory-finished.

PIERS FEETHAM GALLERY

475 Fulham Road, London SW6 1HL ■ Tel: (0171) 381-5958 ■ Fax: (0171) 381-3031 ■ Tue-Fri 10:00-1:00/2:00-6:00, Sat 10:00-1:00 ■ Piers Feetham ■ French spoken ■ Prices medium

Full framing services to conservation standards. Restoration and conservation of paintings and works on paper. Restoration of frames. They also have paintings: contemporary figurative to the abstract.

FIX-YOUR-PIX

269 New King's Road, London SW6 4RB ■ Telfax: (0171) 610-6720 ■ Mon-Sat 9:00-6:00 ■ Andrew Hardings ■ French spoken ■ Prices low to medium ■ Trade discount ■ Major credit cards

Custom frame and print gallery.

FLETCHER GALLERY SERVICES

12 Kinghorn Street, London EC1A 7HT ■ Tel: (0171) 726-4811 ■ Fax: (0171) 606-1826 ■ Mon-Fri 9:00-6:00 ■ Robin Fletcher ■ French, German and Greek spoken ■ Prices medium ■ Trade discount ■ Visa and MC

Hand-finished natural hardwood frames for contemporary works of art on paper. Mounting, framing, hanging and restoration.

FRAMERY LTD

3 Academy Buildings, Fanshaw Street, London N1 6LQ ■ Tel: (0171) 729-7677 ■ By appointment ■ H. Vinson ■ French and German spoken ■ Prices high ■ Trade discount

Bespoke framing for pictures.

CHRISTIAN GEORGET

6 Longyard, Lamb's Conduit Street, London WC1N 3LU ■ Telfax: (0171) 405-9585 ■ By appointment ■ Christian Georget ■ French spoken ■ Prices medium to high ■ Trade discount

Fine art gilding picture frames and restoring. Wide selection of English frames of the late 18th and the 19th century. Reproductions of antique frames to suit the period of a picture. Restoration of gilding. References: Courtauld Institute and many London art galleries.

HERBERT JOHNSON (DRY MOUNTERS/PICTURE FRAMING) LTD

14 Milroy Walk, Stamford Street, Blackfriars, London SE1 9LW ■ Tel: (0171) 928-6202 ■ Fax: (0171) 928-2216 ■ Mon-Fri 8:00-6:00 ■ E.D. Butler ■ Prices medium to high ■ Major credit cards

Fully comprehensive picture framing and mounting. Custom and ready made frames, mounts and prints. Art restoration and dry mounting. Lamination a specialty.

LACY GALLERY

203 Westbourne Grove, London W11 2SB ■ Tel: (0171) 229-6340 ■ Fax: (0171) 229-9105 ■ Tue-Fri 10:00-5:00, Sat 10:00-4:00 ■ Colin, David and Janet Lacy ■ French and Persian spoken ■ Trade discount ■ Major credit cards

Antique picture frames, 1700-1940. Decorative art carvings.

ALEXANDER GEORGE LEY & SONS

13 Brecknock Road, London N7 0BL ■ Tel: (0171) 267-3645 ■ Fax: (0171) 267-4462 ■ Mon-Fri 8:00-6:30 by appointment ■ A.G. Ley ■ Prices high

Carvers and gilders. Makers of fine frames and mirrors and giltwood furniture. Restoration of giltwood.

THE LONDON PICTURE CENTRE

709-723 Fulham Road, London SW6 ■ Tel: (0171) 371-5737 ■ Fax: (0171) 736-7283 ■ Mon-Sun 8:00-5:00 ■ Albert Williams ■ Spanish, Italian and French spoken ■ Prices low to medium ■ Trade discount ■ Major credit cards

Picture framing, mirrors and framed prints.

LONDON WEST TEN GALLERY

485 Latimer Road, London, W10 6RD ■ Tel: (0181) 969-5682 ■ Fax: (0181) 969-4576 ■ Mon-Fri 8:00-5:30, Sat 8:00-1:00 ■ John White ■ Portuguese and Arabic spoken ■ Prices medium ■ Trade discount ■ All credit cards

Picture framing, mirrors, table tops, on-site measuring and installation.

MIND IN TOWER HAMLETS – PICTURE FRAMING WORKSHOP

"A Chance to Work", 125 Poplar High Street, Poplar, London E14 ■ Tel: (0171) 987-4452 ■ Mon & Wed 9:00-5:00 ■ Angela Yphantides ■ Prices low ■ Trade discount

Ready-made and bespoke framing for pictures, photos and mirrors.

NIGHTINGALE & SON

Unit J-202, Tower Bridge Business Complex, 100 Clements Road, London SE16 4DG ■ Tel: (0171) 237-1991 ■ E-mail: nightingales@millhouse.co.uk. ■ Mon-Fri 9:00-5:00 ■ Adam Nightin ■ Prices medium to high ■ Major credit cards

Custom picture and mirror framing using antique reclaimed hardwoods, such as old French railway carriages, London Bridge and old vinegar vats.

OLD CHURCH GALLERIES

320 King's Road, Chelsea, London SW3 5UH ■ Tel: (0171) 351-4649 ■ Fax: (0171) 351-4449 ■ E-mail: sales@old-church-galleries.com ■ Mon-Sat 10:00-6:00 ■ Mati Harrington ■ Spanish, Italian and French spoken ■ Prices medium to high ■ Trade discount ■ Major credit cards

Mounting, framing and restoration of picture frames. Antique maps and prints.

PHILLIPS FRAMING/PHILLIPS-WOOD FINE ART LTD

104 Lower Marsh, Waterloo, London SE1 7AB ■ Tel: (0171) 928-4978 ■ Fax: (0171) 928-4944 ■ Mon-Sat 10:00-5:30 ■ Prices low to high ■ Trade discount ■ Major credit cards

Museum-quality framing and conservation. Limited editions of fine art prints.

F.A. POLLAK LTD

Unit 3, Rosebury House, 70 Rosebury Avenue, Islington, London EC1R 4RR ■ Tel: (0171) 837-6161 ■ Fax: (0171) 837-7676 ■ Mon-Fri 8:30-5:00 ■ Johann Roeder ■ German and French spoken ■ Prices medium to very high

Hand-crafted and hand-carved gilded picture frames. Mounting, fitting, glazing, restoration and conservation.

ROWLEY GALLERY LTD

115 Kensington Church Street, London W8 7LN ■ Tel: (0171) 727-6495 ■ Fax: (0171) 229-5561 ■ Mon-Fri 9:30-5:30 ■ Prices medium to high ■ Trade discount ■ Major credit cards

Custom framing in a wide selection of painted and gilded woods. Mirror frames made and restored. Gilding of small items.

SHAPERO GALLERIES LTD

80 Holland Park Avenue, London W11 3RB ■ Tel: (0171) 727-0462 ■ Fax: (0171) 229-4574 ■ Mon-Fri 10:00-7:00, Sat 10:00-5:00 ■ Rose-Anne and Norman Slater ■ Prices low to high ■ Trade discount ■ Major credit cards

On-site picture framing, including hand-decorated frames and mounts. Antique prints a specialty. Member of The Fine Art Trade Guild.

ROLLO WHATELEY LTD

9 Old Bond Street, 1st floor, London W1X 3TA ■ Tel: (0171) 629-7861 ■ Mon-Fri 9:00-5:00 ■ Rollo Whateley ■ French and German spoken ■ Prices low to high ■ Trade discount

Antique picture frames. Reproduction framing and restoration of frames.

ARNOLD WIGGINS & SONS

4 Bury Street, St. James's, London SW1Y 6AB ■ Tel: (0171) 925-0195 ■ Fax: (0171) 839-6928 ■ Mon-Fri 9:00-5:30 ■ Michael Gregory

Antique and reproduction picture frames. Carving and gilding using traditional techniques. Restoration of carved and gilt-wood furniture.

OUTSIDE LONDON

BLUE JAY FRAMES

Possingworth Craft Workshops, Blackboys, East Sussex TN22 5HE ■ Tel: (01435) 866258 ■ Fax: (01435) 868473 ■ Mon-Fri 8:30-5:30 ■ Simon Hayes Fisher ■ Prices medium

Picture framing to trade customers. All aspects of picture framing, mouldings and mountings. Daily London collection and delivery. Clients are museums, galleries, designers and shops.

FURNITURE

Antique Reproduction

BALLANTYNE BOOTH LTD
Cadogan House, Hythe Road, London NW10 6RS ■ Tel: (0181) 960-3255 ■ Fax: (0181) 960-4567 ■ Mon-Fri 9:00-6:00 ■ Helen Mark ■ Prices medium ■ Possible credit card facility ■ Member of UKIC/Conservation register

Makers of fine reproductions of antique furniture. All aspects of antique and furniture restoration.

♛ BEAUMONT & FLETCHER
261 Fulham Road, London SW3 6HY ■ Tel: (0171) 352-5594 ■ Fax: (0171) 352-3546 ■ Mon-Sat 9:30-5:30 ■ John Crowell, Brian Worthington ■ Prices high ■ Trade discount ■ Major credit cards accepted

Antique furniture reproductions, fabrics, upholstery. Also excellent quality hand carved mirrors and wall lights.

RUPERT BEVAN
40 Fulham High Street, London SW6 3LQ ■ Telfax: (0171) 731-1919 ■ E-mail: rupert@workshop.enta.net ■ Mon-Fri 9:00-6:00 ■ Rupert Bevan ■ Prices medium to high ■ Trade discount

Reproduction and restoration of fine painted and gilded furniture.

CHESTERFIELDS OF LONDON
99 Lisson Grove, London NW1 6UP ■ Tel: (0171) 402-9728 ■ Fax: (0171) 724-8377 ■ Mon-Fri 10:00-5:00, Sat 10:00-1:00 ■ William Kirby ■ American understood ■ Prices medium ■ Trade discount ■ Major credit cards accepted

Reproductions of English furniture. Also contemporary furniture in leather or fabric. Suppliers to British foreign Embassies.

JULIAN CHICHESTER DESIGNS LTD
27 Parsons Green Lane, London SW6 4HH ■ Tel: (0171) 371-9055 ■ Fax: (0171) 371-9066 ■ By appointment

Reproductions of Regency and lacquer and gilt tables and 17th century Dutch tables.

FREUD

198 Shaftesbury Avenue, London WC2 3HB ■ Tel: (0171) 831-1071 ■ Fax: (0171) 831-3062 ■ Mon-Fri 9:30-5:30 ■ Prices medium to high ■ Major credit cards

Reproductions of Charles Rennie Mackintosh furniture.

H.L.C. FITMENTS (REPRODUCTIONS)

305 Kingsland Road, Hockney, London S8 4DL ■ Tel: (0171) 254-8292 ■ Fax: (0171) 923-1439 ■ Tue-Wed, Fri 7:30-4:00, Mon, Thu 7:30-1:00 ■ H.L. Cowen ■ Prices low to very high ■ Trade discount

Reproduction furniture. Their speciality is breakfronts. Furniture made to client's specifications.

♕ HODSOLL MCKENZIE

52 Pimlico Road, London SW1W 8LP ■ Tel: (0171) 730-2877 ■ Fax: (0171) 259-9292 ■ Mon-Fri 10:00-5:00 ■ Alex McKenzie and Mark Butcher ■ Prices high ■ Professional discount

Limited number of reproduction furniture models of high quality and fabrics and wallpapers.

HUMPHREY-CARRASCO

43 Pimlico Road, London SW1W 8NE ■ Tel: (0171) 730-9911 ■ Fax: (0171) 730-9944 ■ Mon-Fri 10:00-6:00, Sat 10:00-5:00 ■ David Humphrey, Marylise Carrasco ■ French and Spanish spoken ■ Prices low to very high ■ Trade discount

Furniture copied or designed to order. First rate antique dealers.

KUWAHARA LTD

6 McNicol Drive, London NW10 7AW ■ Tel: (0181) 963-1100 ■ Fax: (0181) 963-0010 ■ Mon-Fri 9:00-5:00 ■ Shigeru Kuwahara ■ French and Japanese spoken ■ Prices low to high ■ Trade discount ■ Major credit cards

High quality replicas of antique furniture, all hand made. Also traditional hand-crafted leather goods.

ALEXANDER LEY & SONS

13 Breaknock Road, London N7 0BL ■ Tel: (0171) 267-3645 ■ Fax: (0171) 267-4462 ■ Mon-Fri 8:00-6:30 by appointment ■ Mr. A.G. Ley ■ Prices high

Makers of fine giltwood furniture and mirrors. Fine frames as well as restoration of frames and giltwood furniture.

THE PARSONS TABLE LTD

362 Fulham Road, London SW10 9UU ■ Tel: (0171) 352-7444 ■ Fax: (0171) 376-4677 ■ Mon-Fri 10:00-4:00 ■ Maggie Conrad ■ French and Italian spoken ■ Prices medium to high ■ Trade discount

Replicas of fine English and French antique furniture, chests of drawers, tables, chairs, beds, armoires.

RICHARD C. PHILLIPS LTD

3 Ardleigh Road, London N1 4HS ■ Tel: (0171) 923-0921 ■ Fax: (0171) 923-3668 ■ Mon-Fri 8:00-5:00 ■ Richard Phillips ■ Prices high

Fine replicas of antique furniture and four-poster beds.

RESTALL BROWN & CLENELL

120 Queensbridge Road, London E2 8PD ■ Tel: (0171) 739-6626 ■ Fax: (0171) 739-6123 ■ Mon-Fri 8:00-5:00 ■ Susan Brown ■ Prices high ■ Trade discount

Very highest quality English reproduction furniture. Also antique furniture.

ROSTRUM ANTIQUES

115 Portobello Road, London W11 2DY ■ Telfax: (0171) 243-0420 ■ Mobile: 0831 444148 ■ Sat 8:30-5:00 or by appointment ■ Peter Skupien ■ Realistic prices ■ Major credit cards ■ Generous export and trade discounts

Fine replicas of antique dining tables, hand-made to order and to size. Also dressers, chairs, desks. Dining room furniture a specialty.

DAVID SALMON LTD

555 King's Road, London SW6 2EB ■ Tel: (0171) 384-2223 ■ Fax: (0171) 371-0532 ■ Mon-Fri 10:00-5:30 ■ David Salmon ■ Greek spoken ■ Prices medium to very high ■ Professional discount

English Golden Period of furniture all made to order. Living room, dining room and private office furniture. Museum quality replicas. Upholstered antique reproductions. Some of his pieces function as home entertainment centres or computer cabinets.

SHAKER

25 Harcourt Street, London W1H 1DT ■ Tel: (0171) 724-7672 ■ Fax: (0171) 724-6640 ■ 322 King's Road, London SW3 5UH ■ Tel: (0171) 352-3918 ■ Fax: (0171) 376-3494 ■ Mon-Sat 9:30-5:30 ■ Prices medium to high ■ Trade discount ■ Major credit cards

Reproductions of Shaker furniture in maple and cherrywood.

♚ W. THOMAS RESTORATIONS LTD
12 Warwick Place, London W9 2PX ■ Tel: (0171) 286-1945 ■ Fax: (0171) 266-2521 ■ Mon-Fri 8:00-5:30 ■ Raymond Dudman, Partridge Fine Arts ■ Prices medium

Carving and gilding. Reproductions of fine antique furniture. Included in the Register of The Conservation Unit of the Museum and Galleries Commission. Member of the United Kingdom Institute of Conservation.

TINDLE
162-168 Wandsworth Bridge Road, London SW6 2UQ ■ Tel: (0171) 384-1485 ■ Fax: (0171) 736-5630 ■ Mon-Fri 9:30-5:30 ■ Prices medium to high ■ Trade discount

Reproductions of small antique furniture, Chinoiserie tables and painted occasional tables. Ottomans, needlepoint stools two-tier tables and tôle Regency style trays.

TOBIAS & THE ANGEL
68 White Hart Lane, London SW13 0PZ ■ Telfax: (0181) 878-8902 ■ Mon-Sat 10:00-6:00 ■ A. Hughes and A. McLaughlan ■ French and German spoken ■ Prices low to high ■ Trade discount

Made-to-order reproductions of antique furniture as well as soft furnishings, lampshades made from antique textiles.

VILLA GARNELO
26 Pimlico Road, London SW1W 8LJ ■ Tel: (0171) 730-0110 ■ Fax: (0171) 730-0220 ■ Mon-Fri 10:00-5:00, Sat by appointment ■ Maria Francisca Bennloch ■ Prices high ■ Trade discount

Reproduction of Empire and Biedermeier-style furniture made in Valencia, Spain.

Chairs

THE DINING CHAIR COMPANY
4 St. Barnabas Street, London SW1W 8PF ■ Tel: (0171) 259-0422 ■ Fax: (0171) 259-0423 ■ Mon-Fri 10:00-1:00/2:00-6:00, Sat by appointment ■ Patricia Tallon, Alison Jackson, Sacha Jackson ■ Prices medium ■ Major credit cards ■ Trade discount

High quality upholstered seat and back dining chairs at reasonable prices. Special sizes of sofas and upholstered stools. Member of The Guild of Master Craftsmen.

JOHN GANDER (FINE CHAIRS)

7 Wharf Road, Chelmsford, Essex CM2 6LU ■ Telfax: (01245) 287130 ■ Mon-Fri 9:00-6:00 ■ John Gander ■ French spoken ■ Prices high

Fine reproductions of all styles and types of chairs. They also do refinishing.

♕ HOWARD CHAIRS LIMITED

Lymehouse Studios, 30-31 Lyme Street, London NW1 0EE ■ Tel: (0171) 482-2156 ■ Fax: (0171) 482-0068 ■ Mon-Fri 7:30-5:00 ■ George T. Webb ■ Prices high ■ Trade discount

Established in 1820, they have become known as the "Rolls Royce" of furniture. "Howard" chairs and sofas are hand-made, using traditional craft techniques and the highest quality materials. Each piece of furniture is made to order.

PRUE LANE HANDMADE WORLDWIDE

6 Formosa Street, London W9 1EE ■ Telfax: (0171) 266-2629 ■ Tue-Sat 10:00-6:00 ■ Prue Lane ■ French spoken ■ Prices medium to very high ■ Trade discount ■ Major credit cards

A small collection of Louis XV-style chairs.

Children's Furniture

♕ DRAGONS OF WALTON STREET

23 Walton Street, London SW3 2HX ■ Tel: (0171) 589-3795 ■ Fax: (0171) 584-4570 ■ E-mail: dragons@solutions-inc.co.uk ■ Mon-Sat 9:30-5:30 ■ Rosie Fisher ■ French spoken ■ Prices medium to high ■ Amex and Visa

Hand-painted children's furniture and interior design. Everything for the nursery. Curtains, carpets, curtain making. Quite marvellous.

MARK WILKINSON FURNITURE

126 Holland Park Avenue, London W11 4JA ■ Tel: (0171) 727-5814 ■ Fax: (0171) 792-1816 ■ Mon-Fri 9:30-5:30, Sat 10:00-4:30 ■ Richard Jackson ■ Prices high ■ MC accepted

Unique designs of children's furniture. Also designer kitchen, bedroom, bathroom and study furniture.

Contemporary Furniture

STEVE ARMITAGE FURNITURE LTD
21 St. Albans Place, Islington, London N1 0NX ■ Telfax: (0171) 359-0224 ■ Trade discounts ■ Major credit cards

Hand-crafted furniture to their own designs. All free standing.

BYPRODUCT
Unit 11, Stamford Works, Gillett Street, London N16 8JH ■ Telfax: (0171) 923-3430 ■ Rob Melville, James Cannon ■ Prices high ■ Trade discount

Furniture for contract use in plywood and steel. Tables, chairs, stools, beam seats. Standard designs.

CHRISTOPHER HEALY DESIGN
Union Hall, 27-29 Union Street, London SE1 1SD ■ Tel: (0171) 357-7085 ■ Tue-Sun 11:00-6:00 by appointment ■ Christopher Healy ■ Prices high to very high ■ Trade discount ■ Visa accepted

Contemporary English furniture and lighting. Designs exclusive to makers. Custom commissions.

♔ DAVID LINLEY FURNITURE LTD
60 Pimlico Road, London SW1W 8LP ■ Tel: (0171) 730-7300 ■ Fax: (0171) 730-8869 ■ Mon-Fri 10:00-6:00, Sat 10:00-5:00 ■ David Linley and Timothy Gosling ■ French spoken ■ Prices medium to very high ■ Professional discount ■ Major credit cards

Fine hand-crafted furniture made in a classical style and incorporating many other materials. Large choice of stock available in showroom. Excellent choice of accessories such as boxes, desk sets, mirrors and humidors in beautiful hardwoods. Catalogue. Line now available in U.S. through Nieman Marcus.

GUY MALLINSON FURNITURE
7 The Coachworks, 80 Parsons Green Lane, London SW6 4HN ■ Tel: (0171) 731-9010 ■ Fax: (0171) 731-5099 ■ E-mail: g.mallinson.@easynet.co.uk ■ Mon-Fri 9:00-6:00 ■ Guy Mallinson ■ Prices very high

High-quality modern pieces of furniture in wood. Veneering their specialty.

EMILY READETT-BAYLEY LIMITED

St. Luke's Old Rectory, 107 Grange Road, London SE1 3BW ■ Tel: (0171) 231-3939 ■ Fax: (0171) 231-4499 ■ E-mail: emily@emily-readett-b.demon.co.uk ■ Mon-Fri 9:30-5:30 ■ Emily Readett-Bayley ■ French spoken ■ Prices medium to high ■ Trade discount ■ Major credit cards

Pure bamboo and re-claimed teak furniture and lighting.

THIS & THAT FURNITURE

50-51 Chalk Farm Road, London NW1 8AN ■ Tel: (0171) 267-5493 ■ Fax: (0171) 916-4720 ■ 7 Days 10:00-6:00 ■ Prices medium ■ Trade discount ■ Major credit cards

Solid oak furniture, large contemporary sofas, iron and brass bedsteads, wardrobes.

TIS ART DESIGN CRAFT & RESTORATION

2C Queens Road, London E11 1BB ■ Telfax: (0181) 923-2850 ■ By appointment only ■ Tzvetan Stoianov ■ Russian, Polish and Bulgarian spoken ■ Prices very high ■ Possible trade discount

Art furniture: very interesting designs of unusual contemporary furniture. The gentleman is dedicated to bringing fine art to the creation of furniture.

Custom Furniture

ADZE CRAFTSMEN

24 Heriot Avenue, Chingford, London E4 8AP ■ Tel: (0181) 529-4151 ■ By appointment only ■ M.A.Carnell ■ Polish spoken ■ Prices medium to high

Hand-made furniture to any design. Custom joinery and cabinetry.

MICHAEL BERINGER DESIGN

27 Union Street, London SE1 1SD ■ Telfax: (0171) 407-0505 ■ Mon-Fri 8:30-5:30 ■ Michael Beringer ■ French spoken ■ Prices medium ■ Trade discount

Furniture making: design, production and joinery to order.

CHRISTIANS OF KNIGHTSBRIDGE LTD

164 Brompton Road, Knightsbridge, London SW3 1HW ■ Tel: (0171) 581-2271 ■ Fax: (0171) 581-7912 ■ Mon-Sat 9:30-5:30 ■ Celia Warbrick ■ French spoken ■ Prices very high ■ Trade discount

Hand-built English furniture: bed, bath, study and kitchens. Complete design and installation.

♕ EDMUND CZAJKOWSKI

96 Tor-o-Moor Road, Woodhall Spa, Lincs. LN10 6SB ■ Telfax: (01526) 352845 ■ Mon-Fri 9:00-4:30 ■ Michael Czajkowski ■ German spoken ■ Trade discount

Designs and makes individual pieces of furniture. Member of UK Institute of Conservation. Listed on Museum and Galleries Register. BAFRA.

♕ DEACON & SANDYS

Apple Pie Farm, Cranbrook Road, Benenden, Kent TN17 4EU ■ Tel: (01580) 243331 ■ Fax: (01580) 243301 ■ Mon-Fri 8:00-5:30, Sat 8:00-1:00 ■ Jonathan Deacon ■ Prices very high ■ Professional discount

Designer and manufacturer of 17th century-style oak interiors. Oak furniture, wall panelling, staircases. Design, supply and fit.

DETAIL DESIGN

D2 Metropolitan Wharf, Wapping Wall, London E1 9SS ■ Tel: (0171) 488-1669 ■ Fax: (0171) 488-2524 ■ E-mail: natasha@detail.co.uk ■ Mon-Fri 9:30-5:30 ■ Gordon Russell ■ French spoken ■ Prices high

Furniture and kitchen design, production and installation. From one-off to production models. Very distinctive designs.

THE DINING ROOM SHOP

62-64 White Hart Lane, London SW13 0PZ ■ Tel: (0181) 878-1020 ■ Fax: (0181) 876-2367 ■ Mon-Sat 10:00-5:30 ■ Kate Dyson and David Hur ■ French and Spanish spoken ■ Prices low to very high ■ Trade discount ■ Major credit cards

Made-to-measure furniture. Everything for the dining room.

GROVES FURNITURE

6 Waterside, 44-48 Wharf Road, Islington, London N1 7SH ■ Telfax: (0171) 251-6005 ■ Mon-Fri 9:00-6:00 ■ James Groves ■ French spoken ■ Prices low to very high ■ Some trade discounts

Custom-made contemporary furniture, using steel, rubber, glass, laminate and wood, for home, office or garden environments. Works of art on legs, including tables, desks, magazine storage, anything free standing.

HOWARD CHAIRS LIMITED

Lymehouse Studios, 30-31 Lyme Street, London NW1 0EE ■ Tel: (0171) 482-2156 ■ Fax: (0171) 482-0068 ■ Mon-Fri 7:30-5:00 ■ George T. Webb ■ Prices high ■ Trade discount

Established in 1820, they have become known as the "Rolls Royce" of furniture. Their furniture is made using traditional craft techniques and the highest quality materials. Each piece of furniture is made to order. They do superb upholstering, hand-made curtains, drapes, cushions and wall uphholstery.

LAWRENCE KEMP

2A Manor Lane, Lee, London SE13 5QP ■ Tel: (0181) 463-0330 ■ Fax: (0181) 852-3525 ■ Mon-Sat 9:00-7:00 ■ Michael Kemp ■ Prices high ■ Possible trade discount

Architectural bespoke furniture of his own design. Absolutely superb. Unusual and highly figured veneers. His designs are unique, very graceful and beautifully made and finished.

DANIEL NEWLYN UPHOLSTERY

The Vaults, 24 West Street, Covent Garden, London WC2H 9NA ■ Tel: (0171) 379-8680 ■ Fax: (0171) 836-7877 ■ E-mail: daniel@visualeyes.ltd.uk ■ Mon-Fri 9:30-6:00 ■ Prices medium to high ■ Some trade discounts

Bespoke items of furniture design and upholstery.

VICEROY FURNITURE LTD

118 Kensington Park Road, London W11 2PW ■ Tel: (0171) 937-2141 ■ Fax: (0171) 221-2789 ■ Mon-Sat 10:00-5:00 ■ Helga Neter ■ German and French spoken ■ Prices low to very high

Made-to-order traditional and modern furniture. Cabinetry and upholstery.

MARK WILKINSON FURNITURE

126 Holland Park Avenue, London W11 4JA ■ Tel: (0171) 727-5814 ■ Fax: (0171) 792-1816 ■ Mon-Fri 9:30-5:30, Sat 10:00-4:30 ■ Richard Jackson ■ Prices high ■ MC accepted

Designer of furniture for the kitchen, bathroom, bedroom, study. Manufacture and installation of worktops.

Folding Tables

NICHOLAS HERBERT LTD
118 Lots Road, Chelsea, London SW10 0RJ ■ Tel: (0171) 376-5596 ■ Fax: (0171) 376-5572 ■ Mon-Fri 9:30-5:30 ■ Nicholas Herbert ■ French, Italian and Spanish spoken ■ Prices medium to high ■ Trade discount ■ Major credit cards

Folding tables, etc.

Metal Furniture

MARK BRAZIER-JONES
Hyde Hall Barn, Sandon, Buntingford, Hertfordshire SG9 0RV ■ Tel: (01763) 273599 ■ Fax: (01763) 273410 ■ Mon-Thu 9:00-6:00, Fri 9:00-4:00 ■ Mark Brazier-Jones ■ Prices high to very high ■ Trade discount.

Limited editions of cast bronze and aluminium chairs. All other furniture and lighting as well. Commissions taken.

TOM FAULKNER DESIGNS
13 Petley Road, London W6 9SU ■ Tel: (0171) 610-0615 ■ Fax: (0171) 386-0797 ■ E-mail: enquiries@f7designs.demon.co.uk ■ Mon-Fri 9:00-5:00 ■ Prices medium ■ Trade discount

Hand-made metal furniture.

MAIDEN IRON
59-60 Stanworth Street, London SE1 3NY ■ Tel: (0171) 394-6566 ■ Fax: (0171) 250-0650 ■ E-mail: maideniron@msn.com ■ Mon-Fri 9:30-6:00 ■ Penny Speddiny ■ Prices medium to high ■ Trade discount

Metal beds, dining tables, chairs, coffee tables. Sculptural and architectural fittings. In-house design and design service service offered.

MDW DESIGN
Tower bridge Business Complex, Studio J-105-106, 100 Clements Road, London SE16 ■ Telfax: (0171) 374-2882 ■ Mon-Fri 9:00-5:00 ■ Mike Walker ■ Prices high ■ Trade discount

Bespoke furniture and accessories in aluminium and pewter. Chairs, bar stools, architectural items.

♔ J.H. PORTER & SON LTD
13 Cranleigh Mews, London SW11 2QL ■ Tel: (0171) 978-5576 ■ Fax: (0171) 924-7081 ■ Mon-Fri 8:00-5:00 ■ Fred Hodgins ■ Prices low

They make anything in iron, from decorative gates to staircases, railings and furniture.

Rattan, Willow and Wicker Furniture

MALIA LIMITED
C2 and C3 The Chambers, Chelsea Harbour Design Centre, London SW10 0XF ■ Tel: (0171) 352-6656 ■ Fax: (0171) 352-6616 ■ Mon-Fri 9:30-5:30, Sat 10:00-1:00 ■ Osama Al Sayed ■ German, Italian and Arabic spoken ■ Prices high ■ Trade discount ■ Major credit cards

Rattan and Mactanstone products. Furniture in rattan and banana wood with coconut stalk inlay. A wide range of furniture and decorative items.

♔ THE SOMERSET WILLOW COMPANY
Unit 10-12, Wireworks Trading Estate, Bristol Road, Bridgwater, Somerset TA8 2PW ■ Tel: (01278) 424003 ■ Fax: (01278) 446415 ■ Mon-Fri 8:30-5:00 ■ Aubrey and Darrell Hill ■ Prices medium to high ■ Trade discount ■ Major credit cards

Exceptional choice of Willow furniture. Everything woven in willow, from basketware to hot air balloons and even coffins. All items can be made to customers's own specifications.

Upholstered Furniture

BEAUMONT & FLETCHER
261 Fulham Road, London SW3 6HY ■ Tel: (0171) 352-5594 ■ Fax: (0171) 352-3546 ■ Mon-Sat 9:30-5:30 ■ John Crowell, Brian Worthington ■ Prices high ■ Trade discount ■ Major credit cards

Fine traditional handsprung upholstered furniture. Copies of antique furniture.

CHESTERFIELDS OF LONDON

99 Lisson Grove, London NW1 6UP ■ Tel: (0171) 402-9723 ■ Fax: (0171) 724-8377 ■ Mon-Fri 10:00-5:00 ■ William Kirby ■ Prices high ■ Trade discount ■ Major credit cards

Upholstered leather and fabric furniture: sofas, chairs as well as custom-made items.

THE CURTAIN COUTOURIER

285 New King's Road, London SW6 4RD ■ Tel: (0171) 371-9255 ■ Fax: (0171) 371-9261 ■ Mon-Sat 9:30-5:30 ■ Anne Thompson ■ French spoken ■ Prices low to very high ■ Trade discount ■ Major credit cards

Made-to-order sofas, chairs footstools and chaises longues. Can supply top-of-the-range hand-crafted sofas or medium-priced for general domestic or contract use. They also have a line of hand-made furniture from Italy. Member of The Guild of Master Craftsmen.

DELCOR FURNITURE LTD

65 Tottenham Court Road, London W1P 9PA ■ Telfax: (0171) 580-7900 ■ Mon-Sat 9:30-5:00 ■ Ray McClelland ■ Prices medium ■ Trade discount ■ Major credit cards

Full line of upholstered furniture, sofas, armchairs, footstools, sofabeds. They re-upholster.

INTERMURA

27 Chalk Farm Road, London NW1 8AG ■ Tel: (0171) 485-6638 ■ Fax: (0171) 284-4564 ■ Tue-Sun 10:30-5:30 ■ Anne and Christopher Hymers ■ Italian spoken ■ Prices medium ■ Major credit cards

Contemporary upholstered furniture, sofas, chairs, ottomans, chaises longues. Curvaceous with uncluttered simplicity. Very comfortable.

MULTIYORK FURNITURE LIMITED

555 King's Road, Chelsea, London SW6 2EB ■ Tel: (0171) 371-5029 ■ Fax: (0171) 371-5028 ■ Website: www.multiyork.co.uk ■ Mon-Fri 9:30-5:30, Sat 9:00-6:00, Sun 11:00-5:00 ■ Richard Abadioru ■ Prices medium to high ■ Major credit cards ■ Trade discount

Sofas, reproduction furniture, curtains, rugs, lamps, tables, sofabeds.

GEORGE SMITH

587-589 King's Road, London SW6 2EH ■ Tel: (0171) 834-1004 ■ Fax: (0171) 731-4451 ■ Mon-Sat 9:30-5:30 ■ Prices high ■ Professional discount

One of the best selections of classic sofas and chairs. Kilim- and leather-upholstered furniture. Some custom sofa beds.

THE UPHOLSTERERS STUDIO LTD

Unit 6-7, 32 Lawn Road, Hampstead, London NW3 2XU ■ Tel: (0171) 722-2268 ■ Fax: (0171) 722-6673 ■ Mon-Fri 8:00-6:00 ■ S. Bunyan and P. Stemp ■ Prices high ■ Trade discount

New upholstered furniture. Also re-covering and loose covers.

RICHARD JOSEPH WARD FURNITURE

3 Ezra Street, London E2 7RH ■ Telfax: (0171) 729-6768 ■ Mon-Fri 9:00-5:00 by appointment ■ R.J. Ward ■ French and Italian spoken ■ Prices medium to high ■ Trade discount

Design and supply of sofas and seating.

See also: Chelsea Harbour Design Centre
Home Furnishings.

GENEALOGISTS

THE COLLEGE OF ARMS (HERALDS COLLEGE)

Queen Victoria Street, London EC4V 4BT ■ Tel: (0171) 248-2762 ■ Fax: (0171) 248-6448 ■ Mon-Fri 10:00-4:00 ■ Prices medium

Part of The Royal Household. Heraldry and genealogy. Grants of Arms, armorial paintings and copies of family pedigrees. Genealogical research.

OUTSIDE LONDON

ACHIEVEMENTS

79-82 Northgate, Canterbury, Kent LT1 3NA ■ Tel: (01227) 462618 ■ Fax: (01227) 765617 ■ E-mail: achievements@achievements.co.uk ■ Mon-Fri 9:00-5:30 ■ Mrs. A. Humphrey Smith ■ French spoken ■ Prices medium ■ Visa and MC

Family history: heraldry, heraldic design, research, intestacy, coats of arms. Britain's leading genealogist and heraldic craftsman.

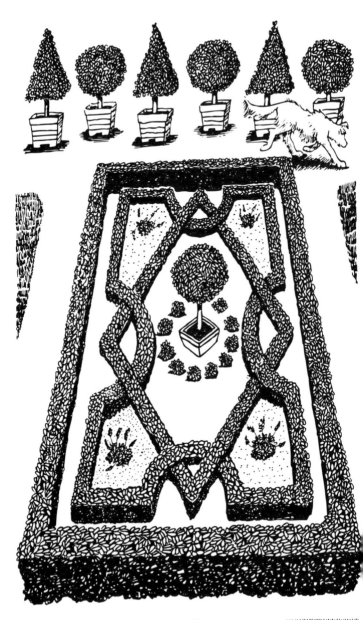

GARDENS

BARTHOLOMEW LANDSCAPES
59 Warwick Way, London SW1V 1QR ■ Tel: (0171) 931-8685 ■ Fax: (0171) 931-8686 ■ E-mail: batholand@aol.com ■ Mon-Sat 9:00-6:00 ■ Barry Burrows, Andrew Coles ■ French and Greek spoken ■ Prices low to very high ■ Trade discount ■ Major credit cards

Design, construction and maintenance of gardens in central London. Shop supplies high quality furniture, sculptures, containers, pots, water features. Plantings.

CAPITAL GARDEN LANDSCAPES LTD
1A Townsend Yard, Highgate Village, London N6 5JF ■ Tel: (0181) 342-8977 ■ Fax: (0181) 341-5032 ■ E-mail: capgar@aol.com ■ Mon-Fri 7:30-6:30 ■ John Edwards ■ Prices high ■ Major credit cards

Mark Enright landscapes. Garden design, construction and maintenance.

JULIAN CHICHESTER DESIGNS LTD
Unit G1, The Old Imperial Laundry, 71 Warriner Gardens, Battersea, London SW11 4XW ■ Tel: (0171) 622-2928 ■ Fax: (0171) 627-2939 ■ Mon-Fri 10:00-5:30 ■ Julian Chichester ■ Prices medium to high ■ Trade discount ■ Major credit cards

A nice selection of 18th to 19th century styles of teak garden furniture and painted Regency style furniture.

ANTHONY DE GREY TRELLISES
Broadhinton Yard, 77A North Street, London SW4 0HQ ■ Tel: (0171) 738-8866 ■ Fax: (0171) 498-9075 ■ Mon-Fri 7:30-6:00 ■ Anthony de Grey ■ French, German and Finnish spoken ■ Prices medium ■ Professional discount

Architectural trellis work. Garden buildings, landscape gardening, trellis work and seats.

JACQUELINE EDGE
1 Courtnell Street, London W2 5BU ■ Tel: (0171) 229-1172 ■ Fax: (0171) 727-4651 ■ Mon-Fri 9:00-6:00, Sat 11:00-4:00 ■ Jacqueline Edge ■ Prices medium to high ■ Major credit cards

A select range of pots and large urns as well as teak furniture. Silk pyjamas and lacquerwork.

S. & B. EVANS & SONS

7A Ezra Street, London E2 7RH ■ Tel: (0171) 729-6635 ■ Fax: (0171) 613-3558 ■ Mon-Fri 9:00-5:00, Sun 9:00-1:30 ■ Stella and Bob Evans ■ Prices low to high ■ Major credit cards

Terra-cotta and glazed gardenware.

THE POT COMPANY

16-20 Raymouth Road, London SE16 2DB ■ Tel: (0171) 394-9711 ■ Fax: (0171) 232-1131 ■ Mon-Sat 7:00-4:00 ■ Kevin McMahon ■ Prices low ■ Negotiable trade discounts

Garden and indoor pottery from around the world, including Greek, Spanish, Chinese, Malaysian, Vietnamese and Moroccan items.

QUESTRITE LTD

113 Portobello Road, London W11 2QB ■ Mobile: 0385 336574 ■ Fax: (0181) 675-4699 ■ Sat only 7:30-3:00 ■ Deborah Cutler ■ Prices low to medium ■ Trade discount

Garden antiques, tools, baskets, terra-cotta pots, beehives, watering cans, florist buckets, vases, baskets, wirework.

THE SCULPTURE FACTORY

21 Perserverence Works, 38 Kingsland Road, London E2 8DA ■ Tel: (0171) 739-7876 ■ Fax: (0171) 739-8095 ■ Mon-Fri 8:30-5:30 ■ John Crisfield ■ French spoken ■ Prices medium to high

Fine art fabrication in bronze and steel: sculpture, fountains, gates, screens, etc.

TIM SNEEZUM LANDSCAPES

181B Lavender Hill, London SW11 ■ Tel: (0171) 223-6903 ■ Tel: (0171) 708-5685 ■ Mon-Sat 9:00-6:00 by appointment ■ Prices medium to high

Garden design and construction service.

SUTHERLAND (EUROPE) LTD

2/20 Chelsea Harbour Design Centre, Chelsea Harbour, London SW10 0XE ■ Tel: (0171) 523-3456 ■ Fax: (0171) 376-5758 ■ Mon-Fri 9:30-5:30 ■ Patricia Stratford ■ Prices high to very high ■ Professional discount

Custom-made teak outdoor furniture and fabric.

WESTLAND & COMPANY

Saint Michael's Church, Mark Street, London EC2A 4ER ■ Tel: (0171) 739-8094 ■ Fax: (0171) 729-3620 ■ E-mail: westland@westland.land.co ■ Mon-Fri 9:00-6:00 /Sat-Sun 10:00-5:00 ■ Geoffrey Westland ■ French and German spoken ■ Prices low to very high ■ Professional discount ■ All credit cards

Fountains, statuary and garden elements in stone and metal, both antique and contemporary.

WORLD'S END NURSERIES

441-457 King's Road, Chelsea, London SW10 0LR ■ Tel: (0171) 351-3343 ■ 7 days 9:00-6:30 ■ J. Lotery ■ French spoken ■ Prices medium ■ Trade discount

Specimen plants, herbs and house plants. Garden statues, terra-cotta pots. Landscaping and maintenance.

OUTSIDE LONDON

STEPHEN CHARLES

8 Clifford Road, Petersham, Richmond, Surrey TW10 7EA ■ Tel: (0181) 940-6769 ■ By appointment

Landscape and contract gardeners. Lawns and tree plantings. Patios, fencing, paving, walls, ponds, turfing. Complete planning and contract maintenance.

GARDEN CRAFTS LTD

Sissinghurst Road, Biddenden, Kent TN27 8EJ ■ Tel: (01580) 292070 ■ Fax: (01580) 292131 ■ Mon-Fri 9:00-5:00, Sat-Sun 10:00-5:00 ■ Stephen Dimmock ■ Prices medium ■ Trade discount ■ Major credit cards

Garden furniture and ornaments in metal and wood.

Conservatories and Orangeries

APEX DOUBLE GLAZING LTD
67 Pound Lane, London NW10 2HH ■ Tel: (0181) 459-5161 ■ Fax: (0171) 459-0023 ■ Mon-Fri 6:00-6:00 ■ Ed Gibson ■ Polish and French spoken ■ Prices medium ■ Trade discount

Conservatories, windows and doors. Secondary glazing for homes, hotels, schools. Hardwood PVCU and aluminium.

LLOYD CHRISTIE GARDEN ARCHITECTURE
63 Islington Park Street, London N1 1QB ■ Tel: (0171) 607-6071 ■ Fax: (0171) 609-6050 ■ Mon-Fri 9:00-5:00 ■ Prices medium to very high

Classic styles in orangeries and conservatories, gazebos and summer houses.

GLASS HOUSES
Barnsbury Street, London N1 1PW ■ Tel: (0171) 607-6071 ■ Fax: (0171) 609-6050 ■ E-mail: design@glass-houses.co.uk ■ Website: www.glass-houses.co.uk ■ Mon-Fri 9:00-5:00 ■ Prices high

Beautiful glass architectural structures, conservatories, orangeries, greenhouses. Portfolio available.

MARSTON & LANGINGER LIMITED
192 Ebury Street, London SW1W 8UP ■ Tel: (0171) 824-8818 ■ Fax: (0171) 824-8757 ■ E-mail: sales@marston-and-langinger.com ■ Mon-Fri 10:00-6:00, Sat 10:00-4:00 ■ Michele Hadlow ■ German spoken ■ Prices low to very high ■ Trade discount ■ Visa and MC

Custom design and construction of garden rooms. Garden room furnishings and accessories. English willow, wirework and metal furniture.

HARDWARE

Door, Window and Cabinet Hardware

A TOUCH OF BRASS

210 Fulham Road, London SW1 9PJ ■ Tel: (0171) 351-2255 ■ Fax:
(0171) 352-4682 ■ Mon-Fri 9:00-5:00, Sat 10:00-5:00

Switches, sockets, door knobs and handles; signs made-to-order; taps and bathroom accessories; locks and security fittings; radiator grilles and cabinets. Wide choice of door and window hardware in Georgian, Regency and Victorian styles.

A & H BRASS

201-203 Edgware Road, London W2 1GS0 ■ Tel: (0171) 402-1854 ■
Fax: (0171) 402-0110 ■ Mon-Sat 9:00-6:00 ■ Prices medium to high
■ Major credit cards ■ Professional discount

Brass and chrome fittings. Architectural ironmongery, bathroom fittings and accessories, door and window fittings, switches and sockets, cabinet fittings and radiator grilles, curtain rails and fittings, locks and engraving.

ARCHITECTURAL COMPONENTS LTD

4-8 Exhibition Road, London SW7 2HF ■ Tel: (0171) 581-2401 ■ Fax:
(0171) 589-4928 ■ E-mail: sales@locks-and-handles.q.uk ■ Mon-Sat
9:00-6:00 ■ G.J. Pearson-Wright ■ Prices low to very high ■ Major
credit cards ■ Trade discount

British brass door, window and cabinet hardware and bathroom accessories. Locks, latches, espagnolettes, ventilator and radiator grilles, electric switch and socket plates, hall and fireplace furniture, They have worked on The Houses of Parliament, Kensington Palace, The Royal Palace of Jordan and The Peninsula Hotel in Hong Kong.

👑 J.D. BEARDMORE & CO LTD

17 Pall Mall, London SW1Y 5LN ■ Tel: (0171) 670-1000 ■ Fax: (0171)
670-1010 ■ E-mail: sales@beardmore.co.uk ■ Mon-Fri 9:00-5:30 ■
William Hudson ■ Spanish, Dutch, German, Italian, French ■ Prices
medium to very high ■ Major credit cards ■ Trade discount

Wide range of traditional door and window hardware, grilles, cabinet hardware, reproduction and restoration.

BRASS FOUNDRY CASTINGS

The Old Wheelwrights, Brasted Forge, Brasted, Kent TN16 1JL ■ (01959) 563863 ■ Fax: (01959) 561262 ■ By appointment only ■ Raymond Konyn ■ Dutch spoken ■ Prices medium ■ Visa and MC accepted ■ Trade discount

Restoration of antique brass hardware, a huge variety of furniture mounts, escutcheon pins, hand-cut nails, kidney bow keys, clock mounts, hand made brass chicken wire, lead sheet, candle sconces, galleries, brass stringing, hinges, feet, castors and many hard-to-find fittings. Hand-made and produced in the lost wax process.

BRASS TACKS FITTINGS LIMITED

177 Bilton Road, Perivale, Middlesex UB6 7HG ■ Tel: (0181) 566-9669 ■ Fax: (0181) 566-9339 ■ E-mail: btacks1358@aol.com ■ Mon-Fri ■ Prices medium to high

Decorative grilles and architectural hardware. Handles, locks, light switches, grilles. Schedules prepared.

JOHN CHURCHILL BLACKSMITH

The New Forge, Capton, Dartmouth, Devon TQ6 0JE ■ Tel: (01803) 712535 ■ Mon-Sat 9:00-1:00, 2:30-6:30 ■ French spoken

Hand-made custom hardware, both architectural and residential, mainly to commission. For doors, windows, furniture and stoves. Commissions of great variety. He has worked on the refurbishment of Plymouth Cathedral and The Evening Standard Garden at Chelsea '97.

COLLIER CASTINGS LTD

Raybar Hooe Battle, East Sussex TN33 9EU ■ Telfax: (01424) 892248 ■ Mon-Fri 7:30-5:30 ■ L. Collier ■ Prices medium

Custom door hardware and lamps. Ormolu brass casting. Lost wax process and sand casting for fine art. Restoration and re-gilding. Top references.

DANICO BRASS LTD

31 Winchester Road, Swiss Cottage, London NW3 3NR ■ Tel: (0171) 483-4477 ■ Fax: (0171) 722-7992 ■ Mon-Fri 9:30-6:00, Thu 9:30-8:00 ■ Ashok Dani ■ French and German spoken ■ Prices medium to very high ■ Visa and MC accepted ■ Trade discount

Large stock of door and window hardware. Also drapery hardware, bathroom fittings, electrical accessories, decorative grilles. Repolishing and refurbishing brass. Plating in gold and chrome.

FRANCHI INTERNATIONAL

Chelsea Harbour Design Centre, Lots Road, London SW10 0XE ■
Tel: (0171) 351-4554 ■ Fax: (0171) 351-2803 ■ Mon-Fri 8:00-6:00,
Sat by appointment ■ Marco Franchi ■ Prices high to very high ■
Major credit cards ■ Trade discount

Traditional and contemporary architectural and builders hardware: door and window fittings, locks, hinges and bolts, door closers, floor springs and fittings, bathroom fittings, grilles, vents and electrical fittings.

HAUTE DECO

556 King's Road, London SW6 2DZ ■ Tel: (0171) 736-7171 ■ Fax: (0171) 736-8484 ■ Mon-Sat 10:00-6:00 ■ Mrs. Swanell ■ French and Italian spoken ■ Prices low to very high ■ Major credit cards ■ Trade discount

Sophisticated designs in cast bronze and resin for door and window hardware, cabinet pulls and other decorative fittings.

SAMUEL HEATH AND SONS PLC

Leopold Street, Birmingham B12 0UJ ■ Tel: (0121) 772-2303 ■ Fax: (0121) 772-3334 ■ Mon-Fri 8:30-5:00 ■ German, French, Spanish and Italian spoken ■ Trade discount

High quality architectural, builders and marine brassware. Door and window hardware. Fittings, faucets, accessories and mirrors for bathrooms. Catalogues available.

LITTLEWOODS OF CRAWFORD STREET

24 Crawford Street, London W1H 1PJ ■ Tel: (0171) 486-7453 ■
Fax: (0171) 487-5011 ■ Mon-Sat 9:00-6:00 ■ Atul Sarin ■ French, German and Hindi spoken ■ Prices medium ■ Major credit cards ■ Trade discount

Retail outlet for all branded door and window hardware. Also plumbing fittings.

LOCKS & HANDLES

8 Exhibition Road, South Kensington, London SW7 2HF ■ Tel: (0171) 584-6800 ■ Fax: (0171) 589-4928 ■ Mon-Sat 9:00-5:00 ■ B. Nugent ■ Prices low to very high ■ Major credit cards ■ Trade discount

Over 1,000 stock items of brass door, window and cabinet hardware.

MARSHALL BRASS

Keeling Hall Road, Foulsham, Norfolk NR20 5PR ■ Tel: (01362) 684105 ■ Fax: (01362) 684280 ■ Mon-Fri 8:00-6:00 ■ Andrew Marshall ■ Prices medium to high ■ MC, Visa

Lost wax casting of reproduction furniture fittings and custom design work. Top of the line. Will copy any piece and make door levers and knobs from old models. Can custom make for complete houses as well as furniture. Antique finishes, gold and silver plating and all other finishes available. Catalogue upon request.

MCKINNEY & CO

Studio P, The Old Imperial Laundry, 71 Warriner Gardens, Battersea, London SW11 4XW ■ Tel: (0171) 627-5077 ■ Fax: (0171) 627-5088 ■ Website: www.i-i.net/mckinney&co ■ Mon-Fri 9:30-5:30 ■ Shona McKinney ■ Spanish and French spoken ■ Prices high ■ Professional discount ■ Visa, MC

Good selection of door and furniture knobs, handles and finials. Excellent selection of drapery hardware.

POOLE, WAITE & COMPANY

3 Clerkenwell Road, London EC1M 5PE ■ Tel: (0171) 253-8117 ■ Fax: (0171) 490-0579 ■ Mon-Fri 8:15-5:00 ■ Alex Mamas ■ German spoken ■ Prices medium to high ■ Major credit cards

Architects and builders ironmongery, since 1936, for both residential and commercial use. Brass, stainless steel, chrome, aluminium. Also specialists in locks, hinges, door closers, floor springs, decorative grilles. Special commission items. Major works for hospitals, schools, the Church of England and private clients. Nationwide delivery service.

RELCROSS LTD

Hambleton Avenue, Devizes, Wiltshire SN10 2RT ■ Tel: (0171) 403-4100 ■ Fax: (01380) 729888 ■ Mon-Sat 8:30-5:00 ■ Trade discount

Residential and commercial door and window hardware. All stocked. Catalogue upon request. Delivery.

ROMANY'S

52-56 Camden High Street, London NW1 0LT ■ Tel: (0171)387-2579 ■ Fax: (0171) 383-2377 ■ Mon-Sat 8:00-5:00, Sat 9:00-5:00 ■ Dilis Bhanderi ■ Prices medium ■ Major credit cards accepted

Architectural ironmongers. Locks, cabinet handles and other brassware.

H.E. SAVILL

9-12 St. Martins Place, Scarborough, North Yorkshire YO11 2QH ■
Tel: (01723) 373032 ■ Fax: (01723) 376984 ■ Mon-Fri 9:00-5:30 ■
Prices medium ■ Trade only

**For antique dealers and restorers only: cabinet hardware for all
English periods available in over 1,000 patterns and sizes.
Antique brass is their standard finish, polished brass also available. They have been in business for the last 100 years. Catalogue upon request.**

♛ J. SHINER & SONS LTD

8 Windmill Street, London W1P 1HF ■ Tel: (0171) 636-0740 ■ Fax:
(0171) 580-0740 ■ Mon-Fri 6:45-3:00 ■ Prices medium ■ Major credit cards ■ Trade discount

**English antique brass handles and locks in stock. Brass
Regency diamond grilles for bookcases, brass mounts for
Empire style furniture. Both supply and restoration of hardware.
One of the best.**

GHISLAINE STEWART

110 Fentiman Road, London SW8 1QA ■ Telfax: (0171) 820-9440 ■
By appointment only ■ Dutch, German and French spoken ■ Prices
high to very high ■ Visa and MC accepted ■ Trade discount

Table lamps, torchères, decorative hardware for doors and furniture. Also fireplace accessories.

LLOYD WORRALL (LONDON)

Unit 17, Sleaford Street Industrial Estate, Battersea SW8 5AB ■ Tel:
(0171) 622-2481 ■ Fax: (0171) 622-2840 ■ Mon-Fri 9:00-5:00 ■
Trade discount ■ Major credit cards

**Architectural hardware specifiers for all aspects of building.
Hardware for residential, commercial and public sector use.
Scheduling, consultants and sales.**

Drapery Hardware

ARTISAN

Unit 4A, Union Court, 20 Union Road, London SW4 6JP ■ Tel: (0171)
498-6974 ■ Fax: (0171) 498-2989 ■ Mon-Fri 9:00-1:00/2:00-5:00 ■
Some French spoken ■ Trade discount ■ Major credit cards

**Iron, wood, aluminium and other types of contemporary style curtain
rails, with glass, resin and porcelain finials. Catalogue available.**

BYRON & BYRON

4 Thane Works, Thane Villas, off Seven Sisters Road, London N7 7NU ■ Tel: (0171) 700-0404 ■ Fax: (0171) 700-4111 ■ Mon-Fri 9:00-6:00 ■ Lorena Dionidous ■ Italian, Portuguese, Spanish and Russian spoken ■ Prices medium ■ Visa, Delta and MC accepted ■ Trade discount

Large selection of gilded and lacquered wood and metal poles and finials. Some with heraldic motifs. There is also a Biedermeier collection.

THE CURTAIN COUTURIER

185 New King's Road , London SW6 4RD ■ Tel: (0171) 371-9255 ■ Fax: (0171) 371-9266 ■ Mon-Sat 9:30-5:30 ■ Anne Thompson ■ French spoken ■ Prices low to very high ■ Major credit cards ■ Professional discount

Most brands of poles and tracks in stock.   Brochures on request. Also expertly crafted made-to-measure curtains, blinds and bedspreads. Member of The Guild of Master Craftsmen.

INTERNATIONAL DRAPERY PRODUCTS

Boulet House, 142A Canbury Park Road, Kingston, Surrey KT2 6LE ■ Tel: (0181) 974-5896 ■ Fax: (0181) 974-5635 ■ Mon-Fri 9:00-5:00 ■ Nick Protts ■ French spoken ■ Prices medium to very high ■ Professional discount

Soft furnishing accessories are their specialty: curtain poles, traverse rods, motorized systems. Made-to-measure products and period reproductions. They are the distributors in the UK of Boulet Frères. Clients include The National Trust, English Heritage, royal palaces, stately homes, department stores.

MCKINNEY & CO

Studio P, The Old Imperial Laundry, 71 Warriner Gardens, Battersea, London SW11 4XW ■ Tel: (0171) 627-5077 ■ Fax: (0171) 627-5088 ■ Website: www.i-i.net/mckinney&co ■ Mon-Fri 9:30-5:30 ■ Shona McKinney ■ Spanish and French spoken ■ Prices high ■ Professional discount ■ Visa and MC

Custom-made finials and curtain accessories. Catalogue available.

MERCHANTS

Olmar Wharf, Olmar Street, London SE1 5AY ■ Tel: (0171) 237-0060 ■ Fax: (0171) 237-8204 ■ Mon-Fri 9:00-5:00 ■ Prices medium to high

Poles, brackets and finials in lacquered steel, bamboo with raffia or copper details. Some reasonably priced metal poles.

SILENT GLISS

Business Design Centre, Suite 325/326, 52 Upper Street, Islington Green, London N1 0QH ■ Tel: (0171) 288-6100 ■ Fax: (0171) 288-6103 ■ Mon-Fri 9:00-5:30 ■ Georgina Michael ■ Prices high ■ Professional discount

High quality curtain fitments and electric systems. Electric and manual decorative window blinds for all windows.

HOME FURNISHINGS

AERO

96 Westbourne Grove, London W2 5RT and 347-349 King's Road, Chelsea, London SW3 5ES ■ Tel: (0171) 221-1950 ■ Fax: (0171) 221-2555 ■ E-mail: shop@aero-furniture.co.uk ■ Mon-Sat 10:00-6:30, Sun 12:00-5:00 ■ Paul Newman ■ Prices medium to high ■ Major credit cards

Stylish utilitarian contemporary design furniture, lighting and accessories.

AFTER NOAH

261 King's Road, Chelsea, London SW3 5EL ■ Tel: (0171) 351-2610 ■ Fax: (0171) 359-4281 ■ Mon-Sat 10:00-6:00, Sun 12:00-5:00 ■ Simon Tarr ■ French and German spoken ■ Prices medium ■ Major credit cards

English Arts & Crafts furniture, American Mission furniture. Vintage and contemporary homeware. Antique furniture reproductions.

AFTER NOAH

121 Upper Street, London N1 1QR ■ Tel: (0171) 351-2610 ■ Fax: (0171) 359-4281 ■ Mon-Sat 10:00-6:00, Sun 12:00-5:00 ■ Major credit cards

One-of-a-kind old pieces: mostly British but some American. Home furnishings and turn-of-the-century Arts and Crafts, clocks, mirrors, 1930s anglepoise lights. Some table arts especially from the 1950s.

ANTA SCOTLAND

Dickens & Jones, 244 Regent Street, London W1A 1DB ■ Tel: (0171) 734-7070 ■ Fax: (0171) 437-1254 ■ Mon-Tue, Fri-Sat 10:00-6:30, Wed 10:00-7:00, Thu 10:00-8:00, Sun 11:00-5:00 ■ Jill Strieder ■ Prices high ■ Major credit cards

100% wool throws and cushions, stoneware and ceramics from Scottish designers.

LAURA ASHLEY

7-9 Harriet Street, Knightsbridge, London SW1X 9JS ■ Tel: (0171) 235-9797 ■ Fax: (0171) 823-2097 ■ Mon-Sat 10:00-6:00 ■ Japanese, French and Urdu spoken ■ Prices medium ■ Trade discount ■ Major credit cards

Home furnishings, fabrics, curtains, cabinets, wallpaper, borders, rugs and glassware.

PERCY BASS

184-188 Walton Street, London SW3 2JL ∎ Tel: (0171) 589-4853 ∎ Fax: (0171) 581-4137 ∎ E-mail: percybass@aol.com.uk ∎ Mon-Sat 9:30-5:30 ∎ Jane Morris ∎ French and Spanish spoken ∎ Prices medium ∎ Professional discount ∎ Major credit cards

151 shop items. Quality custom-made goods, wastebins, tissue boxes, cachepots, sofas and curtains. Everything to do with interior design including furniture, lighting and decorative accessories. Re-upholstery, curtain making, restoration, painting, re-caning, bookbinding, curtain and furniture making. Upholstery cleaning, gilding, drawing service. Full interior design service, etc.

CHARLES CAPEL

72 Cambridge Street, London SW1V 4QQ ∎ Tel: (0171) 821-7668 ∎ Fax: (0171) 821-7467 ∎ Mon-Fri 9:00-5:00 ∎ Brian Worthington ∎ French spoken

Hand-carved and finished furniture and accessories.

CARDEN CUNIETTI

83 Westbourne Park Road, London W2 5QH ∎ Tel: (0171) 229-8559 ∎ Fax: (0171) 229-8799 ∎ Mon-Sat 10:00-5:30 ∎ Audrey Carden, Eleanora Cunietti ∎ French, German, Spanish and Italian spoken ∎ Prices high ∎ Professional discount ∎ Major credit cards

Soft furnishings and antiques, linen, china, glass, lighting, bamboo-shaped candles, hand-stitched cushions, throws, cutlery and antiques.

CONRAN COLLECTION

12 Conduit Street, London W1R 9TG ∎ Tel: (0171) 399-0710 ∎ Fax: (0171) 399-0711 ∎ Mon-Wed, Fri-Sat 10:00-6:30, Thu 10:00-7:30, Sun 12:00-6:00 ∎ Prices low to very high ∎ Major credit cards

Outstanding exclusive homeware collection.

THE CONRAN SHOP

Michelin House, 81 Fulham Road, London SW3 6RD ∎ Tel: (0171) 589-7401 ∎ Fax: (0171) 823-7015 ∎ Mon-Tue 10:00-6:30, Wed-Thu 10:00-7:00, Sat 10:00-6:30, Sun 12:00-6:00 ∎ Prices low to very high ∎ Major credit cards

Home furnishings and accessories, tableware, table linen, bathroom and conservation accessories. Food, gift wrappings and a bridal registry.

THE CONRAN SHOP

55 Marylebone High Street, London W1M 3AE ■ Tel: (0171) 723-2223 ■ Fax: (0171) 535-3205 ■ Mon-Wed, Fri-Sat 10:00-6:00, Thur 10:00-7:00, Sun 12:00-6:00 ■ Prices low to very high ■ Major credit cards

Homeware products including elegant modern furniture, glass, ceramics, lighting, bath items and food. Bridal registry.

CONRAN SHOP CONTRACTS

22 Shad Thames, London SE1 2UU ■ Tel: (0171) 357-7703 ■ Fax: (0171) 357-7704 ■ Mon-Fri 9:00-5:30 ■ Prices medium to high ■ Trade discount ■ Visa and Amex

Contract furniture for hotels, restaurants, airports, offices, etc. Rapid quotes and excellent service.

DECO INSPIRED

67 Monmouth Street, Covent Garden, London WC2H 9DG ■ Telfax: (0171) 240-5719 ■ E-mail: decoinspire@msn.com ■ Mon-Sat 11:00-7:00 ■ Stan and Nicki Chaman ■ French and Spanish spoken ■ Prices medium to high ■ Trade discount ■ Major credit cards

American furniture, lamps and accessories from 1940-1970. Repair and restoration services.

DESIGNERS GUILD

267-271 King's Road, London SW3 5EN ■ Tel: (0171) 243-7300 ■ Fax: (0171) 243-7710 ■ Showroom hours: Mon-Tue 9:30-5:30, Wed-Thu 9:30-6:00, Sat 10:00-6:00 ■ Store hours: Mon-Tue 9:30-5:30, Wed-Sat 10:00-6:00, Sun 12:00-5:00 ■ Tricia Guild

Showroom: Fabric and wallpapers.
Store: Accessories and home furnishings, linen, glassware, china, soft furnishings, furniture, fabric, crockery. Bridal registry.

THE DESIGN NET

3 Rudolf Place, Miles Street, London SW8 1RP ■ Tel: (0171) 820-7771 ■ Fax: (0171) 820-1820 ■ Mon-Fri 9:00-5:30 ■ Diane Morris ■ Prices medium ■ Trade only

Contemporary furniture, lighting and accessories. Large and small projects.

THE DINING CHAIR COMPANY

4 St. Barnabas Street, London SW1W 8PP ■ Tel: (0171) 259-0422 ■ Fax: (0171) 259-0423 ■ Mon-Fri 10:00-1:00/2:00-6:00, Sat by appointment ■ Prices medium ■ Professional discount ■ Major credit cards

Everything for the dining room. High quality dining chairs, glass, china, sofas, upholstered stools and accessories. Custom-made furniture. Member of The Guild of Master Craftsmen.

DKM DESIGNS

43-44 Durant Street, London E2 7BP ■ Tel: (0171) 729-5736 ■ Fax: (0171) 739-4253 ■ Mon-Fri 8:00-6:00 ■ Dek Messelar ■ Prices medium to very high ■ Professional discount

From design to execution: hand-crafted home furnishings and decorative accessories, including furniture.

♛ELIZABETH EATON

85 Bourne Street, London SW1W 8HF ■ Tel: (0171) 730-2262 ■ Fax: (0171) 730-7294 ■ Mon-Sat 9:30-5:30 ■ Prices medium to high ■

A beautiful and complete collection of home furnishings, from reproduction doors and upholstered furniture, to fabrics and trimmings, wallpapers, lighting and lampshades, linens and decorative accessories.

FRONTIERS

37-39 Pembridge Road, London W11 3HG ■ Tel: (0171) 727-6132 ■ Fax: (0171) 229-4835 ■ Mon-Sat 11:00-6:30, Sun 12:00-4:00 ■ Mr. & Mrs. Nall-Cain ■ French, Swiss-German and German spoken ■ Prices low to high ■ Professional discount ■ Major credit cards

Pottery, furniture, decorative accessories and some jewellery. Tribal and ethnographical items from Africa, the Middle East, Asia.

♛THE GENERAL TRADING COMPANY

144 Sloane Street, London SW1X 9BL ■ Tel: (0171) 730-0411 ■ Fax: (0171) 823-4624 ■ Mon-Sat 9:30-6:00 ■ Michael MacRae ■ French and German spoken ■ Prices low to very high ■ Trade discount ■ Major credit cards

Upper end antiques, traditional and contemporary furniture and furnishings. Glass from Bacarrat, Waterford, Dartington and other imported glass. China: Herend porcelain, Raynaud, Wedgewood, Spode, Royal Worcester, Emma Bridgewater, Holdenby Design earthenware. Kitchenware, outdoor living accessories, bed and bath linens, lighting, Oriental department. Wedding lists.

GRAHAM & GREEN

4,7,10 Elgin Crescent, London W11 2JA ■ Tel: (0171) 727-4594 ■ Fax: (0171) 229-9717 ■ 164 Regents Park Road, London NW1 8XN ■ Tel: (0171) 483-2960 ■ Fax: (0171) 483-0901 ■ E-mail: info@grahamandgreen.co.uk ■ Mon-Fri 10:00-6:00 ■ Sat 9:30-6:00, Sun 11:00-5:30 ■ Antonia Graham ■ French and Spanish spoken ■ Prices low to very high ■ Professional discount ■ Major credit cards

An interesting mix of old and new ethnic housewares from around the world. Products from young designers from Asia and the Middle East. Also some kitchen equipment.

HABITAT

196 Tottenham Court Road, London W1P 9LD ■ Tel: (0171) 631-3880 ■ Fax: (0171) 255-6043 ■ Mon-Wed 10:00-6:00, Thu 10:00-8:00, Fri 10:00-6:30, Sat 9:00-6:30, Sun 12:00-6:00 ■ Major credit cards ■ For other branches telephone (0645) 334433

Home furnishings, furniture, kitchenware, lighting, stovetops, storage boxes, curtains, blinds, table linen, rugs and office furniture. Bridal Registry * Tel: (0171) 255-6045 * Fax: (0171) 255-6046.

♛ NICHOLAS HASLAM LTD

12 Holbein Place, London SW1W 8NL ■ Tel: (0171) 730-8623 ■ Fax: (0171) 730-6679 ■ Mon-Fri 10:00-6:00, Sat 12:00-5:00 ■ Paolo Moschino ■ French, Italian, Afrikaans and other European languages spoken ■ Prices high to very high ■ Professional discount ■ Major credit cards

Interior design supply: furniture, fabric, lighting and accessories. Very high quality.

HEAL'S

196 Tottenham Court, London W1 ■ Tel: (0171) 636-1666 ■ Fax: (0171) 637-5582 ■ Bridal Registry fax: (0171) 436-5414 ■ Mon-Wed 10:00-6:00, Thu 10:00-8:00, Fri 10:00-6:30, Sat 9:30-6:30 ■ Major credit cards ■ 234 King's Road, London SW3 ■ Tel: (0171) 349-8411 ■ Fax: (0171) 349-8439 ■ Mon, Tue, Fri-Sat 10:00-6:00, Wed-Thu 10:00-7:00, Sun 12:00-6:00 ■ Major credit cards

Contemporary furniture, a few antiques, fabrics, lighting, mirrors, decorative accessories, china, glassware, table and bath linens, kitchen accessories. Wedding lists.

STEPHANIE HOPPEN LIMITED

17 Walton Street, London SW3 2HY ■ Tel: (0171) 589-3678 ■ Fax: (0171) 584-3731 ■ Mon-Fri 10:00-6:00, Sat 12:00-4:00 ■ Stephanie Hoppen ■ French, Italian and German spoken ■ Prices low to very high ■ Major credit cards

Decorative paintings, both antique and modern. Unique handcrafted frames and accessories for the home. Scented candles, organza curtains, pewter basin plugs.

INDIA JANE

140 Sloane Street, London SW1X 2AY ■ Tel: (0171) 730-1070 ■ Mon-Sat 10:00-6:00 ■ Marguerite Bhasin ■ Prices medium to high ■ Trade discount ■ Major credit cards

Contemporary and old Indian furniture, decorative accessories, lamps, pictures, silverplate and china.

INVENTORY

26-40 Kensington High Street, London W8 4PF ■ Tel: (0171) 937-2636 ■ Fax: (0171) 938-4079 ■ Mon-Sun 10:00-7:00 ■ Prices medium ■ Major credit cards

Stylish home accessories at affordable prices. Bedding, kitchenware, decorative items, lighting, glassware, bathroom accessories.

JERRY'S HOME STORE

163-167 Fulham Road, London SW3 6SN ■ Tel: (0171) 581-0909 ■ Fax: (0171) 584-3749 ■ Mon-Fri 10:00-6:00, Sat 9:30-6:30, Sun 11:30-5:30 ■ Major credit cards

China, glass and flatware. A range of kitchenware, table linen, kitchen and bathroom furnishings and accessories. Inspired by the Pottery Barn in the U.S. One of the best in his field.

KASHMIR

48 South Audley Street, London W1Y 5DG ■ Tel: (0171) 491-2141 ■ Fax: (0171) 491-2149 ■ E-mail: Kashmir@audleyst.force9.co.uk ■ Mon-Sun 9:30-9:30 ■ Riyaz Rather ■ Several languages spoken ■ Prices low to medium ■ Trade discount ■ Major credit cards

Beautiful carpets, antiques and art from Kashmir, together with marble work and handicrafts. Pashmina shawls.

THE LAMP & RUG CO

Nags Head Shopping Centre, 402 Holloway Road, London N7 6PZ ■ Tel: (0171) 700-6744 ■ Mon-Sat 10:00-6:30 ■ C.R. Machon ■ Welsh spoken ■ Prices low to medium ■ Major credit cards

Alternative household furnishings, candles, candle holders, lava lamps, textiles, glassware, ceramics, cards, incense, giftwrappings.

PRUE LANE HANDMADE WORLDWIDE

6 Formosa Street, London W9 1EE ■ Telfax: (0171) 266-2629 ■ Tue-Sat 10:00-6:00 ■ Prue Lane ■ French spoken ■ Prices medium to very high ■ Professional discount ■ Major credit cards

Home furnishings, decorative pieces and hand-made household items from all over the world.

ANDREW MARTIN INTERNATIONAL LTD

200 Walton Street, London SW3 2JL ■ Tel: (0171) 584-4290 ■ Fax: (0171) 589-4957 ■ Mon-Sat 9:00-5:30 ■ Martin Walker ■ Prices medium to high ■ Trade discount ■ Major credit cards

Fabrics, furniture, wallpaper and accessories.

MUFTI MICHAEL D'SOUZA

789 Fulham Road, London SW6 5HD ■ Tel: (0171) 610-9123 ■ Fax: (0171) 384-2050 ■ E-mail: muftiuk@aol.com ■ Mon-Sat 10:30-6:30 ■ Michael D'Souza ■ French, German and Italian spoken ■ Prices high ■ Major credit cards ■ Trade discount

Exclusive collection of original furniture and home furnishings, all hand crafted and using all natural materials. The focus is on shape, colour, serenity and craftsmanship. Furniture is hand crafted from reclaimed teak. Also a range of soft furnishings

ORE DESIGN COMPANY

563-565 Battersea Park Road, London SW11 3BL ■ Tel: (0171) 801-0919 ■ Fax: (0171) 801-0912 ■ Mon-Sun 10:00-6:00 ■ Caroline Musson ■ Prices low to high ■ Trade discount ■ Visa and MC

Furniture and home accessories.

PLANET BAZAAR

151 Drummond Street, London NW1 2PB ■ Telfax: (0171) 387-8326 ■ Tue-Sat 11:30-7:00 ■ Maureen Silverman ■ French spoken ■ Prices low to high ■ Trade discount ■ MC and Visa

Designer furniture from the 1950s to the 1980s, glass, ceramics and lighting. Books and eccentricities.

EMILY READETT-BAYLEY LIMITED

St. Luke's Old Rectory, 107 Grange Road, London SE1 3BW ■ Tel: (0171) 231-3939 ■ Fax: (0171) 231-4499 ■ E-mail: emily@emily-readett-b.demon.co.uk ■ Mon-Fri 9:30-5:30 ■ Emily Readett-Bayley ■ French spoken ■ Prices medium to high ■ Trade discount ■ Major credit cards

Pure bamboo and re-claimed teak furniture and lighting.

RENWICK & CLARKE

190 Ebury Street, London SW1W 8UP ■ Tel: (0171) 730-8913 ■ Fax: (0171) 730-4508 ■ Mon-Sat 9:30-5:30 ■ Several languages spoken ■ Major credit cards

Unique source for all kinds of home furnishings: from furniture and lighting, to linen and tableware. A treat.

THE ROOM

158 Walton Street, London SW3 2JL ■ Telfax: (0171) 225-3225 ■ E-mail: caj@dircon.co.uk ■ Mon-Fri 10:30-6:30, Sat 10:30-5:30 ■ Philip Evans ■ Prices high ■ Trade discount ■ Major credit cards

Contemporary works by British-based designers: silver, glass, ceramics, art objects, furniture and decorative accessories.

STEPHEN RYAN DESIGN & DECORATION

7 Clarendon Cross, Holland Park, London W11 4AP ■ Tel: (0171) 243-0864 ■ Fax: (0171) 243-3151 ■ E-mail: sryandesign@compuserve.com ■ Mon-Sat 10:00-6:00 ■ Stephen Ryan ■ Prices medium to high ■ Major credit cards ■ Trade discount

International design service with their own showroom stocking their own decorative accessories, rugs, furniture, lighting.

SHAKER

322 King's Road, London SW3 5UH ■ Tel: (0171) 352-3918 ■ Fax: (0171) 376-3494 ■ Mon-Sat 10:00-6:00 ■ Pauline Dean ■ Prices medium to high ■ Trade discount ■ Major credit cards

American Shaker-style furniture and accessories. Interior textiles, bedroom and bathroom accessories.

♔ SUSSEX HOUSE & ENGLISH HOME COLLECTION

92 Wandsworth Bridge Road, London SW6 2TF ■ Tel: (0171) 371-5455 ■ Fax: (0171) 371-7590 ■ Website: www.cushion.co.uk ■ Mon-Fri 10:00-6:00, Sat 10:30-5:00 ■ Gaynor Churchward ■ French, Italian and Spanish spoken ■ Prices medium to high ■ Professional discount ■ Major credit cards

Antique-style cushions, throws and bedspreads. Sussex House and English Home Collection. Decorative cushions in appliqued velvets, Aubusson weaving, embroidered raw silk. Bulk orders for floor cushions for parties, fashion shows and theatres.

TOBIAS & THE ANGEL

68 White Hart Lane, London SW13 0PZ ■ Telfax: (0181) 878-8902 ■ Mon-Sat 10:00-6:00 ■ A. Hughes and A. McLaughlin ■ German and French spoken ■ Prices low to high ■ Trade discount ■ Major credit cards

Antique furniture, made-to-order lampshades, soft furnishings made with antique textiles, small antiques, kitchenalia, linens, glass and pottery.

TRADE & CARE

73 Buttesland Street, London N1 6B4 ■ Tel: (0171) 490-2493 ■ Fax: (0171) 253-0663 ■ Mon-Fri 9:30-5:30 ■ Bich Tyler ■ French, Vietnamese, Indonesian and Spanish spoken ■ Visa accepted

Contemporary Vietnamese lacquerware and ceramics.

YOUNG + D LTD

Beckhaven House, 9 Gilbert Road, London SE11 4NL ■ Tel: (0171) 820-9403 ■ Fax: (0171) 793-0537 ■ Mon-Fri 9:30-5:30 ■ S. Young ■ French and Greek spoken ■ Trade discount ■ Major credit cards

UK manufacturers of the Fisherman's Lamp. Full lighting and furniture, candles and tinware.

Historic Furnishings

♔ANN LISTER HISTORIC FURNISHINGS

Cam Laithe, Far Lane, Kettlewell, Skipton, North Yorkshire BD23 5QY ■ Tel: (01756) 760809 ■ Fax: (01756) 760209 ■ By appointment ■ Prices medium to very high

Historic furnishings. Research, supply and making authentic furnishings. Bed hangings, window treatments and other furnishings. From a single room to a whole property. Clients include: The National Trust, English Heritage and privately owned Historic Houses and Museums.

Fine Stationary

THE ITALIAN CORNER COMPANY LTD

16 Royal Arcade, Old Bond Street, London W1X 3HB ■ Tel: (0171) 499-9469 ■ Fax: (0171) 499-9722 ■ E-mail: lucia@italiancorner.co.uk ■ Mon-Sat 10:00-6:00 ■ Lucia Panini ■ Italian and French spoken ■ Prices low to high ■ Major credit cards

Italian stationary, Pineider writing accessories, books, magazines, writing papers, photo albums, leather goods, personal printing, engraving. Worldwide mail order.

ALASTAIR LOCKHART

97 Walton Street, London, SW3 2HP ■ Tel: (0171) 589-0000/581-8289 ■ Fax: (0171) 912-0652 ■ Mon-Fri 10:00-6:00, Sat 10:00-5:00 ■ E-mail: allockhart@aol.com ■ Alastair and Olivia Lockhart ■ French and Italian spoken ■ Prices medium to high ■ Major credit cards

Fine engraved stationary.

THE MEDICI GALLERIES

7 Grafton Street, Bond Street, London W1X 3LA ■ Tel: (0171) 629-5675 ■ Fax: (0171) 495-2997 ■ Mon-Fri 9:00-5:30 ■ Ian Lewis ■ Prices medium to high ■ Major credit cards

Fine art greeting cards, reproduction and limited edition prints, stationary and giftwrap. Oriental contemporary artwork, framing service, overprinted Christmas card service. Member of The Fine Art Trade Guild.

The Department Stores

DICKENS & JONES

224 Regent Street, London W1 ■ Tel: (0171) 734-7070 ■ Fax: (0171) 437-1254 ■ Mon-Tue 10:00-6:30, Wed 10:00-7:00, Thu 10:00-8:00, Fri 10:00:6:30, Sat 9:30-6:30, Sun 11:00-5:00 ■ All price levels ■ Major credit cards

Full range of kitchenware, cutlery, china, glass, table and bed linens, furniture. Bridal registry.

♔ FORTNUM & MASON

181 Piccadilly, London W1A 1ER ■ Tel: (0171) 734-8040 ■ Fax: (0171) 437-3278 ■ Mon-Sat 9:30-6:00 ■ Prices high ■ Major credit cards

After feasting your eyes on the food stalls on the main floor, you might want to make your way to the departments where they offer an excellent selection of cookware, kitchenware, china, glass and silver. Then take a look beyond to their offerings of bed and bath as well as table linens. And don't forget their furniture and especially their garden accessories and tools. Bridal registry.

HARRODS LTD

Knightsbridge, London SW1X 7XL ■ Tel: (0171) 730-1234 ■ Fax: (0171) 581-0470 ■ Mon-Tue, Sat 10:00-6:00, Wed-Fri 10:00-7:00 ■ Most languages spoken ■ Prices high to very high ■ Major credit cards

The full range of home furnishings including antique and contemporary furniture, accessories, lighting, mirrors, bed, bath and table linens, kitchenware and accessories. Silver, china, crystal, glass. Most of the top names. Caution: if you want to spend a penny, be prepared to pay a pound. Bridal registry: Tel: (0171) 225-6500 ■ Fax: (0171) 225-5760.

PETER JONES

Sloane Square, London SW1W 8EL ■ Tel: (0171) 730-3434 ■ Fax: (0171) 730-9645 ■ Mon-Sat 9:30-6:00, Wed 9:30-7:00 ■ Only debit cards accepted.

Home furnishings, tableware and kitchenware. Bridal registry: Tel: (0171) 730-0200 ■ Fax: (0171) 730-9487.

HARVEY NICHOLS

109-212 Knightsbridge, London SW1X 7BJ ■ Tel: (0171) 235-5000 ■ Fax: (0171) 259-6084 ■ Mon-Sat 10:00-7:00, Wed 10:00-8:00, Sun 12:00-6:00 ■ Major credit cards

On the 4th floor, selections of home furnishings including Ralph Lauren Home, Mulberry, Jerry's Home Store, Designer's Guild, Belinda Coote Tapestries. Also lighting, candles and tableware.

JOHN LEWIS

278-306 Oxford Street, London W1A 1EX ■ Tel: (0171) 629-7711 ■ Fax: (0171) 514-5353 ■ Mon-Fri 9:30-6:00, Thu 10:00-8:00, Sat 9:00-6:00 ■ Major credit cards

Seven floors of home furnishings, new furniture and reproductions, decorative accessories, bed and bathroom fittings, kitchen units, china, glass, flatware, silver, carpets. Bridal registry: Tel: (0171) 499-1977 ■ Fax: (0171) 514-5353.

LIBERTY

214 Regent Street, London W1B 6AH ■ Tel: (0171) 734-1234 ■ Fax: (0171) 573-9876 ■ Mon-Sat 10:00-6:30, Thu 10:00-7:30 ■ Major credit cards

Traditional and modern tableware, English and Continental, including china, glass, flatware, cutlery. Also a complete kitchen shop. Home furnishings, fabrics, rugs, lighting and bed, bath and table linens. Bridal registry.

SELFRIDGES

400 Oxford Street, London W1 ■ Tel: (0171) 629-1234 ■ Fax: (0171) 495-8321 ■ Mon-Wed 10:00-7:00, Thu-Fri 10:00-8:00, Sat 9:30-7:00, Sun 12:00-6:00 ■ Major credit cards

Home furnishings including furniture, bed, bath and table linens, kitchenware, tableware, china, glassware, pottery, cutlery and appliances. They carry the Ralph Lauren Home collection. Bridal registry: Tel: (0171) 318-3260 ■ Fax: (0171) 318-3745.

The Designer Home Collections

GUCCI

18 Sloane Street, London SW1X 9NE ■ Tel: (0171) 235-6707 ■ Fax: (0171) 888-9541 ■ Mon-Sat 10:00-6:00, Sat 10:00-7:00 ■ 33 Old Bond Street, London W1X 4HH ■ Tel: (0171) 629-2716 ■ Fax: (0171) 629-4729 ■ Major credit cards

Their location on Sloane Street is the second largest Gucci store in Europe. Their Home Collection includes decorative accessories, table arts, glassware, porcelain, flatware, cookware, cashmere throws and more.

HERMES

179 Sloane Street, London SW1X 9QG ■ Tel: (0171) 823-1014 ■ Fax: (0171) 823-1458 ■ Mon-Sat 10:00-6:00 ■ Major credit cards
155 New Bond Street, London W1Y 9PA ■ Tel: (0171) 499-8856

Furnishings and tableware. Choice of four porcelain patterns, flatware and glassware. The Pippa Collection of small furniture, armchairs and side tables.

VERSACE

34-36 Old Bond Street, London W1X 3AE ■ Tel: (0171) 499-1862 ■ Fax: (0171) 499-1719 ■ Mon-Sat 10:00-6:00 ■ Major credit cards

Their home furnishings collection includes flatware, silver, Rosenthal china, crystal, glassware, special order furniture, lighting, lamps, bed linens, picture frames, fabrics, pillows in various sizes and patterns.

KITCHENS

ABACUS INTERNATIONAL

681-683 Holloway Road, London N18 5SE ■ Tel: (0171) 281-4136 ■ Fax: (0171) 272-5081 ■ Mon-Sat 9:00-5:30, Sun 10:30-1:00 ■ Victor or David Bloom ■ Prices low to very high ■ Major credit cards ■ Professional discount

Kitchens and appliances. Ceramic and marble tile installations. Bathrooms and showers.

NICHOLAS ANTHONY

40 Wigmore Street, London W1H 9DF ■ Tel: (0171) 935-0177 ■ Fax: (0171) 935-1887 ■ Mon-Fri 9:30-6:00, Sat 10:00-4:00 ■ Shaun Lenane ■ French spoken ■ Prices high ■ Professional discount ■ Visa and MC

Kitchens, bedrooms, bathrooms. Full design, planning and installation. They offer German and SieMatic kitchens and a whole range of American appliances – fridges, freezers and cookers.

BARGET KITCHENS & INTERIORS

Contract office: BK House, 3 Biddulph Road, Maida Vale, London W9 1JA ■ Tel: (0171) 286-2109 ■ Fax: (0171) 266-1880 ■ E-mail: bargetkit@aol.com ■ Mon-Fri 9:30-5:30 ■ Christian Huelsen ■ Spanish, Italian, French and German spoken ■ Prices medium to high ■ Professional discount

Specialists in large retail Italian and German kitchens, handmade furniture, American appliances. Delivery and installation. Free design service.

BLACKHEATH DESIGN STUDIO

135 Lee Road, London SE3 9DS ■ Telfax: (0181) 297-8063 ■ Mon-Sat 10:00-5:00, closed Wed ■ N. Grant ■ French spoken ■ Prices low to very high ■ Major credit cards

Kitchen furniture, appliances, installation, tiling, plumbing and electrics.

BROWNS

85 White Hart Lane, Barnes, London SW13 0PW ■ Tel: (0181) 878-9944 ■ Fax: (0181) 878-9494 ■ E-mail: sales@brownskitchens.com ■ Mon-Fri 10:00-6:00, Sat 10:00-4:00 ■ Christian Brown ■ French and Spanish spoken ■ Prices medium to high ■ Professional discount ■ Major credit cards

Bespoke kitchen furniture. American appliances available through catalogues. Full planning, design, building and installation.

BRUTON KITCHENS

122 Brompton Road, Knightsbridge, London SW3 1JD ■ Tel: (0171) 225-2999 ■ Fax: (0171) 225-0445 ■ Mon-Fri 9:00-6:00, Sat 9:00-5:00 ■ Dawn Metcalfe ■ Prices medium to high ■ Professional discount

Specialists in German kitchens. Wide range of American appliances. Design service, delivery and installation.

BULTHAUP – LONDON

37 Wigmore Street, London W1H 9LD ■ Tel: (0171) 495-3663 ■ Fax: (0171) 495-0139 ■ E-mail: 100607.3252@compuserve.com ■ Mon-Fri 9:30-5:30, Sat 10:00-4:00 ■ Alexander Wrighten ■ French spoken ■ Prices very high

Fine contemporary kitchen design. Excellent choice of appliances including Sub-Zero fridges and Thermador cookers. Design and installation.

BUYERS & SELLERS LTD.

120-122 Ladbroke Grove, London W10 5NE ■ Tel: (0171) 229-1947 ■ Fax: (0171) 221-4113 ■ E-mail: sales@buy-sellers.lemon.co.uk ■ Mon-Fri 9:00-5:30, Sat 9:00-4:30 ■ Tim Miller ■ Arabic, French and Hebrew spoken ■ Prices medium to high ■ Professional discount ■ Major credit cards

Retailers for all electrical appliances for the kitchen, cookers, fridges, microwaves, diswashers, washing machines, vacuum cleaners. Will recommend installers.

CHELSEA INTERIORS

27 Wigmore Street, London W1H 9LD ■ Tel: (0171) 408-2230 ■ Fax: (0171) 408-2210 ■ Mon-Sat 9:30-5:30 ■ David Knight ■ Prices high to very high

Full kitchen design and supply of appliances. Most major brands.

CHRISTIANS OF KNIGHTSBRIDGE LTD

164 Brompton Road, Knightsbridge, London SW3 1HW ■ Tel: (0171) 581-2271 ■ Fax: (0171) 581-7912 ■ Mon-Sat 9:30-5:30 ■ Celia Warbrick ■ French spoken ■ Prices very high ■ Trade discount

Complete design and installation service for kitchen, bathroom, bedroom, study.

CONNAUGHT KITCHENS

2 Porchester Place, London W2 2BS ■ Tel: (0171) 706-2210 ■ Fax: (0171) 706-2209 ■ Mon-Thu 9:00-5:30, Fri 9:00-5:00, Sat 10:00-5:00 ■ P. Ozorio ■ Prices medium to high ■ Professional discount ■ Visa and MC

Designers of contemporary and traditional German and English hand-made kitchens. Leading appliance brands. Full design and installation service.

EDWINS

19 All Saints Road, London SW6 3QR ■ Tel: (0171) 221-9340 ■ Fax: (0171) 243-0206 ■ Mon-Fri 8:00-5:00 ■ Bill Wood, Matt Davis ■ Spanish spoken ■ Prices low to high ■ Major credit cards ■ Trade discount

Modern minimalist and traditional kitchens and bathrooms.

F.K. ELLIS & SONS LTD

87 Brixton Water Lane, London SW2 1PH ■ Tel: (0171) 733-4428 ■ Fax: (0171) 733-4034 ■ Mon-Sat 8:00-5:30 ■ Steve Bromley ■ Prices low to high ■ Professional discount ■ Major credit cards

Appliances for kitchens and bathrooms. Fridges, freezers, cookers, dishwashers. Supply to builders and the general public. Will recommend installers.

NORMAN GLEN KITCHENS & INTERIORS

477-481 Finchley Road, London NW3 6HS ■ Tel: (0171) 794-7801 ■ Fax: (0171) 794-1379 ■ Mon-Fri 9:00-6:00, Sat 10:00-5:00 ■ Nicolas Hickson ■ Gujarati spoken ■ Prices high to very high ■ Professional discount ■ Most major credit cards

Fitted furniture for kitchens and interiors. American appliances: Sub-Zero fridges, Thermador ovens. Installations.

HANSENS REFRIGERATION SERVICES LTD

306-306A Fulham Road, Chelsea, London SW10 9ER ■ Tel: (0171) 351-6933 ■ Fax: (0171) 351-5319 ■ E-mail: sales@hansens.co.uk ■ Website: www.hansens.co.uk ■ Mon-Fri 9:00-5:30, Sat 10:00-4:30 ■ Des Proctor ■ French spoken ■ Prices low to very high ■ Trade discount ■ Major credit cards

Supply, design and build kitchens for hotels and restaurants. Large American appliances.

HARRODS LTD

Knightsbridge, London SW1X 7XL ■ Tel: (0171) 730-1234 ■ Fax: (0171) 225-6679 ■ Mon-Tue, Sat 10:00-6:00, Wed-Fri 10:00-7:00 ■ David Lawton ■ Most languages spoken ■ Prices high to very high ■ Major credit cards

Large household appliance department. Amongst the enormous choice you will find Thermador and Sub-Zero. Home delivery.

C.P. HART & SON LTD

Newham Terrace, Hercules Road, London SE1 7DR ■ Tel: (0171) 902-1000 ■ Fax: (0171) 902-1007 ■ Mon-Sat 9:00-5:30 ■ Kitchen Manager: Steve Esdale ■ French, Italian, Spanish and German spoken ■ Prices high ■ Trade discount ■ Major credit cards

Design of SieMatic kitchens. Full range of American appliances: Viking on display. Delivery and installation.

JUST KITCHENS KNIGHTSBRIDGE LTD

172 Brompton Road, Knightsbridge, London SW3 1HW ■ Tel: (0171) 584-2022 ■ Fax: (0171) 584-2160 ■ E-mail: jk1knights@aol.com. ■ Mon-Sat 9:00-6:00 ■ Manager, Lucy Hallett, Contracts Manager, Graham Barnard ■ Italian and French spoken ■ Prices medium to high ■ Professional discount ■ Credit cards for lower priced items

SieMatic kitchens. Large choice of appliances including Sub-Zero and Traulsen. Full design service available and installation.

THE KITCHEN CLINIC LTD

149 St. John's Hill, Battersea, London SW11 1TQ ■ Tel: (0171) 642-8382 ■ Mon-Sat 10:00-5:30 ■ Andrew Barr ■ Prices medium to high ■ Professional discount ■ Most major cards

Bespoke kitchen design. Full range of American appliances. Full design, planning and installation services.

PLAIN ENGLISH

41 Huxton Square, London N1 6PB ■ Tel: (0171) 613-0022 ■ Mon-Sat 11:00-5:00 ■ Katie Fontana, Tony Niblow ■ Prices medium

Hand-made kitchens and kitchen furniture. Designs based on Georgian style joinery.

SELFRIDGES

400 Oxford Street, London W1A 1AB ■ Tel: (0171) 318-2996 ■ (0171) 318-2350 ■ E-mail: jeff.marks@sears-clothing.co.uk ■ Mon-Fri 10:00-7:00, Thu 10:00-8:00, Sat 9:00-7:00, Sun 12:00-6:00 ■ Paul Deacon ■ Most languages spoken ■ Prices high to very high ■ Major credit cards

Large selection of European and American kitchen appliances. Also furniture and accessories for bathrooms, kitchens, bedrooms and living rooms. No installation.

SUPERIOR KITCHENS

255 Rye Lane, Peckham, London SE15 4QN ■ Tel: (0171) 639-8233 ■ Fax: (0171) 277-9740 ■ Mon-Wed, 9:00-5:00, Thu 9:00-8:00, Fri-Sat 9:00-5:00 ■ David Lovatt ■ Prices medium to high

Made-to-measure stainless steel worktops, doors, hob solutions and corner solutions. American appliances including Thermador cookers.

♔ MARK WILKINSON FURNITURE

41 High Street, St. Johns Wood, London NW8 7NJ ■ Tel: (0171) 586-9579 ■ Fax: (0171) 586-8638 ■ Mon-Fri 9:30-5:30, Sat 10:00-5:00 ■ John Day ■ French, Spanish, Finnish and German spoken ■ Prices high ■ Professional discount ■ Most credit cards

High quality custom-made furniture for kitchens, bedrooms and dining rooms. Large choice of American kitchen appliances including Thermador and Amana. Full design and installation.

Kitchenware

BODUM LTD

71 King's Road, London SW3 4NX ■ Tel: (0171) 376-3825 ■ Fax: (0171) 823-3749 ■ Mon-Sat 10:00-7:00, Sun 12:00-5:00 ■ Miriam Koester ■ Prices medium ■ Major credit cards

Specialists in coffee makers.

RICHARD DARE

93 Regents Park Road, London NW1 8UR ■ Tel: (0171) 722-9428 ■ Fax: (0171) 625-7639 ■ Mon-Sat 9:30-6:00 ■ L. Vincent ■ French spoken ■ Prices low to medium ■ Major credit cards

Stainless steel cookware, pottery and faience from Quimper, olive-wood kitchen knives, items for storage, preparation and serving food and wine.

ELIZABETH DAVID

3A North Row, The Market, Covent Garden, London WC2E 8RA ■ Tel: (0171) 836-9167 ■ Fax: (0171) 240-5279 ■ Mon-Sat 9:30-5:30 ■ Major credit cards

A large collection of European cooking and baking accessories, including Le Creuset, Mayer and Fissler. Also Poole pottery and Poterie Francaise. Sabatier knives, drinks accessories and a large selection of cookery books.

DIVERTIMENTI

45-47 Wigmore Street, London W1H 9LE ■ Tel: (0171) 935-0689 ■ Fax: (0171) 823- 9429 ■ Also at 139-141 Fulham Road, London SW3 1SD ■ Tel: (0171) 581-8065 ■ Mail order tel: (0181) 246-4300 ■ Mon-Sat 9:30-5:30 ■ Major credit cards

Great selection of kitchenware, wicker and wooden accessories, stainless steel equipment, small electrical appliances, utensils and cookbooks.

FAIRFAX KITCHEN SHOP

1 Regency Parade, Swiss Cottage, London NW3 5EQ ■ Tel: (0171) 722-7648 ■ Fax: (0171) 722-2333 ■ Mon-Sat 9:30-5:30 ■ Peter Katz ■ French, Italian and German spoken ■ Prices medium to high ■ Major credit cards

Quality cookware, knives, Italian expresso machines and coffee makers. Food preparation equipment. Service and repair of La Pavoni Expresso and cappuccino machines.

LA CUISINIERE

81-83 Northcote Road, London SW11 6PJ ■ Telfax: (0171) 223-4487 ■ Mon-Sat 9:30-6:00 ■ Annie Price ■ French spoken ■ Prices medium to high ■ Major credit cards

A very well-known brand of cookery and tableware. Excellent quality.

DAVID MELLOR

4 Sloane Square, London SW1W 8EE ■ Tel: (0171) 730-4259 ■ Fax: (0171) 730-7240 ■ Mon-Sat 9:30-6:00 ■ David Mellor, Miles Drake ■ Prices low to high ■ Visa and MC

Mellor designs of cutlery: a range of designs in stainless steel and silver plate. Kitchenware, accessories, tableware and glassware.

SUMMERILL & BISHOP LTD

100 Portland Road, London W11 4LN ■ Tel: (0171) 221-4566 ■ Fax: (0171) 727-1322 ■ Mon-Sat 10:00-6:00 ■ June Summerill and Bernadette Bishop ■ French and a little Italian and German spoken ■ Prices medium ■ Professional discount ■ Major credit cards

Functional and decorative kitchen products, old and new. Japanese knives, Cephalon pans, old French table linen, old enamel cafetiers and cannisters.

GILL WING

190 Upper Street, Islington, London N1 1RQ ■ Tel: (0171) 226-5392 ■ Fax: (0171) 354-9641 ■ 7 days 9:30-6:00 ■ Dutch, German, French and Welsh spoken ■ Prices medium to high ■ Visa accepted

White china, cookware, tableware, electrical appliances and barbecues.

LIGHTING

AKTIVA
10B Spring Place, London NW5 3BH ■ Tel: (0171) 428-9325 ■ Fax: (0171) 428-9882 ■ E-mail: info@aktiva.co.uk ■ Mon-Fri 9:00-6:00 ■ Prices medium ■ Trade discount

Contemporary spot lighting and decorative lighting design and manufacture.

AMTIQUES
Unit 3, Admiral Vernon Antique Market, 141-145 Portobello Road, London W11 ■ Fax: (0181) 806-5806 ■ Sat 5:00-5:00 ■ French, German and a bit of Japanese spoken ■ Prices low to medium ■ Major credit cards ■ Trade discount

Quality French, English and European decorative lighting, shades and fittings. Art Deco and Art Nouveau signed figures. Objets d'art and collectibles.

BEAUMONT & FLETCHER
261 Fulham Road, London SW3 6HY ■ Tel: (0171) 352-5594 ■ Fax: (0171) 352-3546 ■ Mon-Sat 9:30-5:30 ■ John Crowell, Brian Worthington ■ Prices high ■ Trade discount ■ Major credit cards accepted

Fine hand-carved mirrors and wall lights.

👑 PETER BELL
78 Albert Street, London NW1 7NR ■ Tel: (0171) 387-8483 ■ Fax: (0171) 387-1704 ■ Mon-Fri 8:30-8:00 ■ Peter Bell ■ French spoken ■ Prices low to medium

Low voltage wire lights. Wonderful minimalist designs. Catalogue available.

👑 COLLIER CASTINGS LTD
Raybar Hooe Battle, East Sussex TN33 9EU ■ Telefax: (01424) 892248 ■ Mon-Fri 7:00-5:30 ■ L. Collier ■ Prices medium

Ormolu brass casting with the lost wax process. Also sand casting for all fine art items such as lamps, lighting. Re-gilding. Works with Sotheby's, museums and major antique dealers.

COLUMBIA GLASSWORKS

13-16 Sunbury Workshops, Swanfield Street, London E2 7LF ■ Tel: (0171) 613-5155 ■ Fax: (0171) 739-7597 ■ E-mail: info@columbia-glass.co.uk ■ Mon-Fri 8:00-6:00 ■ N. Blackmore ■ Prices low to very high

Highly decorative lighting, lamps, vases, glasses, bowls in colourful modern designs.

♛ MRS. M.E. CRICK CHANDELIERS & DENTON ANTIQUES

156 Kensington Church Street, London W8 4BN ■ Tel: (0171) 229-5866 ■ Fax: (0171) 792-1073 ■ Mon-Fri 9:30-5:30 ■ French spoken ■ Prices high to very high ■ Professional discount

Charming and very well informed people. Museum quality chandeliers from the 18th, 19th and early 20th century. Wall lights, lustres, gilded bronze lanterns, sconces, candelabra. Some remarkable cut glass of the 18th to the early 20th century. Beautiful collection of decanters and other unusual art objects.

JOHN CULLEN LIGHTING

585 King's Road, London SW6 2EH ■ Tel: (0171) 371-5400 ■ Fax: (0171) 371-7799 ■ Mon-Fri 9:30-5:30, Sat 10:00-4:00 ■ Colin Brown ■ French, Dutch and German spoken ■ Prices high ■ Trade discount ■ Major credit cards

Discreet lighting for house and garden. A wide variety of light fittings, recessed downlights, surface directional spotlights, uplighting and exterior lighting. Lighting design and special orders. Marvellous lighting for indoor gardens and swimming pools.

DIANE METALWARE

Stall 21A&34A, Westbourne Antique Arcade, 113 Portobello Road, London W11 2QB ■ Tel: (01923) 223287 ■ Sat 7:30-3:30 ■ French spoken ■ Trade discount ■ Visa and MC

Early lighting, Georgian gaslights, Victorian and Edwardian lighting. Brass wall lights, table lamps, ceiling fittings, glass shapes and restoration. Candlesticks, oil lamps, glass shades, wall sconces and ceiling fittings.

EXTRALITE DESIGNS LTD

26 Northways Parade, College Crescent, Finchley Road, London NW3 5DN ■ Telfax: (0171) 722-7480 ■ Mon-Sat 9:30-5:30, Wed 9:30-2:30 ■ Barry Copas ■ Prices medium to high ■ Major credit cards ■ Trade discount

Domestic lighting specialists. Crystal, Tiffany, Italian and Spanish lighting. All types of lamps. Low voltage.

KENSINGTON LIGHTING COMPANY
59 Kensington Church Street, London W8 4HA ■ Tel: (0171) 938-2405 ■ Fax: (0171) 937-5915 ■ Mon-Sat 9:00-6:00 ■ Kevin Kelly ■ Prices low to high ■ Major credit cards

Classical decorative lighting and customized fittings. Beautiful chandeliers, lanterns and wall lights. Outdoor lighting in wood and painted metal. Lamps wired for anywhere in the world.

LA MURRINA
79 Ebury Street, London SW1W 0NZ ■ Tel: (0171) 730-7922 ■ Fax: (0171) 730-7920 ■ Mon-Fri 10:00-5:30, Sat 10:00-5:00 ■ Prices medium to high

Hand-blown and hand-crafted Murano glass lighting, objects and giftware. Vases, bowls and stemware.

LEVITT SHENNAN LIGHTING LTD
17 Clocktower Works, 4 Shearling Way, London N7 9TH ■ Tel: (0171) 609-0002 ■ Fax: (0171) 609-5080 ■ E-mail: post@levitt1.demon.co.uk ■ Website: www.levitt.1.demon.co.uk ■ Mr. Levitt and Mr. Shennan ■ German spoken ■ Prices low to medium

Hi-tech, modern industrial and domestic lighting. Catalogue available.

THE LIGHT STORE
11 Clifton Road, Maida Vale, London W9 1SZ ■ Tel: (0171) 286-0233 ■ Fax: (0171) 286-8133 ■ R. Clift and E. Nicolaides ■ Major credit cards

All types of lighting from traditional to hi-tech.

THE LIGHTING STORE
779-781 Finchley Road, London NW11 8BN ■ Tel: (0181) 201-8628 ■ Fax: (0181) 201-8638 ■ Mon-Sat 9:00-5:00 ■ Kenny Collins ■ French spoken ■ Prices medium to high ■ Major credit cards ■ Trade discount

A collection of lighting from all over the world. Cleaning, design and installation.

DAVID MALIK & SON LTD
5 Metro Centre, Brittania Way, Park Royal, London NW10 7PA ■ Tel: (0181) 965-4232 ■ Fax: (0181) 965-2401 ■ Mon-Fri 10:00-5:00 ■ Sara Malik ■ Prices medium to very high ■ Trade discount

Design, maufacture and restoration of fine crystal chandeliers and wall lights and lustres. In-stock and made-to-order.

♔ MCCLENAGHAN

69 Pimlico Road, London SW1W 8NE ■ Telfax: (0171) 730-4187 ■ Mon-Sat 10:00-6:00 ■ Bob Gilhooly and John McClenaghan ■ Prices medium to very high ■ Major credit cards ■ Trade and export discount

A large selection of 19th century English mirrors and lighting, lamps and an extensive range of hanging lanterns. Lamp conversions and restorations.

MCCLOUD & CO LTD

269 Wandsworth Bridge Road, London SW6 2TX ■ Tel: (0171) 371-7151 ■ Fax: (0171) 371-7186 ■ E-mail: mccloud@ukonline.co.uk ■ Mon-Fri 10:00-5:00, Sat 10:00-4:00 ■ Kevin McCloud ■ Prices high ■ Trade discount ■ Major credit cards

Decorative lighting and furniture. Chandeliers, sconces, lamps, consoles. Commissions undertaken. Experience with historical sites: Shakespeare's birthplace, Edinburgh Castle and The Balmoral Hotel.

ORA LIGHTING

16 Boston Parade, Boston Road, London W7 2DG ■ Tel: (0181) 840-6560 ■ Fax: (0181) 840-8887 ■ Mon-Fri 9:00-5:30 ■ Michael Osborn ■ Prices medium ■ Quantity discount

Their own design and manufacture of leisure lighting: wall lights, uplights and downlights.

W. SITCH & CO LTD

48 Berwick Street, Oxford Street, London W1V 4JD ■ Tel: (0171) 437-3776 ■ Fax: (0171) 437-5707 ■ Mon-Sat 7:30-7:00 ■ Ronald Sitch ■ Prices medium to very high ■ To the trade

Period lighting: manufacture and reproduction of exact copies of chandeliers, free-standing lamps, wall sconces, table lamps, floor standards and lanterns. Rewiring, restoration, polishing, bronzing, silver-plating, ormolu work, brass work, art metal work.

GHISLAINE STEWART

110 Fentiman Road, London SW8 1QA ■ Telfax: (0171) 820-9440 ■ By appointment only ■ Dutch, German and French spoken ■ Prices high to very high ■ Trade discount ■ Visa and MC

Table lamps and torchères. Stock line and her own design of resin and bronze/brass lamps. Finishes can be custom toned.

DAVID TURNER ANTIQUES RESTORATION

24 Tottenham Road, London N1 4BZ ■ Tel: (0171) 241-5400 ■ Fax: (0171) 249-2379 ■ Mon-Fri 9:30-6:00 ■ David Turner ■ French and Italian spoken ■ Prices medium

Restoration of antique metal work, mostly brass and bronze lighting. Reproductions of antique items. Small range of reproduction lamps and lanterns.

WEVER & DUCRE

26 Stove Street, London WC1E 7BT ■ Tel: (0171) 631-1323 ■ Fax: (0171) 631-1224 ■ E-mail: export@wever-ducre.co ■ Mon-Fri 9:00-5:00 ■ Ignace Allaeys ■ French, Dutch and German spoken ■ Prices medium

Manufacturers of architectural lighting fittings.

👑WILKINSON PLC

5 Catford Hill, London SE6 4NU ■ Tel: (0181) 314-1080 ■ Fax: (0181) 690-1524 ■ E-mail: enquiries@wilkinson-plc.com ■ Showroom: 1 Grafton Street, London W1X 3LB ■ Tel: (0171) 495-2477 ■ Fax: (0171) 491-1737 ■ Mon-Fri 9:00-5:00 ■ David Wilkinson ■ Trade discount ■ Visa and MC

Manufacture and restoration of chandeliers. Repair of antique glass. Bespoke glass making. Art metal work. Cleaning and installation of chandeliers. Stock of superb chandeliers in their Grafton Street showroom.

YOUNG + D LTD

Beckhaven House, 9 Gilbert Road, London SE11 4NL ■ Tel: (0171) 820-9403 ■ Fax: (0171) 793-0537 ■ Mon-Fri 9:30-5:30 ■ S. Young ■ French and Greek spoken ■ Prices medium ■ Major credit cards ■ Trade discount

UK manufacturers of the Fisherman's Lamp.

Lampshades

👑ANN'S

34A&B Kensington Church Street, London W8 4HA ■ Tel: (0171) 937-5033 ■ Fax: (0171) 937-5915 ■ Mon-Sat 9:00-6:00 ■ Mandy Goldstein ■ Prices medium to high ■ Trade discount ■ Major credit cards

Hand-made lampshades in fabric or card. Customized specials. Restoration and conversions of lamp bases. Wiring for worldwide shipping.

BESSELINK JONES & MILNE LTD

99 Walton Street, London SW3 2HH ■ Tel: (0171) 574-4068 ■ Fax: (0171) 574-4072 ■ Mon-Sat 10:00-5:30 ■ German and Dutch spoken ■ Prices high ■ Major credit cards ■ Trade discount

Hand-made lampshades and lamps, wall lights, floor lights and table lamps. Repairs, restoration and conversions.

👑 LION, WITCH AND LAMPSHADE

C/O Muriel Michalos Ltd, 57 Elizabeth Street, London SW1W 9PP ■ Tel: (0171) 730-1774 ■ By appointment ■ Nick and Nicky Dixon ■ German spoken ■ Prices medium to high ■ Professional discount ■ MC, Visa

Bespoke lampshade makers of the highest quality, including silk, card, hand-painted metal, hand-painted card as well as glass. Will recover lampshades. Restoration and rewiring of all types of lighting. They are the best at making decorative objects into lamps. Work references include The National Trust. Show-room in the Cotswolds at Northleach: Tel: (01451) 860855. Good selection of lighting.

PATRICK QUIGLEY

24 New Globe Walk, London SE1 9DR ■ Tel: (0171) 633-9933 ■ By appointment

Slightly different lampshades in parchments, crushed velvet and fake fur. For those with "off-the-wall" tastes.

See also: Antique Dealers
            Chelsea Harbour Design Center
            Home Furnishings.

LINEN

Household and Table

COLOGNE & COTTON LTD
39 Kensington Church Street, London W8 ■ 88 Marylebone High Street, London W1 ■ 791 Fulham Road, London SW6 ■ Tel: (01926) 332573 ■ Fax: (01926) 332575 ■ Mon-Sat 10:00-7:00 ■ Victoria Shepherd and Jenny Deeming ■ Prices medium ■ Trade discount ■ Major credit cards

Pure cotton bed and bath linen. Unusual eaux-de-Colognes and bath soaps.

DESCAMPS
197 Sloane Street, London SW1X 9QX ■ Tel: (0171) 235-6957 ■ Fax: (0171) 235-3903 ■ Mon-Sat 9:30-5:30 ■ Prices medium to high ■ Major credit cards

Good selection of French bed and bath linen. Some of it embroidered and scallop edged. Bath mats and robes and a children's line.

♕FRETTE
98 New Bond Street, London W1Y 9LF ■ Tel: (0171) 629-5517 ■ Fax: (0171) 499-2332 ■ Mon-Sat 9:30-5:30 ■ Prices high ■ Major credit cards

Top quality, embroidered bed and table linen and towels. Matching trays and accessories.

GIVAN'S IRISH LINEN STORES
207 King's Road, London SW3 5ED ■ Tel: (0171) 352-6352 ■ Fax: (0171) 351-5645 ■ Mon-Fri 9:30-1:00/2:00-5:00 ■ K.R. Powell ■ Prices medium to high ■ Professional discount ■ Major credit cards

Fine household linens: bed, table, bath and kitchen. Catalogue.

MARY KIRK
31 Linden Avenue, Kensac Rise, London NW10 5RE ■ Tel: (0181) 960-3924 ■ Fax: (0181) 969-7151 ■ E-mail: mk-ah@dircon.co.uk ■ By appointment ■ Mary Kirk ■ Prices medium to high ■ Trade discount

Hand-felted woollen blankets and cushion covers. Throws and baby blankets of 100% merino wool, camel or silk. Will accept commissions for one-off pieces.

THE LINEN CHEST

23 White Conduit Street, Chapel Market, Islington, London N1 9HA
■ Tel: (0171) 833-0418 ■ 7 days 10:00-6:00 ■ Ms. Ferhad ■ Prices
low to medium ■ Trade discount ■ Major credit cards

Bed linens, bath towels, cushions, throws and gifts.

THE LINEN CUPBOARD

21&22 Great Castle Street, London W1N 7AA ■ Tel: (0171) 629-4062
■ Fax: (0171) 491-4576 ■ Mon-Sat 9:00-6:30 ■ G. Green ■ Prices low
■ Major credit cards

**A full range of household linen, including Irish linen and bed,
table and bath linen.**

THE LINEN MERCHANT LTD

11 Montpelier Street, London SW7 1EX ■ Tel: (0171) 584-3654 ■ Fax:
(0171) 584-3671 ■ Ian Southward ■ French and German spoken ■
Mon-Sat 9:30-6:00 ■ Major credit cards

**A wonderful selection of classic and contemporary linens,
many with fine hand embroidery. Also children's bed and cot
linen.**

MONOGRAMMED LINEN SHOP

168-170 Walton Street, London SW3 2JL■ Tel: (0171) 589-4033 ■
Fax: (0171) 823-7745 ■ Mon-Sat 9:30-6:00 ■ French and Italian
spoken ■ Prices medium to high ■ Trade discount ■ Major credit
cards

**All household bed, bath and table linens, accessories and
nightwear. Nice selection.**

THE NURSERY WINDOW

83 Walton Street, London SW3 2HP ■ Tel: (0171) 581-3358 ■ Fax:
(0171) 823-8839 ■ Mon-Sat 9:30-5:30 ■ Prices medium to high ■
Major credit cards

A charming selection of children's bed and bath linen.

PRATESI LINENS UK

Unit 1-2, Chelsea Harbour Design Centre, Chelsea Harbour, Lots
Road, London SW10 ■ Tel: (0171) 349-0090 ■ Mon-Fri 9:30-5:30 ■
Prices high ■ Major credit cards

One of the world's best-known purveyors of fine quality linens.

THE TURKISH BATH SHOP
Unit 2, Main Hall, Camden Lock Market, Chalk Farm Road, London NW1 8AF ■ Telfax: (0171) 267-6000 ■ Website: www.theturkish-bathshop.co.uk ■ 7 days 10:00-6:00 ■ Margaret and Enver Karaali ■ Turkish, Arabic and some French spoken ■ Prices medium ■ Professional discount ■ Major credit cards

Bath robes, towels, Egyptian cotton bed linen, natural sponges, loofahs, pumice, hand-made soaps, ceramic gift boxes.

See also: Department Stores
Home Furnishings.

Antique Linen

JANICE FORD
Shop 48, Admiral Vernon Arcade, 141 Portobello Road, London W11 2DY ■ Telfax: (01892) 822316 ■ Sat only 6:00-4:00 ■ Janice Ford ■ Italian and Spanish spoken ■ Prices low to very high ■ Major credit cards ■ Trade discount

Antique laces and fine linens. Doilies, tray cloths, table centres, tablecloths, napkins, runners, curtains, sheets, pillow-cases, shawls, fans, quilts.

LUNN ANTIQUES LTD
86 New King's Road, Parsons Green, London SW6 4LU ■ Tel: (0171) 736-4638 ■ Fax: (0171) 371-7113 ■ Mon-Sat 10:00-6:00 ■ Stephen Lunn ■ French and German spoken ■ Prices low to very high ■ Trade discount ■ Major credit cards

Antique linen and lace: bedding, tablecloths, nightdresses, clothing. Also restoration for antique linens and lace.

JANE SACCHI
Chelsea, London SW3 ■ Tel: (0171) 589-5643 ■ Fax: (0171) 581-3564 ■ By appointment only ■ LAPADA

Specialists in antique linen: 19th to early 20th century French linen sheets and bed linen. Upholstery and curtains in all qualities.

See also: Antique Markets especially Portobello Road.

MIRRORS

ARTEFACT

36 Windmill Street, London W1P 1HF ■ Tel: (0171) 580-4878 ■ Fax: (0171) 580-0987 ■ Mon-Fri 10:00-5:30, Sat 11:00-5:00 ■ Minda Dowling, Amanda Nightingale ■ Prices low to high ■ Trade discount ■ All major credit cards

Decorative framed mirrors, traditional and custom.

BEAUMONT & FLETCHER

261 Fulham Road, London SW3 6HY ■ Tel: (0171) 352-5594 ■ Fax: (0171) 352-3546 ■ Mon-Sat 9:30-5:30 ■ John Crowell, Brian Worthington ■ Prices high ■ Trade discount ■ Major credit cards accepted

Fine quality hand-carved mirrors and wall lights.

CADOGAN GLASS LTD

214 Battersea Park Road, Battersea, London SW11 4ND ■ Tel: (0171) 720-7466 ■ Fax: (0171) 627-5235 ■ Mon-Fri 9:30-6:00, Sat 10:00-5:00 ■ Prices medium ■ Trade discount

Supply and fit all types of mirrors. Antique bronze and grey mirrors.

CHELSEA ANTIQUE MIRRORS

72 Pimlico Road, London SW1W 8LS ■ Tel: (0171) 824-8024 ■ Fax: (0171) 824-8233 ■ Mon-Sat 9:30-6:00 ■ Andrew Koll ■ Prices low ■ Trade discount ■ Visa and Amex

Custom gilding and carving of mirrors and console tables.

CHELSEA GLASS LTD

650 Portslade Road, Battersea, London SW8 3DH ■ Tel: (0171) 720-6905 ■ Fax: (0171) 978-2827 ■ Mon-Fri 8:30-5:00 ■ Prices medium ■ Trade discount

Made-to-measure mirrors supplied and fitted. Large selection of antique and tinted finishes. Mirrors bevelled and engraved to order.

GRAY & McDONNELL LTD

264-269 Poyser Street, Bethnal Green, London E2 9RF ■ Tel: (0171) 739-4022 ■ Fax: (0171) 739-9424 ■ Mon-Fri 8:00-5:00 ■ Vincent and Gerald McDonnell ■ Prices medium ■ Major credit cards

Mirrors supplied and fitted. Glass bevelling, brilliant cutting, silvering.

ALEXANDER GEORGE LEY & SONS

13 Brecknock Road, London N7 OBL ■ Tel: (0171) 267-3645 ■ Fax: (0171) 267-4462 ■ Mon-Fri 8:00-6:30 by appointment ■ Prices high

Carvers and gilders. Makers of mirrors and fine giltwood furniture. Fine frames.

MINX DESIGN

57 Great Western Studios, Great Western Road, London W9 3NY ■ Telfax: (0171) 289-5621 ■ Mon-Fri 9:00-6:00 ■ Prices medium ■ Professional discount

Mirrors: gilded, aluminium/gold. contemporary frames and simple shapes. Supplier to The Iron Bed Company.

♔ OSSOWSKI

83 Pimlico Road, London SW1W 8PH ■ Tel: (0171) 730-3256 ■ Fax: (0171) 823-4500 ■ Mon-Fri 10:00-6:00 ■ Prices high to very high ■ Trade discount

18th century English giltwood mirrors and consoles. 18th and 19th century decorative giltwood carvings. Restoration of giltwood objects.

OVERMANTELS LTD

66 Battersea Bridge Road, London SW11 3AG ■ Tel: (0171) 223-8151 ■ Fax: (0171) 924-2283 ■ E-mail: seth@overmantels.co.uk ■ Mon-Sat 9:30-5:30 ■ Seth Taylor ■ French spoken ■ Prices low to high ■ Trade discount ■ MC and Visa

Giltwood mirrors in English and French 18th and 19th century styles. Antiques and reproductions of mirrors and consoles.

See also: Antique Dealers.

TABLE ARTS

General

♔ASPREY
165-169 New Bond Street, London W1Y 0AR ■ Tel: (0171) 493-6767 ■ Fax: (0171) 491-0384 ■ Mon-Fri 9:00-5:30, Sat 9:00-1:00 ■ BADA

Antique silver and old Sheffield plate, the big names in fine bone china and crystal.

♔CHRISTOFLE
10 Hanover Street, London W1R 9HF ■ Tel: (0171) 491-004 ■ Fax: (0171) 491-3003 ■ E-mail: christofle@christofle-btinternet.com ■ Mon-Sat 10:00-5:00 ■ Colin Hodgson, John Robinson ■ French spoken ■ Prices medium to very high ■ Trade discount ■ Major credit cards

Silverware and tableware, including crystal, glass, porcelain and china.

FAMOUS NAMES
6-7 Colonnade Walk, 123 Buckingham Palace Road, London SW1N 9SH ■ Telfax: (0171) 233-9313 ■ Mon-Sat 9:00-6:00 ■ Karim Sacoor ■ Spanish, Italian, Portuguese spoken ■ Prices medium to high ■ Major credit cards ■ Trade discount

All the top brand names in table arts, china, pottery, crystal, glassware, tableware.

♔THE GENERAL TRADING COMPANY
144 Sloane Street, London SW1X 9DL ■ Tel: (0171) 730-0411 ■ Fax: (0171) 823-4624 ■ Mon-Sat 9:30-6:00 ■ Michael MacRae ■ French and German spoken ■ Prices low to very high ■ Major credit cards ■ Trade discount

Marvellous choice of porcelain and china from hand-painted Herend and Raynaud to Wedgewood, Royal Worcester, Spode, Emma Bridgewater and Holdenby Design earthenware. Crystal: Waterford, Baccarat, Dartington and many others. Bridal registry.

HERMES
179 Sloane Street, London SW1X 9QG ■ Tel: (0171) 823-1014 ■ Fax: (0171) 823-1458 ■ Mon-Sat 10:00-6:00, Sat 10:00-6:00 ■ Prices high to very high ■ Major credit cards
155 New Bond Street, London W1Y 9PA ■ Tel: (0171) 499-8856

Table arts. Four choices in porcelain patterns, flatware, glassware. Bridal registry possible.

THOMAS GOODE & CO

19 South Audley Street, Mayfair, London W1Y 6BN ■ Tel: (0171) 499-2823 ■ Fax: (0171) 629-4230 ■ Website: www.thomasgoode.com ■ Mon-Sat 10:00-6:00 ■ Prices high ■ Professional discount ■ Major credit cards

An extraordinary experience and a living museum. Superb collection of all the arts of the table. Exclusive patterns of fine bone china, Sevres porcelain, fine crystal, glassware and silver. Bridal registry.

GEORG JENSEN SILVER & ROYAL COPENHAGEN PORCELAIN

15 New Bond Street, London W1Y 9PF ■ Tel: (0171) 499-6541 ■ Fax: (0171) 629-0952 ■ Mon-Fri 9:15-5:30, Sat 10:00-5:00 ■ Prices medium to very high ■ Major credit cards

The great Georg Jensen silver patterns and Royal Copenhagen porcelain. Bridal registry.

OGGETTI

133 and 143 Fulham Road, London SW3 ■ Tel: (0171) 581-8088/(0171) 584-9808 ■ Fax: (0171) 581-9652 ■ Mon-Sat 9:30-6:00, Sun 12:00-5:00 ■ Robin Dawson ■ Italian spoken ■ Prices low to very high ■ Major credit cards

Design table products from Europe and Scandinavia, the big names in porcelain and crystal.

RENWICK & CLARKE

190 Ebury Street, London SW1W 8UP ■ Tel: (0171) 730-8913 ■ Fax: (0171) 730-4508 ■ Mon-Fri 9:30-6:00, Sat 10:00-5:00 ■ Prices high to very high ■ Major credit cards

One of the best and most international selections of the arts of the table. Fine china and porcelain, crystal and silverware, including reproductions of historic silver items. Wedding lists.

TIFFANY & CO

25 Old Bond Street, London W1 3AA ■ Tel: (0171) 409-2790 ■ Fax: (0171) 491-3110 ■ Mon-Fri 10:00-5:30, Sat 10:00-6:00 ■ Major credit cards

Beautiful patterns by the top names in china as well as special designs for Tiffany. More than 20 lines of their silver flatware and a wide choice of stemware and barware. Bridal registry.

GLAZEBROOK & CO

PO Box 1563, London SW6 3XD ■ Tel: (0171) 731-7135 ■ Fax: (0171) 371-5434 ■ 7 days all hours ■ Jonathan Glazebrook ■ Prices medium ■ Major credit cards

Highest quality stainless steel cutlery by mail order. Fine British sterling silver, silver plate. Brochures and price lists available. Free sample service.

♛ DAVID MELLOR

4 Sloane Square, London SW1W 8EE ■ Tel: (0171) 730-4259 ■ Fax: (0171) 730-7240 ■ Mon-Sat 9:30-6:00 ■ David Mellor, Miles Drake ■ Prices low to high ■ Visa and MC

David Mellor's own designs in stainless steel and silver plate cutlery.

REGENCY SILVERWARE LTD

18 Vivian Avenue, Hendon, London NW4 3PX ■ Tel: (0181) 202-9292 ■ Fax: (0181) 202-0008 ■ Mon-Fri 10:00-4:00, Sun 10:00-2:00 ■ David Gubbay ■ Prices low

Sheffield silver and gold-plated cutlery. Stainless steel cutlery plus cutlery sets.

China and Porcelain

CHINACRAFT REJECT CHINA SHOP

134 Regent Street, London W1R 5KA ■ Tel: (0171) 434-2502 ■ Fax: (0171) 287-1558 ■ 7 days 9:00-6:00 ■ French spoken ■ Prices low to high ■ Major credit cards

China, glass and silver. The great brands, Doulton, Spode, Wedgewood, Waterford, Baccarat, sold at discount prices. This company has once-a-year sales in New York at a leading hotel.

DUBARRY (PORCELAIN DE LIMOGES)

Unit 1, Greenwich Centre, 53 Norman Road, Greenwich, London SE10 9QJ ■ Telfax: (0181) 853-0599 ■ E-mail: limoges@dubarry.co.uk ■ Mon-Fri 8:00-5:00 ■ Victor Perera ■ French spoken ■ Prices high ■ Trade discount

Hand-painted Limoges porcelain, collectibles and giftware.

HOCKLEY CHINA AND GLASS FACTORY SHOP

100 East Road, London N1 6AA ■ Tel: (0171) 684-8280 ■ Fax: (0171) 251-0242 ■ E-mail: shop@trauffler.com ■ Mon-Fri 9:30-5:00 ■ Clive Holmes ■ French spoken ■ Prices low to medium ■ Major credit cards

Large selection of porcelain, china, earthenware, glass and crystal. Worldwide mail order.

HOUSE OF HANOVER

13-14 Hanover Street, London W1R 9HG ■ Tel: (0171) 629-1103 ■ Fax: (0171) 491-1909 ■ Mon-Sat 9:30-6:00, Sun 11:00-5:00 ■ Major credit cards

They sell Wedgewood china only.

ROYAL DOULTON & MINTON LTD

167 Piccadilly, London W1V ■ Tel: (0171) 493-9121 ■ Fax: (0171) 499-3561 ■ Mon-Sat 9:30-6:00, Tue 10:00-6:00 ■ All major credit cards

The entire Royal Doulton range, Royal Albert, Royal Crown Derby, Minton. Wedding lists.

ROYAL WORCESTER

Severn Street, Worcester WR1 2NE ■ Tel: (01905) 23221 ■ Fax: (01905) 23601 ■ Mon-Fri 9:00-5:30, Sat-Sun 11:00-5:00 ■ Spanish, German, French and Italian spoken ■ Major credit cards

Two major sales events each year: mid-June through July and in January, where discounts up to 50% apply. They offer first quality and seconds of their wonderful bone china, tableware, porcelain, cookware and giftware.

ROYAL WORCESTER & SPODE

126 Regent Street, London W1R 5FE ■ Tel: (0171) 734-7704 ■ Fax: (0171) 734-7705 ■ Mon-Sat 10:00-6:00 ■ Rebecca Kinnarney ■ French, German and Italian spoken ■ Discounts for quantity ■ Major credit cards

The full lines of Royal Worcester and Spode. Can re-produce old patterns to order.

♛ SPODE FACTORY & MUSEUM

Church Street, Stoke-on-Trent ST4 1DX ■ Tel: (01782) 744011 ■ Fax: (01782) 744-0020 ■ Factory: Mon-Fri 9:00-5:00 ■ Museum: Mon-Sat 9:00-5:00, Sat 10:00-4:00 ■ Major credit cards

Spode ranks amongst the best of the bone china producers in the world. It is sold in many outlets in London. Spode's museum in Staffordshire is open to the public every day. It shows a collection from the company's founding in 1780. The archives can be visited by appointment. The factory is open from Monday to Friday and no appointment is necessary.

VILLEROY & BOCH FACTORY SHOP

267 Merton Road, London SW18 5JS ■ Tel: (0181) 870-4168 ■ Fax: (0181) 871-1062 ■ Mon-Sat 10:00-5:00, Sun 11:00-5:00 ■ Major credit cards

This is a discount store and offers 30% off their regular prices, together with crystal, cutlery and stainless steel flatware. Clients are advised of their sales. The have a concession shop in Harrods.

♛ VON POSCH

100 Jermyn Street, St. James's, London SW1Y 6EE ■ Telfax: (0171) 930-2211 ■ Mon-Fri 10:00-6:00, Sat 10:00-5:00 ■ Gerda von Posch and Jerry Kean ■ German spoken ■ Prices medium to high ■ Major credit cards

Hand-painted porcelain from Europe. Tableware, giftware, figurines, crystal. Most of the well-known names. Mrs. Von Posch is charming and a visit to her shop is a pleasant experience.

♛ WATERFORD WEDGEWOOD RETAIL LTD

158 Regent Street, London W1R ■ Tel: (0171) 734-7262 ■ Fax: (0171) 287-1238 ■ Mon-Sat 9:30-6:30 ■ Major credit Cards
173-174 Piccadilly, London W1V 0PD ■ Tel: (0171) 629-2614 ■ Fax: (0171) 495-2745 ■ Mon-Sat 9:00-6:00 ■ Sue O'Brien ■ Japanese spoken ■ Major credit cards

The Waterford-Wedgewood designs as well as the modern, contemporary designs of Rosenthal, including a wide range of dinnerware and glassware. Wedding lists. The Wedgewood Museum in Staffordshire can be visited by appointment ■ Tel: (01782) 204141.

See: Antique Porcelain under Antique Collectibles.

COSMO PLACE STUDIO

11 Cosmo Place, London WC1N 3AP ■ Tel: (0171) 278-3374 ■ Mon-Sat 10:00-6:00 ■ Josie Firmin, Christopher Strangeways ■ Prices medium to high ■ Visa and MC accepted

Hand-decorated fine English bone china. Vases, tableware, bowls. Special commissions accepted.

STEPHANIE FERNALD CERAMIC DESIGNS

10 Longley Road, Rochester, Kent ME1 2HD ■ Telfax: (01634) 401427 ■ E-mail: stephfernald@hotmail.com ■ 7 days by appointment ■ Trade discount

Hand-decorated English bone china. Complete range of bone china tableware. Commissions undertaken, either from design to completion or using customer's own artwork. Classical designs, sporting, fossils and bugs. Catalogue available.

Ceramic and Earthenware

♛ BRIDGEWATER

739 Fulham Road, London SW6 5UL ■ Tel: (0171) 371-9033 ■ Fax: (0171) 384-2457 ■ E-mail: bridge.water@btinternet.com ■ Mon-Fri 10:00-5:30, Sat 10:00-5:00 ■ Emma Bridgewater ■ Prices high ■ Major credit cards

High quality hand-decorated earthenware. Formal and informal tableware. Clients are invited to come to their studio and decorate their own piece of Bridgewater pottery.

TRAUFFLER LTD

100 East Road, London N1 6HH ■ Tel: (0171) 251-0240 ■ Fax: (0171) 251-0242 ■ E-mail: sales@trauffler.com ■ Mon-Fri 9:00-5:00 ■ Mr. Holmes or Mr. Shute ■ French spoken ■ Prices medium to high ■ Trade discount ■ Major credit cards

Ceramic oven and tableware. Upscale houseware products. They will also customize crockery.

CAROLINE WHYMAN

21 Iliffe Yard, Crampton Street, London SA17 3QA ■ Telfax: (0171) 708-5904 ■ By appointment only ■ Caroline Whyman ■ Prices medium to high ■ Trade discounts

Hand-made porcelain ceramics inlaid in geometric patterns with gold. Vases, bowls, plates. Special commissions undertaken.

Crystal and Glass

♔ BACCARAT

37 Old Bond Street, London W1X 3AE ■ Tel: (0171) 409-7767 ■ Fax: (0171) 409-7717 ■ Mon-Fri 10:00-6:00, Sat 10:00-5:00 ■ Several languages spoken ■ Major credit cards

Baccarat crystal, one of the great names of France. Since 1764, they have been creating stemware, barware, vases, decanters, pitchers, lighting, as well as remarkable chandeliers and decorative objects. The Baccarat Museum in Paris on the rue de Paradis is well worth a visit.

♔ BLUE CRYSTAL (GLASS)

Units 6-8, 21 Wren Street, London WC1X 0HF ■ Telfax: (0171) 278-0142 ■ Mon-Fri 8:45-4:45 ■ D.J. Andrews ■ Prices medium

Rarest amongst the rare: a supplier of the blue glass liners for antique silver. Also provides hand-cut crystal and crystal tableware.

GEORGINA JAY

Crown Arcade, 119 Portobello Road, London W11 ■ Tel: (0171) 792-3619 Fax: (0181) 347-9626 ■ Sat 5:30-4:00 or by appointment ■ French, German and Italian spoken ■ Prices medium ■ Trade discount ■Visa and MC

18th, 19th and early 20th century decanters, glasses, perfume bottles, salts, vases, hand-cut, blown, etched and engraved.

THE GLASSHOUSE

21 St. Albans Place, London N1 0NX ■ Tel: (0171) 359-8182 ■ Fax: (0171) 359-9485 ■ E-mail: 106700.3475@compuserve.com ■ Mon-Fri 9:00-5:00

Glassware of all kinds.

♔ LALIQUE LTD

162 New Bond Street, London W1Y 9PA ■ Tel: (0171) 499-8228 ■ Fax: (0171) 493-7049 ■ Mon-Fri 10:00-6:00, Sat 10:00-5:00 ■ Major credit cards

Blown and cut crystal, stemware, barware, crystal sculptures, china, lighting, tables, mirrors, consoles. Art glass at its best. Bridal registry.

THE LONDON GLASSBLOWING WORKSHOP & GLASS ART GALLERY

7 The Leathermarket, Weston Street, London SE1 3ER ■ Tel: (0171) 403-2800 ■ Fax: (0171) 403-7778 ■ Mon-Fri 10:00-5:00 ■ Peter Layton ■ Prices high ■ Major credit cards

Free blown studio glass. Exquisite colour, texture and form. Tableware and unique decorative items.

SELCO CRYSTAL LTD

88-90 Hatton Garden, London EC1N 8PP ■ Tel: (0171) 242-7216 ■ Fax: (0171) 831-4003 ■ Mon-Fri 9:00-5:00 ■ Philip L. Mayer ■ Spanish, Hebrew and French by arrrangement ■ Prices low to high

Bohemia crystal and glassware. Vases, bowls, clocks, paperweights, glasses, decanters, jugs, tankards. Personal engraving available.

♔ WILLIAM YEOWARD CRYSTAL

336 King's Road, London SW3 5UR ■ Tel: (0171) 351-5454 ■ Fax: (0171) 351-9469 ■ E-mail: office@johnjenkins.co.uk ■ Mon-Fri 9:30-6:00, Sat 10:00-5:00 ■ Prices medium to high ■ Major credit cards

Handmade crystal inspired by great designs of the 18th and 19th century. Remarkable crystal pieces including salt cellars, vases, decanters, bowls and decorative pieces.

See: Antique Glass under Antique Collectibles.

Pewter

♔ JACK CASIMIR LTD

23 Pembridge Road, London W11 3HG ■ Telfax: (0171) 727-8643 ■ Mon-Sat 10:00-5:30 and by appointment ■ M. & R. Casimir ■ Major credit cards ■ BADA, LAPADA

British and European 16th to 19th century brass, copper and pewter. Candelabra, candlesticks, fireplaces and all you can imagine. Third generation of a family business.

HILARY KASHDEN

Outside 171 Portobello Road ■ Tel: (0171) 958-1018 ■ Fax: (0181) 988-2913 ■ Sat only 8:00-4:00 ■ Prices low to very high ■ Major credit cards

Antique pewter from 1600-1850. Flagons, tankards, candlesticks, plates, chargers.

ROYAL SELANGOR PEWTER

14 Burlington Arcade, London W1V 4LP ■ Tel: (0171) 499-2004 ■ Fax:
(0171) 474-5522 ■ Mon-Sat 9:00-6:00 ■ E-mail: r.suk1@dial.pipex.com
■ Virginia Scott-Griffe ■ Prices high ■ Major credit cards

Prestigious pewter giftware.

Silver

ADC HERITAGE LTD

95A Charlwood Street, London SW1V 4PB ■ Tel: (0171) 976-5271 ■
Fax: (0171) 976-5898 ■ By appointment only ■ BADA

Silver and old Sheffield plate.

ARBRAS

292 Westbourne Grove, London W11 2PS ■ Telfax: (0171) 226-5221
■ Mon-Sat 9:30-4:30 ■ Bob Brass ■ Spanish spoken ■ Prices low ■
Trade discount ■ Visa and MC

**Silver photograph frames. Candlesticks, wine coasters, wine
labels, napkin rings, cutlery.**

PAUL BENNETT

48A George Street, London W1H 5RF ■ Tel: (0171) 935-1555 ■ Fax:
(0171) 224-4858 ■ Mon-Fri 9:30-5:30 ■ Prices high ■ Major credit
cards ■ LAPADA

Antique and Modern silver and Sheffield plate.

DANIEL BEXFIELD ANTIQUES

26 Burlington Arcade, London W1V 9AD ■ Tel: (0171) 491-1720 ■
Fax: (0171) 491-1730 ■ E-mail: antiques@bexfield.co.uk ■ Website:
www.bexfield.co.uk ■ Mon-Sat 9:30-5:30 ■ Daniel Bexfield ■ Prices
low to very high ■ Major credit cards

**Antique silver from the 17th to the 20th century, jewellery and
objets de vertu.**

▦ A. & B. BLOOMSTEIN LTD

Bond Street Silver Galleries, 111-112 New Bond Street, London
W1Y 0BQ ■ Tel: (0171) 493-6180 ■ Fax: (0171) 495-3493 ■ Mon-Fri
9:00-5:00 ■ Alfred Bloomstein ■ French, Italian and German spoken
■ Prices high to very high ■ Trade discount ■ Visa ■ BADA

English antique silver from 1720 to 1890 and old Sheffield plate.

BOND STREET SILVER GALLERIES

111-112 New Bond Street, London W1Y 0BQ ■ Tel: (0171) 493-6180 ■ Fax: (0171) 495-3493 ■ Mon-Fri 9:00-5:00 ■ Alfred Bloomstein ■ French, Italian and German spoken ■ Prices low to very high ■ Trade discount ■ Visa accepted

English antique silver 1720 to 1890. Old Sheffield plate circa 1820. The galleries have 16 showrooms dealing with the trade and private clients.

♛ J. H. BOURDON-SMITH LTD

24 Masons Yard, Duke Street, St. James's, London SW1Y 6BU ■ Tel: (0171) 839-4714 ■ Fax: (0171) 839-3951 ■ Mon-Fri 9:30-6:00 ■ Prices high ■ Major credit cards ■ BADA

Silver: specialising in Georgian and Victorian silver.

MARY COOKE ANTIQUES LTD

121A Kensington Church Street, London W8 7LP ■ Tel: (0171) 792-8077 ■ Mon-Fri 9:15-5:30 ■ Prices medium to high ■ Major credit cards ■ BADA, LAPADA

18th century silver and collectibles.

MORELLE DAVIDSON LTD.

38 Conduit Street, London W1R 9FB ■ Tel: (0171) 408-0066/408-0069 ■ Fax: (0171) 495-8885 ■ Mon-Fri 10:00-5:30, Sat 10:00-4:00 ■ Prices medium to high ■ Major credit cards ■ LAPADA

Silver, Russian works of art and old jewellery.

♛ ANTHONY ELSON SILVERSMITHS

Studio 365, 27 Clerkenwell Close, London EC1R 0AT ■ Tel: (0171) 253-0681 ■ Fax: (0171) 490-0063 ■ Mon-Fri 11:00-5:00 ■ Anthony Elson ■ Prices medium to very high

Designing individual silver pieces to customer's requirements. Centrepieces and ceremonial items. Silverware.

GAVINA EWART

Bond Street Galleries, 2nd floor, 111-112 New Bond Street, London W1Y 9AB ■ Tel: (0171) 491-7266/(01242) 254940 ■ Fax: (0171) 491-7211/(01242) 526994 ■ Mon-Fri 9:30-1:00/2:00-5:30 ■ Prices high ■ Major credit cards ■ BADA

Table silver and cutlery, old Sheffield plate and complementary collectibles.

N. & I. FRANKLIN

11 Bury Street, St. James's London SW1Y 6AB ■ Tel: (0171) 839-3131 ■ Fax: (0171) 839-3132 ■ Mon-Fri 9:30-5:30 ■ Prices high to very high ■ Major credit cards ■ BADA

Fine silver and works of art.

O. FRYDMAN

Bond Street Silver Galleries, 111-112 New Bond Street, London W1Y 0BQ ■ Telfax: (0171) 493-4895 ■ Mon-Fri 9:30-5:30 ■ Gerald Barnett ■ Prices low to medium ■ Trade discount ■ Major credit cards

Old Sheffield and Victorian silver plate. Antique silverware.

GARRARD & CO LTD

112 Regent Street, London W1A 2JJ ■ Tel: (0171) 734-7020 ■ Fax: (0171) 734-0711 ■ Mon-Fri 9:00-5:30, Sat 9:30-5:00 ■ Prices high ■ Major credit cards ■ BADA

The Crown Jewellers founded in 1735 offer a huge collection of cutlery and full dinner services in sterling silver, old Sheffield plate and silver plate. Special items to commission.

T.H. GILBERT

Grays Mews, 1-7 Davies Mews, London W1Y 1AR ■ Tel: (0171) 408-0028 ■ Mon-Fri 10:00-6:00 ■ Prices medium to high ■ Major credit cards ■ LAPADA

Antique silver and silver plate.

HANCOCKS & CO LTD

52-53 Burlington Arcade, London W1X 2HP ■ Tel: (0171) 493-8904 ■ Fax: (0171) 493-8905 ■ Mon-Fri 9:30-5:00, Sat 10:00-4:00 ■ Prices medium to very high ■ Major credit cards ■ BADA

Antique silver and a remarkable collection of jewellery and objects.

NICHOLAS HARRIS GALLERY

PO Box 14430, London SW6 2WG ■ Tel: (0171) 371-9711 ■ Fax: (0171) 371-9537 ■ By appointment only ■ BADA

English and American 19th and 20th century silver and art silversmiths.

HARVEY & GORE

41 Duke Street, St. James's, London SW1Y 6DF ■ Tel: (0171) 839-4033 ■ Fax: (0171) 839-3313/493-0324 ■ Mon-Fri 9:30-5:00 ■ Prices medium to high ■ Major credit cards ■ BADA

Silver and old Sheffield plate, miniatures, jewellery, bijouterie and snuff boxes.

HOLMES (JEWELLERS) LTD

24 Burlington Arcade, London W1V 9AD ■ Tel: (0171) 629-8380 ■ Mon-Fri 9:00-5:30 ■ Mon-Fri 9:30-6:00, Sat 10:00-5:00 ■ Prices medium to high ■ Major credit cards ■ BADA

Silver and old Sheffield plate. Jewellery and valuations.

BRAND INGLIS

5 Vigo Street, 4th floor, London W1X 1AH ■ Tel: (0171) 439-6604 ■ Fax: (0171) 439-6605 ■ Mon-Fri 9:00-6:00 ■ Brand Inglis ■ Prices medium to high ■ Some professional discounts ■ BADA

Antique silver.

♛ RICHARD LAWTON LTD

32-34 Greville Street, London EC1N 8TB ■ Tel: (0171) 404-0487 ■ Mon-Fri 8:30-5:00, Sat 8:30-1:00 ■ Richard Lawton ■ Some French and German spoken ■ Prices medium

Manufacturing silversmiths. A full range of tableware and giftware. Complete silver repair service, re-plating, re-polishing, regilding. Replacement of teapot handles, frames backed, rebristling of hairbrushes. Handles and knobs replaced. Flatware re-bladed and re-handled. Blue glass liners, either in stock or blown to special order. He does everything. This is an indispensable address.

MARKS ANTIQUES

49 Curzon Street, London W1Y 7RE ■ Tel: (0171) 499-1788 ■ Fax: (0171) 409-3183 ■ E-mail: marks@marksantiques.demon.co.uk ■ Mon-Sat 9:30-6:00 ■ Anthony Marks ■ Prices medium to very high ■ Trade discount ■ Major credit cards ■ LAPADA

Fine collection of antique silver.

A. PASH AND SON

Bond Street Silver Galleries, 111-112 New Bond Street, London W1Y 9AB ■ Tel: (0171) 493-5176 ■ Fax: (0171) 355-3676 ■ Mon-Fri 9:00-5:30 ■ Arnold and Robert Pash ■ Prices medium to very high ■ Trade discount ■ Major credit cards

Antique silver and old Sheffield plate. Deals with the trade, auction houses and private clients.

PORTOBELLO ANTIQUE STORE

Portobello Road, London W11 2QB ■ Telfax: (0171) 221-1994 ■ Tue-Fri 10:00-4:00, Sat 8:15-4:00 ■ John and Liza Ewing ■ Prices medium to high ■ Major credit cards ■ Trade discount

Old silver and silver plate from 1830 to 1930.

DAVID RICHARDS & SONS

12 New Cavendish Street, London W1M 7LJ ■ Tel: (0171) 935-3206 ■ Mon-Fri 9:30-5:30 ■ Prices medium to high ■ Major credit cards ■ LAPADA

Excellent quality antique silver.

SEARLE & CO LTD

1 Royal Exchange, Cornhill, London EC3V 3LL ■ Tel: (0171) 626-2456 ■ Fax: (0171) 283-6384 ■ E-mail: maul@searleandco.ltd.uk ■ Mon-Fri 9:00-5:30 ■ N.G.D. Bird ■ Prices medium ■ Major credit cards

Silverware, jewellery and unusual gemstones.

SHAPIRO & CO.

Stand 380, Grays Antiques Market, 58 Davies Street, London W1Y 2LP ■ Tel: (0171) 491-2710 ■ Mon-Fri 10:00-6:00 ■ Prices medium to high ■ Trade discount ■ Major credit cards ■ LAPADA

Silver and Russian works of art.

NICHOLAS SHAW ANTIQUES

Bond Street Silver Galleries, 111-112 New Bond Street, London W1Y 0BQ ■ Telfax: (0171) 629-1853 ■ Mobile: 0585 643000 ■ Mon-Fri 9:30-5:30 ■ Prices medium to very high ■ Major credit cards ■ BADA, LAPADA

Scottish provincial silver, Georgian and Victorian silver and small collectors' items.

SILVER

179 New Bond Street, 1st floor, London W1Y 2LP ■ Tel: (0171) 495-3008 ■ Mon-Fri 9:30-5:30 ■ Prices medium to high ■ Major credit cards ■ LAPADA

Antique silver of course.

THE SILVER FUND LIMITED

40 Bury Street, St James's, London SW1Y 6AU ■ Tel: (0171) 839-7664 ■ Fax: (0171) 839-8935 ■ Mon-Fri 9:00-5:30 ■ French and German spoken ■ Prices low to very high ■ Major credit cards

Georg Jensen 20th century silver. A large range of decorative silver objects.

SIMAR ANTIQUES

Antiquarius, Unit C0-B1-B2, 135 King's Road, London SW3 4PB ■ Telfax: (0171) 352-7155 ■ Mon-Sat 10:30-5:30 ■ 6 Bourbon-Hanby Antiques Centre, 151 Sydney Street, London SW3 6NT ■ Tel: (0171) 460-2970 ■ Fax: (0171) 352-7155 ■ Mon-Sun 10:30-5:30 ■ Adrian and Lindsey Cohen ■ Spanish and French spoken ■ Prices low to very high ■ Major credit cards

Silver, silver plate and old Sheffield plate. Decanters and decorative objects.

TESSIERS LTD

26 New Bond Street, London W1Y 0JY ■ Tel: (0171) 629-0458 ■ Fax: (0171) 629-1857 ■ Mon-Fri 10:00-5:00, Sat 10:00-4:00 ■ Prices medium to high ■ Major credit cards ■ BADA

Beautiful silver, silver objects, boxes and jewellery.

WARTSKI LTD

14 Grafton Street, London W1X 4DE ■ Tel: (0171) 493-1141 ■ Fax: (0171) 409-7448 ■ Mon-Fri 9:30-5:00 ■ BADA

Antique silver and 18th and 19th century jewellery. Russian works of art, 18thcentury gold boxes and decorative silver objects.

👑 THE LONDON SILVER VAULTS

Chancery House, 53-65 Chancery Lane, London WC2A 1QS ■ Tel: (0171) 738-0722 ■ Mon-Fri 9:00-5:30, Sat 9:00-12:30

The London Silver Vaults are unique in the world. Established in 1892, there are now 34 shops. Antique and modern silver, silver plate, jewellery, objets d'art, clocks, watches, collectors' items are found there. The vaults are run by families, often with five generations of knowledge and experience passed along. They all offer expert advice and will help match dinner services and cutlery sets. The wall displays can teach one a great deal about the history of English silver and the mysteries of the Guild Marks. Credit cards are accepted.

A.M.W. SILVERWARE

Vaults 52&68 ■ Tel: (0171) 242-3620 ■ Fax: (0171) 381-3923 ■ Alan M. Weisrose

Silverware.

ANTIQUE SILVER

Vaults 31&32, ■ Tel: (0171) 430-1254 ■ LAPADA

Candelabra, candlesticks, medals, coins and silver.

BELMONT

Vault 46 ■ Tel: (0171) 242-3152 ■ Fax: (0171) 831-4629 ■ Alex Belmont

Specialist in antique and modern jewellery, silver, gold and fine watches.

LAWRENCE BLOCK

Vaults 28&30 ■ Tel: (0171) 242-0749 ■ Fax: (0171) 242-4711

Silver and gold jewellery from the 18th century to the present. Silver spoons, forks and giftware. Repairs and engraving.

A. BLOOM

Vault 27 ■ Telfax: (0171) 242-6189

Decorative silver and plate of all kinds, mainly 19th century.

B.L. COLLINS

Vault 20 ■ Tel: (0171) 404-0628 ■ Fax: (0171) 404-1451

Antique and modern silver-plate and art objects.

PAUL DANIEL

Vault 51 ■ Telfax: (0171) 430-1327

18th and 19th century silver and unusual items of silver and plate.

BRYAN DOUGLAS

Vaults 12&14 ■ Telfax: (0171) 242-7073/405-8862 ■ LAPADA

Art Nouveau and Art Deco, clocks, silver, jewellery and decorative objects.

R. FELDMAN LTD

Vaults 4&6 ■ Tel: (0171) 405-6111 ■ Fax: (0171) 430-0126 ■ Raymond Feldman ■ LAPADA

Antique and modern silver, old Sheffield plate and art objects.

I. FRANKS
Vaults 9&11 ■ Tel: (0171) 242-4035 ■ LAPADA

Antique and modern silver and old Sheffield plate: candelabra, candlesticks, desk and writing accessories.

M. & J. HAMILTON
Vault 25 ■ Tel: (0171) 831-7030 ■ Fax: (0171) 831-5483 ■ Mark Hamilton

Antique and modern silver, old Sheffield plate and electro-plate. Large range of flatware available.

GARY HAYAMS
Vault 48 ■ Tel: (0171) 831-4330

Silverware.

S. KALMS
Vaults 31&32 ■ Tel: (0171) 430-1954 ■ Fax: (0171) 405-6206 ■ Stephen Kalms

Fine silver and plated objects from the 18th century to the present.

♕ KOOPMAN RARE ART
Vaults 13-15, 53-64 ■ Tel: (0171) 242-7624/405-9968 ■ Fax: (0171) 831-0221 ■ Lewis Smith and Mickheal Koopman ■ Dutch, Italian, French and Finnish spoken ■ BADA

Fine English and Continental silver of very high quality. An extraordinary collection.

B. LAMPERT
Vault 19 ■ Tel: (0171) 242-4121

Antique silver and silver plate.

♕ LANGFORDS
Vaults 8&10 ■ Tel: (0171) 242-5506 ■ Fax: (0171) 405-0431 ■ E-mail: langfrds@netcomuk.co.uk

Antique and modern silver and silver plate especially cutlery and tableware. Everything, including engraving.

NAT LESLIE LTD
Vault 21 ■ Tel: (0171) 242-4787 ■ Fax: (0171) 242-4504 ■ E-mail: nat.leslie@which.net

20th century table silver and flatware. Also sterling and Sheffield plated ware of all types. Finding discontinued lines a specialty.

LINDEN & CO
Vault 7 ■ Tel: (0171) 242-4863 ■ Fax: (0171) 405-9946 ■ Steven Linden

Medium range silver and silver plate.

I. NAGIOFF (JEWELLERY)
Vaults 63&69 ■ Tel: (0171) 405-3766 ■ I. and R. Nagioff

Jewellery, 18th-20th century, objets d'art of the 19th century.

PERCY'S
Vault 16 ■ Tel: (0171) 242-3618 ■ Fax: (0171) 831-6541 ■ David Simons ■ French, Spanish, Italian and German spoken

Antique English and second-hand English silver. Decorative silver and plate.

DAVID S. SHURE
Vault 1 ■ Telfax: (0171) 405-0011 ■ Sam Shure

Medium-priced table and giftware, including small antique collectibles. Old and new sterling and Sheffield plate. Jewellery and engraving.

SILSTAR
Vault 29 ■ Tel: (0171) 242-6740 ■ Fax: (0171) 430-1745

Silver and silver plate.

⌕ B. SILVERMAN
Vault 26 ■ Tel: (0171) 242-3269 ■ Fax: (0171) 430-1949 ■ R. Silverman and W. Brackenbury

Wonderful selection of antique and modern silver from the 17th century to the present. Objects and flatware.

S. & J. STODEL
Vault 24 ■ Tel: (0171) 405-7009 ■ Fax: (0171) 242-6366

Victorian, Art Nouveau and Art Deco silver. Georg Jensen silver, Chinese Export silver and antique flatware. Very special.

J. SURTEES
Vault 65 ■ Tel: (0171) 242-0518 ■ Fax: (0171) 831-8137

Wide range of small interesting items for special events, birthdays, trophies, presentations. Repairs.

VINCENT ANTIQUES
Vault 58 ■ Tel: (0171) 405-2883 ■ Vincent Saunders

Specialist in haggling: a market trader masquerading as a shop-keeper. A bit of everything.

WILLIAM WALTER ANTIQUES LTD
Vaults 3&5 ■ Tel: (0171) 242-3248 ■ Fax: (0171) 404-1280 ■ BADA, LAPADA

Antique silver and old Sheffield plate. Candelabra, candlesticks. Valuer for probate, insurance, family division.

PETER K. WEISS
Vaults 18&42 ■ Tel: (0171) 242-8100 ■ Fax: (0171) 242-7310

Antique watches, clocks, carriage clocks, objets d'art.

WOLFE JEWELLERY
Vault 41 ■ Telfax: (0171) 405-2101

Victorian and antique jewellery.

UPHOLSTERY

PERCY BASS LTD
184-188 Walton Street, London SW3 2JL ■ Tel: (0171) 589-4853 ■ Fax: (0171) 581-4137 ■ E-mail: percybass@aol.com.uk ■ Mon-Fri 9:30-5:30, Sat-Sun 2:00-5:30 ■ Jane Morris ■ French and Spanish spoken ■ Prices medium ■ Professional discount ■ Major credit cards

Re-upholstery of everything and curtain making. Re-caning, upholstery cleaning.

CHOUMENT UPHOLSTERY CO
26 Sternhall Lane, Peckham, London SE15 4NT ■ Tel: (0171) 639-1775 ■ Fax: (0171) 625-8680 ■ Mon-Fri 9:00-5:30 ■ J. Bailey ■ Prices medium ■ Trade discount

Re-upholstery. Specialist in upholstered headboards. Pelmets made to order.

♔ THE CURTAIN COUTURIER
285 New King's Road, London SW6 4RD ■ Tel: (0171) 371-9255 ■ Fax: (0171) 371-9266 ■ Mon-Sat 9:30-5:30 ■ Anne Thompson ■ French spoken ■ Prices low to very high ■ Trade discount ■ Major credit cards

Expertly crafted made-to-measure curtains, pelmets, blinds and bedspreads. Most brands of poles and tracks in stock. Sofas, armchairs, footstools, chaises longues. Brochures on request. Member of The Guild of Master Craftsmen.

C.H. FROST
67 Abingdon Road, Kensington, London W8 ■ Tel: (0171) 937-0451 ■ Fax: (0191) 451-1049 ■ Mon-Fri 9:00-5:00, Sat 9:30-1:00 ■ C.H. Frost ■ Prices medium ■ Trade discount ■ Major credit cards

Upholstery, curtains, beds, soft furniture.

♔ ANN LISTER HISTORIC FURNISHINGS
Cam Laithe, Far Lane, Kettlewell, Skipton, North Yorkshire BD23 5Qy ■ Tel: (01756) 760809 ■ Fax: (01756) 760209 ■ By appointment ■ Prices medium to very high

Historic furnishings. Research and supply as well as making authentic furnishings: bed hangings, curtains. From single rooms to whole houses. Clients include The National Trust, English Heritage and privately owned historic houses and museums.

MORLEY INTERIORS

84-86 Troutbeck, Albany Street, London NW1 4EJ ■ Tel: (0171) 387-3846 ■ Fax: (0171) 388-0651 ■ Mon-Fri 9:00-5:00 ■ Prices medium to high ■ Trade discount

Antique and modern re-upholstery, hand-made chairs and sofas. Antique restorations, French polishing, leather top tables, leather renovation, cabinet repairs, curtains, bedcovers, pelmets, festoons and wall upholstery.

DANIEL NEWLYN UPHOLSTERY

The Vaults, 24 West Street, Covent Garden, London WC2H 9NA ■ Tel: (0171) 379-8680 ■ Fax: (0171) 836-7877 ■ E-mail: daniel@visualeyes.ltd.uk ■ Mon-Fri 9:30-6:00 ■ Prices medium to high ■ Some trade discounts

Bespoke items of upholstery and furniture design.

PHILLIPS & THORNTON (MFG.) LTD

Unit A, Sapcote Trading Centre, 374 High Road, Willesden, London NW10 2DH ■ Tel: (0181) 459-0569 ■ Fax: (0181) 830-4919 ■ Mon-Fri 9:00-4:30 ■ Mr. & Mrs. Amir Temadi ■ Turkish and Farsi spoken ■ Prices medium ■ Trade discount ■ Barclaycard accepted

Hand-made curtains and decorative accessories: upholstery, cushions, bedspreads. Full range of curtain accessories and fabric. Design service and carpentry. Members of The Association of Master Upholsterers and Soft Furnishers.

♛ CHRISTOPHER HOWE

93 Pimlico Road, London SW1W 8PH ■ Tel: (0171) 730-7987 ■ Fax: (0171) 730-0147 ■ Mon-Fri 9:00-5:30, Sat 10:30-2:30 ■ Christopher Howe ■ French, Spanish and German spoken ■ Prices medium to high ■ Professional discount ■ Major credit cards

Their workshops specialize in re-upholstery of leather furniture and replacement of leather desk tops. One of London's best-known antique dealers.

TOP LAYER LTD

5 Egerton Terrace, Knightsbridge, London SW3 2BX ■ Tel: (0171) 581-1019 ■ Fax: (0171) 589-9043 ■ Mon-Fri 9:30-5:00 ■ Barrie Coppin ■ Prices medium to very high ■ Trade discount ■ Major credit cards

Fabrics, curtain making and wallpapers. They claim to be the best curtain maker in the UK.

THE UPHOLSTERERS STUDIO

Units 6&7, 32 Lawn Road, Hampstead, London NW3 2XU ■ Tel: (0171) 722-2268 ■ Fax: (0171) 722-6673 ■ Mon-Fri 8:00-6:00 ■ Mr. S. Bunyan and Mr. P. Stemp ■ Prices high ■ Trade discount

New upholstered furniture. Recovering and restoration of upholstered furniture. They make loose covers and are able to cope with unusual projects.

WALLCOVERINGS & WALLPAPERS

♔ ALEXANDER BEAUCHAMP
2/12 Chelsea Harbour Design Centre ■ Tel: (0171) 376-4556 ■ Fax: (0171) 376-3435 ■ Mon-Fri 9:00-5:30 ■ Prices medium to high ■ Professional discount

Designers, hand printers and manufacturers of fine wallpapers, hand-printed wallpapers, fabrics and borders. Custom designs and colourings. Extensive archives 1680-1950. Stock wallpapers, stripes and damasks, Chinoiserie and the Victoria House Collection.

BRUNSCHWIG & FILS
10 The Chambers, Chelsea Harbour Design Centre ■ Tel: (0171) 351-5797 ■ Fax: (0171) 351-2280 ■ Bruno Garros ■ French spoken

Founded in France in 1900. Fine fabrics and coordinating wallpapers.

MANUEL CANOVAS LTD
2 North Terrace, Brompton Road, London SW3 2BA ■ Tel: (0171) 225-2298 ■ Fax: (0171) 823-7848 ■ Mon-Fri 9:30-6:00, Sat 10:00-5:00 ■ Prices medium to very high ■ Professional discount ■ Major credit cards

Some fine original contemporary and traditional wallcoverings which match their fabric collection.

COLE & SON (WALLPAPERS) LTD
G9 Chelsea Harbour Design Centre ■ Tel: (0171) 376-4628 ■ Fax: (0171) 376-4631 ■ Mon-Fri 9:30-5:30 ■ Patrick Ball ■ Prices medium to high ■ Professional discount

Handblocked wallpapers made to order as well as stock collections.

COLEFAX & FOWLER
15A Halkin Arcade, London SW1 ■ Tel: (0171) 235-4445 ■ 110 Fulham Road, London SW3 6RL ■ Tel: (0171) 244-7427 ■ Fax: (0171) 373-7916 ■ Mon-Fri 9:30-5:30 ■ Prices high ■ Trade discount ■ Major credit cards

Traditional and contemporary designs of wallpapers coordinating with their fabrics.

♛ DE GOURNAY LTD

14 Hyde Park Gate, London SW7 5DG ■ Tel: (0171) 823-7316 ■ Fax: (0171) 823-7475 ■ E-mail: info@degournay.com ■ By appointment ■ Claud Gurney ■ French and Spanish spoken ■ Prices very high ■ Trade discount

Hand-painted wallpapers in the Chinese Export and European classical styles. Their own designs, or execution of a client's designs. They have an extensive archive in their showroom. One of the very best.

♛ GUY EVANS

96 Great Titchfield Street, London W1P 7AG ■ Tel: (0171) 436-7914 ■ Fax: (0171) 436-2980 ■ Mon-Fri 9:00-5:00 ■ Prices high to very high ■ Professional discount ■ Major credit cards

Historical wallpaper designs from the 18th to the 20th century. Hand-blocked papers, based on French designs. Wallpapers by the American company, Clarence House.

NICHOLAS HERBERT LTD

118 Lots Road, London SW10 0RJ ■ Tel: (0171) 376-5596 ■ Fax: (0171) 376-5572 ■ Website: www.i-i.net/nicholasherbertltd ■ Mon-Fri 9:30-5:30 ■ Nicholas Herbert ■ Major credit cards

French document-based wallpapers and upholstery fabric. Upholstery services.

HODSOLL MCKENZIE

52 Pimlico Road, London SW1W 8LP ■ Tel: (0171) 730-2877 ■ Fax: (0171) 259-9292 ■ Mon-Fri 10:00-5:00 ■ Alex McKenzie and Mark Butcher ■ Prices high ■ Professional discount

Great selection of wallcoverings and fabrics, as well as their furniture line.

LELIEVRE (UK)

101 Cleveland Street, London W1P 5PN ■ Tel: (0171) 636-3461 ■ Fax: (0171) 637-5070 ■ Mon-Fri 9:30- 5:30 ■ Prices medium to high ■ Trade discount ■ Major credit cards

One of the best French fabric houses with a wonderful choice of wide width fabric for wall upholstery.

NOBILIS FONTAN

G3 Chelsea Harbour Design Centre ■ Tel: (0171) 351-7878 ■ Fax: (0171) 376-3507 ■ Mon-Fri 9:30-5:30 ■ Mrs. Gemma Allman ■ Prices medium to very high ■ Professional discount

Textured wallcoverings and upholstery fabrics. Excellent choice.

JOHN OLIVER LTD

33 Pembridge Road, London W11 3HG ■ Tel: (0171) 727-3735 ■ Fax: (0171) 727-5555 ■ Mon-Sat 9:00-5:30 ■ Prices high ■ Trade discount ■ Major credit cards

Eclectic range of wallpapers and fabrics. Their own range of paints in standard as well as historic colours. Expert colour matching. Interior design service.

ORNAMENTA

3/12 Chelsea Harbour Design Centre ■ Tel: (0171) 352-1824 ■ Fax: (0171) 376-3398 ■ Mon-Fri 9:30-6:00 ■ French spoken ■ Prices high ■ Visa and Switch

Hand-painted trompe l'oeil wallpaper, wall decorations, borders and fabrics created by designer Jane Gordon Clark. The papers have the look of antique panelling, stone-block walls or carved architectural friezes and mouldings. 22 carat gold-leaf and sterling-silver-leaf contemporary designs.

OSBORNE & LITTLE PLC

304 King's Road, London SW3 5UH ■ Tel: (0171) 352-1456 ■ (0171) 351-7813 ■ Mon-Fri 9:30-6:00, Sat 10:00-5:30 ■ Tim Walters ■ Prices medium to high ■ Major credit cards

Reproductions of papers from the collection of The Victoria and Albert Museum. Specialist fabrics and wallpapers, borders and trimmings. Also poles, finials and other drapery hardware.

BERNARD THORP

6 Burnsall Street, London SW3 3ST ■ Tel: (0171) 352-5745 ■ Fax: (0171) 376-3640 ■ Mon-Fri 9:00-5:30 ■ Bernard Thorp ■ French and Italian spoken ■ Prices low to very high ■ Trade discount

Custom-coloured and printed and woven fabrics and custom wallpapers.

BRIAN YATES

G27 Chelsea Harbour Design Centre ■ Tel: (0171) 352-0123 ■ Fax: (0171) 352-6060 ■ Mon-Fri 9:30-5:30 ■ Prices medium to high ■ Professional discount

Fabrics and wallcoverings from Europe for both the residential and contract markets. Sole distributors for Arte, Pepe Penalver and Taco Edition.

♔ ZOFFANY LTD

63 South Audley Street, London W1Y 5BT ■ Tel: (0171) 495-2505 ■ Fax: (0171) 493-7257 ■ Mon-Fri 9:00-5:30 ■ Lydia Anikitou ■ Prices medium to high ■ Trade discount

Wallpapers and fabrics based on archival materials from the 18th and 19th century. Also paint and trimmings.

♔ ZUBER (LONDON) LTD

42 Pimlico Road, London SW1W 8LP ■ Tel: (0171) 824-8265 ■ Fax: (0171) 824-8270 ■ Mon-Fri 9:00-6:00 ■ Prices medium to very high ■ Professional discount

Famous, worldwide, for their panoramic, trompe l'oeil and landscape wallpapers, many of which have been in existence since the end of the 18th century.

WINE CELLAR EQUIPMENT

BIRCHGROVE PRODUCTS LTD
Unit 3C, Merrow Business Centre, Merrow Lane, Guildford GU4 7WA ■ Tel: (01483) 533400 ■ Fax: (01483) 533700 ■ E-mail: enquiries@birchgrove.co.uk ■ Mon-Fri 9:00-5:30 ■ D.C. James ■ French spoken ■ Prices low to high ■ Visa and MC
Wine related accessories: corkscrews, decanting cradles, coasters, cellar books, everything for the wine lover. Catalogue available.

CONSORT CONNOISSEUR
Consort House, Bone Lane, Newbury, Berkshire RG14 5SD ■ Tel: (01635) 33993 ■ Fax: (01635) 41733 ■ Mon-Fri 9:00-5:00 ■ Prices medium ■ Trade discount
Wine storage and cellar management.

PATRICA HARBOTTLE
Geoffrey Van Arcade, 107 Portobello Road, London W11 2QB ■ Tel: (01747) 838078 ■ Fax: (01747) 838008 ■ Sat 8:00-3:00 ■ Prices medium to high ■ Trade discount ■ Visa and MC
Decanters, corkscrews, glasses, old bottles. Restoration.

THE HUGH JOHNSON COLLECTION
68 St. James Street, London SW1A 1PH ■ Tel: (0171) 491-4912 ■ Fax: (0171) 493-0602 ■ Mon-Fri 9:30-5:00 ■ Prices medium to high ■ Major credit cards
Everything for the wine lover.

CAROL KETLEY ANTIQUES
PO Box 16199, London N1 7WD ■ Tel: (0171) 359-5529 ■ Mobile: 0831 827284 ■ Fax: (0171) 226-4589 ■ Showroom by appointment ■ Carol Ketley ■ French spoken ■ Prices medium ■ Professional discount ■ Major credit cards
Specialist in antique glassware. Large selection of Georgian decanters in stock.

♔ KOOPMAN LTD & RARE ART (LONDON) LTD

The London Silver Vaults, 53-64 Chancery Lane, London WC2A 1QS ■ Tel: (0171) 242-7624 ■ Fax: (0171) 831-0221 ■ Mon-Fri 9:30-5:30 ■ Prices medium to very high ■ Major credit cards

A fine collection of silver and glass claret jugs, some by Fabergé.

A. & W. MOORE

Quarry Hill Industrial Park, Ilkeston, Derbyshire DE7 4RA ■ Tel: (0115) 944-1434 ■ Fax: (0115) 932-0735 ■ E-mail: www.wineracks.co.uk ■ Prices medium to high ■ Trade discount

Specialists in custom wine racks in any shape or any size. Standard racks in stock. Suppliers of wine display furniture in oak, pine and mahogany. Door-to-door delivery.

♔ CHRISTOPHER SYKES ANTIQUES

The Old Parsonage, Woburn, MK17 9Q ■ Tel: (0152) 529-0259 ■ Fax: (0152) 529-0061 ■ E-mail: sykes.corkscrew@sykes-corkscrews.co.uk ■ Website: www.sykes-corkscrews.co.uk ■ Mon-Sat 9:00-5:00 ■ Sally Lloyd ■ Prices medium to high ■ Trade discount ■ Major credit cards

Wine related antiques, especially antique corkscrews. Silver decanter labels, funnels, tastevin and bar corkdrawers. Catalogue available.

TOUCH OF SWEDEN

Suite 230, 266 Banbury Road, Summertown, Oxford OX2 7DL ■ Tel: (01865) 552198 ■ Fax: (01865) 514656 ■ Mon-Fri 9:00-5:00 ■ Alma Strangby ■ Swedish spoken ■ Prices medium to high ■ Professional discount ■ Major credit cards

Suppliers of Swedish products, noted for the Eco-pac, the soft crate for bottles. An ideal way to protect and transport wine and champagne bottles. Elk-horn wine racks.

TRANSTHERM

52 Larkshall Business Centre, Larkshall Road, London E4 6PD ■ Tel: (0181) 529-9665 ■ Fax: (0181) 529-9666 ■ Website: www.sales@american.appliances.co.uk ■ Prices medium to very high ■ Trade discount

Humidity-controlled wine cellars designed for aging and maturing wines. Compartments for chilling with variable temperatures and multiple zones. They hold from 62 to 233 bottles. In various finishes and colour options, with or without a glass door. They also offer the U-Line brand of ice makers.

THE LONDON STREET MARKETS

Shades of Eliza Doolittle. When you gather up your courage and make your decision to venture into the wilds of London's Street Markets be prepared for an astonishing experience. If you are an early bird, and we mean an early bird, you'll try the Bermondsey Market first. It opens at 5:00 on Friday mornings and by the time a normal English breakfast time comes around, the stalls are being packed up and only the persistent few remain.

There are street markets in every part of London. Most are open one or two days in the week, but many of the merchants either move from one to another or have more-or-less permanent set-ups in two or three.

Do not be put off by the description "street market". Many, like Antiquarius, Alfie's, Grays, The Mall and much of the Covent Garden Market, are in protected arcades or in sprawling old warehouse buildings. Portobello Road, the most famous, is both outdoors and inside several multi-storied buildings.

Some of the markets in London have directories which are available for the asking. Just ask one of the merchants where to find the information stand. Often, the very person you ask will be able to materialize a directory for you. You will find the London Street Markets very friendly places, where great and valuable treasures are often found.

Some of the dealers belong to the important antique dealers' associations and you will be astonished at the wonderful things they have on display.

For these thousands of dealers a separate book would be required. We have listed some of our favourites from the different markets in their various specialties throughout the guide and are unable to resist taking you on a visit to London's famous Portobello Road Market.

"With a little bit a luck" you'll carry off something that will please you for the rest of your life.

Alfie's Antique Market

13-25 Church Street, Marylebone, London NW8 8DT ■ Tel: (0171) 723-6066 ■ Fax: (0171) 724-0999 ■ Tue-Sat 10:00-6:00.

300 stands with over 200 dealers on five floors. Decorative antiques, antique and costume jewellery, old dolls and toys, ceramics and glass, pictures and prints, antique furniture, costume and textile, costume jewellery, silver, Arts and Crafts, Art Nouveau, Art Deco, 1950's, 1960's, 1970's, ephemera and memorabilia. Alfie's is close to the Marylebone Tube Station.

Antiquarius Antiques Centre

131-141 King's Road, London SW3 5PW ■ Tel: (0171) 351-5353 ■ Fax: (0171) 351-5350 ■ Mon-Sat 10:00-6:00

Established 1970. On the corner of King's Road and Flood Street, next to Chelsea Town Hall. There are 120 specialist dealers. Sloane Square Tube Station.

Bermondsey Antiques Market

On the corner of Long Lane and Bermondsey Street, London SE1 ■ Friday 5:00-2:00

This is an important market for the trade. It has been open for 30 years and the cream of the merchandise shows up early with dealers dealing with dealers long before the general public arrives. There are 250 traders. Avoid disappointment and be there early. Borough, Tower Hill or London Bridge Tube Stations.

Bond Street Antiques Centre

124 New Bond Street, London W1 ■ Tel: (0171) 351-5353 ■ Fax: (0171) 351-5350 ■ Mon-Fri 10:00-5:45, Sat depending on the season

Established 1970. Approximately 27 dealers. The Centre specializes in fine antique jewellery and silver. There are also Oriental antiques and paintings, watches, furniture, porcelain and glass. Bond Street/Green Park Tube Stations or walk from Piccadilly.

Camden Passage

The Angel, Islington, London N1 ■ Tel: (0171) 359-9969 ■ Wed & Sat 9:00-3:30

Dating from the 18th century, this interesting area houses over 300 shops and arcades of general and specialist dealers. This is a fun area for a good browse. The Angel Tube Station.

Chalk Farm Market

Chalk Farm Road, London NW1 8AN ■ Sat & Sun 9:00-6:00

You will find some very good country antiques as well as Art Deco and Modern design of furniture and lighting. The whole area is great fun and worth the trip. Make sure to exit at Chalk Farm Tube Station and head for The Stables Market to avoid all the junk and the t-shirts at Camden Town.

Covent Garden Market

41 The Market, Covent Garden, London WC2E 8RF ■ Tel: (0171) 836-9136 ■ Tue-Sat 8:00-6:30

Every Monday and on the first Sunday of each month the antique dealers gather in The Apple Market, where there are lots of good collectibles. On the second and last Sunday of each month there is an Art Market with painters, photographers, cartoonists and printers. A marvellously entertaining atmosphere, with musicians and, of course, flower sellers every day of the week.

Grays Antique Market

58 Davies Street at South Molton Street, London, W1Y 2LP ■ Tel: (0171) 629-7034 ■ Sun-Fri 10:00-6:00.

More than 200 professional and high quality specialist antique dealers. The world's biggest collection of antique jewellery. Close to the Bond Street Tube Station.

The Mall Antiques Arcade

359 Upper Street, Islington N1 0PD ■ Tel: (0171) 354-2839/(0171) 351-5353 ■ Tue, Thu, Fri 10:00-5:00, Wed 7:30-5:00, Sat 9:00-6:00 ■ Rosmarie Donni

Established 1979. Over 35 top quality dealers in one of London's most convenient locations. The Angel Tube Station.

♔ Portobello Road Antiques Market

The Portobello Road Antique Dealers Association ■ 288 Westbourne Grove, London W11 2PS ■ Tel: (0171) 239-8354 ■ Fax: (0171) 243-3419 ■ E-mail: info@portobelloroad.co.uk ■ Website: www.portobelloroad.co.uk ■ Tue-Fri 9:30-2:00

The Portobello Antiques Market has a worldwide reputation with the best choice and variety of merchandise being traded every Saturday to buyers from all over the world. It is London's oldest and biggest street market with more than 1,500 dealers. Action starts at 5:30 in the morning and goes until after lunch although some dealers stay on until 4 or 5 p.m. There are also shops open from Monday to Saturday in the area.

Advertising Memorablia

ANDY'S TIN CITY
Unit 1/2 (Basement), 282 Westbourne Grove ■ Tel: (0171) 727-2027 ■ E-mail: 101735,640@compuserve.com ■ Sat 7:00-2:00

Specialising in tins, old advertising & packaging, showcards and enamels.

Animalier

ELIZABETH BRADWIN
75 Portobello Road ■ Tel: (0171) 221-1121

19th and early 20th century animal subjects including Vienna and French animalier bronzes, Staffordshire, majolica, porcelain and carved wood. Inkwells and tobacco jars.

BETTY & LYN

Units 49,51 & 52, Admiral Vernon Arcade, 141-149 Portobello Road
■ Tel: (0181) 680-7960

Fine table and bed linen, nightdresses, christening gowns, tapestries, embroidery, lace, beadwork, cushions, needlework and collectibles.

BRENDA LINENS

Stand 30, 165 Portobello Road ■ Tel: (012678) 763368

Antique collectibles and good quality linens, bedspreads, pillow cases, cushions, nightdresses, tablecloths, tea cosies and christening dresses.

ANNE BUCKLEY

302 Westbourne Grove, London W11 2PS ■ Telfax: (0171) 229-8786
■ Sat, by appointment during the week

Antique lace, wedding dresses and veils, collars, scarves, gloves, christening gowns, curtains.

MARY EVANS

175 Portobello Road ■ Tel: (01746) 763-463

Linen and lace. Tablecloths, sheets, pillow cases, bedspreads. Lace curtains, fine christening gowns, handkerchiefs, silk shawls.

JANICE FORD

Shop 48, Admiral Vernon Antique Market, 141-149 Portobello Road
■ Telfax: (01892) 822316

Fine antique linens and laces, lace curtains, christening gowns, paisley/silk shawls.

LUNN ANTIQUES LTD.

Unit 8, Admiral Vernon Antique Market, 141-149 Portobello Road ■
Tel: (0171) 736-4638

17th century needlepoints, 18th century Brussels and Valencienne. Dresden whitework. 19th century Honiton point-de-gaze and chantilly. Ayshire whitework. 20thcentury Burano filet and cutwork.

PUNTO IN ARIA

Unit L11, Admiral Vernon Antique Market, 141-149 Portobello Road

Collectors' and decorative lace and linen, collars, scarves, shawls, bed and table linen, curtains and vintage costume.

SCHROCK-CONNER

Portwine Galleries, 173-5 Portobello Road ■ Tel: (0468) 016281

Antique Continental linen, including large pillow cases, early "Shaker- style" check bedcovers and pillow cases, hand towels and hand-woven textiles.

SHIRLEY SHEAH

Outside Chelsea Galleries, 69 Portobello Road ■ Tel: (0171) 624-1514

Linen tablecloths, trolley/tray cloths, hand towels, runners, napkins etc. Also christening robes and children's cloths.

ANNE SWIFT

Street Stall 1, corner of Portobello Road and Westbourne Grove ■ Tel: (0171) 370-6589 ■ E-mail: annephil@msn.com

Antique lace, 17th to 19th century: English, Flemish, Irish, Italian, Maltese. Antique lace bobbins. Christening gowns, embroideries, shawls, linens and fans.

Antiques and Memorabilia

DIDIER MILINAIRE

305 Westbourne Grove ■ Tel: (0171) 243-1373 ■ Fax: (0171) 792-8326 ■ Mon-Sat 10:00-7:00

Antiques, collectibles, memorabilia. Decorative cadeaux d'interieur.

Antiquities

ANCIENT ART

Stand 8, Lipka's Arcade, 286 Westbourne Grove ■ Telfax: (0171) 267-9634 ■ Sat 9:00-4:00 or by appointment

Antiquities from China, Pre-Columbian America, the Near East, Egypt and Europe.

HELIOS GALLERY

Basement, Arbras Gallery, 292 Westbourne Grove ■ Tel: (0411) 955-997

Antiquities and tribal art, Roman, Greek, Egyptian and Mesopotamian objects. Artifacts from all parts of the ancient world.

Arms, Armour, Firearms & Militaria

RONALD E. HOSKINS
Stall 12, 288 Westbourne Grove ■ Tel: (01442) 251-673
Militaria, military headress, medals, uniforms and model soldiers.

♛**PORTOBELLO ARMS & ARMOUR SHOPPE**
117 Portobello Road, Vernons Yard ■ Tel: (01782) 394397 ■ Mobile:
0589 137308
**One of the most interesting shops in the area, with a good
selection of armour, weapons and military curios from most
ages and countries.**

Art Deco, Art Nouveau, Arts and Crafts

R.A. BARNES
D3, D5 and D6, Roger's Gallery, 65 Portobello Road ■ 26 Lower
Richmond Road, London SW15 1JP ■ Tel: (0181) 789-3371
**Glass: Bohemian, Art Nouveau and Art Deco, including Gallé,
Daum and Lalique. Opaline glass and paperweights.**

RICHARD JORDAN - 20TH CENTURY DECORATIVE ART
Crown Arcade, 119 Portobello Road ■ Tel: (0171) 792-3619
20th century fine art, decorative arts and art objects.

Asian Antiques and Art

ASIA ANTIQUES GALLERY
The Admiral Vernon Antique Market, 141-149 Portobello Road ■ Tel:
(0171) 235-6663
**Oriental ceramics and works of art. Bronzes, Buddhas, vases
and silver.**

AURA ANTIQUES
Gallery Arcade, 287 Westbourne Grove ■ Tel: (0171) 495-6083 ■
Fax: (0171) 727-2817
**Specializing in Tibetan, Japanese, Chinese and ethnic works of
art and textiles.**

R.A. BARNES
D3, D5 & D6, Roger's Antiques Gallery, 65 Portobello Road ■ 26
Lower Richmond Road, London SW15 1JP ■ Tel: (0181) 789-3371
**18th and 19th century Chinese and Japanese porcelain and
works of art, also snuff bottles.**

STEPHEN BIRBECK
D1, Roger's Antiques Gallery, 65 Portobello Road

Oriental ceramics and works of art. Also European antiques. Available every second week.

HENRY BROWNRIGG
Stands 2 & 21, The Gallery, 287 Westbourne Grove

Indian, Islamic and South East Asian art and antiques, including metalwork, bronzes, miniature paintings, drawings, manuscripts, topographical and colonial paintings, silver and jewellery.

COHEN & PEARCE
84 Portobello Road ■ Tel: (0171) 229-9458 ■ Fax: (0171) 229-9653

17th and 18th century Chinese and Japanese export porcelain and early pottery

NELLY DAVIES-KATABORI
Back of Grays Arcade, 138 Portobello Road ■ Telfax: (0181) 440-6259

Japanese netsuke and pipe cases. Chinese snuff bottles and bronzes. Oriental works of art. Member of International Netsuke Dealers Association.

DELEHAR
146 Portobello Road ■ Tel: (0171) 727-9860

European works of art, objets de vertu, early jewellery, decorative objects, textiles. Oriental and Victoriana. Established 1919.

J. B. GARRARD
Stand 24, Grays Arcade, 138 Portobello Road ■ Fax: (0181) 847-2349

A spectacular selection of Chinese, Japanese and Continental ceramics and works of art.

S. HYDER ORIENTAL ANTIQUES
Stand 73, Admiral Vernon Antique Market, 141-149 Portobello Road, London W11

Chinese and Japanese works of art and ceramics.

KATIE JONES
195 Westbourne Grove, Portobello Road ■ Tel: (0171) 243-5600 ■ Fax: (0171) 243-4653

Japanese antiques and some contemporary items.

JO DE SOUSA MACEDO
Stand 17, Grays Antique Market, 138 Portobello Road ■ Tel: (0171) 602-1266
Specializing in Oriental, English and Continental porcelain, Delftware, and pottery.

DAPHNE RANKIN & IAN CONN
Stand 28, Lipka's Arcade, 288 Westbourne Grove ■ Mobile: 03744 87713
Main Shop: 608 King's Road ■ Tel: (0171) 384-1847
Specialists in Imari, Satsuma, Rose Medallion, Blue Canton, Chinese export.

PHILIP SNELLEN – IN EASTERN DREAMS
The Gallery, 289 Westbourne Grove ■ Telfax: (01494) 862141
18th and 19th century Oriental antiques. Large selection of Satsuma, Kutani, Imari, Sumida Gawa bronzes, carvings and works of art.

Books and Manuscripts

DENISE ALTMAN ANTIQUARIAN BOOKS, MAPS AND PRINTS
W. Jones & Sons Arcade, 291 Westbourne Grove ■ Telfax: (0171) 727-6054
Antiquarian books: plate books, views, flowers, fashion prints, maps and bindings.

S.K. BILTCLIFFE BOOKS
Gallery 289, Westbourne Grove ■ Weekdays also ■ Telfax: (0181) 740-5326
Specializing in books on 19th century life, labour, social and economic conditions and leisure. Applied arts, sciences and technology. Catalogues.

LAURIE CHRISTIE
Stalls 34-35 (upstairs), Lipka's Arcade, 282 Westbourne Grove
Books on antiques and every kind of collectible: art, bronzes, ceramics, clocks and watches, furniture, glass, Islamic, jewellery, military and more.

PETER KENNEDY
1st floor, John Dale Antiques, 87 Portobello Road ■ Tel: (0171) 243-1416 ■ Fax: (01483) 499006
Illustrated antiquarian books. Natural history, travel, topography, architecture, views, atlases, scrap albums, print folios.

GEORGE MORRIS

Admiral Vernon Antique Market, 141-149 Portobello Road ■ Tel: (0181) 950-9358

Antique books on English literature. First editions of Dickens.

ANTONIO RICHARDS-PERIOD BINDINGS

Stand 16, Lipka's Arcade, 284 Westbourne Grove ■ Telfax (01744) 20804 ■ Mobile: 0410 512225

Antiquarian leather-bound books. Unusual bindings and books by-the- yard.

ST. SWITHIN'S

John Dale Antiques, 87 Portobello Road ■ Tel: (0171) 727-1304 ■ Telfax: (0181) 573-8556 ■ Margaret Davies

Illustrated and children's books, specializing in Victorian movable books, peepshows, panoramas, juvenile prints by well-known book illustrators.

Boxes, Tea Caddies and Writing Slopes

BARHAM ANTIQUES

83 Portobello Road ■ Telfax: (0171) 727 3845 ■ Mon-Fri 10:00-4:30, Sat 7:00-5:00

Boxes, lap desks, tea caddies, stationary slopes, ink wells, silver, silver plate and glass. Fine Victorian furniture and paintings.

DAVID'S BOXES

115 Portobello Road ■ Tel: (0171) 243-0420 ■ Tel: (0171) 419 5011

Large selection of antique boxes, tea caddies, writing slopes, fitted vanity boxes. Jewellery boxes, sewing boxes and travelling inkwells. Cigar boxes and humidors. Also caddie bowls in stock.

GRAHAM FOWLER

Outside the Admiral Vernon Antique Arcade, 141-149 Portobello Road ■ Home: (0181) 889-3083

Victorian writing boxes, tea caddies, humidors and other boxes.

LAWRENCE GOULD

Harris's Arcade, 161-163 Portobello Road ■ Telfax: (0181) 459-7957

English and Continental portrait miniatures. Perfume bottles, enamel boxes and objets de vertu. Watches.

MICHAEL JOHNSON

Chelsea Galleries, 67 Portobello Road ■ Home: (01784) 246169 ■ Mobile: 0836 722-944

Quality antique boxes of the 18th and 19th century. Tea caddies, writing slopes, vanity boxes, decanter boxes, boxes on stands.

TERENCE NEWBERRY

Stall A10, Roger's Antiques Gallery, 65 Portobello Road ■ Tel: (01962) 773393 ■ T. Newberry

18th and 19th century snuff boxes. Pique items in tortoise shell and ivory. Walking canes from the 18th to the 20th century.

COLIN SMITH & GERALD ROBINSON

Geoffrey Van Arcade, 105 Portobello Road ■ Tel: (0171) 225-1163 (daytime)/(0181) 994-3783 ■ Sat 8:30-3:00 or by appointment

Rare and wonderful tortoise shell and silver items including tea caddies and decorator items. Also crocodile, shagreen and ivory items.

JUNE & TONY STONE FINE ANTIQUE BOXES

75 Portobello Road ■ Tel: (01273) 500212 ■ Fax: 01273 500024 ■ E-mail: jts@boxes.co.uk ■ Tue-Fri 10:30-4:30, Sat 7:00-5:00

An astonishing collection of 18th and 19th century boxes of every description. Tea caddies in wood, tortoise shell, shagreen. Cigar humidors, knife boxes, snuff boxes, sewing boxes, dressing cases, writing boxes. Shagreen objects. Colour catalogue.

Brass and Copper

R.A. BARNES

D3, D5 & D6, Roger's Antiques Gallery, 65 Portobello Road ■ 26 Lower Richmond Road, London SW15 1JP ■ Tel: (0181) 789-3371

18th and 19th century copper and brass items, candlesticks, jardinieres, decorative and collectors' items.

PENELOPE BLOGG

Stall D4, Roger's Antiques Gallery, 65 Portobello Road ■ Tel: (01217) 775522

Quality brass, ball-metal and wooden candlesticks. Doorstops, jardiniers, trays and a range of other collectors and decorative items.

ELISABETH & NOEL PULLMAN

Stall 1, Dolphin Arcade, 155 Portobello Road ■ Tel: (01892) 724236

18th and 19th century brass and copper. Large supply of candlesticks, trivets, jardinières, fire irons, bellows and fireplace implements.

WOODRUFF ANTIQUES

Stand 41, Outside 157 Portobello Road ■ Tel: (0181) 458-4170 ■ Mobile: 0421 411123 ■ E-mail: ajd.brudney@virgin.net

English brassware, door knobs, knockers, letter boxes. Candlesticks, fire sets, lamps, pewterware and more.

Carpets and Rugs

IZASH ORIENTAL CARPETS

131 Portobello Road ■ Tel: (0171) 229-7763 ■ Mon-Sat 10:00-6:00

Large selection of kilims and textiles.

Chess Sets

GARRICK COLEMAN

75 Portobello Road ■ Tel: (0171) 937-5524

Fine collectors' chess sets. Also works of art and glass paperweights.

CHANTICLEER ANTIQUES

59/60 Admiral Vernon Antique Market, 141-149 Portobello Road ■Telfax: (0171) 385-0919 ■ S.M. Wilkinson

Tortoise shell, ivory, Continental porcelain, mother-of-pearl, painted boxes, miniatures, chess sets, miniatures and other collectibles.

China, Porcelain & Staffordshire

NORIE ABE

Namba Gallery, 129 Portobello Road ■ Telfax: (0181) 922 0921

Royal Winton, James Kent and Shelly Trios a speciality. Any type of Chintz.

♛ALEXANDRA ALFANDARY

Stand 16, Lipka's Arcade, 290 Westbourne Grove ■ The Mall, Camden Passage, London N1 ■ Tel: (0171) 354-9762 ■ Fax: (0171) 727-4352

Wonderful collection of fine European ceramics, Meissen, Dresden, Sèvres, Vienna and objets d'art.

R.A. BARNES

D3, 5, 6, Roger's Antiques Gallery, 65 Portobello Road ■ 26 Lower Richmond Road, London SW15 1JP ■ Tel: (0181) 789-3371

English and Continental porcelain and pottery including majolica, both English and Continental. Staffordshire animals and figures. Copper lustres, blue and white transferware and mochaware.

J. BERKOFF

Stand 29, Lipka's Arcade, 290 Westbourne Grove ■ Sat 7:30-2:30

Blue and white, flatware and pottery, gaudy china.

GAVIN DOUGLAS

Stand 4, 75 Portobello Road ■ Tel: (0171) 221-1121 ■ Fax: (0182) 572-4418 ■ Mobile: 0860 680521 ■ Website: www.antique-clocks.co.uk ■ Internet http://www.acid.co.uk/gavin

Specialist dealer in porcelain, ormulu clock sets, urns, vases and candelabra.

SABRE GILMARTIN ANTIQUES

Unit 29, Admiral Vernon Antique Market, 141-149 Portobello Road ■ Tel: (0181) 941-0555 ■ Fax: (0181) 873-1315

English and European porcelain, pottery, and glass of all sorts.

RAY & DIANE GINNS

Unit 27, Admiral Vernon Arcade, 141-149 Portobello Road ■ Telfax: (01342) 326041 ■ Sat 7:00-3:00

Majolica, Staffordshire, Masons, animals, figures, cottages and Tobys.

HANNAH'S ANTIQUES

Stand 24, Lipka's Arcade, 288 Westbourne Grove ■ Tel: (0171) 229-0091/ (0171) 580-3513

Early English blue and white transferware.

PAT HUMPHREY & ROGER LITTLE

Unit 18, Lipka's Arcade, 286 Westbourne Grove ■ Home: Pat Humphrey Tel: (01296) 730910 ■ Roger Little Tel: (01865) 762317

English and European pottery, mainly 18th and 19th century. English Delftware, including tiles, early Staffordshire, Whieldon, salt glaze, lead glaze, early creamware, slipware, also some studio pottery (Leach & Cardew) and Weymss ware.

E.Z.A. & S. MAJOLICA
Stand 20, Lipka's Arcade, 290 Westbourne Grove ■ Tel: (0171) 229-0091/(0171) 580-3513
A wide selection of majolica from jardinières to bread plates, tureens, ash trays. 3D majolica such as lobster and animals and good selection of plates.

MARIA'S ANTIQUES
The Gallery, 289 Westbourne Grove ■ Tel: (01722) 742793
Ceramics of basalt and stoneware, lacquer, European papier maché, art objects.

MARIO'S ANTIQUES
Admiral Vernon Antique Market, 141-149 Portobello Road ■ Tel: (0181) 902-1600 ■ Fax: (0181) 900-0810
Specialist in 18th and 19th century Meissen and other Continental porcelain and glass.

MASON'S AT PORTOBELLO - JANICE PAULL
Geoffrey Van Arcade, 105-107 Portobello Road ■ Tel: (01926) 855253 ■ Fax: (01926) 863384 ■ Mobile: 0831 691254
English ironstone, Staffordshire pottery and porcelain.

BARBARA MORGAN ANTIQUES
Unit 6, Lipka's Arcade, 286 Westbourne Grove ■ Tel: (0171) 937-2050 ■ Fax: (0171) 912-0538
European porcelain, Meissen, Dresden, Vienna, Paris and Sèvres.

JACQUELINE OOSTHUIZEN
Unit 10 & 11, Admiral Vernon Antique Market, 141-149 Portobello Road ■ Tel: (0171) 352-6071 ■ Sat 8:00-3:00
Very large selection of Staffordshire figures, animals, cottages and Toby jugs. LAPADA.

MEARS & BOYER
Downstairs 288 Westbourne Grove ■ Tel: (01525) 261401
17th and 19th century English pottery. Early Victorian Staffordshire figures and animals. Blue and white transfer wares, Gaudy Welsh, Mocha, Pratt and lustre wares.

STAFFORDSHIRE DOG CO.

Corner of Portobello Road and Vernons Yard ■ Tel: (01782) 394397
■ Mobile: 0589 137308

Large range of 20th century Staffordshire ware. Blue and white, Toby jugs, Art Nouveau, chamber pots etc.

RAY WALKER

Burton's Antique Arcade, 296 Westbourne Grove ■ Tel: (0171) 727-7920

Staffordshire figures and animals, Sunderland lustre pottery, reference books.

BETTY WILTSHIRE

Portobello Road, Red Lion Arcade, Stall 47/48 and Stall 9, Good Fairy Market ■ Tel: (0181) 668-2418 ■ Fax: (0181) 668-6020

English platters, plates, cup/saucers. Old costume jewellery.

Clocks and Barometers

ARCHAIC TEMPO

Burton Antique Arcade, 296 Westbourne Grove ■ Tel: (0171) 727-7920

Buy or sell. 500 antique clocks in stock.

JOHN CARNIE

Arbras Gallery, 292 Westbourne Grove ■ Tel: (0171) 221-6772 (Sat only) ■ Telfax: (01622) 813304 ■ E-mail: jcarnielbc@aol.com

Barometers, clocks and watches.

EDS CLOCKS

Stall 4, Portwine Galleries, 175 Portobello Road ■ Tel: (0171) 727-4682

Clocks and barometers, mantel, wall, carriage, aneroid, mercury.

GROVE ANTIQUES

220 Westbourne Grove ■ Tel: (0171) 792-8028

Decorative clocks and clock garnitures, Ormulu and bronze, Sevres, candelabra, urns and vases. Music boxes. 19th century furniture.

♛ MAYFLOWER ANTIQUES - JOHN ODGERS

117 Portobello Road ■ Tel: (0171) 727-0381 (Sat)/(01255) 504079 (Mon-Fri) ■ E-mail: mayflower@anglianet.co.uk

Clocks, music boxes, polyphons, scientific, steam, medical and marine items, toys, dolls, photographs, weapons, scrimshaw and pocket knives.

OLD FATHER TIME

Upstairs, Portobello Studios, 101 Portobello Road ■ Mobile: 0836 712088 ■ Telfax: (0181) 546-6299 ■ Fri morn., Sat, or by appointment

Buy or sell, mystery, electric, novelty, skeleton, bracket, carriage clocks. Spares, and glass domes.

TIME STRIKES

Unit 35, Admiral Vernon Antique Market, 141-149 Portobello Road ■ Tel: (0171) 272-5447

A large selection of English and Continental antique clocks.

Coins and Medals

R. GALVIS

John Dale Antiques, 87 Portobello Road ■ Tel: (0171) 727-1304 ■ Mon-Sat 10:00-3:00

Ancient, medieval and modern coins. Ancient and medieval antiquities. War medals, world banknotes. 18th and 19th century antiques and curios.

Collectibles

ARABESQUE ANTIQUES

Unit L11, Lower Trading Floor, Admiral Vernon Antique Market, 141-149 Portobello Road ■ Tel: (0171) 624-7584 ■ Mobile: (0973) 321-530 ■ Sat 7:00-4:30 ■ John Weal

French and English metalwork, ormolu, leather, mirrors, small furniture, objets de vertu, pictures and bronzes.

BERNARD

Outside 282 Westbourne Grove ■ Fri 8:00-5:00 Stall 11, 288 Westbourne Grove ■ Mobile: 0585 098-120

A wide variety of small collectibles, jewellery, watches and silver plate.

MARCO COLACICCO

Outside Portwine Galleries, 175 Portobello Road

Cameras, photographica, golf clubs, sporting luggage, brass binoculars, sewing machines, typewriters. Decorative items for display.

LAURENCE COOPER

Units 15/16, 284 Westbourne Grove ■ Tel: (0171) 727-2027 ■ Fax: (0171) 381-3835

Pharmaceutical antiques, whisky advertising, antique marbles, Christmas items, eye baths and all unusual collectibles.

JOAN & PETER DUNK

Outside 284 Westbourne Grove and 288 Westbourne Grove ■ Tel: (0181) 940-0576

Spectacles and lorgnettes, irons and iron stands, safety razors, whistles, food moulds, small railway relics, tiny toys and toy trains.

GARRICK ANTIQUES

190 Westbourne Grove ■ Tel: (0171) 243-0500

17th, 18th and 19th century ivories, marble and objects.

MICHAEL GOLDSTONE & KLAUS SCHILLING

Chelsea Galleries, 67 Portobello Road ■ Tel: (0171) 828-4237

Objects made of horn, tortoise shell, ivory, silver collectibles 1820-1935 and cigar accessories.

RICHARD & AUDREY JONES

Chelsea Galleries, 67 Portobello Road ■ Tel: (013718) 70201 ■ Fax: (013718) 70601

Sewing items, writing and desk accessories, mauchlin, pottery, brass, glassware, vestas, book marks, bulb vases and decorative objects etc.

R. JORDON

Front stall, outside No. 84 Portobello Road ■ Tel: (0171) 727-3397

Boxes, silver plate and decorative objects. Also a large selection of oleographs, frames and marble plaques. Established over 20 years Portobello Road.

K & G COLLECTIBLES

Unit 27, Ground floor, Admiral Vernon Antique Market, 141-149 Portobello Road ■ Tel: (0181) 445-5618 ■ Kathy and Glynn Gilbert

Doulton, Beswick and other China, limited-edition Teddy bears and other collectibles including advertising memorabilia, bottles, pot lids.

B & B PAGE

153 and 161 Portobello Road

Papier maché, needlework, Tunbridgeware, treen, vesta cases and other 19th century collectors' items.

S & G ANTIQUES

Stouts Antique Gallery, 144 Portobello Road ■ Tel: (0181) 907-7140 ■ Fax: (0181) 909-3277

Miniature cups and saucers, vases, glass, Meissen figures.

VIRAF & CYRUS

Outside Red Lion Arcade, 165 Portobello Road ■ 18 Apple Market, Covent Garden ■ Tel: (0181) 241-3795 ■ Mobile: 0956 225048

Brass nautical surveying instruments: compasses, sextants, theodolites, levels, sundials, telescopes. Also telephones, bank notes, snuff bottles, netsuke, paperweights, watches.

Country Antiques

APPLEBY ANTIQUES

Stand 18, Geoffrey Van Arcade, 107 Portobello Road ■ Telfax: (01452) 741540 ■ Mobile: (0378) 282532

Jelly moulds, pottery and copper.

DECORATIVE & COUNTRY ANTIQUES

Westbourne Antique Gallery, Stand 13A, 113 Portobello Road

Faux bamboo, pine, papier maché, bamboo, enamelware and wire. Shelves, coat hooks and racks, mirrors, frames, pottery, smalls.

KITCHEN & COUNTRY ANTIQUES

300 Westbourne Grove ■ Tel: (0171) 727-7752 ■ Fax: (0162) 848-6172

Pine furniture, kitchen and bathroom accessories circa 1850-1930. Fine linens, patchwork quilts and other decorative items. Wooden countryware, enamel, metalwork, mirrors, bamboo, small furniture, garden tools, pond yachts, corkscrews, pottery.

Cutlery

STEPHANIE
Stall 23, The Good Fairy Market, 100 Portobello Road
Decorative plated tableware, reasonably priced canteen and fish sets. Large selection of general cutlery.

JOHN VINE
Outside Lipka's Arcade, next to 115 Portobello Road
Specialist in flatware, knives, forks, spoons, serving pieces and fish eaters.

JOHN WARNER
Stall 13, The Good Fairy Market, 100 Portobello Road
Antique and decorative cutlery. Serving pieces and a good selection of general flatware. Ebony and horn items always in stock.

Decorative Accessories

ALICE'S
86 Portobello Road ■ Tel: (0171) 229-8187 ■ Mon-Sat 9:00-5:00
Vast selection of painted furniture, decorative pieces, painted advertising boards and antiques.

CHANTRY GALLERIES - DAVID & VICKI
Unit L3, Lower Trading Floor, Admiral Vernon Antique Market, 141-149 Portobello Road ■ Tel: (0421) 075280
18th and 19th century paintings and drawings. Woodcarving, textiles and decorative objects.

JOHN DALE ANTIQUES
87 Portobello Road ■ Tel: (0171) 727-1304
Cameras, stained glass, coins and medals, books, ephemera, prints and decorative objects.

DELEHAR
146 Portobello Road ■ Tel: (0171) 727-9860
European works of art, objets de vertu, early jewellery, decorative objects, textiles. Oriental and Victoriana.

SERGIO GUAZZELLI

Portobello Studios (Ground floor at the back) ■ Mobile: 0956 645492

18th to 20th century decorative objects. Lighting, glass, bronzes, porcelain, marble, wooden candlesticks and sculptures. Victoriana and many unusual items like jewellery made from English cutlery.

JENNIFER MARTIN BROWNE

Stand 63, Admiral Vernon Antique Market, 141-149 Portobello Road ■ Tel: (0171) 221-3998 (Home)

Pictures, lamps, candelabra, linen, candlesticks, tiebacks and rings.

MARIA VILLACAMPA-ASCASO

The Gallery, 289 Westbourne Grove ■ 6:00-5:00

A large range of fine antiques, decorative and collectors' items.

Dolls, Teddy Bears & Vintage Toys

MARION AGNEW

Unit L10, Lower Trading Hall, Admiral Vernon Antique Market, 141-149 Portobello Road ■ Tel: (0181) 660-7632 ■ Mobile: 0802 785675

Toys, dolls, bears, miniature items, lead figures, beaded bags, dolls house accessories, needlework items.

THE DOLL CUPBOARD

Admiral Vernon Antique Market, Unit 64, 141-140 Portobello Road ■ Telfax: (0181) 559-8176

A unique selection of antique dolls, bisque, from miniature to large scale.

GEORGE FECHTER

Admiral Vernon Antique Market, 141-149 Portobello Road ■ Tel: (0181) 673-4542

Teddy bears, dolls and vintage toys.

HEATHER'S TEDDYS

World Famous Market, 177 Portobello Road ■ Mon: Apple Market, Covent Garden, Stand 28 ■ Tel: (0181) 204-0106

Many interesting old bears and soft toys.

MR. PUNCH'S OLD TOYS

Unit 18, Admiral Vernon Antique Market, 141-149 Portobello Road ■
Telfax: (0181) 878-0773/(01372) 456044

Vehicles, boats, aeroplanes, automata and novelty toys. Teddy bears, composition dolls, character items, old wooden jigsaws and games. Lead and diecast figures.

VICTORIANA DOLLS

Portobello Studios, 101 Portobello Road ■ Tel: (01737) 249525

A large selection of antique dolls, doll accessories and clothes.

English Enamels

LAWRENCE GOULD

Harris's Arcade, 161-163 Portobello Road ■ Tel: (0181) 459-7957 ■
Lawrence and Nicky Gould

17th to 19th century English and Continental portrait miniatures and objets de vertu. 18th to 19th century perfume bottles, enamel boxes and objects. 18th century watches.

STEWART ANTIQUES

Stall 18, Ground floor, Lipka's Arcade, 282 Westbourne Grove ■ Tel: (0171) 727-2027/(0181) 446-2537 (Home)

Large selection of Staffordshire, enamel boxes, bonbonnières, étuis, perfume bottles, mosaics, papier maché boxes.

Ephemera

VALERIE JACKSON-HARRIS TRADING AS QUADRILLE

146 Portobello Road ■ Tel: (01923) 829079

Rare antique ephemera, including Valentines, Christmas cards, trade cards, commemorative items, prints, theatrical advertising, performing arts memorabilia and unusual items relating to the history of London.

Ethnological and Tribal

AFRICAN ESCAPE GALLERY & BOOKSHOP

127 Portobello Road ■ Tel: (0171) 221-6650 ■ Mon-Fri 10:30-6:00, Sat 8:30-6:00

African tribal art from all parts of Africa: masks, figures, stools, tribal jewellery and beads. New and old African books on African tribal art.

ANCIENT, MEDIEVAL, RENAISSANCE, ORIENTAL & TRIBAL WORKS OF ART

Stand 29, Grays Antique Market ■ Mobile: (0831) 373154

The name of the stand says it all.

RAM CHANDRA

Grays Arcade, 138 Portobello Road ■ Tel: (0181) 741-1764

Specialist in Tibetan and Nepalese jewellery and artefacts. Turquoise, coral, amber, cornelian and Azi beads. Jewellery made to order.

♛ ANTHONY JACK

Antique Arcade, 293 Westbourne Grove ■ Tel: (0171) 272-4982 ■ Mon-Fri 9:30-5:30

Specialist dealer since 1965 in old ethnographic artefacts with emphasis on tribal weaponry, and the material culture of Islamic Africa.

DAVID LEWIN

Geoffrey Van Arcade ■ 105-107 Portobello Road ■ Mobile: 041 319809 ■ Fax: (0181) 673-0692 ■ E-mail: schneeky@atlas.co.uk

Ethnographic artifacts and tribal art for the decorator and the collector. Also folk art items.

MICHAEL TELFER-SMOLLETT

88 Portobello Road ■ Tel: (0171) 727 0117 ■ Wed&Fri 10:00-4:00, Sat 7:30-5:00

Specialist in Islamic furniture and tribal art.

Fountain Pens

BATTERSEA PEN HOME

Unit 50, Admiral Vernon Antique Market, 141-149 Portobello Road ■ Telfax: (0171) 652-4695

Vintage fountain Pens, Parker, Waterman, Swan and others. Repairs.

PHYLLIS GORLICK-KING

Stand No. 1, Portwine Gallery, 173-175 Portobello Road

Vintage fountain pens, mechanical pencils, authentic paintings and prints, early drawings, watercolours. Repairs.

CAELT GALLERY

182 Westbourne Grove ■ Tel: (0171) 229-9309 ■ Fax: (0171) 727-8746 ■ Mon-Sat 9:30-6:00, Sun 10:30-6:00, or by appointment

Hand-made quality frames to measure at reasonable prices. Also re-lining and restoration and a stock of 1000 oil paintings.

CHARLES DAGGETT: DAGGETT GALLERY

153 Portobello Road ■ Tel: (0171) 229-2248 ■ Mon-Sat

Always at least 200 old frames stocked. Restoration, cut-downs and new framing.

FRAME

137 Portobello Road ■ Telfax: (0171) 792-1272 ■ Mon-Fri 9:30-6:00, Sat 8:00-5:30

Huge range of frames made to bespoke standards from fine quality mouldings.

PAUL TRADEAWAY

Stand 4A, Jones Arcade, 291 Westbourne Grove ■ Tel: (01494) 716313 ■ Mobile: 0850 621507

Antique frames, hand-made water-gilded frames, verre-eglomese mounts, sanded squadrels made to order.

WHITCHER & WADE

Stand 8, Geoffrey Van Arcade, 105 Portobello Road ■ Tel: (0181) 458-6347

Large selection of period French ormolu photograph frames, decorative silver items and match strikers.

Furniture

BEAGLE GALLERY

303 Westbourne Grove ■ Tel: (0171) 229-9524 ■ Tue-Sat 10:00-5:00

Furniture: Asian, Chinese and decorative art.

BUTCHOFF ANTIQUES

229 & 233 Westbourne Grove ■ Tel: (0171) 221-8174 ■ Fax: (0171) 792-8923

Established 1964. 4000 sq. ft. of fine 18th and 19th century English and Continental furniture. LAPADA.

TERENCE MORSE & SON LTD.

197 and 237 Westbourne Grove ■ Tel: (0171) 229-4059 ■ Fax: (0171) 792-3284 ■ Mon-Fri 10:00-6:00, Sat 11:00-2:00

Fine 18th and 19th century English furniture. Desks, bookcases and dining tables a speciality. Established over 40 years.

ROSTRUM ANTIQUES

115 Portobello Road ■ Telfax: (0171) 243-0420

18th and 19th century fine English and Continental furniture. Hand-made, high-quality replicas to order.

LOUIS STANTON

299-301 Westbourne Grove ■ Tel: (0171) 727-9336 ■ Fax: (0171) 727-5424 ■ Mon-Sat 10:00-5:30 and by appointment ■ BADA

English and Continental furniture 1600-1830. Specialists in Early Oak and ancillary items.

TRUDE WEAVER (ANTIQUES)

71 Portobello Road ■ Tel: (0171) 229-8738 ■ Wed-Fri 10:00-5:00, Sat 8:00-5:00 and by appointment ■ LAPADA

English furniture 1780-1920, fireplaces, Oriental textiles, treen, and works of art.

Gardening

QUESTRITE LTD

Stand 33a, 113 Portobello Road ■ Mobile Tel: 0385 336574 ■ Fax: (0181) 675-4699 ■ Deborah Cutler

Gardening antiques and bygones. Country garden and barn look. Hundreds of gardening items including cloches, watering cans, tools and pots.

Gifts for Gentlemen

PROPERTY OF A GENTLEMAN

Front stall, "The Big Red Teapot," 101 Portobello Road ■ Tel: (0171) 434-3482 ■ Fax: (0171) 494-1127

Decanters, Dunhill table lighters, cufflinks. Chess sets and other games, photo frames, paperweights, desk items.

GEORGINA JAY

Crown Arcade, 119 Portobello Road ■ Tel: (0171) 792-3619

18th and 19thcentury scent bottles, Bohemian, Georgian, Victorian and Edwardian glass.

ALAN MILFORD

Stand 5/6, Dolphin Arcade, 155 Portobello Road ■ Tel: (0370) 851136

Antique drinking glasses. Delft, European and Chinese pottery, porcelain and paperweights.

RETRO GALLERY

Unit L2, Lower Trading Floor, Admiral Vernon Antique Market ■ Telfax: (0115) 967-4381 ■ Mobile: 0802 445814

Art glass from 1910-1970: specializing in Italian and Scandinavian glass from 1940-1960 including Seguso, Avem, Venini, Orrefors and Kosta.

SHARON & ANTHEA'S GLASS

Burton's Arcade, 296 Westbourne Grove ■ Tel: (0181) 599-8145

Victorian, Georgian and decorative glass. Opaline, Bohemian, enamelled, gilded, hand-cut and engraved glass.

S & G ANTIQUES

Stall 16, Stout's Arcade, 144 Portobello Road ■ Tel: (0171) 229-2178 (Sat only)/(0181) 907-7140 ■ Fax: (0181) 909-3277

Miniature cup/saucers, vases. Glass, Meissen figures, hardstone carvings.

PHILIP SMALL

Telfax: (0181) 699-1619 ■ Mobile: 0956 33795

Antique glass restorer. Specializes in the replacement of WMF liners, claret jugs, ink wells, glass grinding, chandelier, wall light and candelabra parts. All shades and colour of glass available.

TREVOR SMITH

Stall 37, The Good Fairy, 100 Portobello Road ■ Tel: (01453) 886068

Old and collectible glass.

SUSAN ANTIQUES
Crown Arcade, 119 Portobello Road ■ Tel: (0171) 792-3619/(0171) 419-5011
18th, 19th and early 20th century Georgian, Victorian and decorative glass. English and Continental gilded crystal and glass, small silver items

JOSCELYN VERECKER
Downstairs, Arbras Gallery, 292 Westbourne Grove ■ Telfax: (01743) 790747 ■ Mobile: 0378 291181
Georgian and Victorian glass.

Glass Domes

OLD FATHER TIME
Upstairs, Portobello Studios, 101 Portobello Road ■ Telfax: (0181) 546-6299 ■ Mobile: 0836 712088
Antique glass domes, many shapes and sizes.

Knobs and Knockers

WOODRUFF ANTIQUES
Stall 41, outside Dolphin Arcade, 157 Portobello Road ■ Tel: (0181) 458-4170 ■ Mobile: 0421 411123 ■ E-mail: adj.brudney@virgin.net
Antique and modern pewter, silver plate, copper and brass, door knockers, fire sets, cutlery. Flasks and lamps.

Lighters and Smoking Objects

RICHARD
Unit 6, Admiral Vernon Antique Market, 141-149 Portobello Road ■ Tel: (0181) 665-9578 (Mon-Fri) ■ Fax: (0181) 665-9579
Lighters, lighters and lighters. Member LCGB.

TOM CLARKE
Unit 36, Admiral Vernon Antique Market, 141-149 Portobello Road ■ Telfax: (0181) 802-8936
Cigarette lighter specialist. Publicity Director for Lighter Club of Great Britain.

AMTIQUES
Unit 6, Admiral Vernon Antique Market, 141-145 Portobello Road ■
Fax: (0181) 806-5806

Quality lighting, shades and fittings. Cherubs, Moreaux, signed figures, objets d'art and collectibles.

DIANE METALWARE
Stands 21A/34A Westbourne Antique Arcade, 113 Portobello Road ■ Tel: (01923) 223287 ■ French spoken

Early lighting, Georgian gaslights, Victorian and Edwardian lighting. Brass wall lights, table lamps, ceiling fittings, glass shapes and restoration.

JONES ANTIQUE LIGHTING
194 Westbourne Grove ■ Telfax: (0171) 229-6866 ■ Mon-Sat 9:30-6:00

They claim to have the largest selection of its kind in the world, spanning the period 1860-1960. No reproductions, including the glass lampshades.

Luggage

SEAN ARNOLD
21-22 Chepstow Corner ■ Tel: (0171) 221-2267 ■ Fax: (0171) 221-5464

Vintage leather luggage, hat boxes, trunks etc. Early Louis Vuitton. Also excellent selection of old sporting equipment and memorabilia.

A. JOHN GREY
82B Portobello Road ■ Tel: (0171) 229-2544 ■ Mon-Fri 10:00-5:00, Sat 8:00-4:00

Period leather luggage, trunks, hatboxes, attache cases, in hide and crocodile. Early Louis Vuitton. Also antique sporting equipment.

👑 HILARY PROCTOR
34 Admiral Vernon Antique Market, 141-149 Portobello Road ■ Bourbon-Hanby Antiques Centre, 153 Sydney Street, Chelsea SW3 ■ Tel: (0171) 376-5921

Antique luggage and handbags. Petit-point bags, crocodile luggage and accessories.

MARC-ANTOINE DURY

Westbourne Antique Arcade, 113 Portobello Road ■ Telfax: (0171) 267-9669

Specialist in illuminated manuscripts, early painting and stained glass, from 1200-1520. Some of the oldest Western art in Portobello.

Musical Instruments

MAYFLOWER ANTIQUES

117 Portobello Road ■ Tel: (0171) 727-0381/(01255) 504079 (Mon-Fri) ■ E-mail: mayflower@anglianet.co.uk ■ John and Kevin Odgers ■ Sat 7:00-4:00

Antique mechanical music, polyphons, clocks, scientific, steam, medical and marine items, toys, dolls, photographs, weapons, scrimshaw and pocket knives.

Paintings, Watercolours and Drawings

ACROBAT FINE ART

Unit 71, Admiral Vernon Antique Market, 141-149 Portobello Road ■ Mobile: 0370 946464 ■ Telfax: (01273) 738502 ■ Barry Chapman MCSD

Large selection of quality oils at trade prices. Also stipple engravings, watercolours and drawings.

ANGLIAN ART

Spectus Gallery, 298 Westbourne Grove ■ Tel: (0171) 221-6557 ■ Home: (01553) 760627

Decorative oil paintings, watercolours and prints, 1750-1950, usually within their own period frames. Subjects can be found for specific collector's requirements.

BOSTOCK

82 Portobello Road ■ Tel: (0171) 229-8164 ■ Fax: (0171) 221-8175

Oil paintings, reproductions, oleographs and wooden gilt frames at lowest wholesale prices.

CAELT GALLERY

182 Westbourne Grove ■ Tel: (0171) 229-9309 ■ Fax: (0171) 727-8746 ■ Mon-Sat 9:30-6:00, Sun 10:30-6:00

1,000 oil paintings: all periods, all subjects. Sections of Orientalists and Impressionists. Also re-lining, restoration and framing.

CARTER & BRADY

Crown Arcade, 119 Portobello Road ■ Tel: (0181) 870-8996

Oils, watercolours, bronze and other sculpture, prints and art objects. 19th and 20th century.

CHARLES DAGGETT GALLERY

153 Portobello Road ■ Tel: (0171) 229-2248 ■ Fax: (0171) 229-0193

British pictures 1740-1850C, specializing in Arcadian, Neo-Classical and country-house landscapes, portraits, etc.

FLEUR DE LYS GALLERY

227A Westbourne Grove ■ Telfax: (0171) 727-8595 ■ E-mail: fleur@art-connection.com ■ Website: www.fleur-de-lys.com

19th century oil paintings: British, Dutch, European.

GARDEN HOUSE GALLERY

Admiral Vernon Antique Market, 141-149 Portobello Road ■ Roberta Boud

Watercolours from the 19th and 20th century. Prints of animals.

PHYLLIS GORLICK-KING

Stand 1, Portwine Gallery, 173-175 Portobello Road

Authentic paintings and prints, original fountain pens, magnifiers, early drawings, watercolours. Repairs.

RICHARD JORDON

Crown Arcade, 119 Portobello Road ■ Tel: (0171) 792-3619 ■ Home: (0171) 352-6980 ■ Sat 7:30-4:30

20th century fine art, decorative art and objects.

THE PARK HOUSE GALLERY

The Gallery, 287 Westbourne Grove ■ Tel: (0171) 727-2817

Antique and decorative paintings, Arabic and European.

STERN ART DEALERS

46 Ledbury Road ■ Tel: (071) 229-6187 ■ Fax: (0171) 229-7016 ■ Website: www.pissarro-stern.euro-index.co.uk

19th and 20th century English and European oil paintings. On one floor over 300 Victorian oil paintings.

Paperweights

GARRICK COLEMAN

75 Portobello Road ■ Tel: (0171) 937-5524

Collectors' glass paperweights: French, English and Bohemian. Also works of art. Fine chess sets.

Perfume Bottles

ACCENT SCENT BOTTLES

Unit 37, Admiral Vernon Antique Market, 141-149 Portobello Road ■ Mobile: 0370 851136

19th and 20th century scent bottles at trade prices. Bohemian, Georgian, Victorian and Art Deco.

LAWRENCE GOULD

Harris's Arcade, 161-163 Portobello Road ■ Tel: (0181) 459-7957 ■ Mobile: 0860 875150

Large selection of 18th and 19th century English and Continental perfume bottles always in stock. Glass, opaline, lythalin, ceramic, enamel, wedgewood, precious metals, Venetian, etc.

SHIRLEY BRUNNING

Stand 14, Geoffrey Van Arcade, 105-107 Portobello Road

Scent bottles, cologne bottles, small decorative silver and collectibles.

Pewter

HILARY KASHDEN

Outside Portobello Star Pub, 171 Portobello Road ■ Tel: (0171) 958-1018 ■ Fax: (0181) 2913

A fine collection of pewter.

Photographs

HISTORICAL IMPRESSIONS

Portwine Gallery, 175 Portobello Road ■ Tel: (0171) 727-4681 ■ Telfax: (01953) 850253 ■ E-mail: ben@histimp.demon.co.uk ■ John Benjafield

Photographs and photographic books. Speciality: history of photography.

THE MODEL YACHT CO

Portwine Gallery, 173-175 Portobello Road ■ Tel: (01747) 812009 (Mid-week) ■ Tel: (0171) 727-4681 (Sat)

Specialist dealers in fine quality model-racing yachts, steam boats, maritime works of art. Restoration service available.

Portrait Miniatures

LAWRENCE GOULD

Harris's Arcade, 161-163 Portobello Road ■ Tel: (0181) 459-7957 ■ Mobile: 0860 875150

Large selection of 18th and 19th century English and Continental miniatures on ivory, enamel and porcelain. Also portrait boxes.

STEWART ANTIQUES

Stall 48, Ground floor, 282 Westbourne Grove ■ Tel: (0171) 727-2027 ■ Home: (0181) 446-2537 ■ Sat 9:00-2:00

Large selection of 17th, 18th and 19th century miniatures on ivory and enamel: English and Continental. Also portrait boxes.

Posters

LIZ FARROW/TRADING AS DODO

L26, lower trading floor, Admiral Vernon Antique Market, 141-149 Portobello Road ■ Tel: (0171) 706-1545

Posters and old advertising signs.

Prints, Engravings and Maps

MIKE CASSIDY

Denbigh Close, off Portobello Road by Alice's. Shop:"Cassidy's Gallery", 20 College Approach, Greenwich, London SE10 9HY ■ Telfax: (0181) 858-7197 ■ Mobile: 04100 12128

Large selection of inexpensive antiquarian prints.

UMBERTO COLACICCO

Outside Portwine Galleries, 175 Portobello Road ■ Tel: (0171) 727-4681

Antique prints, engravings, framed pictures, quality reprints, restrikes and paperweights.

CRANBORNE ANTIQUES/DEBORAH CUTLER

Stall 32a and 33a, Westbourne Antique Arcade, 113 Portobello Road ■ Tel: (0181) 675-4699 (Weekdays)

Natural history, 17th to 19th century, prints, good selection of botanical. Botanical print search service. Gardening equipment.

DECORATIVE PRINTS

Stall 52, Good Fairy Market, 100 Portobello Road

Old and decorative prints in hand-decorated mounts at trade prices.

JULIE GREGORY

World Famous Market, 177 Portobello Road ■ Tel: (0171) 727-8781

Large collection of topographical prints, maps, watercolours and some oils. Natural history, theatrical and caricatures. 18th to the 20th century. Conservation and restoration available.

PETER KENNEDY

1st floor, John Dale Antiques, 87 Portobello Road ■ Tel: (0171) 243-1416 ■ Fax: (01483) 499006

Antique and decorative prints. Animal, views, birds, landscapes, fruits, flowers, classical subjects. Architecture, atlases, illustrated books.

ALISTAIR MILNE DECORATIVE PRINTS

Crown Arcade, 119 Portobello Road ■ Tel: (0181) 968-6807 Mon-Fri ■ Mon-Fri 9:00-6:00

Wide range of prints. Mount decoration and framing.

THE PORTOBELLO PRINT ROOMS

109 Portobello Road ■ Tel: (0181) 858-2560 (weekdays)/(0171) 243-2203 (Sat only) ■ Fax: (0181) 858-5776

Old prints, engravings and maps.

MANOU SHAMA-LEVY

Jones Arcade, 291 Westbourne Grove ■ Home: (0171) 485-7069 ■ Fax: (0171) 485-7075

Old Master, decorative and 20th century British prints.

SANDRA TALANTI

Jones Arcade, 291 Westbourne Grove ■ Home: (0171) 372-0199

Decorative lithographs, topographical, sporting. Natural history prints from the 17th to the 20th century. Drawings, watercolours, books.

👑 **WESTBOURNE PRINT & MAP SHOP**
297 Westbourne Grove ■ Shop: Tel: (0171) 792-9673 ■ Home: Tel
(0181) 852-2717 ■ Tue-Sat or by appointment
A wide variety of antique prints and maps from throughout the world.

Scientific and Medical Instruments

PETER DELEHAR
146 Portobello Road ■ Tel: (0171) 727-9860 (Sat)/(0181) 866-8659
(Home) ■ Website: www.mikronet.demon.co.uk/pdelehar
Unusual scientific and medical instruments. Physics, chemistry, mathematics, navigation optics, acoustics, electricity diagnostics, electromagnetism. Special objects found for collectors and museums worldwide. Est. 1919.

P. HAMILTON
Chelsea Galleries, 67 Portobello Road ■ Tel: (0973) 618187or (0171)
352-4113
Specializing in scientific, marine and all types of related items. Est. 1973.

B.A. NEAL OF BRANKSOME ANTIQUES
Stand D2 and D7, Roger's Antiques Gallery, 65 Portobello Road ■
Tel: (01202) 763324 (day) or (01202) 679932 (evenings)
Scientific, marine and medical items.

JOHN ODGERS
117 Portobello Road ■ Tel: (0171) 727-0381/(01255) 504079 (Mon-Fri) ■ E-mail: mayfloweer@anglianet.co.uk
Scientific, medical, marine items, music boxes polyphons, clocks, steam, toys, dolls, photographs, weapons, scrimshaw and pocket knives.

DESMOND & ELIZABETH SQUIRE
Stall Nos. 23-25, Lipka Gallery, 285 Westbourne Grove (Downstairs)
■ Tel: (0181) 946-1470 ■ Fax: (0181) 944-7961 ■ Mail: P.O. Box
4252, London SW20 0XS UK
All scientific and medical instruments also slide rules, calculators, globes, electrical, telegraphy and wireless apparatus and related books. Mail order catalogues published.

MICHAEL DENTON & SON

Outside Silver Fox Gallery, 121 Portobello Road ■ Tel: (0181) 207-6456 ■ Mobile: (0956) 321-866

Antique fob seals and watch keys, many engraved with armorials. Antique jewellery and small objets d'art.

Silver and Silver Plate

TONY BOOTH

135 Portobello Road ■ Tel: (0181) 810-6337 ■ Fax: (0181) 810-6339

Victorian and more recent silver.

BOSTOCK

82 Portobello Road ■ Tel: (0171) 229-8164 ■ Fax: (0171) 221-8175 ■ Wed-Sat 11:00-4:00 or by appointment

Silver photo frames. Antique silver, silver plate.

CAPEL ANTIQUES

Front middle stall, The Good Fairy, 100 Portobello Road ■ Tel: (01202) 519330

Cutlery, silver, silver plate and tableware.

JEANNE & KEN CARPENTER

Stand C10, Roger's Antiques Gallery, 65 Portobello Road ■ Tel: (01753) 888296

Quality silver picture frames and small collectible items.

CHARLOTTE'S ANTIQUES

Stall C5, Roger's Antiques Gallery, 65 Portobello Road ■ Tel: (0181) 390-1844 ■ Sat 7:00-2:00

Dutch and Continental silver and collectibles. Wide selection of jewellery, glass and porcelain.

IRIS CREMER-PRICE ANTIQUES

Outside Lipka's Arcade, 282 Westbourne Grove ■ Tel: (0171) 370-1236 ■ Fax: (0171) 460-8814

English sterling silver and silver plate. Silver mirrors, frames, perfume bottles, enamels, purses, match strikers and inkwells. Watchcases, flasks, candlesticks.

TONY CREMER-PRICE

Outside Lipka's Arcade, 282 Westbourne Grove ■ Tel: 0836 291791■ Fax: (0181) 546-1618

All English silver and silver plated pieces, especially posy holders, novelty vesta matchcases, perfume bottles, coasters and place card holders.

D & D ANTIQUES

Stall 3, Outside Lipka's Arcade on Portobello Road ■ Tel: (01628) 825223

Georgian and Victorian silver trays, teasets, candlesticks, flatware, vinaigrettes, snuff boxes, enamels, and foreign silver.

NIGEL DIMMICK

Outside 304 Westbourne Grove ■ Tel: (01425) 275705 ■ Mobile: 0831 338289

Objects, jewellery, collectibles, antique to 1960's.

H. DINERSTEIN

Outside 282-284 Westbourne Grove ■ Tel: (0181) 445-3224 ■ Sat 8:00-5:00

Antique silver and silver plate, foreign silver, babies' rattles, cutlery, vinaigrettes, teasets, individual teapots, old picture frames candlesticks.

J. FREEMAN

85A Portobello Road ■ Tel: (0171) 221-5076 ■ LAPADA

Candelabra, candlesticks, lighting and silver.

GARRET AND HAZLEHURST ANTIQUES

Unit 25, Admiral Vernon Antique Market, 141-149 Portobello Road ■ Tel: (01273) 735953

18th and 19th century silver, decorative antiques, jewellery, arms, English and European ceramics.

GOLDSMITH & PERRIS

Jones Arcade, 291 Westbourne Arcade ■ Tel: (0171) 724-7051 ■ Mobile: 0831 447432

Antique and modern silver and silver plate. Silver frames, unusual cocktail shakers and interesting collectibles.

E.D. GREEN

Stands C20 & C21, Roger's Antiques Gallery, 65 Portobello Road ■ Tel: (01895) 673925 ■ Fax: (01895) 851416 ■ Sat 7:00-4:00

Silver suppliers to the trade of magnifying glasses, letter openers, antique and modern silver jewellery and small collectible items.

HENRY GREGORY

82 Portobello Road ■ Tel: (0171) 792-9221 ■ Mon-Fri 10:00-4:00, Sat 8:00-5:00

Antique Victorian and Edwardian silver and silver-plated items. Dining items. Decorative and sporting objects. Victorian jewellery.

HILLTOP COTTAGE ANTIQUES

Portobello Studios, 101 Portobello Road ■ Tel: (01451) 844362 ■ Mobile: 0860 504707 ■ Sat 6:30-2:00 ■ Peter and Patsy Dawson

Antique and modern silver, specializing in canteens of silver cutlery.

♔KLEANTHOUS ANTIQUES

144 Portobello Road ■ Tel: (0171) 727-3649 ■ Fax: (0171) 243-2488 ■ E-mail: antiques@kleanthous.com ■ Sat 8:00-4:00 and by appointment ■ Chris and Costas Kleanthous ■ Greek spoken ■ LAPADA

British 18th to 20th century silver, porcelain, furniture, clocks and objets de vertu. Vintage watches by the big names and Georgian, Victorian, Art Nouveau and Art Deco Jewellery.

SARA LEVY FINE SILVER

"The Big Red Teapot", 101 Portobello Road ■ Tel: (0181) 946-2374 ■ Fax: (0181) 944-6570 ■ Mobile: 0802 864068

Wide range of British hallmarked silver. Teasets, bowls, candlesticks, salvers, flatware and collectors' items.

JOHN MANASSEH

Chelsea Galleries, 73 Portobello Road ■ Tel: (0171) 405-1056 ■ Mobile: 0410 077916

Antique silver. Hand-crafted modern silver. Commissions.

ANGELA & STEPHEN MARSH

"Big Red Teapot", 101 Portobello Road ■ Telfax: (0276) 675388 ■ Mobile: 0411 032381 ■ Sat 6:30-3:30

Antique and modern silver. Tea and coffee sets, candlesticks and cutlery.

TED ORME

Outside Dolphin Arcade, 155 Portobello Road ■ Home: (01628) 31960

Silver and silver plate. Watches, pen knives, fountain pens, canes and objects.

PORTOBELLO ANTIQUE STORE

79 Portobello Road ■ Telfax: (0171) 221-1994 ■ Tue-Fri 10:00-4:00, Sat 8:15-4:00 ■ John & Liza Ewing

A large and varied selection of old silver and silver plate, 1830-1930.

SCHREDDS OF PORTOBELLO

Geoffrey Van Arcade, 107 Portobello Road ■ Tel: (0181) 348-3314 ■ Fax: (0181) 341-5971 ■ E-mail: silver@schredds.demon.co.uk ■ Website: www.schredds.com/schredds

Antique silver collectibles and some wedgewood, ranging from early spoons to the occasional teapot with most pieces prior to 1890.

JEANNIE & DAVID SLATER

Stall 33, Portobello Road, outside Grays Antique Market ■ Shop: David Slater Antiques, 170 Westbourne Grove ■ Tel: (0171) 727-3336

Silver jars, perfumes, napkin rings, vestas, mirrors, prayer books, frames, collectibles, magnifying glasses and letter openers.

Stained Glass

E.S. PHILLIPS & SONS

99 Portobello Road ■ Tel: (0171) 229-2113 ■ Fax: (0171) 229-1963 ■ Neil Phillips

Stained glass specialists. Antique stained glass and new designs commissioned. Repairs, alterations and advice.

Stamps

PORTOBELLO STAMP COMPANY

World Famous Market, 177 Portobello Road ■ Tel: (0171) 727-2903

Great Britain stamps and overprints from 1840, plus Europe and U.S.A.

Tartanware

EUREKA ANTIQUES
Geoffrey Van Arcade, 105 Portobello Road ■ Tel: (0171) 229-5577

The largest selection of tartanware available in the U.K. Snuff and patch boxes.

Textiles

EVA MARTIN
Westbourne Antique Arcade ■ Tel: (0171) 221-8900 ■ Fax: (0171) 229-2449

Antique textiles from Europe and Asia, silks, tapestries, printed toiles, Chinese embroideries, large and small.

ANN ROSENTHAL
Stand 5b, Westbourne Antique Arcade, 113 Portobello Road ■ Tel: (01905) 641406 (Anytime)

Samplers, shawls, cushions, 17th to 19th century tapestry, beadwork and more.

BRIAN TAPPLY & MARTYN CORBETT
88 Portobello Road (Basement) ■ Tel: (0171) 722-4001

Indian, Islamic, Oriental and European textiles and antiques.

BRYONY THOMASSON
Westbourne Antique Arcade, 283 Westbourne Grove ■ Tel: (0171) 731-3693 ■ Sat 7:30-5:00

Rustic handwoven textiles, with or without holes, darns, patches, linen and hemp sheets, sacks, agricultural working clothes to 1939. Lanterns, ropes, game bags, nets for theatre and film.

ADRIENNE TURNER
The Gallery, 289 Westbourne Grove ■ Tel: (01442) 878460

Oriental hand-embroidered robes, skirts, rank badges, shoes and hats. Framed and unframed. Sleeve panels, Kossu and Chinese Rice paintings.

👑 RHONA VALENTINE
Admiral Vernon Antique Market, 141-149 Portobello Road ■ Tel: (01372) 726931

European decorative textiles of the 17th, 18th and 19th centuries.

IRENE WILLIAMS
Arbras Gallery, 292 Westbourne Grove ■ Tel: (01797) 344526
Bed canopies and other French decorative antiques, lace, tôle, papier maché, pre-1940s.

Thimbles and Needlework Tools

JUDY POLLITT
Chelsea Gallery, 67 Portobello Road ■ Tel: (0831) 454225/(01905) 381739 ■ Fax: (01905) 381158
Thimbles and needlework tools, objets de vertu, étuis and sewing sets, chatelaines, lace bobbins, small silver items, collectibles, jewellery and buttons. Also large selection of blue and white pottery.

Tins

COLLECTORS HAVEN
Unit 1 & 14/15 (Basement), 290 Westbourne Grove
Tobacco and cigarette tins from all over the world, everything in tobacco ephemera, showcards, mirrors, cigarette packets and ashtrays.

GAMMAGES
82A Portobello Road
Specialists in advertising and commemorative tins.

Toys & Games

FLATAUS FIGURES
Stall 30, 290 Westbourne Grove ■ Home: (0181) 997-4170
Toys, lead and plastic soldiers, farm, zoo, civilian, ships, cars, trains, aircraft, tin plate, space, jigsaw and cigarette cards. Books on toys.

BRUNO LENISA
Stall 14, Stouts Arcade, 144 Portobello Road ■ Tel: (0171) 603-3706 ■
Giocattoli di latta, macchinette e treni. Periodi diversi.

LILY MORANT
Street Stall 5, Portobello Road ■ Tel: (0171) 229-4359
Dinky, Corgi, Matchbox and various diecasts. Lead soldiers, civilians, zoo and farm figures by various makers. Antique dolls and trains.

THE OLD TOY SHOP

Stand 33, World Famous Market, 177 Portobello Road ■ Tel: (0181) 878-0773 ■ Sat 8:00-4:00

Bears, vehicles, boats, aeroplanes, lead figures, diecasts, dolls, character items, games and jigsaws.

YONNA

Unit L 34, lower trading floor, Admiral Vernon Antique Market, 141-149 Portobello Road ■ Home: (0171) 435-0595 ■ Fax: (0171) 431-9359

Rare, unusual and amusing toys and childhood related antiques. Early Disney characters, black memorabilia, Bonzo. Also specialists in tin-plate toys from the turn of the century to 1960's.

Treen

♔ DAVID LEVI ANTIQUES

Stands 3 & 4, downstairs, Lipka's Arcade, 282 Westbourne Grove ■ Tel: (0171) 727-2027

Treen: a wide range of wooden bygones, metalware, glass and earthenware. English 19th century and earlier.

Tunbridgeware

SARICE ANTIQUES

Stands 13 & 14, 284 Westbourne Grove ■ Mobile: (0850) 374510

Tunbridgeware, antique furniture, decorative and collectors' items.

Vintage Clothing & Costume

ANNE & MARIA

173 Portobello Road ■ Tel: (0171) 381-5674/(0171) 727-4681

Linens, fans, Chinese shawls, curtains, lace, christening and night gowns. 1920's and 1930's dresses, shawls etc. Cut velvet, lamé, beaded, chiffon.

THE ANTIQUE CLOTHING SHOP

282 Portobello Road, London W10 ■ Tel: (0181) 964-4830/(0181) 993-4162 ■ Fri-Sat 9:00-6:00 or by appointment

A large collection of 1860s to 1960s costume and accessories for men, women and children, for sale or hire. Some fabrics, trimmings and needlepoint.

SHEILA COOK

Market Stall, 77 Portobello Road ■ Shop: 42 Ledbury Road, London W11 2AB ■ Tel: (0171) 792-8001 ■ Fax: (0171) 229-3855

18th to 20th century decorative textiles and costume. Interesting embroideries, shawls, chintz, linen and lace, samplers, fans, costume and accessories.

DELEHAR

146 Portobello Road, London W11 2DZ ■ Tel: (0171) 727-9860

Antique needlework of the 16th to 19th century. Specialists in costume accessories and jewellery of the 16th to the 19th century and 19th century shawls.

DOLLY DIAMOND'S VINTAGE FASHION

51 Pembridge Road, Notting Hill Gate ■ Telfax: (0171) 792-2479 ■ Mon-Sat 10:30-6:30

Represents chic and unique styles in costume and accessories 1920s to 1970s. Specializing in evening wear for ladies and gentlemen. Top international designers have been inspired by her collection.

♔ DAVID IRELAND

Westbourne Antique Arcade, 283 Westbourne Grove ■ Tel: (0181) 968-8887

Antique costumes and textiles from Europe, Asia and North Africa, including printed cotton and chintz. Ikats, Kente cloth, Chinese robes and embroideries. 18th and 19th century waistcoats, brocades, paisley shawls.

THE OLD HABERDASHER

Units 19&20, Admiral Vernon Antique Market, 141-149 Portobello Road ■ Tel: (0181) 907-8684

Ribbons, laces, braids and trims. Collectors' lace, costume, tassels. Antique doll hats and trimmings. Needlework items, jewellery, hatpins, hatstands, curios and artificial flowers.

Watches, Pocket and Wrist

ABOUT TIME

Chelsea Galleries, 75 Portobello Road ■ Tel: (01784) 452411/(01626) 355322 ■ Sat 7:30-3:00

Wide variety of wrist and pocket watches.

ATLAM SALES & SERVICE
Stalls 1-2-3, 284 Westbourne Grove ■ Tel: (0171) 221-5230 (Sat)/(0171) 371-6960 ■ Fax: (0171) 602-3398

Verges, repeaters, enamel watches, interesting and unusual watches, gold watches.

CLIVE
"The Big Red Teapot", 101 Portobello Road ■ Sat 7:00-3:00

Antique pocket watches, enamels and jewellery.

LAWRENCE GOULD
Harris's Arcade, 161-163 Portobello Road ■ Tel: (0181) 459-7957 ■ Mobile: (0860) 875150

Pocket watches, repeaters, Hunters.

LEON
Stall 4, Stouts Antique Gallery, 144 Portobello Road

A large collection of pocket and wristwatches and mantel clocks.

PASTIME, WRISTWATCHES FOR THE COLLECTOR
Portobello Studios, 101 Portobello Road ■ Tel: (0171) 794-3836/(0836) 233170 ■ Fax: (0171) 4314183

Rolex from 1905 to 1960, also Longines, Omega, Cartier and Patek Philippe.

NINO SMITH
Stand 30, Lipka's Arcade, 282 Westbourne Grove ■ Telfax: (0171) 629-3008

Wrist watches and antique pocket watches.

RIC SAUNDERS
"The Big Red Teapot", 101 Portobello Road

Rolex and early wristwatches, 1910-1960.

Wedgewood

APPLEBY ANTIQUES
Stand 18, Geoffrey Van Arcade, 107 Portobello Road ■ Telfax: (01452) 741540 ■ Mobile: (0378) 282-532

A good selection of 18th and 19th century Wedgwood.

R.A. BARNES

D3, D4 & D5, Roger's Antiques Gallery, 65 Portobello Road ■ 26 Lower Richmond Road, London SW15 1JP ■ Tel: (0181) 789-3371

18th, 19th and 20th century Wedgewood. All colours. Wedgewood and Bently, Fairyland lustre and signed pieces.

♛WEDGEWOOD COLLECTION

Namba Art, 129 Portobello Road ■ Tel: (0171) 243-8653 ■ Telfax: (01753) 866620 ■ Mobile: 0370 833330 ■ Sat 6:00-4:00 or by appointment

Antique and modern. All colours, green, black, yellow, lilac, black basalt.

Wine Related Collectibles

PATRICIA HARBOTTLE

Stand 16, Geoffrey Van Arcade, 107 Portobello Road ■ Tel: (0171) 731-1972 ■ Fax: (0171) 731-3663

Wine funnels, corkscrews, glass, decanters, coasters, flasks, bin labels, wine labels, old wine bottles, measures.

Woodwork Tools

"BYGONES"

Stall 108, outside Admiral Vernon Antique Market, 141-149 Portobello Road ■ Tel: (01727) 860753

Collectible and user woodworking tools. Pond yachts, aeronautica, scientific instruments, wooden lawn bowling balls and modern glass.

JOHN KING

Stall 41, The Good Fairy Market, 100 Portobello Road ■ Tel: (0181) 868-8363 ■ Mobile: 0956 405319

Woodworking and watch-makers tools. Miniatures, planes, chisels and carvers.

TRADITIONAL WOODWORKING TOOLS

Outside Chelsea Galleries, 67 Portobello Road ■ Home: (0181) 291-0807

Antique woodworking tools for the user and the collector.

VICTORIA ANTIQUES

Unit 27, Admiral Vernon Antique Market, 141-149 Portobello Road ■
Tel: (0973) 963424/(0976) 353039

Woodworking tools, specializing in rules and levels. Lighting, brass, copper, treen and decorative objects.

Works of Art and Art Objects

DEREK GREENGRASS

Chelsea Galleries, 67 Portobello Road ■ Home: (01276) 857582 ■
Fax: (01276) 855289 ■ Mobile: 0860 399686

Vienna bronzes, works of art, scientific instruments. Specialist walking sticks and other collectibles.

SHIPPERS AND PACKERS

ANGLO PACIFIC INTERNATIONAL PLC
Unit 2, Bush Industrial Estate, Standard Road, London NW10 6DF ■ Tel: (0181) 838-8008 ■ Fax: (0181) 965-4950 ■ E-mail: gerry@anglopacific.co.uk ■ Mon-Fri 8:00-6:00 ■ Gerry Ward ■ Prices medium ■ Visa and MC
Specialist in packing art, antiques and complete exhibitions, and shipping by road, sea or air to anywhere in the world.

ART SERVICES
134 Queens Road, London SE15 2HR ■ Tel: (0171) 635-7555 ■ Fax: (0171) 732-2631 ■ Website: www.artservices.co.uk ■ Mon-Fri 9:00-5:00 ■ Rees Martin ■ Visa and MC
Fine art packing, storage and transport for the contemporary art market. Climate controlled storage, cataloguing, import, export, custom cases, site suveying and installation .

ALAN FRANKLIN TRANSPORT
26 Black Moor Road, Verwood, Dorset BH31 6BB ■ Tel: (01202) 826539 ■ Fax: (01202) 827337 ■ Mon-Fri 8:30-5:30 ■ Alan Franklin ■ French and Spanish spoken ■ Prices medium
Transportation of fine art and antiques for clients who buy in Europe. Expert packing services provided.

GANDER & WHITE SHIPPING LTD.
21 Lillie Road, London SW6 1UE ■ Tel: (0171) 381 0571 ■ Mon-Fri 8:30-5:30 ■ Prices medium to high
Well-known transporter of art and antiques.

HEDLEYS HUMPERS LTD.
3 St. Leonards Road, London NW10 6SX ■ Tel: (0181) 965-8733 ■ Fax: (0181) 965-0249 ■ E-mail: alllondon@hedleyshumpers.com ■ Mon-Fri 8:00-7:00 ■ S.C. Hedley ■ French, Italian and Spanish spoken ■ Prices medium ■ Visa and MC
Export packing and shipping by air, road or sea. Case making. Import and export.

THE PACKING SHOP

6-12 Ponton Road, London SW8 5BA ■ Tel: (0171) 498-3255 ■ Fax: (0171) 498-9017 ■ E-mail: sales@thepa ■ Mon-Fri 8:00-6:00 ■ K. Tassell ■ French, Spanish, Japanese, Arabic and Thai spoken ■ Prices medium ■ Trade discount ■ Major credit cards

Shipping, packing and storage. Weekly collections in Europe.

VEHO INTERNATIONAL TRANSPORT

Unit 1, London Stone Business Estate, Broughton Street, London SW8 3QR ■ Tel: (0171) 622-3141 ■ Office: 1 Denbigh Road, London W11 2SJ ■ Tel: (0171) 221-5963 ■ Fax: (0171) 498-4308 Bostrans SRL: Via Papa Giovanni XX111, No.6, 40056 Crespellano, Bologna ■ Tel: (39-051) 969367/9695544 ■ Fax: (39-051) 969133

Packing and shipping worldwide of art and antiques.

VULCAN INTERNATIONAL SERVICES GROUP LTD

Unit13-14 Ascot Road, Clockhouse Lane, Feltham, Middlesex TW14 8QF ■ Tel: (01784) 244152 ■ Fax: (01784) 248183 ■ E-mail: vulcan-group.co.uk ■ Mon-Fri 8:30-5:30 ■ Brian Bedingfeld, Andrew Morton Hunt ■ French and Japanese spoken ■ Prices medium ■ Visa and MC

Packing, handling, storage and shipping of fine art and antiques. Bonded warehouses. Import and export services including customs brokerage. Scheduled European van service.

WORLDWIDE SHIPPING

Drury Way, Brent Park, London NW10 0JN ■ Tel: (0181) 784-0100 ■ Fax: (0181) 459-3376 ■ Mon-Fri 8:30-5:30 ■ Prices medium to high

Trans-Euro fine art division. Packing and shipping to any destination, by sea, air and road, at competitive rates. Instant quotations.

PACKING MATERIALS

LEONARD DRAY – DRAY PACKING

139 South Lane, New Malden, Surrey KT3 ES ■ 121 Portobello Road, London W1 2DY ■ Tel: (0181) 949-0988 ■ Mon-Sat 9:00-6:00 ■ Leonard Dray ■ Some German spoken ■ Trade discount ■ Major credit cards

Packing materials, bubble wrap, tissue paper. Packing tapes, printed and plain labels, shopping bags, plastic carrier bags, paper bags and all other materials for packing.

Alphabetical Index

The Towe.